# IN-SERVICE EDUCATION:

## A Guide to

## Better Practice

**Ben M. Harris**
*Professor of Educational Administration*
*The University of Texas at Austin*

**Wailand Bessent**
*Associate Professor of Educational Administration*
*The University of Texas at Austin*

*in collaboration with* **Kenneth E. McIntyre**
*Professor of Educational Administration*
*The University of Texas at Austin*

PRENTICE-HALL, INC., *Englewood Cliffs, New Jersey*

Prentice-Hall International, Inc., *London*
   Prentice-Hall of Australia, Pty. Ltd., *Sydney*
Prentice-Hall of Canada, Ltd., *Toronto*
   Prentice-Hall of India Private Ltd., *New Delhi*
Prentice-Hall of Japan, Inc., *Tokyo*

# Acknowledgements

THE AUTHORS are indebted to literally thousands of men and women who have, knowingly or not, made important contributions to this book. The teachers, administrators, and supervisors who served as field trial participants deserve special mention even though they are too numerous to designate by name. Their enthusiastic endorsement of the laboratory approach has encouraged us to share our developments more widely. The enthusiasm of these thousands of participants was not unanimous, however, and many of their critical reactions and suggestions resulted in the elimination of some laboratory sessions and revision of all of them.

Another group deserving special mention includes those graduate students, research assistants, and secretaries who edited and analyzed evaluation reports, transcribed protocols, and assisted in field tests. These sorely over-worked but enthusiastic faithfuls include Mrs. Janie Patterson, Mrs. Betty Porter, Mrs. Camille Kateley, Mrs. Faye Dysart, Mrs. Sylvia Hodges, Mrs. Cathie Erskine, Mrs. Margaret Charlton, Dr. Chester Raun, Mr. Howard Pickle, Mr. Kelly Hamby, and Dr. Robert Brown.

Professor Kenneth E. McIntyre has been involved in the development, field testing, and evaluation of nearly all of these laboratory sessions. His creative ability was instrumental in the design and conception of the laboratory approach and his advice and encouragement to the authors as they prepared this manuscript has been invaluable. Of no less significance has been his willingness to release certain materials for publication.

The South Park School District in Beaumont, Texas, R. A. Permenter,

Superintendent, has been most cooperative in permitting us to use their video-tapes in order to prepare some of the protocols in Chapter VIII. The Research and Development Center for Teacher Education funded under contract O.E. 6–10–108, Division of Laboratories and Research Development, U.S. Office of Education has assisted in preparing and analyzing protocols and other materials contained herein.

Still another word of thanks to Professor William Barron, Director, Extension Teaching and Field Services Bureau, University of Texas who made many of these materials available for extended field trials.

Our families deserve more than the usual credit for their sacrifices in connection with this book. If we were certain of the price Jana, Tommy, David, Jan, and Kim have paid to allow their fathers time for writing, we might have changed our minds. Rachel Bessent and Mary Lee Harris have encouraged us much and refrained as much as good wives can from complaining of the neglect they suffered to get this writing accomplished.

# Preface

THIS IS A BOOK for practitioners and those learning to become practitioners of the art and science of instructional leadership. The authors have not attempted a comprehensive treatment of principles of instructional supervision. On the contrary, we have restricted ourselves to conceptualizing in-service education as a crucial function of educational leadership, describing one major approach in some detail, and specifying basic activities which are useful in designing and implementing programs in schools and colleges. The ideas presented are illustrative rather than comprehensive in nature. They were selected, however, for their proven effectiveness and because they illustrate both basic and new approaches to in-service education programs.

Part I is an attempt to develop a conceptual framework for in-service education in the instructional area and to relate it to the problem of program design.

Part II describes procedures and techniques for employing the laboratory training approach with instructional staff members for a few instructional improvement purposes.

Part III attempts to define, describe, and suggest criteria for selecting basic activities for use in in-service programs. As in other parts of the book, practical procedures are emphasized as guidelines for administrators, supervisors, and teachers.

Exhibits are extensively included as samples of a variety of instruments and materials described Part II. Some materials are included in the Appendices to avoid exhibits that are rather bulky. Many of these are essential to understanding the laboratory sessions being described.

Special attention is directed to the supplement to this volume entitled *In-Service Education: Materials for Laboratory Sessions*. This publication contains materials for participants to use in each of the laboratory sessions described in Part II. The reader who wishes to use these in-service sessions with a group should have this supplement in hand and review it along with this work.

# Contents

**Acknowledgements** . . . iii

**Preface** . . . v

*One.* **Introduction** . . . 1

Defining In-Service Education . . . 1
The Importance of In-Service Education . . . 3
Some Mistakes in Practice . . . 4
STAFF NEEDS AND PROGRAM PLANS . . . 5
ACTIVITY SELECTION . . . 5
STAFF AND RESOURCES . . . 6
Leadership for Planning and Implementation . . . 7
Involvement as a Key . . . 9
PLANNING FOR INVOLVEMENT . . . 9
THE LABORATORY APPROACH . . . 9
*Selected References* . . . 10

**I. PERSPECTIVES ON INSTRUCTIONAL CHANGE**

*Two.* **In Search of a Conceptual Framework** . . . 15

A Process for Change . . . 17
A DISTRICT-WIDE CHANGE . . . 17

A SMALL GROUP CHANGE . . . 17
AN INDIVIDUAL CHANGE . . . 18
Planned Change . . . 18
The Organizational Context of In-Service . . . 21
A HIERARCHY OF AUTHORITY . . . 22
RELIANCE ON RULES . . . 23
FUNCTIONAL SPECIALIZATION . . . 23
Sources of Change in Organizations . . . 23
ENVIRONMENTAL CHANGE . . . 24
STRUCTURAL CHANGE . . . 25
FUNCTIONAL CHANGE . . . 25
PERSONNEL CHANGE . . . 25
Organizational Controls . . . 26
Personnel Development—Everybody's Job . . . 27
*Selected References* . . . 28

*Three.*  **Designing In-Service Programs . . . 29**

Objectives and Activities . . . 30
ANALYSIS OF OUTCOMES . . . 31
ANALYSIS OF ACTIVITIES . . . 34
Relating Activities to Objectives . . . 36
DESIGN I: COGNITIVE OUTCOMES . . . 37
DESIGN II: AFFECTIVE OUTCOMES . . . 38
DESIGN III: BROAD-SPECTRUM OUTCOMES . . . 39
In-Service Education as a Component in a Larger Design . . . 40
Summary . . . 42
*Selected References* . . . 43

*Four.*  **The Laboratory Approach . . . 44**

Laboratory Approach Defined . . . 45
Characteristic Elements of the Design . . . 46
INVOLVEMENT IN PROBLEM SOLVING . . . 47
REALISTIC PROBLEMS . . . 47
DATA PRODUCTION . . . 47
FEEDBACK ON DATA ANALYSIS . . .
GENERALIZATIONS AND IMPLICATIONS CONSIDERED . . . 48
OTHER FEATURES . . . 48
Principles of Learning Involved . . . 50
Reality Simulation . . . 51
Limitations of the Approach . . . 52
Past Experience with Laboratory Sessions . . . 53
Summary . . . 54
*Selected References* . . . 55

*ILLUSTRATIVE LABORATORY SESSIONS*

*Five.* **Analyzing the Evaluation of Pupil Performance . . . 60**

Problems of Marking Pupils' Work . . . 61

BACKGROUND ON THE PROBLEM . . . 61

 *Determination of criteria . . . 61; measurement . . . 61;*
 *analysis . . . 61; interpretation . . . 62; valuing . . . 62;*
 *representing the value . . . 62.*

PROCEDURE . . . 63

SEQUENCE OF ACTIVITIES . . . 64

DESCRIPTION OF INSTRUMENTS . . . 64

 *English themes . . . 65; an arithmetic test item . . . 66;*
 *a spelling test . . . 66.*

REVIEW OF CONCEPTS ILLUSTRATED . . . 67

CAUTIONS AND LIMITATIONS . . . 78

SUGGESTED RELATED ACTIVITIES . . . 78

SUMMARY . . . 78

Analyzing Teacher-Made Tests . . . 79

BACKGROUND ON THE PROBLEM . . . 79

ACTIVITIES . . . 80

PROCEDURES . . . 80

SEQUENCE OF ACTIVITIES . . . 81

A SAMPLE ANALYSIS OF THE TEST ITEMS . . . 81

 *Test format . . . 82; multiple choice items . . . 83; true-*
 *false items . . . 85; the matching item . . . 86; completion*
 *items . . . 87; the essay items . . . 89.*

CAUTIONS AND LIMITATIONS . . . 90

SUGGESTED RELATED ACTIVITIES . . . 91

SUMMARY . . . 91

*Selected References . . . 93*

*Six.* **Individualizing and Grouping for Instruction . . . 94**

Grouping Pupils for Effective Instruction . . . 95

BACKGROUND ON THE PROBLEM . . . 95

ACTIVITIES . . . 96

PROCEDURE . . . 96

SEQUENCE OF ACTIVITIES . . . 102

SPECIAL ARRANGEMENTS . . . 102

CAUTIONS AND LIMITATIONS . . . 104

SUGGESTED RELATED ACTIVITIES . . . 104

SUMMARY . . . 106

Diagnostic Flexible Grouping . . . 106

BACKGROUND ON THE PROBLEM . . . 106

ACTIVITIES . . . 107

PROCEDURE . . . 108

Divide participants into working teams . . . 108; using the "Worksheet for Mechanics of English" . . . 108; instruct each team to group students . . . 111; distribute the "Worksheet for Diagnosing Learning Needs" . . . 115.

SEQUENCE OF ACTIVITIES . . . 115

CAUTIONS AND LIMITATIONS . . . 116

SUGGESTED RELATED ACTIVITIES . . . 117

SUMMARY . . . 118

Individualized Analysis of Achievement . . . 118

BACKGROUND ON THE PROBLEM . . . 118

ACTIVITIES . . . 119

PROCEDURE . . . 119

Introduce the activities of the session . . . 119; ask participants to read and study . . . 119; consider the scores of one pupil . . . 121; instruct participants to prepare "Individual Profile Charts" . . . 121; relate mental maturity data . . . 121; analyze growth scores . . . 121; summarize . . . 123; undertake item analysis . . . 123; summarize . . . 125.

SEQUENCE OF ACTIVITIES . . . 125

CAUTIONS AND LIMITATIONS . . . 125

SUGGESTED RELATED ACTIVITIES . . . 128

Summary . . . 128

Selected References . . . 129


Seven.  Observing and Analyzing Instruction . . . 131

Administrative decision-making . . . 132; program evaluation and planning . . . 132; direct in-service experience . . . 132.

Discovering Observation as Professional Skill . . . 133

BACKGROUND OF THE PROBLEM . . . 133

Purpose selection . . . 133; observation skill . . . 134; instruments for observing and recording . . . 134; systematic procedures . . . 136; analysis and interpretation of data . . . 137.

ACTIVITIES . . . 137

PROCEDURE . . . 137

SEQUENCE OF ACTIVITIES . . . 141

SPECIAL ARRANGEMENTS . . . 142

CAUTIONS AND LIMITATIONS . . . 142

SUGGESTED RELATED ACTIVITIES . . . 143

SUMMARY . . . 144

Training in the Use of Observation Guides . . . 144

BACKGROUND ON THE PROBLEM . . . 144

ACTIVITIES . . . 145

PROCEDURE . . . 145

Studying the guide . . . 146; presenting recording procedures . . . 147; visiting in classroom . . . 148; recording and studying evidence . . . 149; discussing and analyzing evidence . . . 149.

SEQUENCE OF ACTIVITIES . . . 150

SPECIAL ARRANGEMENTS . . . 150

Selecting a classroom . . . 151; planning with the teacher . . . 151; providing information . . . 151; making physical arrangements . . . 151; planning the schedule . . . 151; other arrangements . . . 151.

CAUTIONS AND LIMITATIONS . . . 152

SUGGESTED RELATED ACTIVITIES . . . 152

SUMMARY . . . 153

Other Observation Guides . . . 153

THE TEACHER QUESTION INVENTORY . . . 154

Recognition . . . 154; recall . . . 154; demonstration of skill . . . 154; comprehension . . . 156; analysis . . . 156; synthesis . . . 156; opinion . . . 156; attitude or value . . . 156.

THE PUPIL RESPONSE INVENTORY . . . 157

SELECTING AND DEVELOPING OTHER GUIDES . . . 160

SUMMARY . . . 161

Selected References . . . 161

Eight. Analyzing Lesson Protocols . . . 163

Protocol Analysis Using Special Observation Guides . . . 164

BACKGROUND ON THE PROBLEM . . . 164

ACTIVITIES . . . 165

PROCEDURE . . . 165

SEQUENCE OF ACTIVITIES . . . 168

INSTRUCTOR'S GUIDE PROTOCOL . . . 168

The Russian Revolution Lesson . . . 169

Introduction . . . 169; the lesson . . . 169.

SPECIAL ARRANGEMENTS . . . 176

CAUTIONS AND LIMITATIONS . . . 176
SUGGESTED RELATED ACTIVITIES . . . 176
Guides for Protocol Analysis . . . 177
THE TEACHER BEHAVIOR INVENTORY (TBI) . . . 177
*Encouraging . . . 178; presenting . . . 178; assisting . . . 178; analyzing . . . 179; directing . . . 179; discouraging . . . 179.*
BALES INTERACTION ANALYSIS . . . 182
Other Lesson Protocols . . . 184
APPENDIX VIII-D: THE ELEMENTARY SCIENCE LESSON . . . 184
APPENDIX VIII-E: THE LEAKING BOTTLE LESSON . . . 184
APPENDIX VIII-F: A CREATIVE WRITING LESSON . . . 184
Summary . . . 184
*Selected References . . . 185*

## *Nine.* Studying Communication Patterns . . . 186

Three Styles of Interviewing . . . 187
BACKGROUND ON THE PROBLEM . . . 187
ACTIVITIES . . . 188
PROCEDURE . . . 188
*Directive critical role . . . 190; laissez-faire role . . . 188; non-directive constructive role . . . 190; session plan . . . 190; the reactionnaires . . . 192; discussion . . . 192.*
SEQUENCE OF ACTIVITIES . . . 194
SPECIAL ARRANGEMENTS . . . 194
CAUTIONS AND LIMITATIONS . . . 195
SUGGESTED RELATED ACTIVITIES . . . 195
SUMMARY . . . 195
Three Styles of Group Communication . . . 196
BACKGROUND ON THE PROBLEM . . . 196
ACTIVITIES . . . 197
PROCEDURE . . . 197
*Role A: controlling style . . . 199; Role B: parliamentary style . . . 199; Role C: open discussion style . . . 199.*
SEQUENCE OF ACTIVITIES . . . 201
SPECIAL ARRANGEMENTS . . . 201
CAUTIONS AND LIMITATIONS . . . 201
SUGGESTED RELATED ACTIVITIES . . . 202
SUMMARY . . . 202
The Effect of Feedback in Communications . . . 202
BACKGROUND ON THE PROBLEM . . . 203
ACTIVITIES . . . 204

PROCEDURE . . . 204
SEQUENCE OF ACTIVITIES . . . 210
SPECIAL ARRANGEMENTS . . . 211
CAUTIONS AND LIMITATIONS . . . 211
SUGGESTED RELATED ACTIVITIES . . . 212
Summary . . . 212
Selected References . . . 213

## Ten. Setting Instructional Objectives . . . 214

BACKGROUND ON THE PROBLEM . . . 214
ACTIVITIES . . . 216
PROCEDURE . . . 217
Introducing the exercise . . . 217; pretesting beliefs . . .
218; stating outcomes . . . 218; stating objectives in per-
formance terms . . . 220; clarifying conditions for objec-
tives . . . 222; stating criteria . . . 222; post-test on
objectives . . . 225; feedback on outcomes . . . 225.
SEQUENCE OF ACTIVITIES . . . 227
SPECIAL ARRANGEMENTS . . . 228
CAUTIONS AND LIMITATIONS . . . 228
SUGGESTED RELATED ACTIVITIES . . . 229
Selected References . . . 229

## DESCRIPTIONS OF BASIC ACTIVITIES

## Section One. Brainstorming . . . 234

DEFINITION . . . 239
PURPOSES . . . 234
PROCEDURE . . . 234
Orientation . . . 234; established time period . . . 235;
ideas permitted to "flow" . . . 235; ideas recorded . . . 235;
ideas repeated . . . 235; silence allowed . . . 235; feed-
back session . . . 235; ideas slightly edited . . . 236.
SUGGESTED FOLLOW-UP ACTIVITIES . . . 236
ARRANGEMENTS . . . 236
Group size . . . 236; facilities . . . 236; personnel . . . 236.
ILLUSTRATION . . . 236
CAUTIONS AND LIMITATIONS . . . 237
SUMMARY . . . 238

## *Section Two.*  Buzz Sessions . . . 239

DEFINITION . . . 239
PURPOSES . . . 239
PROCEDURE . . . 239
> *Specific location . . . 239; specific topic . . . 239; time limit . . . 240; "recorder" designated . . . 240; free interaction . . . 240; "discussion leader" appointed . . . 240; brief notes . . . 240; notes turned over to appropriate officials . . . 240; leaders circulate . . . 240.*
SUGGESTED FOLLOW-UP ACTIVITIES . . . 240
ARRANGEMENTS . . . 240
> *Group size . . . 240; facilities . . . 241; personnel . . . 241; name tags . . . 241.*
ILLUSTRATION . . . 241
CAUTIONS AND LIMITATIONS . . . 244
SUMMARY . . . 244

## *Section Three.*  Demonstrations . . . 245

DEFINITION . . . 245
PURPOSES . . . 245
PROCEDURE . . . 245
> *Focus of demonstration . . . 246; demonstrator(s) selected . . . 246; planning detailed . . . 246; maximum use of viewing . . . 247; select participants carefully . . . 247; brief introduction . . . 247; immediate follow-up . . . 247.*
SUGGESTED FOLLOW-UP ACTIVITIES . . . 247
ARRANGEMENTS . . . 247
> *Group size . . . 247; facilities . . . 248; personnel . . . 248; special note . . . 248.*
ILLUSTRATION . . . 248
CAUTIONS AND LIMITATIONS . . . 251
SUMMARY . . . 252

## *Section Four.*  Group Discussions . . . 253

DEFINITION . . . 253
PURPOSES . . . 253
PROCEDURES . . . 253
> *Problem/topic analyzed . . . 254; appropriate discussants used . . . 254; discussion leader selected . . . 254; leader*

*trained . . . 254; initial discussion organized . . . 254;*
*basic elements/specific problems focused on . . . 254;*
*references provided . . . 255; group decisions encour-*
*aged . . . 255; openmindedness encouraged . . . 255;*
*planning and scheduling encouraged . . . 255; group*
*outcomes recorded . . . 255.*

CASE DISCUSSION . . . 256
LEADERLESS DISCUSSION . . . 256
SUGGESTED FOLLOW-UP ACTIVITIES . . . 257
ARRANGEMENTS . . . 257
*Group size . . . 257; facilities . . . 257; personnel . . . 258.*
ILLUSTRATION . . . 258
CAUTIONS AND LIMITATIONS . . . 259
SUMMARY . . . 260

**Section Five.  Role-Playing . . . 261**

DEFINITION . . . 261
PURPOSES . . . 261
PROCEDURES . . . 261
*Participants should be comfortable with each other . . .*
*262; role players directed to specific problems . . . 262;*
*assigned roles specified . . . 262; role-playing terminated*
*by leaders . . . 262.*
SUGGESTED FOLLOW-UP ACTIVITIES . . . 263
ARRANGEMENTS . . . 263
*Group size . . . 263.*
ILLUSTRATION . . . 263
CAUTIONS AND LIMITATIONS . . . 264
SUMMARY . . . 264
*Selected References . . . 265*

**Appendix III.  Locator for Laboratory Sessions and Materials . . . 270**

**Index . . . 427**

# Exhibits

2.1     The Organizational Context for In-Service . . . *16*
2.2     Planned Change in School Organizations . . . *24*
3.1     Ideals, Selected Goals, and Specified Objectives . . . *32*
3.2     Experience Impact of Activities . . . *35*
3.3     In-Service Design Grid . . . *37*
3.4     Design for Cognitive Objectives . . . *38*
3.5     Design for Affective Objectives . . . *39*
3.6     Design for Broad-Spectrum Objectives . . . *40*
4.1     Design for Learning . . . *46*
5.1     Instructions and Worksheet for "The Best Teacher I Have Ever Had" . . . *68*
5.1 (cont.)   Theme: "The Best Teacher I Have Ever Had" . . .*68*
5.2     Instructions and Worksheet for "Equality of Man" . . . *69*
5.2a    Theme: "Equality of Man" (Neat version) . . . *69*
5.2b    Theme: "Equality of Man" (Sloppy version) . . . *70*
5.3a    Instructions and Worksheet for "The Job I Would Like to Have Ten Years From Now" (Good citizen) . . . *71*
5.3b    Instructions and Worksheet for "The Job I Would Like to Have Ten Years From Now" (Poor citizen) . . . *72*
5.3b (cont.)  Theme: "The Job I Would Like to Have Ten Years From Now" (Auto mechanic version) . . . *72*
5.4a    Instructions and Worksheet for "The Day Pedro Met Tiny" (Low I.Q. boy) . . . *73*
5.4b    Instructions and Worksheet for "The Day Pedro Met Tiny" (High I.Q. boy) . . . *73*
5.5     Instructions and Worksheet for "Arithmetic Test" . . . *74*
5.5 (cont.)   Arithmetic Test . . . *47*
5.6a    Instructions and Worksheet for "Test Over Selected Spelling Demons" . . . *75*
5.6a (cont.)  "Test Over Selected Spelling Demons" . . . *75*
5.6b    Key to Spelling Demons Test . . . *76*
5.6c    Spelling Demons Test—Percentage and Letter Marks . . . *76*
5.6d    Spelling Demons Test—Janice's Class . . . *77*
5.6e    Spelling Demons Test—Nine Classes . . . *77*
6.1     Sample Data on One Pupil . . . *97*
6.2     Instructions for Grouping . . . *98–100*
6.3     Worksheet for Analyzing Individual Differences . . . *102*
6.4     Worksheet for Analyzing Individual Differences (Four Class Sections) . . . *105*
6.5     Sample Sheet Diagnostic Outline—Language Test . . . *109*
6.6     Worksheet for Mechanics of English . . . *110*
6.7     Worksheet for Language Sub-Test A—Capitalization . . . *112*
6.8     Worksheet for Diagnosing Learning Needs . . . *113–14*
6.9     Achievement Test Report . . . *120*

6.10    Sample Worksheet for Test Report . . . *120*
6.11    Pupil Record Card (Howard J. Abbe) . . . *122*
6.12    Individual Profile Chart . . . *122*
6.13    Mental Maturity Record . . . *124*
6.14    Pupil Growth Scores . . . *124*
6.15    Growth Profile Chart . . . *126*
6.16    Item Analysis Worksheet . . . *126*
6.17    Answer Sheet—Charts . . . *127*
7.1    Sample Entries on the Comprehensive Observation Guide . . . *135*
7.2    Sample of Group Test Results on Film Clip Observations . . . *139*
7.3    The Reliability of Observations as a Function of Number of Visits . . . *140*
7.4    Levels of Observation Related to Skills Employed . . . *141*
7.5    Sample Questions from Each Section of the Comprehensive Observation Guide . . . *146*
7.6    Four Problems in Recording Evidence . . . *149*
7.7    Sample Lesson Analysis Using the Teacher Question Inventory . . . *155*
7.8    Sample Lesson Analysis Using the Pupil Response Inventory . . . *159*
8.1    Sample Protocol Analysis Using the Teacher Question Inventory . . . *167*
8.2    Sample Protocol Analysis Using the Pupil Response Inventory . . . *168*
8.3    Sample Tabulation On the Teacher Behavior Inventory . . . *181*
8.4    Categories and Illustrations for Bales' Interaction Analysis . . . *183*
9.1    Vignette, "Being a Parent Is Too Much Work" . . . *189*
9.2    Summary Form for Group Reactions to Three Styles of Interview . . . *193*
9.3    Schedule for Problem Solving Sessions . . . *198*
9.4    Tabulation Worksheet for Summary of Reactionnaire Results . . . *198*
9.5    Summary Analysis of Reactionnaire Results . . . *200*
9.6    Directions for Communicator . . . *205*
9.7    Directions for Communicator . . . *206*
9.8    Directions for Receiver . . . *207*
9.9    Directions for Receiver . . . *209*
9.10    Directions for Scoring Feedback Exercise . . . *210*
10.1    Content, Activities, Objectives and Goals . . . *216*
10.2    Preparing Instructional Objectives . . . *218*
10.3    Specifying Outcomes . . . *219*
10.4    Stating Objectives in Performance Terms . . . *221*
10.5    Clarifying Conditions for Objectives . . . *223*
10.6    Stating Criteria . . . *224*
10.7    Evaluating Outcomes . . . *226*

# Chapter One

# INTRODUCTION

THIS BOOK about in-service education was written primarily for practitioners; its purpose is to provide the superintendent, principal, supervisor, curriculum director, academic dean, or college consultant with practical guidelines for planning and implementing in-service education activities for instructional staff members. Aside from a few milestone publications, such as the 56th NSSE Yearbook entitled *Inservice Education* (9), there is not much available for the practitioner in his in-service education efforts. Research in this field is meager. Reports of practices are sketchy and tend to be reported as local "success" stories rather than as objective descriptions. Good case studies are a rarity, and to the authors' knowledge a handbook describing practices in any extensive way simply does not exist.

The authors have no illusion about solving all of the problems regarding the scarcity of good literature in this field. We do wish, however, to make a limited, but, hopefully significant contribution to the literature of supervision in this practical guide to in-service education.

### Defining in-service education

In-service education is usually distinguished from pre-service education simply by the time and sequence. It is not uncommon for in-service education to be confused with supervision. This is understandable since the term *supervision* is itself used with a great variety of meanings. A distinction, however, needs to be drawn.

The range of supervision activities tends to be rather broad, including public relations, instructional materials development, curriculum development, and evaluation of instruction. In-service education, on the other hand, is concerned with much more limited tasks, namely the development of instructional staff members as professional practitioners, in such ways as to have a reasonably direct impact upon the quality of instruction offered in the school or college. It is the emphasis upon *instruction* which separates supervision from many other facets of the school operation, but it is the emphasis on the *development of instructional staff members* as practitioners which distinguishes in-service education from the larger function of instructional supervision.

It is important, also, to distinguish programmatic efforts at staff improvement from individual efforts for professional growth. This is not intended to denigrate the importance of individual efforts, but to reflect an emphasis on the crucial importance of planned programs if in-service needs are to be met. Broadly defined, in-service education must include all activities aimed at the improvement of professional staff members. Since this conception is too broad to be useful for the purposes of this book, however, we are defining in-service education as *planned activities for the instructional improvement of professional staff members.*

It should be noted at this point that in-service education is being defined here to exclude staff development programs which would be directed toward noninstructional staff members. Much of what will be presented in this book would have direct reference to personnel development programs in noninstructional areas, but the concerns of the authors are for the major responsibility of the school—the instruction of students. Our concerns will be directed, accordingly, only toward in-service education for the instructional staff, including administrators and supervisors concerned with instruction.

To understand the term *in-service education* (as it will be used in this book), it is important to keep in mind that many of the tasks of supervision tend to be closely interrelated with the in-service education task. Curriculum development often contributes to in-service education. The selection and development of instructional materials is rarely accomplished without concomitant in-service education also occurring. The planning of new or remodeled physical facilities is seldom undertaken by staff members without some in-service growth. The distinction here must be recognized in terms of major purpose. When the major purpose is to develop a new curriculum or to provide a new facility or to secure new and better materials for instruction, in-service education is a by-product. We are concerned with in-service education activities as they are planned and directed *primarily* toward the development of instructional staff members. This does not diminish the importance of professional growth that may occur as a secondary outcome. It is our conviction that these secondary outcomes are often less real than imagined. However real they may be, in-service education is sufficiently difficult and important to warrant special attention.

A note concerning our inclusion of college personnel in the introductory statement of this chapter is in order. Though over the years college personnel have been very much involved and are increasingly so in *leading* in-service activities for elementary and secondary staff members, they have steadfastly avoided anything approximating in-service education for themselves. There have been noteworthy exceptions to this generalization, however—for example, the University Council for Educational Administration's career development seminars for professors of educational administration and supervision. Generally, however, in-service education in any formal, organized sense is relatively unknown at the college level. There is no reason why this has to be the case, and many of the activities which will be described here and many of the ideas expressed will be applicable at the college and university level with only minor variations.

The use of the term *instructional staff* instead of *teacher* is an important part of our thinking when defining in-service education. Teachers are usually the direct focus of in-service programs, and so it should be, since they are the ones most directly involved in the instructional program, and they comprise the most numerous staff group. It is extremely important, however, to keep in mind that there are others who have enormous influence upon the instructional program and who require in-service education too. They include such people as librarians, counselors, principals, supervisors, deans, and superintendents. In fact, there is some reason to believe that unless in-service education is planned to include high status personnel, even the best conceived programs may lack effectiveness. Wendell Wolfe (21), for example, found that principal's mastery of concepts presented in a year-long in-service program was positively related to the superintendent's or curriculum director's attendance at in-service sessions.

### The importance of in-service education

The reasons for in-service education hardly need recounting, for they have been widely described in the literature for more than thirty years. A brief review brings to mind several key points. Fundamentally, in-service education programs are important for the following reasons:

1. Pre-service preparation of professional staff members is rarely ideal and may be primarily an introduction to professional preparation rather than professional preparation as such.

2.  Social and educational change makes current professional practices obsolete or relatively ineffective in a very short period of time. This applies to methods and techniques, tools and substantive knowledge itself.

3.  Coordination and articulation of instructional practices require changes in people. Even when each instructional staff member is functioning at a highly professional level, employing an optimum number of the most effective practices, such an instructional program might still be relatively uncoordinated from subject to subject and poorly articulated from year to year.

4.  Other factors argue for in-service education activities of rather diverse kinds. Morale can be stimulated and maintained through in-service education, and is a contribution to instruction in itself, even if instructional improvement of any dynamic kind does not occur.

### Some mistakes in practice

The in-service education program is not only a tool of progress; it is also a symbol of faith in the improvability of the individual. As such, it is especially unfortunate that these programs, in practice, often fail to live up to expectations. Any number of research studies and surveys attest to the precarious reputation of in-service programs (6, 9).

In a summary of interview studies of beginning teachers conducted in twelve states, Hermanowicz (10) found a general dissatisfaction with in-service programs. Most of those interviewed believed that in-service programs were greatly needed, but that existing programs were severely inadequate. Some frequently expressed criticisms were that programs were dull and useless because they were too general, poorly timed, or devoted mainly to administrative housekeeping.

Rigorous studies are rarely reported, forcing practitioners to speculate concerning the mistakes that others have made. It seems fairly safe, however, to suggest a number of areas in which serious mistakes occur. Among these are the following:

1.  Failure to relate in-service program plans to genuine needs of staff participants.

2.  Failure to select appropriate activities for implementing program plans.

3.  Failure to implement in-service program activities with sufficient staff and other resources to assure effectiveness.

Many specific problems or mistakes could be subsumed under each of these three categories and still others might be considered, but attention to these three is warranted.

## STAFF NEEDS AND PROGRAM PLANS

A major theme in nearly all writing for many years has centered on the notion that the needs of teachers and other staff members should be central to all in-service efforts. Practice still violates this basic idea in many ways:

1. Sometimes in-service programs are dictated by the superintendent, school board, principal, or other official with only superficial consideration of staff needs.
2. Sometimes in-service plans are based on superficial surveys of teacher interests. These are then interpreted to be genuine interests, reflecting real needs.
3. Individual differences are widely ignored. Even when real interests reflecting real needs of groups are identified, the variations within a staff group are great, and simple, in-service programs designed for uniform participation cannot suffice.
4. Careful evaluations of a program *in progress* and at its termination are rarely undertaken to determine the degree to which needs are being met.

There is no simple method of program planning to avoid these violations, but to be conscious of them may be helpful. Certainly, in-service programs should be planned with the active participation of those who are to be the benefactors. Surveys of interest should be only one approach to determining needs and interests. Leaders should recognize the need to stimulate interest and assist staff members in recognizing needs. All in-service programs should be designed to maximize freedom of response by individuals. This can be accomplished in a variety of ways. In brief, freedom of response is maximized by activities which are voluntary, various, and unstructured, or structured for maximum involvement.

## ACTIVITY SELECTION

From a number of studies, findings suggest problems with the kinds of in-service activities selected for use with staff members. The excessive use of staff meetings (6) and the frequent use of lectures (12) are isolated examples. They illustrate, however, several tendencies in program planning which violate good supervision practice.

1. An otherwise appropriate in-service activity is sometimes used excessively.
2. Little consideration is given to the unique purposes which a given activity might serve effectively (8).

3. An in-service program plan tends to take stereotyped forms, as a series of meetings or a lecture followed by discussions or a film followed by buzz sessions with no real designing involved.
4. The requirements of a program as to time, staff, and other resources tend to be ignored.

Here again, it is easier to point out violations of good practice than to propose solutions, but program planning can be undertaken with careful consideration of basic requirements, and efforts can be made to design for results. No activity is so effective in serving a given purpose nor so broad-gauge in its effectiveness for a variety of purposes that it should be used repeatedly to the exclusion of a variety of other activities. Each activity tends to be distinctive in serving a limited array of purposes. Each activity, like each craftsman's tool, should be selected for use in terms of its uniqueness.

There is no perfectly logical sequence for a program of in-service activities. A highly logical sequence is often psychologically unsound for the participants. Adult learning, like that of children, is not promoted well by a rigid or overly simplified pattern of activities. Instead, in-service plans should be structured for diversity of activities, time schedules should be guidelines to progress, flexibility within structure should be encouraged, and there should be planning for revising the structure itself.

STAFF AND RESOURCES

Finally, it is fundamental that one does not get something for nothing. In-service education involves costs in terms of time and money for staff, materials, and facilities. Short faculty meetings lasting less than an hour after a long hard teaching day will not suffice. Staff members must be freed by whatever administrative devices are necessary so that individuals and groups can engage in in-service activities in earnest. This means a few hours for some purposes, a day for other purposes, and a week, a month, or even a year on occasion when the need demands it. The hourly meeting once every week for in-service purposes is as old-fashioned as the box social. Staff members must be assigned in-service leadership responsibilities with high priority labels attached. Furthermore, budgetary allocations of significant amounts to provide for released time, visiting specialists, and materials must be provided.

### Leadership for planning and implementation

"Schools exist for the purpose of providing effective instruction." Let this statement be made (as it usually is) at a conference of teachers, supervisors, or administrators, and none will be so foolish as to question it. After all, why quibble about the obvious? The only problem is that the centrality of instruction is not always obvious when one examines the administration and supervision of schools. Whereas most of the personnel and funds of public schools are devoted to teaching, many school systems give little more than lip service to the up-grading of instructional personnel. One indicator of the problem is the fact that only 14,097 consultants or supervisors of instruction were reported for public elementary and secondary schools in the 48 states and the District of Columbia in 1957–58 (19). This figure represents approximately 1 per cent of the total instructional staff in public schools, some states running well above the 1 per cent level and others far below it. Burnham and King (2) report supervisor-teacher ratios as high as 1 to 300. Harris (8) studied four comparatively well organized small city school districts, indicating that supervisor-pupil ratios ranged as high as 1 to 3,000.

In recent years school principals have been charged with increasing responsibilities for providing leadership in the improvement of instruction in their buildings. No trend in expectations for the principalship has held greater implications for making the position one of real significance and importance, but accompanying the new expectations are new demands for increased competencies on the part of principals. But the preparation programs of most principals now on the job did not adequately prepare them for this demanding task of improving instruction. Consequently, the typical school principal finds himself in the uncomfortable position of being expected to serve in a capacity for which neither pre-service nor in-service education has prepared him.

Superintendents are also becoming aware of the importance of their role in the instructional improvement process. The chair-borne superintendent who directs the campaign from his office and sees no need for getting into the thick of the activity himself is as derelict in his duty as is the general who sends his troops into battle and then retires to the local bistro. Both the superintendent and the general have unique roles to play, both are exceedingly important to the success of the operations they lead, and both must thoroughly understand the personnel, material, methods, and design needed to achieve their objectives. When a superintendent does not know at least the basic rudiments of instruction, he is in danger of becoming an obstacle in the path of instructional improvement in the system. This is not to say that administrators should be "experts" in every field that teachers represent, but they *should* be competent engineers of the improvement process.

The importance of competent, dynamic leadership to the success of in-service education programs deserves much attention. In the planning and implementing of programs for in-service education, the quality of leadership is a crucial determiner of outcomes. The few points below highlight in a practical manner some guidelines for leadership.

It should be recognized that teachers' expectations of the role of administrators and supervisors must be known and taken into account. In some cases, those expectations will have to be changed if any substantial change in teaching outcomes is to be accomplished. In order to change his teachers' expectations, the principal will have to gain the respect of his faculty through the way he handles *all* aspects of his position: the managerial, public relations, and other tasks, as well as those directly related to instruction. This applies equally to deans, supervisors, or department chairmen. Leaders cannot be equally effective in all things, but neither can they become accepted as instructional leaders if they neglect other essential responsibilities. A gradual reallocation of time as the leader develops new competencies and finds ways of streamlining the more routine tasks would appear to be the sensible way for a principal, supervisor, director, or superintendent to approach the problem of changing teachers' expectations of his role.

Any administrator, supervisor, or other leader should avoid being panicked into doing "something" in a hurry, before he knows what he is doing. Some superintendents make the mistake of decreeing that principals and supervisors must visit classrooms or hold meetings a certain number of times each year without considering whether such activities are likely to produce anything more than ill will and insecurity on the part of the teachers. The superintendent who wants to improve teaching through the in-service activities of his staff leaders should first be convinced that they have the understanding and tools to do the job. If the principals or supervisors are not so equipped, the superintendent should make available the necessary in-service training for them. Otherwise, he is likely to create more problems than he alleviates.

Another pitfall is that of expecting to find a quick and easy way to develop instructional leadership competencies. Such competencies are extremely difficult to attain, and to expect them to burst forth as a result of having taken a course in supervision or having studied this book is to expect the next-to-impossible. A more realistic undertaking would be to make a start with a well-designed year or two of intensive leader development work, launching a long-range, continuous program, supported by ample allocations of funds and personnel. A "quickie" course is not adequate for anything as complex as instructional leadership.

Most school officials frankly admit their shortcomings with respect to instructional leadership knowledge and skills. Some superintendents, however, are unaware of the feelings of inadequacy that prevail among their subordinates. The assertion, "Those other school systems need a lot of help, but our principals are already doing well in instructional matters and need only a little brushing up," has been made or implied many times in the authors' presence. Although some groups of principals and other staff members are far ahead of other groups, even those who "need only a little brushing up" usually turn out to need a complete, two-coat paint job.

The superintendent's or dean's participation in programs of in-service education seems to be a crucial element in their success. When the status leader enters into the activities fully, as a learner and not just as an observer, and when he provides enthusiastic leadership and shows by example that he is serious about setting a climate for self-improvement, the program has a much greater than average chance for success. Where the leader merely tolerates the program or sets it in motion and then remains aloof from it, his subordinates tend to catch the spirit and little is accomplished. Instructional leadership is a team affair. At best, the entire administrative and supervisory staff of a school system will be hard-pressed to provide the leadership required for top quality education.

### Involvement as a key

Throughout this book, suggestions are made for getting the teachers actively involved as the subjects rather than merely the objects of instructional improvement efforts. The shores of in-service education programs down through the years are strewn with the wrecks of ships that sailed forth with only the officers on them, while the crew remained behind. One of the few certainties in the field of human endeavor is the relationship between involvement in an enterprise and commitment to its goals. The mystery that has so commonly surrounded in-service education and what supervisors or administrators are "up to" when they launch a program is as unnecessary as it is destructive to morale.

#### PLANNING FOR INVOLVEMENT

Eventually everything mentioned in this book must penetrate the barrier between the teacher and her principal or supervisor if any improvement is to come of it. From initial planning to final evaluation, the staff members must be intimately involved in the activities of a program in a meaningful way. Involvement is an important key to success. There are others, perhaps, but none so basic nor more important.

In Part I the chapters are devoted to conceptualizing in-service education in relation to other organizational functions and to suggesting a possible framework to assist in planning in-service programs. While recognizing the wide range of activities useful in in-service efforts, emphasis is placed on the use of laboratory experiences. The final chapter of Part I describes the laboratory approach and presents a rationale for its use as a vehicle of great power and versatility for in-service education.

#### THE LABORATORY APPROACH

Throughout Part II of this book the authors concentrate on laboratory experiences rather than exhortation, in the firm belief that one learns best that which he derives from experience. When a participant *finds out*, for example, that feedback is important to effective communication or that nondirective parent interviews produce different results from those produced by directive interviews, he is much more likely to remember and to use his learning than he would be if he had to take it on somebody else's experience. Consequently, the chapters describe carefully designed and well-tested laboratory training exercises from which the participants derive important learnings.

Because of the highly structured characteristics of most laboratory sessions, involvement is secured by offering a very stimulating, realistic experience with which individuals with diverse needs and interests can identify. Involvement is active and purposeful rather than passive and routine. Although the experiences are highly structured, a variety of basic activities is employed to maintain interest, and participant responses are relatively free.

The laboratory approach is, then, a rather unusual approach to in-service education. It offers many of the advantages of the highly organized, structured, carefully focused in-service session, but a high level of involvement is maintained with a wide array of interests and needs served. These advantages have been confirmed through several years' experience with in-service programs in which the laboratory experience has been the principal technique used for leadership training of instructional personnel (17). The materials and techniques derived from this experience comprise the basis for this book.

## Selected references

1. Boardman, Charles, W., H. R. Douglass, and R. K. Bents, *Democratic Supervision in Secondary Schools.* Boston: Houghton Mifflin Company, 1961, Chapters 2, 3, and 4.
2. Burnham, Reba M., and Martha L. King, *Supervision in Action.* Washington, D.C.: Association for Supervision and Curriculum Development, N.E.A., 1961, p. 43.
3. Crockett, W. H., "Emergent Leadership in Small, Decision-Making Groups," *Journal of Abnormal and Social Psychology,* LI (November, 1955), 378–83.
4. Curtin, James, *Supervision in Today's Elementary School.* New York: The Macmillan Company, 1964, Chapters 6 and 7.
5. Franseth, Jane, *Supervision as Leadership.* Evanston, Ill.: Row, Peterson and Company, 1961, Chapter 13.
6. Frazier, A. *et al.*, "Sample Studies in Supervision," *Educational Leadership,* XVI (May, 1959), 517–20.

7. Gwynn, J. Minor, *Theory and Practice of Supervision.* New York: Dodd, Mead and Company, 1961, Chapters 16 and 17.

8. Harris, Ben M., *Supervisory Behavior in Education.* Englewood Cliffs, N.J.: Prentice-Hall, Inc., 1963, Chapter 3.

9. Henry, Nelson B., ed., *Inservice Education for Teachers, Supervisors, and Administrators.* Fifty-sixth Yearbook of The National Society for the Study of Education. Chicago: The University of Chicago Press, 1957, 376 pp.

10. Hermanowicz, Henry J., "The Pluralistic World of Beginning Teachers," in *The World of Beginning Teachers,* National Commission on Teacher Education and Professional Standards, The National Education Association, 1966, pp. 16–25.

11. Heywood, Stanley J., "What's Wrong with Faculty Meetings?" *Administrator's Notebook,* Midwest Administration Center, I (December, 1952) 5.

12. Leavitt, H. J., and R. A. H. Mueller, "Some Effects of Feedback on Communications," *Human Relations,* IV (1951), 401–10.

13. Levine, J., and J. Butler, "Lecture vs. Group Decision in Changing Behavior," *Journal of Applied Psychology,* XXXVI (February, 1952), 29–33.

14. Linder, Ivan H., "The Secondary School Principal and Staff Morale," *The American School Board Journal* (October, 1955).

15. Lippitt, Ronald, J. Watson, and B. Westley, *The Dynamics of Planned Change.* New York: Harcourt, Brace and World, Inc., 1958.

16. Lucio, William H., and John D. McNeil, *Supervision—A Synthesis of Thought and Action.* New York: McGraw-Hill Book Company, 1962, Chapter 5.

17. McIntyre, Kenneth E., "The Laboratory Approach," in *Designs for Inservice Education,* ed., E. W. Bessent. Austin: "The University of Texas Printing Division, 1967.

18. Neagley, Ross L., and N. D. Evans, *Handbook for Effective Supervision of Instruction.* Englewood Cliffs, N.J.: Prentice-Hall, Inc., 1964, Chapters 9 and 10.

19. Schloss, Samuel, and Carol J. Hobson, *Statistics of State School Systems, 1957–58,* Biennial Survey of Education in the United States. Washington, D.C.: U.S. Office of Education, p. 28.

20. Swearingen, Mildred E., *Supervision of Instruction: Foundations and Dimensions.* Boston: Allyn and Bacon, Inc., 1962, pp. 138–45.

21. Wolfe, Wendell W., *A Study of a Laboratory Approach to In-Service Development Programs for School Administrators and Supervisors.* Unpublished Ph.D. dissertation, The University of Texas, 1965.

# PART ONE

# Perspectives on
# Instructional Change

# Chapter Two

# IN SEARCH OF A
# CONCEPTUAL FRAMEWORK

NO WORD is so likely to be met with a sigh or a groan as "in-service." Many teachers have developed an understandable distaste for the chop suey of practices and purposes often stirred together in a common pot by those who cook up in-service programs.

Some of the reasons for the groan response to in-service were suggested in the previous chapter. There it was noted that many in-service programs suffer from the following:

1. Inappropriate activities—selected without regard for purposes to be achieved.
2. Inappropriate purposes—a failure to relate in-service programs to genuine needs of staff participants.
3. Lack of skills among program planners and directors who design and conduct instructional improvement efforts.

These deficiencies may be due, in part, to the lack of a clearly conceptualized view of the nature and function of in-service education. It seems clear that the concept needs to be more sharply defined, its unique contribution to the operation of the educational enterprise needs to be specified and the purposes of in-service education must be placed in the total perspective of other organizational processes. The intent of this chapter is to accomplish these tasks—in short, to create a framework for the concept of in-service education.

Four generalizations form the basis for the analysis that is to follow.

**15**

They are stated here as propositions that are to be linked together at a later point in the chapter. Taken together, they establish the authors' point of view toward the meaning and function of in-service education. They are as follows:

1.  In-service education is a process for change.
2.  Changes through in-service education take place in an organizational context.
3.  In-service education is a process for planned change.
4.  In-service education is one of several organizational changes and takes place through personnel development.

Each of these propositions will be examined in turn. Before doing so, however, it may be helpful to view them schematically. The following diagram is constructed to indicate the function of in-service education as a fundamental task for bringing about change in the school organization.

**Exhibit 2.1**
**THE ORGANIZATIONAL CONTEXT FOR IN-SERVICE**

THE FORMAL ORGANIZATION

Organizational Maintenance — Organizational Change

Unplanned Change — Planned Change

Physical Change — Rule Change — Structural Change — Functional Change — Personnel Change

Replacement — Reassignment — In-service Education

Stated briefly from the bottom up, the perspective in Exhibit 2.1 is that in-service education is seen as one of several means for bringing about personnel changes. Personnel change is only one of the several classes of planned change in organizations. Changes may be unplanned as well as planned, and formal organizations such as school districts have both maintenance and change operations. In-service education, then, is defined as being for both change and maintenance; planned and goal-directed rather than unplanned; achieved through personnel changes, not changes in procedures and rules, structure, function, or physical environment; and accomplished through retraining, not replacement or reassignment. Furthermore, the material presented in this book is focused on the instructional improvement of professional staff members. Let us now examine each of these propositions more fully.

### A process for change

The intent of in-service education is to change instructional practices or conditions by changing people. To illustrate this assertion, let us look at three familiar examples of in-service programs for change at different organizational levels; one of a district-wide change, one of change in a small group, and one of an individual change.

#### A DISTRICT-WIDE CHANGE

Let us suppose that a school board has accepted the superintendent's recommendation that instructional television (ITV) be used to supplement the program of instruction in all of the schools of the district. As a result, an in-service education program is planned to give teachers the new knowledge needed to initiate the use of the new instructional tool with maximum effectiveness. A district-wide meeting is held at which the superintendent tells four or five hundred teachers, supervisors, and administrators the purpose of the new system, how the program will operate, and what the district expectations are. A representative of the television network appears to explain the program format and to show excerpts from each of the program series. Finally, program guides and schedules are passed out to teachers.

In the weeks that follow, the regular weekly "in-service" meeting of each faculty is devoted to discussion of the changes necessary to adopt the new instructional tool, and teachers begin using instructional television with varying degrees of understanding, commitment, and success.

#### A SMALL GROUP CHANGE

Some teachers in a small elementary school become disturbed over inequities in their intra-class grouping procedures. A small group voluntarily meets weekly during the fall semester to study the problem. During this time, they decide that grouping should be flexible and should be based on analysis of individual test results. To learn how to do this, they ask a supervisor to plan a series of meetings to teach them the needed skills.

At the meetings, the supervisor uses some of his laboratory training materials in analysis of individual test results. The group members practice with the laboratory materials and then try their hands at forming instructional groups in their own classes. The supervisor returns periodically to confer with individuals and assist them as problems arise. At the end of the year, they have greater skill in analysis of test results for intra-class grouping.

AN INDIVIDUAL CHANGE

A principal of a secondary school wants to take his role in instructional improvement seriously, but realizes he has few supervisory skills and little understanding of the supervisor's role. He begins a reading and study plan for himself that includes a summer practicum in supervision. During this period, he decides that becoming a skilled observer of instruction is his first task.

Using a series of classroom observation procedures he learned in the practicum, he plans a program of classroom observation for himself. During the fall semester, he visits a classroom every day, records his observations, and discusses them with teachers. At the end of this time he has become a knowledgeable observer of instruction, has a close acquaintance with the instructional program in his school, and a new awareness of his staff's strengths and weaknesses.

## Planned change

In all the examples cited, it is clear that the in-service efforts were intended to bring about some change—another medium of instruction will be put into use, grouping procedures will be based on test results, or different supervisory behavior will be employed.

Furthermore, the changes will have occurred through change in people's behavior. Teachers planning for and guiding pupils' learning from television represents altered teaching-learning behavior; teachers analyzing test results for grouping are engaged in different teaching activity, and the principal's supervisory behavior has changed. They are all doing some things they didn't do before in ways that represent some adaptation of behavior. Finally, in each example, the change wasn't accidental, it was intended and planned by someone, with the intent to intervene in the normal course of events. These conditions are fundamental to all in-service education in the way in which this term is being defined (2).

It might be noted that one of the changes in adoption of instructional television resulted from external inputs to the school organization. The availability of the change depended upon another organization, the television network, and the acceptance of it by the district's board of education was dependent upon societal approval of this as a legitimate educational activity for schools. This is mentioned because this book is largely devoted to a consideration of *internal* sources of change rather than *external* ones. This is not to deny the reality or importance of extra-organizational influences for changes in instructional practices. Professional associations, governmental policies, social changes, and scientific developments all have a profound effect on instruction in schools.

Our intent to concern ourselves with internal sources of change is based on a belief that these are the ones that can be planned, directed, and controlled by those to whom this book is addressed and that external change forces will ultimately find their expression in internal change efforts. Planned change implies an agent of change; someone who examines the existing state of affairs in the light of some future desired conditions. He then intervenes in some manner intended to change the course of events to reach the desired goal. Since this intervention is goal directed, it is purposeful activity based upon some plan of action aimed toward some desired future state of affairs. That is to say, the intervention represents a planned change.

The change agent may be any person who is in a position to exert influence for the change. In the examples given above, the superintendent intervened as a change agent to bring about the adoption of television for instruction; the teachers who initiated the study of grouping intervened in the procedures for assigning children for instruction; and in the last example, the principal intervened to change the climate and procedures for supervision in his school. All these interventions were directed toward deliberate, planned changes. There are, of course, many changes that are unplanned. Like all things that change over time, organizations experience fortuitous events that result in an altered set of conditions at a future point in time.

Historical events, environmental changes, maturation of people and programs, innovations, new or obsolescent buildings, and other cause-effect chains in progress at a point in time will result in an altered state at a later time. These result in unplanned changes that might be thought of as *organizational drift.*

The point of introducing this analysis is that it makes it possible to define in-service education as a planned goal-directed change process introduced through a deliberate intervention aimed at some altered future condition.

Incidental learning through experience or casual experiences, though important, is part of organizational drift and, not being planned or goal-directed, is not included in the meaning of the term "in-service education."

A second, and perhaps more fundamental, idea is being advanced as well. That is, while in-service education is always aimed at changes in people, the intent at the organizational level may be directed toward maintenance as well as change. A complex organization has great need for reliability in its operations; its members must behave in predictable ways according to standard operating procedures and routines. Accordingly, some in-service activities are for the purpose of securing appropriate adaptations of the individual to the organization. For example, a preschool orientation program held every year for new personnel is for the purpose of *maintaining* existing conditions by inducting newcomers into the organization's pattern of operation.

Despite the importance of in-service education for organizational maintenance, however, the employment of in-service education for organizational *change* may mean the difference between successful adaptation and failure of the organization to respond to needed change.

The last decade has seen a new emphasis on change in education. The recognition by the federal government of public education as an instrument of national defense, the development of curriculum by national task force groups, the increasing impact of technology on schools, and the activities of foundations in underwriting vast programs aimed at changing education, all have brought tremendous pressures on schools to change their practices.

In-service education has become, to a great extent, an instrument for bringing about changes in education. To cite only one example of this, a major effort has been carried on through summer and year-long institutes for in-service education in mathematics, science, languages, and guidance. These have been supported by the National Defense Education Act, the National Science Foundation, and other foundations (6).

With the national interest in innovation and the focus of public attention on school improvement, school districts have increased the number of in-service programs and, though no one has documented this, in the experience of the authors, the sense of urgency for program change has brought an increase in the proportion of in-service programs which are based not so much on needs identified by staff members, but on a demand for organizational change. As often as not, this demand is based on some organizational response to outside sources of change.

In-service education as an instrument for organizational change becomes a nonrepetitive process similar to research and development activities. Once developed and institutionalized, the procedures become part of existing conditions or standard operating procedures.

Finally, it must be made explicit that the concept of change proposed is a general statement intended to include change processes other than in-service education. There are many different ways of intervening in a given state of affairs in an organization. The selection of means is a matter of design on the part of the change agent. He selects from among available means those that are most likely to bring about the desired end. Changes in people, though fundamental to any organizational change, represent only one kind of change. Furthermore, in-service education is only one means among several which may be used to bring about personnel changes (1).

As indicated in Exhibit 2.1, personnel changes may result from replacement, reassignment or in-service education. It is not a very likely occurrence in schools, but people are occasionally fired and replaced. More often they are transferred to other positions. Most likely, change efforts focus on personnel improvement through in-service education.

Let us now look at some alternative designs for change in organization and some different ways in which personnel change may be brought about.

## The organizational context of in-service

To adopt a mechanistic analogy, those directing an organization are sometimes bewildered by the problems of making it go; those who are the cogs and pulleys that make it go are often frustrated by improper linkages and lack of fuel or oil. Most important, those for whom the machine is intended may have real fears that they may be run over by it. During their darker moments, all these people probably feel that it would be better if they could get rid of the organization and get their tasks done some other way.

As understandable as these feelings are, the inescapable fact is that the very nature of complex undertakings involving a number of different people working at interrelated tasks means that the parts must be brought into some organic relationship. That is, they must be organized.

Though there is a lot of variation among school districts in specific organizational characteristics, several aspects of organizations are worth noting because they describe the setting in which in-service education takes place. Space does not permit a thorough treatment of this, but several excellent sources are available for an introduction to the literature on organizations (3, 5).

First, the school system is not a monolithic structure nor an aggregation of disparate individuals, but may be conceptualized as a set of subsystems. The school districts exist within larger systems (community, state, etc.) that comprise an external environment from which inputs are derived. In turn, the system may be seen as having school units as subsystems. The advantage to be gained by keeping in mind the systemic structure of the school district is to avoid the simplistic assumption that in-service programs can be successful independent of changes required in other subsystems (4).

For example, in the first illustration given earlier, the district-wide adoption of instructional television will demand changes far beyond the simple in-service approach used. To mention only a few things affected, the schedules will have to be changed in some schools, the school services subsystem will have to add an electronics repair capability, courses of study may produce conflicts, materials of instruction will need to be revised or developed, and the individuals in the supervisory subsystem will need to learn new skills and develop new understandings.

The school district shares several characteristics that have been termed the bureaucratic form with other large formal organizations. These characteristics determine, in part, the organizational context for all school operations including in-service programs and establish the basis for controlling the behavior of individuals in ways other than professional development through in-service. They are as follows:

1. A hierarchy of authority.
2. Reliance on rules and regulations.
3. Functional specialization.

### A HIERARCHY OF AUTHORITY

The status relations in schools are arrayed in the familiar pyramidal form with those responsible for the direction of the total enterprise at the apex of the structure. In successive strata going down to the broad base of the pyramid are people with successively more restricted amounts of the organization under their direction. The authority relations are thus structured in a chain of superior-subordinate relations going from superintendent to assistant superintendent to director, to principal, to teacher. Any dyad in this chain is an authority relationship in which the subordinate is expected to comply with requests from his superior.

In the example of the district-wide adoption of ITV, the authority relations are clearly seen as the superintendent determines the change to be effected and sets up the plan for putting it into effect. Principals and teachers were expected to comply.

Authority relations are less visible, though present, in the second illustration given. Although the group of teachers initiated the change in grouping, it had to be carried out with the consent of the principal and could not be contrary to district policy. In the third in-service illustration, the principal-teacher relationship was implicit—the principal's concern with his supervisory responsibility was the manifestation of his formal authority.

It should be noted that within the formal authority structure, an informal structure exists in which coalitions of individuals are formed that establish influence structures which may be independent of the formal structure. Consistent with an emphasis on controlled changes through in-service, we will not deal with the informal, largely uncontrolled, structures except to note their existence and to recognize that they may exert influence on all organizational operations including in-service education.

RELIANCE ON RULES

The second characteristic of formal organizations noted was a reliance on rules. As can be seen from the discussion of authority relations, some control must be exercised to insure that authority is not abused, that capricious decisions will not be made, and that the efforts of the total organization may be coordinated. The device for accomplishing this is the use of rules which take the form of policies and procedures for the organization. Thus, rule-making is both a source of the authority relations and a constraint on authority. Since rules specify constraints on the behavior of individuals, the use of rules is one possible device for bringing about change in the organization. In the last example given, the self-development efforts of the principal may be seen as his response to the rule in his district that principals perform the supervisory function.

FUNCTIONAL SPECIALIZATION

The third salient feature of organizations noted was functional specialization. That is, since the services to be provided by the school are complex, they may be better accomplished by having specialists highly trained in rather limited task areas. Thus, the district will have such specialists as subject matter specialists, teachers, supervisors, counselors, and secretaries. Each of them carries out a specific part of the total task of providing education. Since, as we have seen, the subsystems are interdependent, changes in one functional specialty require adaptive changes in other parts. Thus, *changing functional specialization* is one source of change.

In the third example given, the principal has developed his responsibility for the tasks of the supervisor. This will require a changed response to him from not only teachers with whom he works, but also from the supervisory specialist who sometimes visits him. It also requires changes in his functional relationship to other tasks demanded of him or his assistants.

In summary, we have depicted the organizational setting in which in-service takes place as a set of interdependent subsystems structured in a hierarchy of authority relations. The authority is created in rules; and rule-making is the device used to secure reliability of the operation. Finally, the organization is characterized by functional specialization of roles which give individuals limited but interrelated responsibilities.

## Sources of change in organizations

The branching diagram in Exhibit 2.1 was presented in order to separate various components from each other so that the meaning would be clarified. The diagram tends to obscure more complex interrelationships, however. For example, changes in the organization may be sought through changing the organizational structure. This change means that functional roles of superintendents and principals may need to change as well. Similarly, a change introduced by means of a new building design will need to be accompanied by an in-service program designed to change the teaching practices required to make use of it.

Exhibit 2.2 is presented as a way of identifying the in-service education component in the different ways through which organizational change may be accomplished. In Exhibit 2.2, four sources of change are arrayed in panels going from left to right. Those farther to the left are the more impersonal, involving a primary intent of changing things (buildings or facilities) or abstractions (positions or jobs). The panels to the right are those concerned with *personal* change. That is to say, change in the individual who occupies the position, not the position itself. Perhaps this distinction will become clearer as we define the terms used to identify the panels.

## Exhibit 2.2
## PLANNED CHANGE IN SCHOOL ORGANIZATIONS

| ORGANIZATIONAL CHANGE | | | | |
|---|---|---|---|---|
| ENVIRONMENTAL CHANGE | STRUCTURAL CHANGE | FUNCTIONAL CHANGE | PERSONNEL CHANGE | |
| | CHANGE IN AUTHORITY RELATIONS | JOB REDEFINITION | REPLACEMENT | Organizational Controls |
| | | PERSONNEL DEVELOPMENT | RETRAINING | |
| ADAPTATION | ADAPTATION TO STRUCTURAL CHANGE | | | In-Service Education |

Impersonal ← ──────────── → Personal

### ENVIRONMENTAL CHANGE

The first panel to the left is that of physical environmental change. This concerns all the "things" of instruction—buildings, facilities, equipment, and materials of instruction. There are also environmental changes that are external to the organization, but these are not included in the term as used here. Such things as changed societal demands or legal constraints on schools are the conditions that may bring about some organizational response, but we are concerned in this analysis with only the response mode, not the stimulus. In other words, the environment of interest is the internal environment of the organization—the physical setting in which instruction takes place.

## STRUCTURAL CHANGE

The second panel concerns structural change. Structure alludes to the pattern of the hierarchy of the organization; what positions there are, and how these are structured with respect to authority relations. The familiar organization chart depicts the structure of an organization. The structure may be flat, with few levels between the top and the bottom, or peaked, with several layers of authority. Structural change affects people, but this is placed toward the impersonal end of the scheme because the structure concerns the position, not the incumbent.

## FUNCTIONAL CHANGE

Functional change occupies the next to last panel. Functional roles are specifications for what a person who occupies a given organizational position is expected to do—what tasks and activities he is required to perform.

Job descriptions are the formal manifestation of functional roles, but informal manifestations based on expectation of other persons exert a strong influence on behavior and are a powerful personal component in functional role specification.

## PERSONNEL CHANGE

The final panel, personnel change, is located at the personal end of the continuum because it concerns change of individual behavior—not merely change of the job held by the person. This panel is intended to include all ways in which personnel are changed—replacement, reassignment, and retraining. For reasons we shall consider in more detail later, retraining is the most important of these means for personnel change in school organizations. For this reason, in-service education occupies a central position.

To summarize briefly: environment concerns the physical setting for instruction; organizational structure specifies relative status in the hierarchy—whom a person supervises and to whom he is accountable; function specifies what the incumbent of a given position is expected to do; and the personnel dimension identifies the person who occupies the position and performs the assigned tasks in the organizational structure.

This brings us to the remaining feature of the diagram—the area defined by the irregular diagonal line. The shaded area indicates that in-service education is by far the most important component in personal change in school organizations. It is a major part of changes in functional roles, it is a minor component in structural changes, and it is least involved in changes brought about through change in the physical environment. Whether or not this contention is a true statement of reality will depend upon further investigation. At this point, let us consider this to be a model presented to help define terms, specify relationships, and give a point of view.

### Organizational controls

It should be apparent from the foregoing analysis that in-service education is but one of several sources of change in organizations. A major source of change comes through the use of authority. Some would suggest that authority is an overused and somewhat ineffective means of getting change, but the fact remains that all change in the organization must take into account authority relations. Furthermore, some changes can be brought about by use of authority alone. Changes in goals that may change the organization in dramatic ways are clearly functions of authority.

The illustration of the district adoption of ITV is an example of a change brought about by use of authority. The school board accepted the superintendent's recommendation and adopted ITV for use in all schools in the district. With no changes other than this and the provision of TV sets, *some* adoption of ITV would likely result.

A closely related process for effecting change is through the use of rules. If organizations are structured on authority relations, they operate according to a set of rules—some explicit, some implicit. One way of changing some part of the operation is to change the rules. The reason this process is so difficult to separate from authority relations is that the rule making is in the hands of those higher in the authority hierarchy.

We are using *rules* in the somewhat limited sense, meaning a set of specifications for behavior such as might be comprised by policy manuals, courses of study, administrative procedures, teachers' handbooks, and other standard operating specifications.

In one of the examples, the use of test results for grouping that was achieved through in-service could also have been brought about to some extent by an explicit set of rules and procedures adopted by the school and enforced by close supervision. There are many reasons, of course, why this is a less desirable and less effective procedure, but the point is that some change can be effected through rule change alone.

Another way of obtaining change is by means of the functional specialization described above. Since responsibility for a given function may reside in specially defined positions, it is possible to bring about change by creating a new position or by redefining an existing one.

For example, in the illustration in which the goal was to use television for instruction, the district could create the position of TV coordinator with responsibility for preparing pretelecast activities, setting up viewing arrangements, and handling testing and evaluation. This person's position would be defined by rule under the authority of some superior to assume certain specialized responsibilities. His behavior would be a product of the interacting influences of the authority, the rules, and his own personal skills, knowledge, and relationships.

### Personnel development—everybody's job

A final source of change, and the one which involves in-service education most directly, is that of personnel development. Since individuals carry out the tasks of the organization, change can be effected by changes in the manner in which they function. An almost total reliance is sometimes placed on personnel development for change, although, as we have seen, other supporting change processes should be involved. The importance of personnel development in the promotion of instructional change can hardly be overemphasized however.

All organizational changes depend to some extent on the willingness and ability of people to change their ways of doing things. In some institutions, such as schools, the human factors are crucial. Whether change is coercive or whether it is done willingly may greatly affect the genuine acceptance with which people proceed to change, thereby affecting the quality of the change outcome. Whether they have adequate opportunities to develop the necessary knowledge, skills, or related attitudes and values to carry out the change will also affect the quality of the outcome. Personnel development programs, skillfully handled, can affect both the ability and the willingness of the person to change.

Unlike the other change processes we have noted, personnel development may be initiated at any level in the hierarchy. This makes it a highly adaptive procedure. In our examples, the in-service introduction to the use of ITV was initiated by the superintendent, the study of the use of test results for grouping was a voluntary effort initiated at the school unit level, and the principal's self-development program was initiated by the individual.

Of all the change processes noted, only in-service for personnel development may be employed by everyone in the organization. Of course, school district-wide plans or school unit programs depend on authority relations and changes in district rules, building a new building, or hiring of new people for new jobs are strategies available only to the superintendent and board, but personnel development is open to all.

A few teachers may voluntarily undertake a plan of action or any individual may devise a self-study plan aimed at changing existing conditions. To the extent that this is successful, organizational change results.

In an organization such as a school, where members aspire to professional autonomy and status, personnel development is seen as everybody's job. Members may feel a responsibility to meet their own needs either individually or in small voluntary groups. To the extent that this is true, programs described by authority are likely to be seen as irrelevant, coercive, and demeaning. These assertions, reflecting the familiar experiences of teachers and principals, help account for the low state of in-service education and lead to a groan response when in-service is mentioned. The resolution of these two needs—organizational and personal—is a major challenge to leadership personnel in designing in-service education programs.

In summary, we have asserted that to put instructional change in its proper perspective the processes for achieving that change must be clearly in view. Change may be brought about by use of authority, by changes in the physical environment (facilities, materials, buildings), through use of rules and regulations, through changes in functional specialization, and through in-service development of personnel. Though it cannot stand alone, in-service development is the most fundamental of the change processes, since it is concerned directly with the individual, is aimed at some change in his knowledge and behavior, and can affect his willingness to accept the change.

## Selected references

1. Bennis, Warren G., Kenneth D. Benne, and Robert Chin, eds., *The Planning of Change*. New York: Holt, Rinehart and Winston, 1966.
2. Coffey, Hubert S., and William P. Golden, Jr., "Psychology of Change Within An Institution," in *In-Service Education for Teachers, Supervisors, and Administrators*, ed. Nelson W. Henry, Fifty-sixth NSSE Yearbook. Chicago: The University of Chicago Press, 1957, 376 pp.
3. Katz, Daniel, and Robert L. Kahn, *The Social Psychology of Organizations*. New York: John Wiley and Sons, Inc., 1965.
4. Lippett, Ronald, Jeanne Watson, and Bruce Westley, *The Dynamics of Planned Change*. New York: Harcourt, Brace, and World, Inc., 1958.
5. March, James G., ed., *Handbook of Organizations*. Chicago: Rand McNally and Co., 1965.
6. Reynard, Harold E., "Pre-Service and In-Service Education of Teachers," *Review of Educational Research*, XXXIII (October, 1963), 369.
7. Taylor, Bob L., "Factors Influencing In-Service Teacher Education Programs," *Journal of Educational Research*, LII (May, 1959), 336–38.

# Chapter Three

# DESIGNING IN-SERVICE PROGRAMS

IN PREVIOUS chapters, in-service education was defined as being directed toward the improvement of instructional staff members. It was asserted that in-service education is a goal-directed activity concerned with changes in individuals and organizational systems and achieved through changes in people, rather than in rules, structures, function, or physical environment (although these may be associated changes); and accomplished through training, rather than replacement or reassignment.

Parts II and III of this book describe an array of laboratory exercises and basic activities that provide useful approaches to in-service programs. The present chapter is intended to assist the planner to select from among avialable techniques those that are most likely to achieve the desired results—in short, to *design* in-service programs.

Though it is a fashionable term (1, 3), the authors have consciously avoided the use of the term *strategy* because it connotes a gaming or conflict situation in which there is a strategist and an antagonist. Usually, but not always, the intended result of the strategy is that somebody wins and somebody loses. Even if its military origin is overlooked, the term still connotes a clever scheme or stratagem that may convey a sinister intent to the person against whom the strategy is employed. Imagine the effect of telling a group of teachers that "The strategy for our in-service program this year is. . . ." A more neutral term is *design*. A still more neutral term is *plan*, and these two terms will be used more or less interchangeably.

A somewhat oversimplified conception of the task of the in-service designer underlies this chapter. Perhaps the oversimplification is justified if it helps the planner with an overall conception of his task, for he must select from available activities and content those that are most likely to result in the desired learning. To cite an extreme example, if the objective is for the learner to be able to construct transparencies for an overhead projector, a lecture will likely leave him as unskilled as he was before. A demonstration, when combined with some practice with reproduction process, may accomplish the objective. In other words, the design of an in-service program should take into account the relationship of means to ends.

Let us hasten to add that we do not presume to present a recipe book for cooking up in-service programs. Changing people in significant ways is a complex leadership task involving many difficulties for professional leaders such as principals, supervisors, and superintendents. Goals must be selected for their genuine significance, and staff members must be guided and stimulated toward these goals. The selection of activities that stimulate appropriate changes in staff requires careful planning. The use of selected activities and the active, purposeful involvement of people in them demands the highest kind of leadership.

Improvement programs for optimum effectiveness must be designed with an understanding of the kinds of changes that may reasonably be expected from a given activity. It is not enough to approach important changes in professional people either by presenting a cafeteria of in-service delicacies from which to choose or a rigid diet of lectures or course credits. Poorly designed programs may be ineffective or even produce undesirable results. The need for improvement programs that are designs for human growth and development is imperative for leadership (4).

### Objectives and activities

If it weren't violated so much in practice, it would seem too obvious to require mentioning that the first task of designing a program is to get clearly in mind what the program is to achieve. When this has been done, it seems equally elementary to suggest that the next step is to discover some means for reaching the desired outcome. On these two dimensions, both appearing deceptively simple, a generalized approach to design will be suggested.

The two dimensions are variously thought of as means and ends, process and product, or input and output (if one wants to adopt the jargon of the systems analyst). We will find it convenient to think of the immediate outcome as the *objective* and the means for getting there as the *activity*. These terms have some utility in the meanings they connote. Means and ends imply a more direct relationship between the activity and the objective than can usually be counted on in the complex business of human learning. Secondly, the typical in-service program takes place over a period of weeks or months and may have a number of different procedures that may be properly thought of as activities. Finally, the term *objective* is intended to be helpful in conveying the meaning that the program should have some predetermined result that may be expressed in terms of the behaviors of people relating to some instructional procedure (6).

Much experience with in-service programs suggests that the activity is frequently confused with the objective. It is not unusual to find an in-service program in which the only identifiable objective is to have an in-service program. The planners of such programs may have some vague notion that what they are doing will result in some good somehow, but when the program is concluded, the aura of unevaluated feelings of "success" that results suggests that the real purpose was to conduct the program.

In the sections that follow, we hope to clarify and differentiate objectives and activities and offer a way of conceptualizing the two terms in such a way as to assist the designer. First, objectives will be defined and some generalized outcomes will be presented. Second, some basic learning activities will be presented. Finally, activities will be related to objectives in a grid that will suggest their interrelationships. The latter section will be suggested as a kind of designer's guide.

### ANALYSIS OF OUTCOMES

One of the reasons that in-service programs frequently seem to have fuzzy objectives is that too little attention is given to the definition of desired outcomes. Even when time is given to this important activity, long-range goals may be confused with immediate objectives.

To help in clarifying outcomes, let us call the broad general outcomes of the in-service activity *goals*. These may be such things as "To improve the teaching of reading," or "To individualize instruction." These goals serve to give direction to the long-range in-service efforts and to assist in the selection of more specific objectives for planned activities. Goals specify objectives that the program should add up to in the long run.

As may be seen in Exhibit 3.1, goals are a functional expression of some larger *ideals*, which are the social expectations for the school. Ideals are frequently found in statements such as "To educate each child to the limit of his potential," "To produce effective citizens," or, "To educate for economic effectiveness." The goals for an in-service program are the instructional expression of these ideals.

**Exhibit 3.1**
**IDEALS, SELECTED GOALS, AND SPECIFIED OBJECTIVES**

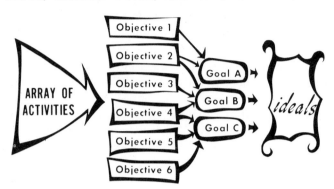

Goals can be further defined as statements of objectives that are specific statements of behavioral outcomes for in-service activities. Thus, if Goal A is to improve instruction in reading, there may be two or more objectives relating to that goal. The first might be that successful participants in the in-service program will be able to identify reading difficulties using diagnostic tests. A second objective might be that participants will be able to apply appropriate instructional procedures for diagnosed reading difficulties. The same objective may relate to several goals. In the example just given, the second objective might also apply to Goal B if that goal is to individualize instruction.

The relationships shown in Exhibit 3.1 illustrate one function of objectives—to guide the selection of appropriate activities. To continue the example just given, some appropriate activities for reaching the objective of diagnosing reading difficulties might be (1) to see a demonstration of someone administering and interpreting diagnostic tests, (2) to hear an expert discuss the uses and limitations of the procedures, and (3) to participate in directed practice in their use with different kinds of problems.

When the focus is on the immediate objective, it is easy to see how learning activities are directly related to the objective, but when only the broad goal—to improve reading—is in view, then any number of activities could have been selected which might or might not have resulted in increased skill in diagnosing reading problems.

Since objectives are such a pivotal part of the design of programs, it might be well to look at the statement of objectives in greater detail. The same principles that are given in Chapter 8, concerning the statement of instructional objectives, apply here, but it might be helpful to cite at least one of them briefly at this point. That is, the objective should be stated in terms of what the participant in the in-service program is *to be able to do* when he completes the program. To say that he should "Understand the place of linguistics in the teaching of English," or that he must "Appreciate the advantages of the inquiry method in science" tells little about what changes in behavior are desired.

Instead, the objective should be stated in performance terms such as, "To select from a list of topics in English teaching, all of the topics that are most effectively taught using the linguistics approach," or "To identify questions that exemplify the principles underlying the inquiry method in teaching science when given a teaching protocol that contains examples of teachers' questions."

To state objectives in performance terms not only offers more help in selection of specific learning activities that will reach the objective, it also helps in evaluating whether or not the objective has been reached. It is almost impossible to determine if someone "appreciates" something, but it is relatively easy to find out if he can "contrast" the thing which he prefers with some standard of comparison.

Note the differences between the two sets of objectives given below. The utility of stating objectives in performance terms should be readily apparent. The objectives given here are not intended to illustrate *all* the principles of good statements of objectives presented in Chapter 10. They are presented only as brief illustrations of the point being made.

| *Not Stated in Performance Terms* | *Stated in Performance Terms* |
|---|---|
| To understand the reasons for using the overhead projector | To state the advantages of using the overhead projector |
| To appreciate flexible grouping | To contrast flexible grouping with single group instruction |
| To know how to interpret achievement test results | To demonstrate the interpretation of achievement test results |
| To understand the responsibilities of the homeroom teacher for guidance and counseling | To identify the guidance and counseling responsibilities of the homeroom teacher |

Perhaps the most important advantage to be gained from stating objectives in performance terms is that when they are so stated the appropriate activities for reaching the objective are clarified. In the list just mentioned, for example, if the objective is that participants will be able to demonstrate the interpretation of achievement test results, it follows that some time should be planned in the in-service program for an analysis of some sample achievement test data, and participants should be led in some directed practice following a demonstration in which different configurations of achievement test results are shown.

ANALYSIS OF ACTIVITIES

A number of activities are presented in detail in the remaining chapters of this book. They were selected because they include some effective but little-used methods and provide means for achieving a broad range of learning outcomes that may be desired in in-service programs.

No attempt will be made at this point to explicate the activities thoroughly. The reader may want to see Part III for a detailed analysis and come back to this chapter afterward. Our purpose here is to order the activities in terms of the experience impact they can be expected to have on the learner so that they can be related to the kind of learning outcome desired.

With no intent to defend the order as absolute, activities may be arrayed from those with low experience impact to those with high experience impact on the learner. By *experience impact* we mean that the learner is more likely to interact with the learning situation in such a way that the experience will have some impact that will affect his later behavior. This is, of course, an extremely complex relationship which is being oversimplified in order to make possible a rather gross categorization of common in-service activities.

The impact which the learner experiences may be thought of as being related to three characteristics of the learning situation. The first of these is the extent to which he can control the content of the experience. If he has some influence on the content of what is being presented, there is a greater chance that it can be made relevant to his past experience—an important principle in learning. The second characteristic is whether or not the learning experience is multisensory. Use of multisensory stimuli increases the probability that the learner will become involved in the learning situation. Finally, whether communication is one-way or two-way will influence the accuracy of perception and affect confidence in what has been communicated.

Several basic activities are presented in Exhibit 3.2 to illustrate the way in which they are ordered according to their experience impact. For a somewhat different treatment of basic activities, see McIntyre (7) and Harris (4).

In the lecture, the learner is essentially passive. The lecturer controls the structure and content of the activity and the learning is primarily (though not entirely) single-sensory. The illustrated lecture is much the same as the straight lecture with the exception that a visual stimulus has been added.

The participant in a demonstration is usually passive also, although he is experiencing a pattern of activity that he may later seek to emulate. In many ways, the demonstration resembles the illustrated lecture except that what is being witnessed is intended as a model and so usually takes

## Exhibit 3.2
## EXPERIENCE IMPACT OF ACTIVITIES

| ACTIVITIES | CONTROL OF CONTENT | MULTI-SENSORY | TWO-WAY COMMUNICATION | |
|---|:---:|:---:|:---:|---|
| Lecture | | | | |
| Illustrated Lecture | | X | | LOW EXPERIENCE |
| Demonstration | | X | | IMPACT |
| Observation | | X | | |
| Interviewing | X | | X | |
| Brainstorming | X | | X | |
| Group Discussions | X | | X | |
| Buzz Sessions | X | | X | |
| Role-playing | X | X | X | HIGH EXPERIENCE |
| Guided Practice | X | X | X | IMPACT |

place in a setting which includes equipment, materials, and realia with which the participant later will have firsthand experience.

Observation involves both visual and aural stimuli but it is like the lecture in that the observer exercises no influence over what he is experiencing and he has no means of communicating with others during the observation. Observation is also like some kinds of demonstrations. The major differences would seem to be that the demonstration is a simulation while the observation is normally thought of as taking place in some real situation. In this sense, content is more highly focused in the demonstration.

When used in a laboratory exercise, interviewing may be a demonstration for those who are watching, but from the viewpoint of those engaged in the interview, it is a special form of role playing. In this sense, content is extemporized and communication is two-way. Since the interview is usually limited to verbal communication, it may be considered single-sensory although some visual stimuli are no doubt present in the "silent language" of gestures and facial expressions. Interviewing is also a useful in-service technique for leadership training. In this use, the interviewer seeks to gain skill in getting information needed to diagnose a problem situation and to prepare an effective supervisory plan.

Brainstorming and buzz sessions are similar in that content, though focused, depends upon the contributions of group members and that communication is completely unrestricted. The learner may influence the content of activity although it may be somewhat restricted by the group leader and there is a two-way flow of communication.

Role playing is listed as a high experience impact activity in Exhibit 3.2 because participants control the content to the extent that they extemporize the interchange. The learning situation is multisensory in that it involves physical movement and may have various props which serve as visual stimuli to learning. Communication, of course, is two-way in two-person role playing and multichannel in situations involving more than two people.

Guided practice has the same sources of experience impact as role playing except that now the role is being played "for real." In this sense, internships, student teaching, and other forms of guided practice have maximum experience impact.

The differences among the various activities mentioned above would suggest that some of them are better for certain in-service purposes than others. In general, those that have higher experience impact take more time and skill and require more materials and equipment. The question confronting the designer is what activities will give the desired outcomes at the least cost? It will be the purpose of the following section to suggest a relationship between activities and objectives that will have some utility in the design of in-service programs.

### Relating activities to objectives

Objectives of in-service programs and activities that might be planned for reaching those objectives are depicted in Exhibit 3.3 as the two dimensions of a grid that might be considered the *design grid* for planning in-service programs.

The horizontal dimension lists the objectives that might be sought. Beginning at the left are those objectives that lie lowest in the cognitive domain: (1) outcomes that concern recall or recognition (knowledge), (2) outcomes that demand that the learner can relate various knowledges to each other or to possible applications (comprehension), (3) outcomes that demonstrate that the learner *will* exhibit the desired behavior given the opportunity to do so (application), (4) outcomes that require that the learner demonstrate that he can recognize the appropriate use of the new behavior in relation to the total configuration of the teaching task—that he knows *when* to use it (synthesis). In the order mentioned, each

**Exhibit 3.3**
**IN-SERVICE DESIGN GRID**

| ACTIVITIES | OBJECTIVES | | | | | |
|---|---|---|---|---|---|---|
| | Knowledge | Compre-hension | Appli-cation | Synthesis | Values & Attitudes | Adjust-ment |
| Lecture | | | | | | |
| Illustrated lecture | Design I Cognitive Objectives | | | | | |
| Demonstration. | | | Design III Broad-Spectrum Objectives | | | |
| Observation | | | | | | |
| Interviewing | | | | | | |
| Brainstorming | | | | | | |
| Group Discussion | | | | | | |
| Buzz Sessions | | | | | | |
| Role-Playing | | | | | | |
| Guided Practice | | | | Design II Affective Objectives | | |
| | | | | | | |

category of objective is higher in the cognitive domain, with synthesis being the most complex. It will be recognized that the ordering has been adapted from the *Taxonomy of Educational Objectives* (2, 5).

Although there is not a clear demarcation among the categories, the remaining two classes of objectives lie in what is ordinarily considered to be the affective domain—those that concern the feelings of the learner. These are popularly called attitude and value.

DESIGN I: COGNITIVE OUTCOMES

To illustrate a design in which the objectives lie in the lower ranges of the cognitive domain, let us suppose that a group of teachers has planned to learn something about the Initial Teaching Alphabet as a way of introducing reading. At present they are not interested in putting the ITA into use or even trying it out in a limited way. These may be later objectives, but for the moment, the group is interested only in contrasting its advantages and limitations with their present program to see if further experience is desired.

This, then, is a very limited objective and can be met with a design based on isolated activities. Since it concerns factual content at the level of recognition and comprehension, a low experience impact activity is indicated. From the design grid, it appears that lecture, demonstration, and perhaps discussion would be appropriate activities.

Perhaps a resource person might be contacted to bring an illustrated lecture and follow this with a demonstration. Finally, a report on research results might be presented and then discussed. The design might look something like that shown in Exhibit 3.4

## Exhibit 3.4
## DESIGN FOR COGNITIVE OBJECTIVES

| ACTIVITIES. | OBJECTIVES | | | | | |
|---|---|---|---|---|---|---|
| | Knowledge | Compre-hension | Application | Synthesis | Values Attitudes | Adjustment |
| Lecture | | | | | | |
| Illustrated Lecture | x | | | | | |
| Demonstration | | | x | | | |
| Interviewing | | | | | | |
| Brainstorming | | | | | | |
| Group Discussion | | | x | | | |
| Buzz Sessions | | | | | | |
| Role-Playing | | | | | | |
| Guided Practice | | | | | | |

**DESIGN II: AFFECTIVE OUTCOMES**

There are times when the emphasis is not on new information to be imparted in the in-service program, but on changing the feeling tone of participants. Let us suppose, for example, that a group of teachers has spent some time in study of effective parent-teacher interviews, but the principal is still not completely satisfied with the feedback he is getting from some parents concerning their responses to interviews. From the results of a questionnaire, he decides that the problem is that most teachers are not able to empathize with the parent who comes to the conference. Perhaps some teachers are treating the conference too logically and in too highly structured a way, without giving the parent the opportunity to deal with his own anxieties about his child's progress. The objective in this event might be "That teachers will be able to contrast the effects of directive and nondirective interview techniques and will demonstrate acceptance of both methods when appropriate in conferences with parents."

The activities selected for this objective must have great experience impact on participants since the outcome requires some alteration in their pattern of behavior. This would suggest a series of sessions in which teachers role-play interview techniques, using different approaches. The role-playing might be followed by buzz sessions in which the effectiveness of the interviews is discussed. The program might culminate with guided practice in which a resource person gives a critique of how effectively the person playing the role of teacher allows the parent-player to discuss his concerns for his child.

When the activities are related to the objective of the program, the design will appear as in Exhibit 3.5.

### Exhibit 3.5
### DESIGN FOR AFFECTIVE OBJECTIVES

| ACTIVITIES | OBJECTIVES | | | | | |
| --- | --- | --- | --- | --- | --- | --- |
| | Knowledge | Compre-hension | Application | Synthesis | Values Attitudes | Adjustment |
| Lecture | | | | | | |
| Illustrated Lecture | | | | | | |
| Demonstration | | | | | | |
| Interviewing | | | | | | |
| Brainstorming | | | | | | |
| Group Discussion | | | | | x | |
| Buzz Sessions | | | | | | |
| Role-Playing | | | | x | x | |
| Guided Practice | | | | | | x |

DESIGN III: BROAD-SPECTRUM OUTCOMES

Often a program will not have a single objective that can be met with limited activities. Most instructional problems are so complex that they require a variety of activities to meet several objectives ranging from knowledge outcomes to values and adjustments in practice. A good example of broad spectrum outcomes is found in the laboratory exercise concerned with homogeneous grouping. In that exercise the objective might be for a group of teachers to contrast the results of homogeneous grouping with its intended purposes (knowledge), to demonstrate the limited extent to which a range of abilities is reduced in homogeneous grouping (application), and to determine the effect of grouping on criteria other than those used as a basis for grouping (attitudes). For a detailed account of that laboratory exercise, see Chapter 6.

The activities suggested by these objectives range from low experience impact to high experience impact. First, teachers are organized into work teams, divided into buzz groups, and given a deck of cards containing pupil data that might be used as a basis for grouping. The small groups work as teams to form homogeneous groups of students. In the buzz sessions, they role-play the teacher's task of deciding on membership of instructional groups.

Following the role-playing, a group discussion is held in which the group leader feeds back the results from the buzz groups and has the total group contrast the results of the grouping with original objectives. Finally, the range of abilities on a number of different criteria is examined.

The final session is one in which the leader may summarize the experience and deliver a short lecture on homogeneous grouping as demonstrated by outcomes of the laboratory session.

When analyzed, the design of this broad-spectrum program forms a diagonal as shown in Exhibit 3.6.

**Exhibit 3.6**
**DESIGN FOR BROAD-SPECTRUM OBJECTIVES**

| ACTIVITIES | OBJECTIVES | | | | | |
|---|---|---|---|---|---|---|
| | Knowledge | Compre-hension | Application | Synthesis | Values Attitudes | Adjustment |
| Lecture | x | x | | | | |
| Illustrated Lecture | | x | | | | |
| Demonstration | | | x | x | | |
| Interviewing | | | | | | |
| Brainstorming | | | | | | |
| Group Discussion | | | | x | x | |
| Buzz Sessions | | | x | x | | |
| Role-Playing | | | | | | |
| Guided Practice | | | | | x | x |

**In-service education as a component in a larger design**

Too many efforts at instructional change through personnel development fail because they are single-element programs. A larger design is frequently needed to take into account all the organizational systems that must be adjusted to give the change a supportive environment.

Teachers may be exhorted to try new methods, but unless all system modifications which are necessary to put the methods into practice are made, the new practice is impeded. For example, grading, marking, and reporting practices may underlie resistance to modifications in instruction, and unless organizational rules are relaxed, teachers may be reluctant to change. In other instances teachers may find it impossible to accept the organizational consequences of adopting the new instructional practice. This may be illustrated by the demand of team teaching on planning time and the differentiation of teaching responsibilities. Similarly, staffing patterns may not be flexible enough to permit the introduction of the program that is being promoted by an in-service effort.

School improvement problems range widely for most staff groups and the design of programs should be equally diverse. Problems relating to instruction are commonly related to curriculum, organizational structure, facilities, resources or personnel. Many problems involve all of these elements. Curriculum inadequacies may call for new curricula or revisions of the old. Necessary facilities may be nonexistent, too limited, or inadequate for quality instruction. Organizational arrangements—grouping, departmentalization, or testing schedules—may be impeding good instructional practice. Resources, both human and material, may be inadequate. Personnel may be too busy or simply unavailable to implement certain improvements.

Whatever the type of problem faced and whatever the specific objective selected for instructional improvement, alternative procedures are available. A point developed in the previous chapter may be reiterated here. There are several avenues open to bringing about organizational change. These include adopting new rules, prescribing new procedures, changing materials provided, altering structure and function of the organization, or creating temporary organizational structures such as experimental or pilot programs. None of these approaches obviates the need for encouragement, stimulation, and morale-building directed toward acceptance of improved practices. More than in most other organizations, the school must depend upon systematic personal development of people through in-service education for major improvements in its functioning.

The difficulties mentioned above are usually abundantly clear to the staff members who are experiencing them, and lounge conversations may offer precise and caustic diagnosis. The problems might be equally clear to the planners of the in-service program if they were to set out to identify all the changes that would have to take place before the objective of the in-service program could be reached.

Such preplanning is imperative, and the planning group should include someone who is influential enough in the organization to bring about needed changes in the organization when they are identified. A checklist might even be developed to help in determining whether all important elements have been considered. Some of the following questions should be included in any such list.

1. Is adequate supervisory staff available to support the early hard-to-manage period of trying out a new instructional approach?
2. Is clerical assistance, if needed, available?
3. Are necessary materials available?
4. Is a continuing supply of materials planned?
5. Are necessary items of equipment readily available?
6. Is maintenance of necessary equipment provided for?
7. Are there formal organizational policies that must be modified?
8. Are there informal procedures that must be supplanted?
9. Are there administrative regulations and procedures that conflict with the objective of the in-service program?
10. Will remodeling of facilities be required?
11. Should additional facilities be planned?
12. Will special furnishings in the facility be needed?
13. Has adequate time been made available for the leaders and participants to become thoroughly familiar with new approaches?
14. Have all members of the organization been made aware of the program and how its objectives relate to their areas of concern?
15. Have people outside the organization been informed of ways in which the program might concern them?

The above questions are only starters and each could be amplified considerably. It is not within the scope of this book to develop a total organizational approach to the design of in-service programs, but it is important to keep in mind that such an approach is essential to the success of any program. A favorable balance in the design can be achieved only by considering the organizational context in which the in-service program is to take place.

## Summary

The design of in-service programs has been presented in terms of the selection of available activities to reach the objectives of the program. Objectives, in turn, were stated in terms of larger goals for the in-service program and the school.

A number of activities that are useful in conducting in-service programs were presented, and they were ordered in terms of their experience impact—the extent to which they might be expected to affect the behavior of the learner.

Objectives were defined as being the desired behavior of the participant in the program, and a set of generalized objectives was developed. These objectives were ordered from those demanding a relatively low order of cognition to those which require a high order of response from the learner.

Design was illustrated by showing three typical patterns: one dealing with cognitive objectives, one dealing with affective outcomes, and the last illustrating broad-spectrum outcomes.

## Selected references

1. Association for Supervision and Curriculum Development, *Strategy for Curriculum Change.* New York: The Association, 1966.
2. Bloom, Benjamin S., ed., *Taxonomy of Educational Objectives, Handbook I: Cognitive Domain.* New York: David McKay Company, Inc., 1956.
3. Blanke, Virgil E., and Blaine R. Worthen, eds., "SEC Newsletter of the Conference on Strategies for Educational Change," Ohio State University.
4. Harris, Ben M., *Supervisory Behavior in Education.* Englewood Cliffs, N.J.: Prentice-Hall, Inc., 1963, pp. 71–73.
5. Krathwohl, David R., Benjamin S. Bloom, and Bertram B. Masia, *Taxonomy of Educational Objectives, Handbook II: Affective Domain.* New York: David McKay Company, Inc., 1964.
6. Mager, Robert F., *Preparing Objectives for Programmed Instruction.* San Francisco: Fearon Publishers, 1962.
7. McIntyre, Kenneth E., *Learning in a Block-of Time Program.* The University of Texas, Austin: Southwest School Administration Center, 1957.

# Chapter Four

# THE LABORATORY APPROACH

THIS CHAPTER describes in detail the rationale and essential features of a design or a class of designs referred to as the *laboratory approach*. The authors do not presume that this is the best or even completely adequate approach for accomplishing all in-service objectives. Considerable experience with a variety of laboratory sessions with teachers, administrators, and supervisors leads us to believe that this is a distinctive approach. When laboratory activities are properly incorporated into a suitable design, participants are highly stimulated and report significant gains in understanding (8).

Chapters 5 through 9 provide descriptions of specific laboratory sessions. This chapter is intended to provide a rationale for those types of sessions. The procedures suggested for using an in-service design are likely to be effective only when the rationale is understood by those leading the sessions. It is hoped that this chapter will provide the basis upon which leaders of in-service training programs can design laboratory sessions that have special relevance to their own situations and problems.

The authors are not attempting to provide a leader-proof package for in-service education. On the contrary, it is our belief that in the years ahead in-service education programs must be more imaginative and reflect a larger variety of designs. This will require more and better leadership than ever before. However, the laboratory approach, like others before it (action research, workshops, intervisitation, and so on), may fall far short of its potential for improving instructional practice unless

44

those planning and leading laboratory sessions are professionally knowledgeable and skilled.

## The laboratory approach defined

The laboratory approach is characterized as a basic design for one or more in-service education sessions with design elements as follows:

1. The participant is actively involved in solving a problem.
2. The problem situation is simulated as realistically as possible.
3. Quantifiable data are produced and recorded to reveal the nature of the response of the participants.
4. Feedback on data is provided to permit each participant to contrast his reactions with those of the larger group or other groups.
5. Data are discussed and analyzed so as to lead to generalizations and implications for practice.

Each of these characteristic elements of the laboratory design is discussed below in greater detail. It is important to note at this point some of the differences in characteristics of commonly used designs. A lecture-questioning design, for instance, makes no attempt to simulate reality, involvement is very limited, no data are produced, and feedback (via questions) is directed toward the presenter rather than toward the participants. The design using brainstorming (4) along with discussion still involves no reality simulation, but involvement is more highly individual and data are produced. In a brainstorming-discussion design the kind of data produced is rarely suitable for systematic analysis, and a structured situational context is not provided. Since brainstorming data do not grow out of a simulated reality, it is very difficult for participants to generalize and to see direct applications for the ideas.

In designs making use of firsthand experience, it is interesting to note that reality does not have to be simulated. For example, in-service designs such as those described in Chapter 7 (observing in classrooms) substitute reality for simulation. However, most in-service designs using firsthand experience fail to take advantage of a high level of involvement to produce recorded data, and then feedback is limited and lacks the impact possible when systematic analysis of data is undertaken for feedback purposes. A further limitation of firsthand experience is the excessive amount of time required. For these reasons, laboratory experiences may actually be superior to reality in certain respects.

Exhibit 4.1 presents a schematic flow chart of a design for learning. This is essentially the design of the laboratory approach except that the first and last steps may be separated from the others in both time and space. Planning is an essential part of all laboratory sessions, and, in fact, it is much more detailed for such designs than for most others. The last step, on the other hand, is not an integral part of the laboratory approach.

**Exhibit 4.1**
**DESIGN FOR LEARNING**

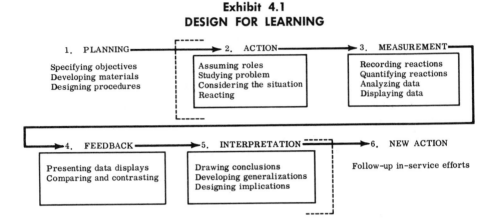

## Characteristic elements of the design

Each of the five elements of the laboratory approach listed above is essential in an in-service design of the laboratory type. To make these ideas more tangible, they will be related to the specific illustration described below as well as to sessions described in Part II.

An in-service session designed to deal with certain concepts regarding evaluation of pupil performance begins with the distribution of a copy of a pupil's spelling paper to each participant. Each individual is asked to score the paper of an eighth-grade girl. (See Chaper 5 for details of this session.) A scoring key is provided to aid the patricipants as each assumes the role of teacher. The scores are recorded, collected, and tabulated while participants individually compute a percentage score and assign a letter grade. These new data are in turn collected and tabulated while participants are given new information concerning the scores of the pupils in the entire class. With the scores for the class in view, participants are again asked to assign a letter grade. This process is repeated a third time on the basis of new information showing scores of 250 pupils in several class sections. Once these various sets of data are tabulated and fed back to participants, they show (1) a high incidence of scoring errors, (2) a continuous shift of the letter grades assigned as more information is made available, and (3) a wide variation in the letter grades assigned regardless of information provided. These data are then discussed, appropriate generalizations are drawn, and possible implications are considered for improving the practice of evaluating pupil performance.

### INVOLVEMENT IN PROBLEM SOLVING

Each participant is asked to assume a role and act in a certain way toward a solution of the problem. The kinds of acts may vary, but *action* is required in response to specific stimuli in a simulated situation and distinct role or position. In the illustration cited above, the situation is structured so that each participant must take the spelling paper and the key and actually check every word and mark it as correctly or incorrectly spelled. The role assumed is that of teacher evaluator. Subsequently, each participant is called upon to make a series of independent decisions regarding appropriate letter grades to be assigned to this girl's spelling test.

As may be seen in Chapter 9, involvement is obtained in the session on interview styles by asking each participant to complete a reactionnaire following each demonstration. Similarly, in the sessions described in Chapter 7, involvement comes about by using observation instruments which require continuous looking, deciding, and recording actions.

### REALISTIC PROBLEMS

Problems are presented in forms that can be readily identified as having been taken from reality. Instead of relying on verbal descriptions, facsimiles of materials are used. In the illustrations above, a sheet of paper which looks very much like a spelling test paper from a student's folder is used. The handwriting is real and the errors are the kind one would expect on a student's paper. As a matter of fact, we have used real materials in most of the sessions described.

In Chapter 7 the first laboratory session provides simulated reality by using a film of classroom teaching for classroom observation. In a session in Chapter 9 simulated interview styles are presented by the use of role-playing or sociodrama, and specific problems are described to provide the situational context.

### DATA PRODUCTION

Each participant records reactions and ideas or in some way produces data that reflect his efforts to solve the simulated problem. The data are in quantifiable form to make analysis and feedback possible. In the illustration above, the data consist of the raw score on the spelling test, the percentage scores, and the letter grades assigned by each participant. In all instances, simple frequency tabulations are employed for analysis.

In Chapter 8 the session on studying teacher questions using lesson protocols provides data for subsequent analysis in the form of code symbols recorded opposite each question. These symbols are then analyzed using frequency tables.

### FEEDBACK ON DATA ANALYSIS

Participants are given an opportunity to view a data display in which raw data have been analyzed to provide insights into the problem under consideration. The data may be analyzed by the leader and his assistants and then presented to participants. However, it is sometimes useful to guide participants in analyzing their own data. In still other instances, the participants are provided with a certain amount of pre-analyzed data to facilitate the analysis of their individual sets of data.

In the illustration above, simple tabulations of scores and letter grades are presented as frequency tables for each participant to see and contrast with his own results. In Chapter 7 the test on specific events observable in a teaching film is scored by each participant, and these scores are combined to form a frequency table for all to see. On the other hand, in the last session described in Chapter 6 standardized test scores are provided to participants, and each individual prepares data displays in the form of line graphs.

### GENERALIZATION AND IMPLICATIONS CONSIDERED

The leader guides the participants in interpreting the data. The group is led in discussing these interpretations so as to discover possible generalizations that can be drawn. Finally, implications for practice in dealing with similar problems are considered.

In the previous illustrations, tables showing the several frequency tables would be displayed on a chalkboard, on a projection screen, or on charts. Each table would be considered individually, and then several tables would be compared. Participants would recognize that each table reveals a wide range of scores and grades assigned. This leads to the generalization that "students with identical performance may receive different letter grades." A comparison of the distributions of letter grades when the student's paper is considered in isolation, compared with classmates, and compared with other class groups, leads to the generalization that "grades assigned by teachers are influenced by the knowledge the teacher has of other pupils' performances." Such generalizations are drawn without satisfactorily controlled experimentation, but the fact that the outcome is inescapably the work of the participant provides him with a sense of satisfaction and confidence in his findings.

### OTHER FEATURES

The characteristic elements of the laboratory approach described above are accompanied by other special features which make these kinds of in-service sessions enthusiastically accepted by the teacher, administrator, and supervisor groups which we have worked with. Some special design features are suggested by the following terms:

1. Structured activity.
2. Restricted focus.
3. Freedom of response.
4. Tension control.

Each of these features is discussed briefly below.

Structured rather than unstructured activity characterizes laboratory sessions. The participants' involvement in problem solving as discussed above is rather highly structured by the nature of the materials used to simulate a problem. The recording of participant responses adds structure to the experience. Furthermore, most laboratory sessions are designed so as to require a specific sequence of activities for all participants. In a sense they are programmed activities.

Focus is obtained in laboratory sessions by producing and analyzing data. Since prompt feedback is an essential characteristic, it demands that the purposes to be served by the session be very narrowly focused. The many kinds of purposes which might be served by having participants engage in problem-solving activities are necesarily delimited by the need to produce a specific array of data for prompt analysis and feedback to participants.

Freedom to respond in one's own way is assured in well-designed laboratory sessions despite the narrow focus and highly structured involvement. For instance, in the case of the evaluation of the spelling test, despite the restriction that the focus is limited to scoring and assigning a letter grade and the activities are closely supervised to insure that every participant will proceed rapidly from step to step, every participant is completely free to assign any letter grade from A through F. In this way, the individuality of each participant is expressed.

Tension control to avoid embarrassment and assure full use of the freedom to respond is important when feedback is to occur in a group context. Laboratory sessions are likely to produce some tension among participants as they realize that they must face their own responses in comparison with those of others. They must be assured, therefore, that such tension will not become excessive. This assurance is built into the design of every laboratory session in several ways.

1. Recorded responses are submitted anonymously, using a personal code or carrying no identifying information.
2. Data are tabulated or otherwise analyzed as frequency distributions, mean scores, ranges, or profiles which reflect responses of a group, not those of individuals.

3.  When either of these precautions is not possible, small groups of
    individuals work together in producing the data, so that they need
    not stand alone when interpretations are discomforting.

### Principles of learning involved

The foregoing description of the laboratory approach implies certain
assumptions about the way people learn, and it is appropriate to consider
them directly. Certain principles of learning seem to be nicely incorporated into the laboratory approach while others are not. Specifically, the
relationship of learning to interest, involvement, success, feedback, discovery, stress, and transfer are worth considering.

Interest in the topic or problem in focus cannot be assured by the
design of the session itself. However the use of realistic problem situations tends to stimulate interest.

Involvement has been discussed at length. These laboratory sessions
produce active involvement and are structured so as to make it very difficult for participants to avoid being fully involved.

Success for participants is assured in laboratory sessions not only by
the highly structured nature of the activities, but also by the freedom of
responses permitted. Activities are structured for easy accomplishment
by the average instructional staff member. Responses require no specialized skills and, if necessary, group leaders work closely with individuals to facilitate their participation.

Feedback is a basic element in each of these sessions and is provided
as quickly as possible, usually delayed only by a coffee break. Since data
are in simple quantitative form, frequency tabulations, graphs, and
tables are used for brief but meaningful feedback sessions. While feedback is not usually immediate in these laboratory sessions, it is prompt
in the sense that only an hour's delay is common. This builds interest
while retaining the full value of the feedback effect.

Discovery rather than exhortation is involved in each session because
each participant gets involved, deals with real problems, produces unique
data, and is assisted in drawing inferences by a highly structured sequence which leads to a data display to be considered. While the approach is inductive rather than deductive, it does not provide for the
unstructured exploration usually associated with discovery learning (3).

Emotional stress is controlled by several devices discussed above, but
a minimum level of stress is assured by the requirement that responses
be recorded individually or in small groups. The fact that the individual's
response becomes part of a group record stimulates interest, but it also
makes each participant somewhat anxious. As he submits his response, he
almost always turns to others to see how they compare.

Transfer is not fully assured by the laboratory approach, but the realistic context in which participants face problems gives some chance for transfer of training to similar situations. The simulation offered by these sessions may well be similar to that encountered in real school situations. The strength of transfer is weakened, however, by the highly structured responses which are not likely to be closely related to those on the job.

### Reality simulation

The effort to simulate reality in designing laboratory sessions has been emphasized in a variety of ways. The extensive use of role-playing, demonstrations, films, vignettes, and realia is calculated to give the participant as many opportunities as possible to relate the activities of the sessions to past experience. Various other in-service designs also call upon reality simulation, but the importance of this element in laboratory sessions makes careful consideration of this term worthwhile.

One question which should be asked is "Why use simulated reality instead of reality itself?" Various reasons clearly argue against the use of real experience for some in-service purposes. The economical use of time or the inaccessibility of some situations may make reality less than feasible. But even when these are not barriers, simulated situations can be more highly structured, comparable data can be produced, extraneous factors can be controlled, and group processes can be employed in dealing with problems which in reality might involve only one or two persons. Furthermore, an excessively high level of stress is sometimes associated with firsthand experience. Last but not least is the costliness of errors; sometimes, as in a parent-teacher interview, the school cannot afford the consequences of learning (and making mistakes) via firsthand experiences.

In choosing simulation one has to design an in-service session with careful attention to those elements of reality which are essential or at least most important to maintain. The central purpose or purposes of the session will dictate such decisions, and it is usually convenient to eliminate certain elements which are not crucial to the accomplishment of the purpose. Within the limits of feasibility, reality probably should be maintained wherever possible, but sacrificed wherever the cost in time and materials is too great or extraneous to the purpose. In general, reality as it relates to the time dimension almost always has to be sacrificed, since one of the very important and almost essential advantages of reality simulation is that of collapsing the time span that would be required for a real experience. On the other hand, reality should be maintained as far as is possible when it relates to the kind of data to be gathered, the sources of the data, and the sequence of activities. Participants need to sense reality as they proceed with the activities, and having a fairly normal sequence of experiences seems to facilitate this. On the other hand, the data produced, if realistic, facilitate discussion in terms of related problems and might well facilitate transfer.

Reality simulation must be such as to maintain credibility in the eyes of the participants. They tend to respond to reality, but unless it is a relevant kind of situation and problem it will not be readily accepted by them. If the problem situation is such that transfer to other related problems is quite feasible, participants are more receptive. Even though involvement encourages consideration of the ideas being presented, the design needs to avoid oversimplified situations and problems. Professional staff members tend to resist the use of their valuable time for dealing with the superficial.

Because reality is simulated, its limitations need to be made quite apparent and explicit to participants. There should be no pretext that simulation *is* reality. Where simulation has been seriously sacrificed, it should be openly acknowledged. Finally, the designs should conform with appropriate research and theory so that participants can be given assurances that insights gained in the simulated experience are supported by more rigorous studies of related problems.

### Limitations of the approach

The laboratory approach described above is no panacea for all in-service education programs. In-service sessions designed along the lines described can be extremely useful for building a variety of understandings, overcoming certain misconceptions, and, in many instances, stimulating an interest in new approaches to problems. On the other hand, the laboratory approach does not lend itself particularly well, as far as we know, to the development of a variety of skills. Likewise, we have not been able to design sessions that seem to have any significant impact on restructuring of value systems or provide relatively efficient ways to present new information.

Even within the domain of effectiveness which the laboratory approach seems to possess, some weaknesses should be clearly recognized. The highly structured nature of these sessions makes it very difficult to involve participants in preplanning. We rely heavily upon the face validity of the activities, and a high level of involvement in them to stimulate interest and gain acceptance; whereas involvements in preplanning often suffices to do this with other in-service designs.

Since laboratory sessions are not designed to produce high-level skill development, there may be a tendency for participants to accept and appreciate their new insights without being motivated to take the next steps required to restructure behavior.

Because these designs call for high levels of involvement in a simulated problem situation with thorough data production analysis and feedback, the result is a fairly time-consuming type of in-service education. Laboratory sessions are rarely effectively presented in less than two hours and often three or more hours are desirable.

Many of the laboratory sessions that have been designed call for groups of no less than fifteen participants. This is both a limitation and an advantage. It restricts the use of these training sessions to those situations where a group of similarly interested and concerned professional staff members is available. There is an advantage to be found in that many of the laboratory sessions have been successfully used with unusually large groups, ranging up to as many as 500 participants.

## Past experience with laboratory sessions

The illustrative sessions described in Part II have been developed over the past five or six years in connection with an in-service education project directed by Professor Kenneth E. McIntyre at the University of Texas. This project was initially concerned with the development of school principals as more effective instructional leaders. Gradually, it became evident that principals, like teachers, need in-service opportunities to learn about some very fundamental concepts of teaching, learning, human growth and development, testing, etc. The authors accepted this challenge to broaden their thinking and focus upon in-service program development as related to crucial concerns about instructional practices. As a result, laboratory sessions have been developed over the years in response to questions and concerns expressed by teachers, principals, and supervisors. With a particular instruction-related concept or problem in mind, the authors began to explore possible laboratory designs. Once a design was developed in preliminary form, a "tryout" with colleagues and graduate students provided experience for use as a basis for revising the materials and procedures. Field trials of all sessions were subsequently conducted before the materials and procedures were available for general distribution.

The laboratory sessions described in this book have all had extensive field testing. Unlike many published materials intended for use in elementary and secondary schools, those described in these chapters were developed in response to the expressed interests and concerns of practitioners, designed with these staff people in mind, and tested widely in the field. Understandably, perhaps, these laboratory sessions have also been well received in graduate education courses on several college campuses.

Field trials have been conducted with many groups. The administrative and supervisory staffs in more than 20 school districts have used this approach in in-service groups and several large school systems have given the authors opportunities to use certain laboratory sessions with 150 to 300 staff members. Entire high school and elementary school faculty groups have been involved using certain materials. On still other occasions 20 or more elementary and secondary school teachers have formed in-service groups. Other groups have consisted of superintendents, supervisors, curriculum directors, and college professors. Programs using a variety of sessions have been conducted in Virginia, Alabama, New Mexico, Florida, and Missouri, as well as in Texas where the authors have conducted extended field trials. Limited evaluations have been undertaken with nearly every session as well as programs involving a whole series of sessions (6, 8). Reactions of participants secured anonymously immediately following a session have produced uniformly high ratings when compared with other in-service experience. At the end of year-long programs, rankings of individual in-service sessions including a variety of kinds of activities have resulted in high rankings for laboratory sessions as compared with other types. Evidence on change in behavior of participants is very limited, but before and after tests of knowledge do show significant gains, and self-reports from participants regarding follow-up efforts are frequently received even several years later.

## Summary

The laboratory approach is a category of in-service design which is quite different from those approaches commonly in use in in-service programs in the United States today. The special characteristics of involvement, reality simulation, data production, feedback, and interpretation, while found in certain instances in other in-service designs, are brought together in the laboratory approach to form a unique sequence of structured experiences for group participants. Perhaps the most unique features of this design are reality simulation, quantifiable data production, and prompt feedback. With due regard for the limitations that this and all other in-service designs have, there appear to be almost no limits to the variety of concepts and related problems that can be dealt with effectively for the production of understanding and new attitudes using this design.

## Selected references

1. Bartholomew, Wm., "Place of Demonstration in Supervision," *National Elementary Principal*, XXXV (Sept. 1935), 189–91.
2. California Council on Teacher Education, *Toward Better Schools*, Bul. 26, No. 3. Sacramento: California State Department of Education, 1957.
3. Glaser, Robert, "Variables in Discovery Learning", in *Learning by Discovery: A Critical Appraisal* by Lee S. Shulman and Evan R. Keislar, eds., Chicago: Rand McNally and Company, 1966.
4. Harris, Ben M., *Supervisory Behavior in Education*. Englewood Cliffs, N.J.: Prentice-Hall, Inc., 1963, Chapter 3.
5. Harris, Ben M., "The Teaching Demonstration Model," in *Designs for Inservice Education*, E. W. Bessent, ed., The University of Texas, 1967, Chapter 4.
6. McIntyre, Kenneth E., "The Laboratory Approach," in *Designs for Inservice Education*, E. W. Bessent, ed., The University of Texas, 1967, Chapter 2.
7. Thomas, Michael P., *Strategies in the Preparation of School Administrators*. Report of the National Conference of Professors of Educational Administration, August, 1964.
8. Wolfe, Wendell W., *A Study of a Laboratory Approach to In-Service Development Programs for School Administrators and Supervisors*. Unpublished Ph.D. dissertation, The University of Texas, 1965.

PART TWO


Illustrative Laboratory Sessions

The following six chapters present a number of laboratory exercises that have been developed in recent years in working with in-service groups of school leadership personnel. All of the exercises were developed jointly or individually by Professors Wailand Bessent, Ben M. Harris, and Kenneth E. McIntyre, with the assistance of a number of graduate students who have worked in the School Principalship Project at the University of Texas.

Our experience in using these exercises has been highly gratifying. The fact that the content has been largely collected from real-life situations in schools gives the material authenticity that school people recognize and appreciate. For example, the test items in the Teacher-Made Test exercise in Chapter 5 are actual items taken from classroom tests. Extensive field testing and development over the past ten years have yielded a series of exercises that are feasible for use within the practical constraints of time, setting, and group membership found in typical in-service groups in the field. An even more important aspect of the laboratory exercises included is that they deal with problems of immediate interest to teachers and instructional leaders—grading, marking, reporting, testing, observing and analyzing instructions, stating instructional objectives, and communicating with others.

The selection of laboratory sessions included is not intended to suggest that these are the only or even the best ones for use in in-service programs. They are important and broad enough in scope so that, if used properly, they could constitute a significant in-service effort.

We have attempted to give instructions for use that are complete enough to enable the reader to duplicate the session if he desires, although we urge the person interested in using the materials to adapt them to his own locally-developed objectives and to modify procedures. To that end, we hope the following chapters will provide a useful model and stimulus for further development.

58

*Throughout the chapters that follow, the group leader will be referring participants to* forms *that appear as* exhibits *and* appendices *in this book. In every instance the same exhibit number in this book is retained in the materials the participants will use out of the supplementary volume,* In-Service Education: Materials for Laboratory Sessions. *Exhibits are identified by means of Arabic numerals (e.g., Exhibit 6.1) and appendices are identified by Roman numerals (e.g., Appendix VI-A); for this reason it will be important for the session leader to clearly identify the form to which he is directing participants as Form 6.1 or VI-A, whichever is appropriate.*

*The participants may find the page numbers by using the "Locator" in the front of the workbook or materials volume (see Appendix III in this book). If participants have any difficulty in finding materials rapidly, the session leader may want to look up the page number of each form he will use and announce it at the proper time.*

Chapter Five

# ANALYZING THE EVALUATION OF PUPIL PERFORMANCE

THE EVALUATION of any complex endeavor is difficult, and evaluating learning is perhaps the most complex of all endeavors that most of us deal with directly. Throughout the teaching-learning process, from the setting of goals to the measurement of performance and the determination of criteria, obstacles arise to complicate evaluation. To make matters even more difficult, our efforts to make obviously needed changes are thwarted by well-established tradition—a long history of confusion and near chaos, especially in the indiscriminate mixing of measurement, analysis, interpretation, valuing, and reporting in the totality called evaluation.

Much can be done, however, to improve the evaluation of pupil performance. Although it will never be characterized by the precision achieved in certain fields, a great deal of improvement is possible.

The purpose of this chapter is to describe laboratory exercises designed to expose the most persistent problems of performance evaluation and to provide a basis for discussing and alleviating them. The first session consists of a series of tasks in which each participant is asked to evaluate several examples of pupil work. Analysis of the group's marks brings out many of the most troublesome problems of evaluation. In the second session, the meanings conveyed by evaluation symbols are considered. In the third session, teacher-made tests are the focus of attention. Several items from various teacher-made tests, and a few complete tests, are presented for analysis and discussion.

## Problems of marking pupils' work

BACKGROUND ON THE PROBLEM

Evaluation is essential to progress in education. It begins with the determination of criteria and follows with description or measurement, analysis, and interpretation of data, and, finally, by the valuing of the performance or product and the representing of that value with some kind of abstract symbol.

*Determination of criteria*  Before one can tell how well his new sports car is performing, he must have an idea of what a good sports car performance is like; similarly, before one can evaluate a pupil's essay on "The United Nations," he must decide what a good essay on this topic would be like. Without criteria, evaluation is aimless and often meaningless. A meaningful measure of performance is not possible unless specified criteria are used.

*Measurement*  One could make a convincing argument that the measurement aspect of evaluation in the schools is the weakest link in the entire chain. How often we attempt to "evaluate" without having carefully measured the phenomena that we are trying to judge! We have a strong hunch that Miss Smith is a good teacher, but, if challenged to support our hunch with concrete evidence, we wouldn't have it. Or, we place a mark on a pupil's paper—say that we give him an "A"—indicating that we like his work, but we haven't systematically measured in order to have a more defensible basis for our judgment of value.

We are so accustomed to indiscriminate mixing of measurement, on the one hand, and "valuing," on the other, that it is sometimes difficult to convince teachers that there is a difference between the two processes. For instance, when we say that Mary typed 56 words per minute, or Willie broad-jumped 16 feet, 5 inches, or Joe misspelled 4 words out of 20, or Susie's response to Item 1 on an essay test met the criteria for that item to the extent that her paper was placed in the next-to-highest of five stacks (for that item only)—for all of these performances we have merely described or measured something so that we are in a better position to judge it later. We haven't said that any of the efforts mentioned above were "good" or "bad." When we do get to the valuing phase of the process, the quality of our evaluation will be dependent in large measure on how well we have measured or described something.

*Analysis*  When we measure or describe something, we must find ways to arrange it or organize it or "take it apart" so that we can study what we have. Usually it is advisable to arrange pupils' scores on a test so that we can see how the group as a whole performed, so we make a frequency distribution of the scores. We might want to know how the boys' scores compared with the girls' scores, or which items were answered incorrectly by the most pupils, so we analyze the test results to find out. We can compute a mean score in order to draw comparisons. We can place our measures in rank order. We can contrast one set of measures with an earlier set by the same pupil. Any and all of these manipulations of data provide the evaluating teacher (or student) with ways of viewing the measurements.

*Interpretation*   Once we have our data arranged so that we know what we have, we can interpret the results. Willie's broad jump of 16 feet, 5 inches looks different if he is the only person in the group to jump more than 12 feet, or if he was jumping only 10 feet at the beginning of the year. To interpret a pupil's performance, we relate it to other relevant information so that we can value it. When viewing Mary's typing as the third fastest in a class of 35 students, it has more meaning. If Joe's spelling of 16 words correctly places him in the middle of one hundred students, it has some meaning.

*Valuing*   Too often we begin evaluation by valuing or passing judgment without having gathered the evidence, analyzed or interpreted it. Sometimes we suffer for this—as when we flunk a pupil without the evidence to back up our action, and the injured person protests—but regardless of our own troubles, everybody suffers when such an important process as evaluation is poorly done. Valuing is an essential step in the process of evaluation. Having established criteria, measured, analyzed, and interpreted to the best of their ability, evaluators are in a position to make limited judgments about the value or worth of the measured performance. Interpretations will have been drawn based on the comparisons which seem most relevant. A judgment of worth can then be made. The teacher may call Mary's typing "excellent," Willie's jump "good," and Joe's spelling "fair."

*Representing the value*   A value judgment can be represented in various ways in written or symbolic form and can be conveyed orally as well as in written symbols. Graphic representations are also possible alternatives. Generally, we use a symbol (A, B, C, etc.) to represent our judgments of worth.

No attempt is made in this session to treat all of the problems involved in the marking of pupils' work. Rather, a few of the most troublesome aspects of the problem are highlighted to serve as a basis for discussion and further study. This session is intended to provide evidence to support the following statements:

1. The high degree of variability among persons when they evaluate pupil performance.
2. Teachers' measurement errors influence pupils' marks.
3. Pupils' marks are influenced by the performances of the groups with which they are compared.
4. Ability grouping affects the marks assigned to pupils' work.
5. Extraneous factors such as the appearance of a paper, the pupil's I.Q., and the pupil's behavior and background influence the marks a pupil receives.
6. There is an "objectivity" fallacy in marking arithmetic, spelling, or similarly "factual" work.
7. Measurement is only one component of evaluation.
8. Single symbols have serious limitations as conveyors of meaning concerning pupils' performances.

PROCEDURE

During the first part of the session, participants are seated at tables or desks in a way that will facilitate the distribution and collection of papers, but with enough space between individuals so that each person will work independently. During the discussion phase of the session, the seats should be arranged to facilitate discussion.

After announcing the basic purpose of the session, the leader immediately distributes an English theme, the first of a series of instruments. (They are shown later in this chapter.) This theme (Exhibit 5.1) is an exact copy of one submitted by a high school student. Each participant has the same theme and the same instructions—to play the role of the student's teacher, and mark the theme. As marking is completed, the papers are collected for tabulation with assurances that feedback will be given shortly. Another piece of work by a pupil is distributed for "marking," then another, and so on until several evaluations have been made by all participants. The mark on each instrument is tabulated as it is completed, but these tabulations are not revealed until all instruments have been marked. Once the participants "catch on" to the pattern of responses to any one of the instruments, they might be influenced in the way they respond to subsequent instruments. Therefore, *it is necessary to complete all of the marking before any of the results are revealed.* Some of the samples of pupil work being distributed come in two versions. The leader must study these exhibits with great care and follow procedures described below for distributing these to alternate tables and rows, if desired results are to be obtained.

Unless the group is quite large, the tabulation of responses to each instrument can be handled by one person while the next instrument is being filled out. If the group is large, it might be necessary to recruit more than one tabulator or to provide a coffee break after the marking phase in order to finish the tabulations.

Before the tabulations are fed back to the group for discussion, it is advisable to have a consultant or some other informed person present a brief lecture on the history of the problem, including the various attempts at its solution through changing symbols, manipulating the form of report cards, adding criteria, and the like. After perhaps 10 or 15 minutes of this sort of background, the leader acknowledges that most of the historical problems are still with us and proceeds to illustrate his point by revealing the first of the tabulations or responses by the group itself.

## SEQUENCE OF ACTIVITIES

| Time | Activity and Materials |
|------|------------------------|
| 3 min. | Brief introductory comments. |
| 5 min. | Distribute instrument shown in Exhibit 5.1. Review instructions. Circulate to assist as needed. Collect marks assigned. (Start tabulation while instrument is being studied.) |
| 5 min. | Distribute instruments shown in Exhibits 5.2a and 5.2b. Be sure each participant has only 5.2a *or* 5.2b, not both. Review instructions (Exhibit 5.2a) briefly. Collect marks assigned, keeping marks of those reacting to Exhibit 5.2a separate from those reacting to Exhibit 5.2b. (Continue tabulations while other instruments are being marked.) |
| 6 min. | Distribute next instrument selected for use. (The instruments shown in Exhibits 5.3 and 5.4 may be eliminated if a short session is planned.) |
| 6 min. | Distribute instrument shown in Exhibit 5.5. Show scoring system on chalkboard or overhead transparency. Be sure that participants understand scoring from zero to ten. |
| 5 min. | Distribute instruments shown in Exhibits 5.6a and 5.6b. Assure group that the key is correct. |
| 10 min. | Distribute instruments shown in Exhibits 5.6c through 5.6e in sequence, collecting each set of marks as next instrument is being distributed. |
| 10 min. | Break for coffee or stretch. (Complete all tabulations as quickly as possible.) |
| 10 min. | Brief lecture on problems with marks and parent reporting systems. |
| 10 min. | Feed back results of tabulation of all instruments showing distributions of marks assigned. |
| 10 min. | Discussion of principles and implications. |
| 10 min. | Summary. |

*Total Time:* 1 hour and 30 minutes

## DESCRIPTION OF INSTRUMENTS

Each of the examples of pupil work that is available for use in this session is described below. Each instrument will bring out a different concept, which can serve as the focus of discussion for a few minutes during or following feedback on the tabulations.

*English themes* The first theme is marked twice by participants, once assuming heterogeneous grouping and once assuming homogeneous grouping. This instrument (Exhibit 5.1) usually produces a distribution of marks ranging from B through F for the heterogeneous group and a distribution ranging from A through D for the low ability group. The first concept to be discussed is that of the variability of ratings and the difficulties arising from this variability. The second concept is that of the effect of grouping on marks and the fact that a given paper tends to receive a higher mark if the pupil is in a low ability group.

The material in Exhibits 5.2a and 5.2b should be arranged before distribution to the group, so that every other person or row receives 5.2a, and the alternate persons or rows receive 5.2b. In order that the participants will not notice the difference in handwriting and become suspicious, the alternating of rows is preferable. We recommend that the books being used by participants (*In-Service Education: Materials for Laboratory Sessions*) be kept in the possession of the group leader between sessions. This means that all of the materials to be used in this particular session can be distributed by the leader or his assistants in the proper sequence. By tearing all of the materials for this session from these books in advance, the leader can hand out each instrument as it is needed. He can be sure that two-version themes are passed down alternate rows or tables without revealing the fact that the effects of a certain variable are being tested. The leader should announce, in any case, that the papers are not identical (which is true because of the difference in handwriting—although this is the only difference.) The concept illustrated by the use of these two instruments is that of the influence of extraneous factors in scoring pupil work; although the scorers are instructed to evaluate the essay on the basis of content and organization only, the average score on the neat theme is usually higher than that on the sloppy theme.

Another aspect of the problem of extraneous factors is illustrated by the instruments shown in Exhibits 5.3a and 5.3b. Again, the two response sheets and themes should be alternated among the participants. The theme in Exhibit 5.3a is identical to the one in Exhibit 5.3b except for the occupation about which "Pete" is writing; however, in Exhibit 5.3a Pete is described as a wholesome sort of "All-American boy," and in 5.3b he is described as a slob. Be sure to have one part of the group use Exhibit 5.3a while the other uses 5.3b.

Although in actual practice it is doubtful that the slob would receive higher marks for his work, he usually does in this exercise, probably because the scorers have compassion for a slob in the abstract. At any rate, something other than the essay itself is entering into the scoring process because the essays are essentially identical. In the discussion, the point might be made that there is some research evidence indicating that children from the wrong side of the tracks actually tend to receive lower marks than do middle-class youngsters for the same quality of work. Then what is responsible for Pete's higher scores when he is described according to the stereotype of a lower-class youngster? Is it surprise that a youngster of his type wrote as well as he did? Is it sympathy for the underdog? Would it happen that way if Pete were a physcial reality, instead of a character of fiction.

Exhibits 5.4a, and 5.4b also illustrate the concept of extraneous factors, this time by revealing the writer's score on an "I.Q." test. Half of the group of participants should receive 5.4a, the writer of which is said to have scored 85 on a mental maturity test; the other half should receive 5.4b written by a pupil who scored 127 on the test. This is the only difference between the two instruments, and the participants, of course, are not aware of this difference at the time they place a mark on the paper. The paper written by the child with the lower I.Q. usually gets a higher average score than does the paper written by the child with the higher I.Q. During the discussion session, the group should be asked whether knowledge of I.Q. scores *should* influence those who mark pupils' papers.

*An arithmetic test item*   The myth of the objectivity of scoring arithmetic papers will be shattered through the use of the instrument shown in Exhibit 5.5. In most groups, the range of scores is from 0 through 7 or 8, out of a possible 10 points. In the discussion period, different points of view will be vigorously defended; several people will insist that the product (the correct answer) is the only important consideration, whereas others will argue that the entire process should be evaluated, and the pupil credited with those parts that he handled correctly.

*A spelling test*   Exhibits 5.6a through 5.6e constitute a series of steps in an exercise designed to bring out the problem of inaccuracy on the part of scorers, as well as the importance of norm groups in interpreting scores. These materials are shown in Exhibits 5.6a through 5.6e. The materials shown in Exhibits 5.6a and 5.6b should be distributed together, with instructions (Exhibit 5.6a) to each participant to score Janice Henry's spelling test. When each person has finished checking the pupil's paper against the key, the score (number correct) should be placed in the designated place, and the papers should be handed in for tabulation. Then the sheet shown in Exhibit 5.6c should be distributed, with instructions to calculate the percentage score and a letter mark, which should then be handed in for tabulation. The sheet shown in Exhibit 5.6d should be distributed, completed, and handed in, followed finally by the instrument shown in Exhibit 5.6e.

Most groups will be surprised when the results of this exercise are revealed. With most groups, the scores placed on Janice's paper will vary widely; usually only slightly more than one third of the group will give her a 37, which is the correct score. The percentage scores given to her paper will vary even more widely, sometimes from less than 30 per cent to more than 80 per cent—even after the participants have been informed of the number of words that Janice spelled correctly!

Most participants will mark the paper with a D or an F on the instrument shown in Exhibit 5.6c; the average will go up to a B on Exhibit 5.6d and then nearly to an A on Exhibit 5.6e. There are sometimes some holdouts for giving Janice a D or even an F, even on the instrument shown in Exhibit 5.6e.

Remember to follow the directions given above for distributing and collecting the various instruments in this exercise and do not discuss the group's responses until the entire exercise—5.6a through 5.6e—has been completed. Then feed back results in the order given, discussing the results of each instrument as they are presented to the group.

**REVIEW OF CONCEPTS ILLUSTRATED**

| EXHIBIT | OUTCOME | CONCEPT |
|---|---|---|
| 5.1<br>English Theme | Participants raise the grade when they learn the student is in a slow group. | Teacher makes unwarranted assumptions about an individual's work based on knowledge about the group.<br><br>Teachers let expectations of group influence valuations of individuals. |
| 5.2a–b<br>English Theme | Participants mark neat papers higher than sloppy papers. | Teachers allow attitudes toward neatness to influence valuing even when neatness is not a criterion of evaluation. |
| 5.3a–b<br>English Theme | Participants give better marks to student described as a culturally disadvantaged boy. | Teachers allow feelings for student to influence their valuations. |
| 5.4a–b<br>English Theme | Participants give better marks to the student with the low I.Q. | Teachers tend to allow expectations of pupils to influence their evaluations.<br><br>High ability students have difficulty getting objective valuations.<br><br>Low ability students tend to get unrealistically positive valuations. |

## INSTRUCTIONS AND WORKSHEET

### "The Best Teacher I Have Ever Had"

This is a required theme written by a student in a 10th grade English class.

Read it and then assign two marks to it (with an $\underline{A}$, $\underline{B}$, $\underline{C}$, $\underline{D}$, F marking system, $\underline{D}$ being the lowest passing mark).

1. The mark you would give the theme if this were in a completely normal community and school situation and a typical heterogeneous group of students:

   (circle one)

   A    B    C    D    F

2. The mark you would give the theme if this were in the same situation above except that the class is the lowest of three ability groups:

   (circle one)

   A    B    C    D    F

As soon as you have completed the marking as instructed, hand in this sheet for tabulation.

**Exhibit 5.1**

---

The Best Teacher I Have Ever Had

At eight o'clock every morning a lady about five-feet seven inches tall arrives at school. She walks into her speech class and then proceeds to the teacher's lounge to get a cup of coffee. At about eight-fifteen she returns to her room to find it full of students. These students keep her busy answering questions until the 8:25 bell rings which means all the students should go to their advisory.

In another five minutes her room is full again with kids needing help in acts and plays.

During the school sponsored assemblies no one else but this busy teacher directs them. The assemblies are programs of-off rather smooth considering the fact that the audience sometimes hisses and boos.

This teacher is the best teacher I have ever had because she can handle all of the plays, assemblies, and her classes which number five and still be the nice, kind and meet teacher you like to be around. She is always friendly to everyone and never gets mad or upset, unless her class gives her good reason. Truly she is the best teacher I have ever had.

**Exhibit 5.1 (continued)**

INSTRUCTIONS AND WORKSHEET

"Equality of Man"

This is an essay submitted by a student in a 10th grade English class.

The assignment was to write an original essay on some aspect of democracy, approximately 250 words in length, giving special attention to original thinking, creative expression, and effective organization.

Evaluate this essay very carefully on the basis of original thinking, creative expression, and effective organization. Then assign a mark to it, assuming that there is an A, B, C, D, F marking system, D being the lowest passing mark. Circle one of the following:

A

B

C

D

F

As soon as you have completed the marking as instructed, hand in this sheet for tabulation.

**Exhibit 5.2**

---

*Equality of Man*

"...We hold these truths to be self-evident: that all men are created equal; that they are endowed by their Creator with certain inalienable rights; that among these are life, liberty, and the pursuit of happiness." Every American holds this thought of the Declaration of Independence to be at least a part of the great American ideal. Everyone probably believes it. We want to. How can we argue it?

We would like arguing against the principals of democracy that our forefathers introduced in the earliest beginnings of America as a free nation.

Who were our forefathers? The earliest Americans were the Indians who first discovered and settled the land. When the European explorers discovered America and overran the Indians, they became Americans. Actually, the word "American" means a mixture of cultures and races; these people immigrated to America from all over the world. Therefore the only people who are inclined to call themselves full-blooded Americans are the Indians who first settled the land.

Consequently, when I see people who immigrated here from another country as they arrived, did discriminate against newcomers, I wonder why the people who are fleeing the discrimination think they have the right to do so.

The reason so many people immigrate to America each year is that America was founded on the principle of freedom to all. I believe in this principle in order to solve our problems, we should all be among ourselves, and our fellow Nations.

**Exhibit 5.2a**

## Exhibit 5.2b

*Equality of Man*

"...We hold these truths to be self-evident: that all men are created equal; that they are endowed by their creator with with certain unalienable rights. that among these are life, liberty, and the pursuit of happiness..." Every American holds this excerpt of the Declaration of Independence to his heart as one of the great American ideals. Everyone probably believes it, for how can we argue it? We would be ~~arguing~~ against the principals of Democracy ~~that our~~ forefathers introduced in the earliest beginning of America as a free nation.

Who were our forefathers? The earliest Americans were the Indians who first discovered and settled the land. When the European explorers discovered America and overran the Indians they became Americans. Actually, the word "American" means a mixture of culture and races, because people immigrated to ~~....~~ America from all over the world. Therefore, the only people who are qualified to call themselves full-blooded Americans are the Indians who first settled the land.

Consequently, when I see people who immigrated here from another country just as my ancestors did discriminated against and not allowed certain unalienable rights, I wonder why the people who are doing the discriminating think they have the right to do so.

The reason so ~~....~~ many people immigrate to America each year is that America was ~~....~~ founded on the principle of freedom for all men. I believe in the upholding of this principle in ~~....~~ order to insure peace among ourselves and our fellow nations.

INSTRUCTIONS AND WORKSHEET

"The Job I Would Like To Have Ten Years From Now"

Pete, the writer of this theme, is a 10th grade student. He generally works diligently at his studies, and he is considered to be a good school citizen. Pete is popular with his fellow students, being elected as the student council representative from his homeroom. He is one of the student managers for the football team, and he played on the "B" squad in basketball. He also plays trombone in the school band. Pete usually wears white levis and colorful sport shirts, and he keeps "boyishly" well groomed and clean. Although he has been known to be involved in a few mischievous episodes, he has never caused any serious trouble for his teachers or parents. His favorite interests are athletics and jam sessions.

The class was asked to write a theme of one or two pages on the topic, "The Job I Would Like To Have Ten Years From Now." Assign a mark to Pete's paper, assuming that there is an A, B, C, D, F marking system, D being the lowest passing mark. Circle one of the following:

A    B    C    D    F

As soon as you have completed the marking as instructed, hand in this sheet for tabulation.

**Exhibit 5.3a**

---

The Job I Would Like to Have
ten years from now

Ten years from now I would like to be an engineer. I would not like a job that would keep me indoors much of the time, like a store clerk or a banker. Also I want a job that will permit me to make a good living and not worry about having enough money for my family to have a furthings. There will always be plenty of work for engineers to do some proper choose a line of work because it is easy. I dont mind hard work so long as its the kind of work I like to do. Another reason for my choice is that an engineer can be his own boss and run his own business. These are the reasons why I would like to be an engineer ten years from now.

If I couldnt be an engineer I think my second choice would be an airline pilot.

**Exhibit 5.3a (continued)**

INSTRUCTIONS AND WORKSHEET

"The Job I Would Like To Have Ten Years From Now"

Pete, the writer of this theme, is a 10th grade student. He frequently comes to classes late; sometimes he arrives as much as forty minutes after school begins in the morning. Some of the girls in class complain about his use of profane language in the halls. The teachers often have to reprimand him for his manners. He is sometimes curt and impolite toward teachers. On hot spring days, students are especially antagonistic toward Pete because of his repulsive body odor. His clothes are usually dirty and sloppily worn, with shirt out and pants hanging low on his hips. He lets his black hair grow long around his ears and uses gobs of grease or oil to keep it in place. His favorite sport is hot-rodding.

The class was asked to write a theme of one or two pages on the topic, "The Job I Would Like To Have Ten Years From Now." Assign a mark to Pete's paper, assuming that there is an A, B, C, D, F marking system, D being the lowest passing mark. Circle one of the following:

A    B    C    D    F

As soon as you have completed the marking as instructed, hand in this sheet for tabulation.

**Exhibit 5.3b**

---

The Job I Would Like to Have Ten Years From Now

Ten years from now I would like to be an auto mechanic I would not like a job that would keep me indoors much of the time, like a store clerk or a teacher. Also I want a job that will permit me to make a good living and not worry about having enough money for my family to have a few things. There will always be plenty of work for mechanics to do. Some people choose a line of work because it is easy. I dont mind hard work as long as its the kind of work I like to do. Another reason for my choice is that a mechanic can be his own boss and run his own business. These are the reasons why it would like to be a mechanic ten years from now.

If I couldn't be a mechanic I think my second choice would be a filling station operator.

**Exhibit 5.3b (continued)**

## Exhibit 5.4a

The Day Pedro Met Tiny

(handwritten story)

It was a beautiful day and Pedro... This was the day Pedro's Mama boke (broke) her leg... but full. Pedro's father would... him full when she was around this was... the day...

the little Bill Tiny... had named... knew that some day he did not... a giant of a bird. One day Pedro's... father had a bad harvest and needed... money bad. It was a terrible thing for... Pedro when papa had to sell Tiny for... right he would never forget the...

T....

INSTRUCTIONS AND WORKSHEET

"The Day Pedro Met Tiny"

This is an original story written by Henry Alderson, a 6th grade pupil, as a homework assignment to be done by each pupil in the class. His I.Q., as measured by the California Test of Mental Maturity, is *Low*. He generally works diligently at his studies.

Read the story and then assign a mark to it, assuming that there is an A, B, C, D, F marking system, with D being the lowest passing mark. Circle one:

A    B    C    D    F

**Exhibit 5.4a**

## Exhibit 5.4b

The Day Pedro Met Tiny

(handwritten story)

It was a beautiful day and Pedro... a little Mexican boy was crying for joy. This was the day Pedro's Mama broke her leg... but full. Pedro's father would... him full when she was around this was... the day...

the little Bill Tiny... although he did not... knew that some day he... a giant of a bird. One day Pedro's... father had a bad harvest and needed... money bad. It was a terrible thing for... Pedro when papa had to sell Tiny for... right he thought he would n.....

INSTRUCTIONS AND WORKSHEET

"The Day Pedro Met Tiny"

This is an original story written by Henry Alderson, a 6th grade pupil, as a homework assignment to be done by each pupil in the class. His I.Q., as measured by the California Test of Mental Maturity, is High. He generally works diligently at his studies.

Read the story and then assign a mark to it, assuming that there is an A, B, C, D, F marking system, with D being the lowest passing mark. Circle one:

A    B    C    D    F

**Exhibit 5.4b**

INSTRUCTIONS AND WORKSHEET

Arithmetic Test

This is the first of ten items in a 6th grade arithmetic test. Each item is worth a maximum of ten points.

Read the teacher's directions to the pupils and then examine the response of this particular pupil. Evaluate the pupil's work by circling the number of points that you would award him for his response. Circle one:

0   1   2   3   4   5   6   7   8   9   10

As soon as you have completed the marking as instructed, hand in this sheet for tabulation.

**Exhibit 5.5**

---

ARITHMETIC TEST

Directions (to the pupils): Work the following problems and show your steps in arriving at the solutions:

1. If 3 apples cost 13¢, how much will 7 apples cost?

$$\begin{array}{r} 4.56 \\ 3\overline{)13.00} \\ \underline{12} \\ 10 \\ \underline{8} \\ 20 \end{array}$$

$$\begin{array}{r} 4.56 \\ \times 7 \\ \hline 31.92 \end{array}$$

Answer: 31.92

**Exhibit 5.5 (continued)**

## INSTRUCTIONS AND WORKSHEET

### Test Over Selected Spelling Demons

This is an 8th grade pupil's performance on a test over 54 spelling demons, together with the key giving the correct spelling of the words. Check the pupil's performance on each word against the key and enter her score (the number correct) in the space below.

_____
Score

As soon as you have completed the marking as instructed, hand in this sheet for tabulation.

**Exhibit 5.6a**

---

### TEST OVER SELECTED SPELLING DEMONS

NAME _Janice Henry_    DATE _Jan. 4, 1964_

CLASS _English 8_    PERIOD _3rd_

1. accommodate
2. aeronautics
3. apparatus
4. beginning
5. cemetary
6. chauffer
7. completion
8. conscientious
9. cylinder
10. defense
11. decent
12. desert
13. dicipline
14. ecstasy
15. embarass
16. exaggerated
17. foreign
18. grammer
19. grievous
20. hieght
21. interrupt
22. lieutenant
23. livable
24. maintenance
25. mathmatics
26. mileage
27. mischievous
28. misspell
29. murmur
30. noticeable
31. nuisance
32. occurrance
33. original
34. pamphlet
35. parliment
36. personnel
37. prejudice
38. privilege
39. professor
40. psychology
41. recommend
42. referred
43. restaurant
44. sacreligious
45. seize
46. seperate
47. similar
48. sophomore
49. therefore
50. they're
51. tobacco
52. unnecessary
53. vengance
54. yield

**Exhibit 5.6a** (continued)

Key to Spelling Demons Test

| | | |
|---|---|---|
| 1. accommodate | 19. grievous | 37. prejudice |
| 2. aeronautics | 20. height | 38. privilege |
| 3. apparatus | 21. interrupt | 39. professor |
| 4. beginning | 22. lieutenant | 40. psychology |
| 5. cemetery | 23. lovable | 41. recommend |
| 6. chauffeur | 24. maintenance | 42. referred |
| 7. complexion | 25. mathematics | 43. restaurant |
| 8. conscientious | 26. mileage | 44. sacrilegious |
| 9. cylinder | 27. mischievous | 45. seize |
| 10. defense | 28. misspell | 46. separate |
| 11. descent | 29. murmur | 47. similar |
| 12. dessert | 30. noticeable | 48. sophomore |
| 13. discipline | 31. nuisance | 49. therefore |
| 14. ecstasy | 32. occurrence | 50. they're |
| 15. embarrass | 33. original | 51. tobacco |
| 16. exaggerated | 34. pamphlet | 52. unnecessary |
| 17. foreign | 35. parliament | 53. vengeance |
| 18. grammar | 36. personnel | 54. yield |

**Exhibit 5.6b**

Spelling Demons Test--Percentage and Letter Marks

If you scored Janice's test correctly, you found that she spelled 37 of the 54 words correctly. The Haven Cove Junior High School uses an A, B, C, D, F marking system, with D being the lowest passing mark. When marks are expressed as percentages, teachers are given considerable freedom in assigning the marks, but general practice is to regard 70 as barely passing.

Calculate Janice's percentage mark    _____ %

Give her a letter mark (A, B, C, D, or F)    _____

As soon as you have completed the marking as instructed, hand in this sheet for tabulation.

**Exhibit 5.6c**

## Spelling Demons Test--Janice's Class

Following is some information about the scores earned on this Spelling Demons Test by students in Janice's classroom:

| | |
|---|---|
| Highest score | 41 |
| Lowest score | 26 |
| Average score | 33 |
| Janice's score | 37 (one of the top four) |

Give Janice a letter mark (A, B, C, D, or F)  _____ (Mark)

As soon as you have completed the marking as instructed, hand in this sheet for tabulation.

**Exhibit 5.6d**

## Spelling Demons Test--Nine Classes

There are nine eighth grade English classes at Haven Cove Junior High School.

All nine classes (250 students) took the Spelling Demons Test and scored as follows:

| | |
|---|---|
| Highest score | 42 |
| Lowest score | 0 |
| Average score | 22 |
| Janice's score | 37 (one of the top five) |

Give Janice a letter mark (A, B, C, D, or F)  _____ (Mark)

As soon as you have completed the marking as instructed, hand in this sheet for tabulation.

**Exhibit 5.6e**

REVIEW OF CONCEPTS ILLUSTRATED (*cont.*)

| EXHIBIT | OUTCOME | CONCEPT |
|---------|---------|---------|
| 5.5 Arithmetic Test | Scores for this one problem in long division range widely (usually 0–9). | Teachers select different evaluative criteria (accuracy, knowledge of process, and correct answer) when valuing a very "objective" performance. |
| 5.6a–e Spelling Demons Test | Participants tend to make errors in correcting the test even with a key, marks assigned vary widely, but most participants raise the mark steadily as their information about others increases. | Teachers are not infallible. Teachers tend to accept artificial norms like 70 per cent without considering the appropriateness of such a norm. Teachers are willing to use other norms when they are appropriate and available. The information available about performances of others at a learning task strongly influences valuations of teachers. |

CAUTIONS AND LIMITATIONS

Participants may react negatively to this session if they assume that the leader is being critical of them as evaluators. It must be emphasized that the problems being illustrated are persistent problems which require attention but are not easily resolved. In fact, participants may react to these exercises by saying, "Well, what's the use. No evaluations are reliable so why evaluate?"

SUGGESTED RELATED ACTIVITIES

Participants can gain much by working in teams to specify criteria for evaluating work and to check how much agreement can be reached.

SUMMARY

This series of instruments and the discussions growing out of their use will provide no simple answers to the complex problems involved. In fact, the point of the entire exercise is to show that there are no simple answers to these questions, so we had better face up to the facts and not act as if the evaluation of pupil performance could be reduced to anything less than a difficult, extremely complicated responsibility. Only when we have forsaken the quest for "quack" remedies will we settle down to our proper role—consisting of setting clear goals, collecting accurate information, diagnosing difficulties, planning and executing programs, evaluating outcomes, and making the necessary corrections before taking further action.

## Analyzing teacher-made tests

A teacher's tests reveal a lot about his teaching, particularly with respect to what he considers important. If Mr. Chips tests for nothing but the memorization of trivia, then one might well assume that he values the memorization of trivia; certainly his grade-conscious pupils will value it and will operate accordingly.

In addition to focusing attention upon the types of learning measured by tests, the following exercise deals with such matters as the arrangement of items and responses so as to facilitate maximum utilization of teacher and pupil time; the avoidance of common errors in test construction; and the evaluation of teacher-made tests. In fact, most of the difficulties encountered by teachers in the construction and use of tests are included.

The strategic importance of exercises such as the one described here should not be overlooked. Teachers enjoy examining the test items that are included, and they take considerable delight in searching for the "boners" therein. They also tend to see this type of activity as being quite practical—the sort of thing that can be used immediately. The administrator or supervisor thereby gains entree to teachers by an interesting and favorably perceived activity, and he can follow through with other activities that might have less initial appeal.

**BACKGROUND ON THE PROBLEM**

Systematic study of many tests devised by teachers for use at various levels and in various subjects reveals several types of problems. These are problems of which many teachers are simply unaware. A first step in improving teacher-made tests is developing a sense of awareness of problems. This solves many minor difficulties almost simultaneously. Other more difficult problems require skill development, training in procedures, and development of new insights.

Basic problems in test construction include the following:

1. Inconsequential content being tested.
2. Learning being tested only at superficial recognition or recall levels.
3. Test format creates confusion or wastes time on the part of the *pupil.*
4. Test format creates confusion or wastes time on the part of the *teacher.*
5. Test items are constructed so as to be nondiscriminating.
   a. Non-functioning distractors convert multiple-choice items to simple choice items.
   b. Trick wording misleads those who know.
   c. A word used is a specific determiner of appropriate answer.
   d. Items tend to be too easy.

6.  Test items are negatively discriminating.
7.  Guessing ability or simple use of deduction is tested instead of the intended content.
8.  Inappropriate type of item used for testing a certain kind of learning.
9.  Unrealistic responses required in time available.

ACTIVITIES

Discussing the importance of formal testing in the evaluation of instruction.

Demonstrating the ways in which teacher-made tests reflect and inflect pupil learnings.

Demonstrating some of the important characteristics of good tests and good test items.

Developing skills in identifying weaknesses in teacher-made test items.

Developing skills needed to improve teacher-made test items.

PROCEDURES

At the beginning of the meeting it is advisable for someone who is knowledgeable in the field of test construction to make a brief introductory statement concerning the importance of teacher-made tests, the general characteristics of good tests (validity, reliability, and usability), and the purposes of the meeting. Then the instrument should be distributed to the group with instructions to respond to the items as indicated in the following section. After approximately 20 minutes, most of the participants will have completed Part I and will have studied Part II. The remainder of the meeting can be devoted to a discussion of the items. The entire exercise requires a minimum of approximately 90 minutes.

A collection of several objective and essay type test items, representing several subject areas and grade levels, is presented to the participants in the form of a test (see Appendix V–A: *A Collection of Items From Teacher-Made Tests*). The instructions are to respond to the items as in a real test situation and, also, to note weaknesses in the items for later discussion. Participants are asked to answer each test item just as though they were in a classroom where such content had been taught. The group is assured that the purpose of the test is strictly instructional and that the papers will not be scored or collected.

Part I of the test consists of objective items of the multiple-choice, true-false, matching, and completion types. Part II contains three sections, each representing one or more of the common weaknesses in essay test construction, and a final section contains several essay test items that have certain commendable features.

Time is called after most of the participants have completed Part I and have begun Part II. The group is then instructed to take approximately five more minutes to examine the remaining essay type items in order to be ready to discuss them.

The laboratory activity using the instrument described here can be carried on in groups of various sizes, although the discussion of the items is increasingly limited as the group increases in size. School faculty and administrator-supervisor groups of no more than 30 persons are of manageable size for this purpose.

The physical arrangements will depend on the size of the group and the availability of facilities. Since this exercise is used for discussion only, the usual precautions followed in administering a measuring device need not be observed. If facilities and group size permit, an arrangement whereby the participants face each other is desirable, because the likelihood of greater involvement in the discussion will be increased.

SEQUENCE OF ACTIVITIES

| Time | Activity |
|------|----------|
| 5 min. | Briefly introduce the topic. Distribute the instrument shown in Appendix V–A; *A Collection of Items from Teacher-Made Tests.* |
| 5 min. | Give instructions on completing all of Part I and study items in Part II. |
| 30 min. | Test session. |
| 25 min. | Discuss items section by section. |
| 25 min. | Consider follow-up activities. |

*Total time:* 1 hour and 30 minutes

A SAMPLE ANALYSIS OF THE TEST ITEMS

It is interesting to note that almost all of the items in the collection presented here were taken from actual tests constructed by teachers in various school systems. Although a few items were included to illustrate strengths, most of the items represent weaknesses that are quite common. Undoubtedly the greatest weakness to be found in these items, as in most teacher-made tests, is the lack of significance of the subject matter being tested. In the first item, for example, who cares or will ever need to know the exact date on which the Battle of Chattanooga ended? This pursuit of trivia, as revealed in most teacher-made tests, is the important handle that can be grasped by alert supervisory personnel as they analyze tests with teachers.

Having made this point, we shall proceed to our analysis of the test items without repeatedly belaboring the point just mentioned. Although we shall concentrate on the technicalities of test construction, we remind the reader once more that the primary consideration with this test or any other test is the type of learning it measures and, hence, motivates. The technical matters with which we shall deal here are important to be sure, and, also, they are useful in capturing the interest of the teacher to work on whatever problems are revealed.

*Test format*   The discussion might well begin with the point that no directions are given other than "answer the following questions to the best of your ability," an exhortation that is of doubtful value. This is likely to cause confusion and to waste time while the teacher explains what might have been included in writing at the beginning of the test. Even more serious is the possibility that one or more of the children will be confused but will remain silent and never learn what the teacher expects. Should the pupil guess if he isn't sure of the correct response, or will a correction formula be used that will make guessing inadvisable? In the multiple-choice section, is there one and only one correct option per item? These are the kinds of questions that should be answered in writing, before the pupil begins to take the test.

Another question that might or might not be raised by the pupils after they receive the test pertains to the way in which responses are to be made. If the question arises, valuable time is lost in answering it; if not, more time is lost—to the teacher in scoring the test and to the pupils in response modes that require considerable unnecessary writing. For example, consider the time lost in writing the words "true" or "false" instead of using a simple mark, or in copying essay questions that are already written.

The matter of saving time for the teacher deserves further comment. Whenever one can show a teacher how to accomplish the same ends in less time, the teacher tends to be justifiably interested. It becomes a matter of strategic importance, then, to be able to show teachers that their time, as well as their effectiveness, is involved in the way their tests are constructed. Whenever pupil responses are made in a uniform way, the time required for scoring the tests is reduced, and the saving in time is increasingly substantial as the number of items or the number of pupils taking the test is increased.

For true-false items, a simple device for facilitating scoring is to place a column of $T$'s and $F$'s at the left-hand side of the page corresponding to the items on the page and instruct the pupils to circle either the $T$ or the $F$. If an extra space is left after every fifth item, it will serve to cluster the responses—making scoring even easier. For multiple-choice items, columns of letters for each option provide a similar medium for responses. In either case, the pattern of circles on the teacher's scoring key, which designate correct responses, permits the scoring of entire pages of items almost at a glance when placed alongside the pupil's responses. For other types of objective items, similar arrangements can be contrived to reduce the amount of time required for scoring.

It is enlightening to contrast the task of scoring tests as described in the preceding paragraph and the task that is encountered when no provision is made for a uniform mode of responses. When no directions are given for a true-false test, for example, it is not uncommon for some pupils to write the entire word *true* or *false*, for others to write *T* or *F*, and for others to use such symbols as + or *0*. Some pupils place their responses at the left and others at the right. The scoring task consequently becomes an arduous, item-by-item chore.

Before considering the individual items in the simulated test, one further comment is in order concerning the matter of directions. Spaces designated for the pupil's name, the class, the section, the date, and any other information needed by the teacher will make for ease in handling the papers, recording the grades, and distributing the papers to the pupils.

*Multiple choice items* Following is a brief analysis of the multiple choice items in the test instrument:

1. The Battle of Chattanooga ended
   (a) December 9, 1935
   (b) November 25, 1863
   (c) July 4, 1923
   (d) February 30, 1492

Aside from the inconsequential nature of the subject matter, this item suffers from the presence of three nonfunctioning distracters. The purpose of a distracter (an option that is not a correct response) is to *distract*. If it is not as attractive as the correct response to the pupil who is guessing, then it is not serving its purpose. In this case, the correct answer would be obvious even to the pupil who knows almost nothing about the subject.

2. Man differs from birds in that man has a
   (a) four-chambered heart
   (b) hair
   (c) warm blood
   (d) eyes

This was either intended to be a trick question, or it turned out to be one unintentionally. The alert pupil will notice that only one of the four options fits the stem grammatically, but it is not the correct option! This will be an effective distracter, but it will be likely to distract some of the pupils who know the subject matter as well as those who do not. "Hair" is the correct response, but not "a hair" as it is in this item.

3. The Frenchman who developed a cure for rabies was
   (a) Harvey
   (b) Banting
   (c) Pasteur
   (d) Leeuwenhoek

All an alert pupil would need to do here is to recognize that Pasteur's name is the only one of the four that is French. The guessing pupil would need to know nothing about Pasteur's work in order to answer the item correctly (with respect to the teacher's key); on the other hand, the informed pupil would know that none of the four options is really correct, in that Pasteur did not develop a "cure" for rabies, as the test item suggests.

4. The person who made the first American flag was
   (a) Samuel Adams
   (b) Paul Revere
   (c) John Hancock
   (d) Betsy Ross

Assuming that Betsy Ross really did make the first American flag, which is not accepted by all historians, this item requires the pupil to remember only that it was a *woman* who made the first flag. As in the preceding item, the problem is one of heterogeneity of the options. Whenever one option stands out as being basically different from the others, the gambler has the odds in his favor if he selects the different one, and he will usually win.

5. An 8-sided polygon is an
   (a) octagon
   (b) pentagon
   (c) hexagon
   (d) decagon

Another grammatical clue, a very common one in teacher-made tests, gives the answer away in this item. The use of the article *an* in the stem requires an option beginning with a vowel, and only the option *octagon* meets this requirement. Validity is again the victim, because it is grammar and not mathematics that the item actually involves.

6. Which of the following state aid systems would favor school districts in which few pupils reside?
   (a) a uniform grant per census pupil
   (b) a uniform grant per pupil in average daily attendance
   (c) a uniform grant per enrolled pupil
   (d) a uniform grant per teacher

This was selected from a test at the college level. Assuming that the subject matter in the item was not covered previously in its present form, this could be a good thought question. The student who understands state aid systems could think through this problem and determine the correct answer. Although the correct option (a uniform grant per teacher) is not completely homogeneous with the three distracters, all of which deal with pupil units, this is not a serious weakness in this case. Several analyses of this item have revealed that the distracters are selected frequently by the less knowledgeable students.

7. Because of the time in which each of the following men lived, which one could have been present during the Battle of the Alamo?

   (a)  Daniel Boone
   (b)  Kit Carson
   (c)  George Rogers Clark
   (d)  George Armstrong Custer

For the most part this is a good item. Although it requires only the ability to recall facts, a correct response (Kit Carson) presumably depends upon the recall of information in a new context. The options are all homogeneous, which is desirable. On the other hand, the possibility of negative learning is present in that the pupils might get the impression that one of the four men *was* involved in the Battle of the Alamo.

8. Adding the same number to the numerator and denominator of a fraction

   (a)  decreases it
   (d)  increases it
   (c)  may either increase or decrease it
   (b)  leaves it the same

This item is likely to cause the teacher some difficulty. If the teacher has in mind a proper fraction (denominator greater than numerator), then she would assume that the correct answer is "increase it"; however, wide-awake pupils will recognize that the answer would be "may either increase or decrease it," since the teacher did not indicate whether the fraction is proper or improper.

*True-false items*  Following is a brief analysis of the true-false items in this instrument:

1. The Battle of Lexington was fought in 1775 B.C.

This is a trick item in which the "B.C." is a trap that the teacher has set for unwary pupils. One often hears as a justification for trick items the argument that pupils must learn to be careful. This is hardly a defensible way to teach such an objective. The teacher who uses trick items usually succeeds only in teaching pupils to look for (and often find) arguable points in every test item.

2. The most famous American general in World War I was John James Pershing.

This is another example of a trick item, which is true except for Pershing's second name (Joseph, instead of James). What is the author of this test item really teaching?

3. The value of pi is 3.14.

Is this item true or false? One could make a good argument either way. Heaven help the teacher who tries to defend this item from attack by an irate parent.

4. A child with a weak heart may be given aspirin.

Why not? The teacher probably meant "should" instead of "may," but even then the item would not be very useful. As it is, "true" is the only defensible response.

5. All dogs have a keen sense of smell.

"All" is one of several specific determiners (always, never, etc.) that usually tip off the respondent that a "false" is called for. A gambler would welcome the odds that such clues provide.

6. No mammals fly.

"No" is another specific determiner, and an alert pupil will mark "false" whether or not he knows that bats are mammals.

7. All squares are rectangles.

This item, taken from a mathematics test, was keyed as "true." This would forgive the use of the specific determiner; however, what will the teacher say to the pupil who argues that the square his father uses in carpentry work isn't a rectangle?

8. A married high school student may be expelled from school.

The teacher intended this item to be "false," on the grounds that marriage alone has been ruled by the courts to be insufficient reason for expelling a person from school. However, the item does not say this. A married student or an unmarried student may be expelled from school for various reasons.

*The matching item*   This matching exercise was copied verbatim from a test given by a high school teacher. It is a notable example of just about all of the mistakes one can make in matching exercises. In fact, in its original form it contained some errors that do not appear here, such as retesting factual matter already treated twice in the same test and being continued on a second page. Another shortcoming is the fact that the premises and responses are equal in number, which facilitates guessing. Spelling and punctuation are also incorrect in several instances, and capitalization and verb usage are inconsistent.

The major weakness in this matching exercise is the almost complete heterogeneity of the material in each column. Names of persons, events, organizations and groups, officials, places—all are thrown together in one hodgepodge. As a result, every item in the exercise can be answered without any knowledge of the subject matter! Following is an explanation of how this can be done:

1. *First battle of the Civil War took place here.* This has to be Fort Sumter, the only *place* listed.
2. *Made the famous march through Georgia.* Only two names of individuals are listed, one of which is *General* Sherman. A general would be likely to make a march.
3. *Set the slaves free.* If the student knows the meaning of *emancipation*, he can guess that the Emancipation Proclamation set the slaves free.
4. *Assassinated Abraham Lincoln.* Only one person's name is left (John Wilkes Booth).
5. *Term applied to freed slaves.* Why not *freed*men?
6. *Used to discourage Negro voting.* If the student knows the meaning of the word *poll*, he can associate it with the word *voting.*
7. *Was set up to help the Negro who was free.* The student already established that the freed Negroes were *freedmen,* so the *Freedmen's* Bureau would be the logical answer to this item.
8. *Are heads of military districts. Military governors* would be the only sensible answer.
9. *Persons who came from the North.* This would have to be *carpetbaggers,* because it is the only plural word left in the response column.
10. *Made the Negroes citizens.* Since there were ten items in each column and nine have been accounted for, the tenth would have to be the only one remaining, the *Fourteenth Amendment.*

Although most matching exercises are not as faulty as this one, many contain enough of these errors to destroy most of their usefulness.

*Completion items*  Each of the completion items is analyzed below:

1. The force of gravity causes water to flow _____.

Presumably the teacher who constructed this item was attempting to determine whether her sixth-grade pupils knew something about gravity. Scientists who know a great deal about gravity confess that even they do not know all there is to know about this highly complex phenomenon. The fact that water flows downward is about all that a pupil would need to know to answer this question; he would not need to know anything about gravity other than that it has something to do with the downward flow of water. He would not even need to recall the word *gravity*; he would, at most, need merely to recognize it.

The problem with this item is one of inappropriateness. The very least that the teacher should do is to reword the item so that recall of the word *gravity* is required. It would be better to use an essay type item and ask for a discussion of what gravity *does*.

2.   The Battle of New Orleans was fought in _____.

Ambiguity is the principal weakness of this item. The teacher probably had the date of the battle in mind, but how many other answers would be equally correct?

3.   The Nile River is _____ miles long.

As long as a teacher feels that the length of a river is important knowledge for pupils to possess, she can at least frame a more manageable test item to measure such knowledge. One wonders whether *anybody* knows exactly how long the Nile is. And how precise does the answer have to be? Wouldn't it be better to use a multiple-choice item and ask the respondents to identify the number most closely approximating the length of the Nile?

4.   A child who is 10 years old should _____ _____ _____ every night.

The teacher who conceived this item might have been a humorist. Let us hope so—some of the wags in her class will have a good time with it!

5.   The Continental Congress chose well when it made George Washington _____ _____ _____ of the army.

Why give clues in the length of the lines? Some teachers even show how many *letters* are in each word in the blanks, which is even more absurd.

6.   Match these proper nouns with a common noun:
     a. Canada _____
     b. July _____
     c. Easter _____
     d. Arizona _____

Here again, the pupils will undoubtedly wonder what the teacher wants. What kind of common noun would "match" with Canada? Almost any common noun would seem to be appropriate for any of these blanks.

7.   When Washington became commander-in-chief, the British held _____.

Teachers sometimes inadvertently answer one item with another item. After reading Item 7, will any pupil wonder how to answer Item 5?

*The essay items*   The first two items illustrate a common failing of many essay tests. When a pupil is asked to "discuss what is needed for good health," or "what Edison did," he has a right to ask for clarification and more specific instructions. One wonders what the teacher's key for these items contains, although it would be safe to assume that teachers who write this type of item would reconsider if they took the trouble to outline the elements of an acceptable response. Certainly the use of such items for diagnostic purposes—which good instruction would presuppose —would be difficult.

The third item (Give a brief sketch of Lincoln, telling where and when he was born, offices he held, and how and when he died.) shows how one can attempt to avoid one type of difficulty and get into another. Here we have none of the ambiguity or vagueness of "What did Edison do?" but we now have a series of minute fragments of information that could be tested much better with objective items.

"List the four causes of the depression of the 1930's!" This type of test item (which isn't an essay item at all, as it was classified in the test from which it was taken) should have gone out with the nickel beer. When a teacher asks for *the* four causes of anything as complex as a major depression, is she stimulating *thought* or *rote memory?*

When students are asked why they do or do not appreciate our American heritage, one might wonder what criteria will be used to evaluate the responses. Do you suppose that the students in this class have really made a penetrating study of American history—its valleys as well as its many peaks? Does the student really have the alternatives implied in "why you do or do not?" If he does not actually have these alternatives, then why ask the question? If he does have both alternatives, how will his response be judged?

The eight items listed under the heading "American History, 1789–1860" were copied verbatim from a test given in a high school class. The individual items need not be discussed because the unreasonableness of the test as a whole is the important point. Any one of these items could well occupy the time of a thoughtful student for at least a half day. All the teacher could possibly get with a test of this kind is oversimplification and superficiality. How much better it would be to devise two or three items that would reveal a real grasp of a few important historical concepts.

The comparison of two essay examinations in Section C reveals two quite different approaches to the same subject matter. In the first examination, the teacher (Perkins) is placing a premium on listing, naming, and recalling isolated bits of information. One can easily imagine the type of study that this type of examination will encourage students to do.

The second examination (that of teacher Brown) is unrealistically long and involved, but assuming that the students have not encountered the items in this same form before, the intellectual demands made here are much different than the ones in the previous example. Here the students must recall subject matter as before, but now they must show relationships, causes and effects, and trends. Studying for this type of examination would be quite a different thing from merely memorizing lists and fragments of historical trivia.

The last section, entitled, "What Do You Think of These Questions?" contains questions selected from several sources in order to illustrate an approach to teaching and testing that is somewhat unusual. In each case, the student is required to do something more with subject matter than merely remember it.

In the first question, common elements must be found in several bodies of recalled information; in the next two questions, the student is asked to compare the knowledge that he has gained from his study with the knowledge that he presumably has of the present.

The fourth and fifth questions call for the application of knowledge to specific problems.

Questions six and seven require the student to use his knowledge in predicting conditions under a prescribed set of circumstances.

The eighth and ninth questions call upon the student to demonstrate his understanding of subject matter.

Regardless of the other merits or shortcomings of these questions, they have one desirable characteristic in common: they go beyond merely requiring the recognition or recall of subject matter by asking the student to demonstrate deeper levels of understanding or ability to apply his knowledge to the solution of new problems.

CAUTIONS AND LIMITATIONS

The central purpose of this activity should be kept in focus throughout the meeting. Participants seem to enjoy picking the test items to pieces, and this, of course, is to be encouraged. However, it is possible for the group to waste time quibbling over unimportant aspects of particular items and to neglect more relevant considerations. The main point is not whether one of the options of an item is a good one or a poor one, but rather the implications of the whole experience for the improvement of instruction.

Teachers are constantly on the alert for "practical" suggestions—techniques that can be applied in the classroom tomorrow morning. This activity tends to satisfy this need and is therefore quite enthusiastically received by teachers and other groups of professional people. Although immediate applicability is not to be scorned, the administrator or supervisor who leans too heavily on the bag-of-tricks approach is likely to be disappointed with the results. On the other hand, if the help that teachers get in the mechanics of test construction is merely the prelude to a thorough study of measurement with respect to motivation, incentives, and the learning process, then much more value can be gained from the experience. In other words, a satisfying meeting which "gives some answers" to the relatively simple problems of test construction can be the foot-in-the-door to more fundamental and complex considerations.

### SUGGESTED RELATED ACTIVITIES

It is obvious that test construction itself is much too complicated to master in one meeting; further work in that area might be needed by individuals or groups after the initial exposure to the possibilities. Follow-up studies of the tests constructed in a given situation after the initial meeting will reveal the types of problems requiring further attention. This involves using the test instrument in the manner recommended previously in this chapter.

One of the instruments included in Chapter 7, the *Teacher Question Inventory*, was designed primarily for purposes of analyzing oral questions in a recitation or discussion. The same instrument could well be used in analyzing items on written tests. In fact, some such analysis would be highly appropriate as a part of one's supervisory activities with an individual teacher if she seemed to have a problem in getting meaning into subject matter.

After interest is stimulated in a group meeting involving teachers, individual or small group activities can be planned according to need. A grade level or department group might well plan a series of laboratory work sessions around systematic analysis of items in the test they are currently using.

Laboratory sessions with teacher groups can be planned to develop understanding of and skill in other analytical procedures. A set of locally prepared tests can be used to demonstrate *content balance analysis*, procedures, and item discrimination analysis.

Still another promising follow-up activity involves organizing and planning for the development of an item pool. High quality items can be selected, categorized, and organized in a card file to provide a group of teachers with a teaching resource of great value.

### SUMMARY

The activity proposed and described in this section was designed to acquaint participants with some of the rudiments of test construction. A collection of test items in the form of a simulated test is administered to the group. The items are then discussed, and their strengths and short-comings are revealed. Several ways of evaluating teacher-made tests are then presented.

Although one objective of this activity is to improve competencies in test construction, a more central objective is to reveal ways in which test analysis can be used as a supervisory technique to improve instruction.

## Selected references

MARKING PUPILS' WORK

1. *Encyclopedia of Educational Research* (3rd ed.). New York: The Macmillan Company, 1960, pp. 783–89, 1253, 1439–40.
2. Cook, Walter W., "The Gifted and the Retarded in Historical Perspective," *Phi Delta Kappan* (March, 1958), pp. 249–55.
3. Douglass, Harl R., *Modern Administration of Secondary Schools*, (2nd ed.). Boston: Ginn and Company, 1963, Chapter 17.
4. Harris, Ben M., and Kenneth E. McIntyre, *A Manual for Evaluating Pupil Performance*, Instructional Leadership Training Materials, Series No. 2, Austin, Texas: Extension Teaching and Field Service Bureau, The University of Texas, 1964.
5. Johnson, Mauritz, Jr., "Solving the 'Mess in Marks,'" *Education Digest* (February, 1962), pp. 12–14.
6. Stanley, Julian C., *Measurement in Today's Schools* (4th ed.). Englewood Cliffs, N.J.: Prentice-Hall, Inc., 1964, Chapter 2.
7. Wrinkle, W. L., *Improving Marking and Reporting Practices in Elementary and Secondary Schools*. New York: Holt, Rinehart, and Winston, Inc., 1956.
8. Yauch, Wilbur A., "School Marks and Their Reporting," *NEA Journal* (May, 1961), pp. 50, 58.

TEACHER-MADE TESTS

9. Chauncey, H., and J. E. Dobbin, *Testing: Its Place in Education Today*. New York: Harper and Row, 1963.
10. Lindquist, E. F., ed., *Educational Measurement*. Washington, D.C.: American Council on Education, 1951, Chapters 7 and 13.
11. *Making the Classroom Test*. Evaluation and Advisory Service, Series No. 4. Princeton, N.J.: Educational Testing Service, 1959.
12. *Multiple-Choice Questions: A Close Look*. Princeton, N.J.: Educational Testing Service, 1963.
13. Odell, C. W., *How To Improve Classroom Testing*. Dubuque, Iowa: William C. Brown Company, 1958, Chapters 5 and 6.
14. Remmers, H. H., N. L. Gage, and J. F. Rummel, *A Practical Introduction to Measurement and Evaluation*. New York: Harpers, 1960, Chapter 8.
15. *Short-cut Statistics for Teacher-made Tests*, Evaluation and Advisory Service, Series No. 5. Princeton, N.J.: Educational Testing Service, 1960.
16. Stanley, Julian C., *Measurement in Today's Schools* (4th ed.). Englewood Cliffs, N.J.: Prentice-Hall, Inc., 1964, Chapters 7 and 8.

17. Stanley, Julian C., "The ABCs of Test Construction," *NEA Journal* (April, 1958), pp. 224–26.
18. Tyler, Leona E., *Tests and Measurements*. Englewood Cliffs, N.J.: Prentice-Hall, Inc., 1963.
19. Wrightsone, J. Wayne, Joseph Justman, and Irving Robbins, *Evaluation in Modern Education*. New York: American Book Company, 1956, Chapters 5 and 6.

# Chapter Six

# INDIVIDUALIZING AND GROUPING FOR INSTRUCTION

A GREAT variety of problems face instructional staff members as they attempt to cope efficiently with individual differences among pupils. The problems posed by individual differences are widely discussed by teachers, but approaches to instruction that are consistent with this reality are rarely practiced. Increasingly, teachers, administrators, and supervisors are making vigorous efforts to individualize instruction more fully. The use of organizational arrangements such as interclass grouping, team teaching, and tracking seems steadily on the increase. These arrangements are presumed either to facilitate individualized approaches or to compensate for the diverse needs of individuals. Whatever the organization arrangements, they tend to be concerned with groupings of pupils on either an interclass or intraclass basis.

The complexity of the instructional problems relating to variations in individuals is very commonly underestimated and oversimplified. Often, relatively simple grouping arrangements are adopted on the false assumption that they resolve the complex problems created by individual differences. The laboratory sessions described in this chapter deal with three different and important aspects of the problem suggested above. These are sessions which deal with significant concepts of human variability. They suggest possible approaches to improving instruction while attempting to destroy the oversimplified notions and misconceptions that might be held by some staff members.

The first session deals specifically with the problem of interclass grouping—possibly the most widely used approach to the problems of individual differences among pupils. This session is designed primarily to come to

94

grips with misconceptions regarding efforts to produce homogeneity and to clarify the limits to which grouping might serve to improve instruction. This session provides participants with a better basis for understanding the consequences of various grouping approaches and the conditions under which various consequences can be expected.

The second laboratory session described in this chapter also deals with grouping. In this session, however, the concern is for flexible diagnostic grouping in contrast to interclass groupings or more traditional kinds. This session guides the participants through a series of activities designed to help them gain insights into the nature of diagnostic groupings and the flexibility requirements for making such grouping useful for instructional improvement purposes. It also attempts to develop skills in the analysis of standardized achievement data for diagnostic purposes.

The third session deals with only one of many approaches to the individualization of instruction. It emphasizes still further the trait variability of individual pupils and attempts to develop an understanding of the use of standardized achievement data for identifying individual learning needs while avoiding some of the oversimplified uses of test data. In this session participants are given opportunities to review basic techniques and procedures for working with data to produce the most useful kinds of analyses and profiles.

## Grouping pupils for effective instruction

**BACKGROUND ON THE PROBLEM**

It is not only necessary for practical purposes, but desirable for educational reasons that pupils be grouped for instruction for a significant portion of their time in school. Grouping can be flexible or inflexible, ranging from one-to-one tutorial arrangements, in which a teacher works with a single pupil for a brief period of time, to comparatively large group arrangements in which one or more teachers deal with 30 or more pupils for a semester or more. The question is not whether interclass grouping is desirable or undesirable, but what system of assignment of pupils to teachers and classrooms will best facilitate the accomplishment of the school's instructional objectives? Most interclass grouping is relatively inflexible and assumes that a high degree of similarity or "homogeneity" is produced, which in turn is assumed to facilitate learning. For a variety of reasons, both assumptions are generally unwarranted. The wide range of pupil differences found in schools and the nature of the distribution of these differences makes anything approximating homogeneity unrealizable in most situations. On the other hand, there is little evidence to support the assumption that better teaching or more learning occurs even when a more homogeneous group is formed.

The most serious limitation to interclass inflexible grouping as traditionally practiced is posed by the realities of trait variability within each pupil. In simple terms, the problem is one of grouping for homogeneity when the individual pupils are not homogeneous within themselves. Most grouping systems either ignore this bit of reality or underestimate its effect.

### ACTIVITIES

In this session we are concerned only with the problem of grouping pupils into appropriate class sections. We shall not be concerned directly with what the teacher does to teach her pupils after they are assigned to her, although this is ultimately the most important consideration of all. Rather, we shall limit our concern to an investigation and analysis of the extent to which various grouping criteria are effective in accomplishing the results that are usually assumed. Specifically, the following purposes are intended to be served through this exercise:

1. Demonstrating the extent of trait variability within individual pupils and the implications of this variability for grouping practices.
2. Demonstrating the effectiveness of various ability and achievement criteria in reducing the variability within the resultant groups, both on the criteria themselves and on related measures.
3. Providing data to stimulate thinking on the effects of other considerations on the feasibility of various grouping practices—such factors as the objectives of the class for which grouping is being done, the number of sections to be formed, and the level of the school (elementary, secondary, or higher).
4. Identifying alternative procedures for assisting teachers in meeting individual differences among pupils, including alternative grouping procedures.

### PROCEDURE

To set the stage for this laboratory session, the instructor should make a few comments about the problems of individual differences in most school situations. The wide range of pupil abilities and interests, increasing as pupils ascend the educational ladder, is "felt" by most teachers and administrators but seldom comprehended in its real magnitude. For example, the fact that a group of pupils will naturally vary several years in their ability to do school work, even in the elementary grades, is not always known, or, if known, is not accepted by many school people.

The instructor may mention the fact that one administrative device for dealing with the problem is that of grouping the pupils into class sections based on one or more ability or achievement criteria. Then the questions can be asked: "Why might we place pupils into class sections based on measures of ability or achievement? What are we really attempting to do by such a procedure?" Encourage the participant group to talk about these questions.

After a short time the group will usually agree that the purpose of such procedures is to assist the teacher in dealing with individual differences by reducing the variability within the different classes. This sort of statement will provide a useful basis for the subsequent activity. The laboratory session can show the extent to which this desired *variability reduction* has taken place with each of several criteria for grouping.

The next step might be to introduce the activities themselves by saying that the participants, in teams of two or more members, will assume the roles of teachers or other school personnel who are responsible for assigning pupils. Emphasize that each team will actually do some grouping to find out what happens with respect to the variability problem. Each team should be given a set of cards (Appendix VI-A) containing actual data on 100 pupils selected at random from a total of 5,000 pupils in four school districts. A sample card is shown in Exhibit 6.1 below. When a set of these cards is in the hands of each team, it is advisable to have each team member study a card to be sure he knows how to interpret the information. Review the meaning of stanine scores if the participants are not familiar with this kind of data. Emphasize that for each measure a stanine score of "1" is low and presumably undesirable while "5" is average and "9" is highest. Blanks or zeros indicate that no usable score was available for that student.

### Exhibit 6.1
### SAMPLE DATA ON ONE PUPIL

| | | | | | |
|---|---|---|---|---|---|
| 7 | Grade-point average | | Divergent thinking | 6 |
| 6 | Science | | Convergent thinking | 5 |
| 6 | Social studies | | Mental maturity | 6 |
| 3 | Total arithmetic | | Achievement drive | 7 |
| 3 | Arith. fundamentals | | Peer status | 7 |
| 4 | Arith. reasoning | | Social status | 8 |
| 5 | Total language | | Social inadequacy | – |
| 5 | Spelling | | Personal adjustment | 7 |
| 5 | Mechanics of English | | Study habits | 6 |
| 6 | Total reading | | Schol. motivation | 7 |
| 5 | Reading comprehension | | Self confidence | 6 |
| 6 | Vocabulary | | Procrastination or. | 6 |

Girl
M14

Card #40

As soon as the cards have been discussed, the leader should distribute the sheet entitled *Instructions for Grouping* shown in Exhibit 6.2 and go

## Exhibit 6.2

INSTRUCTIONS FOR GROUPING

Your deck of cards contains real data on 100 school pupils.
For each pupil you have a separate card which shows his scores
on 24 different measures. These scores are expressed in stanine
(standard nine) units, the high scores being at the "desirable"
end of the continuum. The cards also indicate the sex of the
pupils, although no sex differentiation is suggested in this
particular exercise.

You are to play the role of a principal whose job is to
divide into class sections the 100 pupils whose cards you have.
You want them grouped in the best way possible to help the teachers to provide for individual differences. You may make whatever assumptions you wish concerning the grade level or subject
involved; for purposes of realism, however, think of an actual
situation and select your criterion and related measures accordingly.

Specific Steps

1. Look over the different measures available on the cards
in order to choose the single measure that you feel will serve
as the best criterion for grouping the pupils into class sections.
Unless another team has already selected the criterion that you
want, get permission of the session leader to proceed, and record
your criterion in Section 1 of the worksheet.

**(Exhibit 6.2 cont.)**

2. Sort the cards into nine groups on the basis of the
stanine scores achieved by the pupils on the criterion measure.
Use the cards numbered 1 through 9 to designate a stack for each
stanine. Count the number of cards for each stanine and record
these numbers in Section 2 of the worksheet.

3. Group the pupils into three class sections on the basis
of the distribution of scores: "slow," "middle," and "fast."
If the class sizes do not come out to at least 30 and not more
than 36, divide the stack for the stanine in question simply
on the basis of the card numbers, the higher numbers going into
the "faster" sections. In general, the card number indicates
the pupil's rank on a combination of several academic and cognitive measures. Record in Section 3 of the worksheet the number
of pupils and the stanines included in each of the three class
sections. Keep the cards for each class section separate from
now on, using the cards marked "slow," "middle," and "fast" to
identify the three sections. Now that you have grouped the
pupils into class sections on the basis of the criterion measure,
you will want to look at the distribution of scores made by
the pupils in each section on some of the other measures in order
to see how effectively you have narrowed the range of individual
differences.

## (Exhibit 6.2 cont.)

4. Select two or three other measures that you consider
important in teaching the subject or grade that you have in
mind, and record the names of these measures in Section 4 of
the worksheet. Then, using the blanks provided on the worksheet, tally for each class section the scores of the pupils
on these related measures.

5. Examine the distributions of scores you obtained on
the related measures. How effectively has the range of individual differences been reduced? What differences would it make
if you were dealing with 500 pupils instead of 100? What portion of pupils in each "section" could justifiably be in any
of the three sections? If parents complained about the sections
to which their child had been assigned, what percent of the
assignments could be defended as "definitely correct"? How
does the normalcy of the distribution complicate this kind
of grouping? For which section is the variability reduction
purpose best accomplished?

through the instructions carefully with the entire group. When the leader arrives at Item 2 in the instruction sheet, he should make one copy of the *Worksheet for Analyzing Individual Differences* (Exhibit 6.3) available to each team. At this point each team should select its criterion for grouping, and as the selections are made they should be listed on the chalkboard so that there will be no duplications. It is advisable to suggest that only the achievement or ability measures be selected as criteria (the measures in the left-hand column of the card, together with the top three in the right-hand column). The other measures might be used as related variables, but would hardly be used as grouping criteria.

The remainder of the instructions should be fairly clear after the leader has gone through the instruction sheet with the group. He will need to move about the room for the first few minutes to help clear up any confusion that might exist while the teams are getting started.

Most teams will finish tabulating the scores on all three related measures within 30 to 45 minutes. Others who lag far behind need not be required to finish all three of the related measures. As soon as each team finishes, the worksheet should be handed in so that one of the three related measures can be selected for presentation to the entire group. As the work sheets are handed in, the teams can be given a coffee break until the entire group has finished and the selected data have been processed for presentation to the group.

During the coffee break the leader selects a variety of distributions to present to the entire group. These distributions should be selected to show a variety of grouping criteria with a variety of related measures analyzed. As the group re-convenes, the leader needs to point briefly to the distinct features of each distribution. An example of a completed worksheet, using total arithmetic as the criterion, is provided in Exhibit 6.3. Different criteria will produce somewhat different results, but a very similar pattern emerges. There is a tendency for median scores to increase from the slow to the middle and from the middle to the fast groups. The increase will usually be about one stanine in magnitude. A second general characteristic of the data will be a tendency for the overlap among the three groups to be striking. For example, the highest scores in the slow group are usually two or three stanines higher than the lowest scores in the fast group. Quite often, all but eight or nine pupils will be included in the same stanine categories in all three groups.

After several worksheets have been reviewed, a discussion should direct attention to the generalizations that can be developed and the implications suggested. For example, it becomes obvious that variability is reduced only slightly by grouping on any one criterion. Even a combination of several criteria doesn't change the situation. (See number 2 in the instructions for Suggested Related Activities below.) The teacher still has a wide range to deal with, regardless of the label of the group.

If the teacher has the impression that pupil differences have been substantially reduced by grouping, and if the teacher proceeds on this assumption, a serious disservice has been done to the pupils.

**Exhibit 6.3**

WORKSHEET FOR ANALYZING INDIVIDUAL DIFFERENCES

1. Criterion Used for Grouping into Class Sections *Total Arithmetic*

2. Number of Pupils in Each Stanine on Criterion Used for Sectionizing:

| 1 | 2 | 3 | 4 | 5 | 6 | 7 | 8 | 9 |
|---|---|---|---|---|---|---|---|---|
| 1 | 2 | 10 | 33 | 29 | 20 | 2 | 2 | 1 |

3. Distribution of Pupils into Class Sections

| Section | Number of Pupils | Stanines Included |
|---|---|---|
| Slow Group | 33 | 1 -2 - 3 - 4 * |
| Middle Group | 33 | 4 - 5 * |
| Fast Group | 34 | 5 - 6 - 7 - 8 - 9 |

*Stanines 4 and 5 had to be split to form the three sections. In this case, pupils' scores on arithmetic reasoning and fundamentals were used to determine the sections in which the cards would be placed.

4. Tabulation of Scores on Related Measures:

| Related Measure | Section | Lowest 1 | 2 | 3 | 4 | 5 | 6 | 7 | Highest 8 | 9 |
|---|---|---|---|---|---|---|---|---|---|---|
| Science | Slow | | 2 | 9 | 3 | 9 | 8 | 2 | | |
| | Middle | | 1 | 3 | 7 | 10 | 7 | 4 | 1 | |
| | Fast | | | | 4 | 7 | 9 | 5 | 6 | 3 |
| Mental Maturity | Slow | | 3 | 6 | 9 | 7 | 8 | | | |
| | Middle | | 1 | 2 | 11 | 7 | 11 | 1 | | |
| | Fast | | | 1 | 1 | 3 | 15 | 10 | 4 | |
| Divergent Thinking | Slow | | 1 | 8 | 11 | 5 | 5 | 2 | | 1 |
| | Middle | | 4 | 11 | 4 | 8 | 4 | 2 | | |
| | Fast | | | | 6 | 8 | 10 | 6 | 3 | 1 |

The discussion can turn in any one of several fruitful directions after the data have been presented and analyzed. The question concerning what would happen if more than 100 pupils were involved should be presented; actually, although the data generated in this exercise will not answer the question, one might advance the hypothesis that except for a section or two of extreme highs and lows, the situation would not be a lot different had there been several hundred pupils. Likewise, although the concomitant social and emotional factors are not involved in the data produced in this exercise, the discussion might include some of the findings of the research in this area. Other alternatives, such as flexible, temporary, and diagnostic grouping, should be explored during the discussion period.

Should ability grouping be abandoned because of the relatively disappointing results revealed in this exercise? This should be thoroughly discussed, and the answers might well depend on the purposes for which pupils are grouped. If a football coach has only one overriding purpose for his efforts—to win games—then the best ability grouping he can do is obviously imperative. However, once other objectives are added, then the efficacy of the grouping becomes less apparent. For instance, if cultivation of good sportsmanship and building physical stamina are also objectives of the football program, then rigid ability grouping is less useful. Also, it should be pointed out that in a practice session any good coach takes his highly selected, "homogeneous" group and spends most of his time working on their *individual weaknesses*—which any good teacher should do regardless of the grouping practices.

**SEQUENCE OF ACTIVITIES**

| *Time* | *Activities* |
|---|---|
| 5 min. | Introduce the problem. |
| 15 min. | Make available a set of cards (Appendix VI-A) and the instruction sheets (Exhibit 6.2) to each item. |
| 40 min. | Participants sort cards and prepare frequency tabulations on three related measures (Exhibit 6.3). |
| 20 min. | Coffee break while the leader selects tabulations for presentation to total group. |
| 20 min. | Leader presents selected tabulations showing a variety of criteria and related measures. |
| 30 min. | Discussion of generalizations and implications. |
| 5 min. | Summary. |

*Total time*: 2 hours and 15 minutes.

**SPECIAL ARRANGEMENTS**

Groups of various sizes can participate in a session of this kind, although facilities will limit the number than can feasibly be handled. In most situations, a group of 30 to 40 participants, divided into 10 to 15 teams, is about as many as one leader can guide and one room can accommodate. Since each team must work with cards spread out over an area at least 4 feet by 2 feet in size, and preferably somewhat larger, it is essential that tables be provided in adequate numbers to permit the activity to take place. A chalkboard or overhead projector is necessary for presenting the data accumulated.

Grouping pupils is a topic which tends to be viewed with much emotion on all sides. The leader should remain very objective, allowing the data to speak for themselves.

Be careful not to overgeneralize about "homogeneous" grouping as a result of this exercise. Since grouping of pupils into sections must be accomplished in schools employing more than one teacher, the use of an ability or achievement criterion may well be useful for some purposes. This session should emphasize the strict limitations from which an inflexible grouping system suffers.

The following two laboratory sessions are very useful for building upon the ideas developed above. Other follow-up activities that are more directly related to this session may be required, however. Some staff members who have strong prejudices regarding "ability" or "homogeneous" grouping may resist the generalizations demonstrated here. They may need opportunities to analyze data in still other ways. Several sessions can be planned to meet such needs.

(1) Repeat the activities described above allowing for four instead of three class sections. Many advocates of homogeneous grouping argue that small classes are also essential to make the scheme "really work." Exhibit 6.4 gives an example of such a grouping arrangement. As participants have a chance to try this, the leader can help them see that class size has little to do with homogeneity until that size becomes one pupil. Individual differences are truly individual.

(2) Plan a session that allows participants to try a variety of combinations of scores as a criterion for grouping. Many homogeneous grouping advocates believe that combinations such as mental ability, language achievement, and arithmetic achievement will produce groups with very similar instructional needs. In order to facilitate an analysis of such multiple criteria, each card contains a designation such as "S12," "M18," or "F23." These refer to the total score of the pupil on the three measures mentioned above. The S, M, and F stand for "slow," "middle," and "fast" groups. The numbers are the sum of the three stanine scores. When these

## Exhibit 6.4

### WORKSHEET FOR ANALYZING INDIVIDUAL DIFFERENCES

1. Criterion Used for Grouping into Class Sections _____

2. Number of Pupils in Each Stanine on Criterion Used for Sectionizing:

| 1 | 2 | 3 | 4 | 5 | 6 | 7 | 8 | 9 |
|---|---|---|---|---|---|---|---|---|
| / | 2 | 10 | 33 | 29 | 20 | 2 | 2 | / |

3. Distribution of Pupils into Class Sections:

| Section | Number of Pipils | Stanines Included |
|---|---|---|
| Slow Group | 25 | 1 - 2 - 3 - 4* |
| Low Middle Group | 25 | 4 - 5* |
| High Middle Group | 25 | 5 |
| Fast Group | 25 | 6 - 7 - 8 - 9 |

4. Tabulation of Scores on Related Measures

| Related Measure | Section | Lowest 1 | 2 | 3 | Stanine Scores 4 | 5 | 6 | 7 | Highest 8 | 9 |
|---|---|---|---|---|---|---|---|---|---|---|
| Science | Slow | | / | 8 | 3 | 6 | 7 | | | |
| | Low Middle | | / | 2 | 6 | 7 | 5 | 4 | | |
| | High Middle | | / | 2 | 3 | 9 | 5 | 4 | / | |
| | Fast | | | 2 | 4 | 7 | 3 | 6 | 3 | |
| Mental Maturity | Slow | 3 | 4 | 7 | 4 | 7 | | | | |
| | Low Middle | | / | 3 | 9 | 6 | 6 | | | |
| | High Middle | | | / | 4 | 5 | // | 4 | | |
| | Fast | | | / | / | 2 | 10 | 7 | 4 | |
| Divergent Thinking | Slow | / | 7 | 8 | 4 | 3 | 2 | | | |
| | Low Middle | | 4 | 7 | 2 | 8 | / | 2 | / | |
| | High Middle | | | / | 9 | 6 | 3 | 4 | / | |
| | Fast | | | | 4 | 5 | 9 | 5 | 2 | |

groups are formed by sorting the S, M, and F cards, tabulations on related measures such as "Divergent Thinking," "Reading Comprehension," "Spelling," and "Science" can be most revealing. The combining of scores to provide a multiple criteria grouping system results in even *less* distinct differences between groups.

(3) Take a sample of data from a local school situation and have participants repeat some of these activities with their own data. Test profiles or answer sheets can be used for this purpose by eliminating names, if necessary, and preparing multiple copies on a copying machine.

(4) Analyze what grouping systems do to sex ratios and socioeconomic distributions in the classroom by using local data as described in number 3 above or by using appropriate measures on the cards in Appendix VI-A. Have a counselor, principal, or teacher estimate socioeconomic status for each sampled pupil on a three-point scale—1-lowest, 2-middle, and 3-highest if local data are used. When an academic criterion is used for grouping, girls tend to fall into the "fast" section while boys predominate in the "slow" section. Similarly, pupils with lower socioeconomic backgrounds tend to predominate in "slow" sections, which produces a kind of social segregation.

SUMMARY

Interclass grouping or "sectionizing" is necessary in organizing schools for instruction. When such inflexible organizational arrangements are employed to deal with individual differences, many misconceptions may be involved. By involving participants in this series of activities, a variety of grouping arrangements can be studied. In this process, participants can be more objective and can come to understand that individual differences among pupils are not easily organized away. Trait variability within the individual makes any grouping arrangement on one criterion almost useless when other measures are considered.

### Diagnostic flexible grouping

BACKGROUND ON THE PROBLEM

Any group of students inevitably includes individuals with a wide variety of learning needs. When groups are relatively large, small subgroups often share certain specific learning difficulties. Teaching plans based upon diagnosed needs of small groups or individuals tend to be much more effective in eliminating specific difficulties and in promoting steady growth in an area of study than plans based simply upon prescribed scope and sequence or a vague impression of need. Even achievement test scores offer only crude guidelines for lesson planning as compared with systematic diagnostic data derived from standardized achievement tests for assigning students to teaching groups for specific learning purposes.

The session described here is aimed at demonstrating specific procedures for diagnostic analysis of individual learning needs. Procedures are suggested for making use of diagnostic data derived from standardized achievement tests in assigning students to teaching groups for specific learning purposes. This is flexible, diagnostic grouping as distinguished from the inflexible, ability, or achievement grouping analyzed in the previous session.

One of the most widely debated and rigorously researched areas of educational practice has to do with the grouping of students. The variability of each individual within himself is generally so great that he can be assigned to a group for an array of learning purposes with full assurance that he will still be in an extremely heterogeneous group (4, 8, 9, 10, 18, 19). Nearly all research studies having to do with ability grouping using criteria such as intelligence, reading achievement, total achievement, grade-point average, or teacher judgment produce similar findings.

Little progress is made with regard to achieving homogeneity, even within traditional subject fields, by any known general ability grouping procedures. Alternatives must be sought if grouping is to serve instructional purposes. One alternative to such widespread and relatively futile efforts is what might be referred to as *flexible diagnostic grouping* (2, 11, 23). In essence, this is a matter of taking a fairly large group, which represents some similar chronological age or general achievement level with all the diversity implied, and using diagnostic analysis procedures to determine the specific learning needs of the individuals in the group. When the specific learning needs of individuals have been diagnosed, clusters or subgroupings of individuals who have related needs can be placed into temporary teaching groups for these diagnosed learning purposes.

ACTIVITIES

This session demonstrates diagnostic and flexible grouping procedures, using a set of language achievement tests of senior high school pupils. Specific activities are:

1. Demonstrating intragroup variability, specifically showing how much similarity there is between language scores of 10th, 11th, and 12th grade pupils.

2. Illustrating the persistence of intragroup variability even when *subtest scores* are used.

3. Demonstrating the reality of trait variability as reflected in various levels of learning within a single area of English language content.

4. Showing procedures for identifying diagnostic groups on the basis of a specific learning need.

5. Illustrating procedures for organizing a program of flexible diagnostic grouping within a school.

Briefly introduce the activities planned for the session. Mention the central focus of the session as being the diagnosis of learning needs of individuals by using standardized achievement data. Mention also the emphasis being given to the important problem of organizing to meet individual needs through grouping procedures. Refer to the fact that rigid ideas about pupil grouping have provided little help, but that more flexible grouping procedures might well be promising.

*Divide participants into working teams* Teams should consist of at least three members. Four or five may serve as a team if necessary but three persons per team are preferable. Make a set of diagnostic outline materials available to each team. Fifty-nine sheets are included in a set. Each sheet is entitled "Diagnostic Outline—Language Test." This set of sheets is shown in Appendix VI-B. A sample sheet is shown as Exhibit 6.5.

Ask each team member to take one of the sheets to become familiar with the kind of material included. Suggest that sheets be kept together in a stack whenever they are not specifically being separated for some special purpose. Emphasize also that nothing is to be written upon these sheets, as they must be used by other groups.

Tell each team member that there are 59 students represented by the sheets in the set. These are students enrolled in the English classes of a high school. They are in three separate classes, taught by three separate teachers, but they are all scheduled in the same second period of the day.

Discuss the diagnostic outline sheets. Point out that each sheet represents one student—these are real, not fictional, cases. Refer to the source of the data as "standardized achievement test in English language." Review the types of scores at the top of each page. Ask participants to take special note of the material on the lower part of the sheets. Tell them that this is derived from item analyses that were completed using the answer sheets. Point out also that each student's name and the grade to which he is assigned are shown at the bottom.

*Using the "Worksheet for Mechanics of English"* Be sure each item has only one copy of the worksheet (Exhibit 6.6). Ask each team to go through all 59 sheets and tabulate the scores for "Mechanics of English" on this sheet. Emphasize that they are to tabulate 10th grade students separate from 11th, and 11th grade students separate from 12th. When tabulations are completed, ask for a brief discussion of the results. How well did these grade groups do as compared with national norms? How homogeneous are these grade groups? How different are the apparent needs of 10th, 11th, and 12th grade students as far as "Mechanics of English" measured in this test are concerned? (See a sample of the worksheet in Exhibit 6.6 as it will appear when completed.)

**Exhibit 6.5**

DIAGNOSTIC OUTLINE--LANGUAGE TEST

Test 5--Mechanics of English     Advanced Form     Grades 9 to 14

| Battery Summary | Raw Scores | Grade Placement Scores | Sub-test A--Capitalization |
|---|---|---|---|
| Total Language . . . . . . | *94* | *9.2* | |
| Mechanics of English . . . | *85* | *9.2* | *32* correct out of 40 |
| Spelling . . . . . . . . . | *9* | *8.5* | |

Item Analysis for Capitalization

1. Names of institutions and organizations . . . . . . 2 19 23 27 38 39

2. Titles of persons . . . . . . . . . . . . . . . 3 18 24

3. Titles of literature and drama . . . . . . . . . . 4 (14) (32) 35

4. First words of sentences . . . . . . . . . . . . 5 15 (28)

5. Names of persons . . . . . . . . . . . . . . . 6 22 36

6. Names of cities . . . . . . . . . . . . . . . . 7 10 13

7. Names of rivers, streets, islands, etc. . . . . . . 20 25 37

8. Days and months . . . . . . . . . . . . . . . (9) 16 30

9. First words of quotations . . . . . . . . . . . . (11) (21) (33) (40)

10. Names of languages . . . . . . . . . . . . . . 31

11. Over-capitalization . . . . . . . . . . . . . . . 1   8 12 17 26     29 34

Student's Name *Doyle, Richard*     Grade   9 10 (11) 12

## Exhibit 6.6

WORKSHEET FOR MECHANICS OF ENGLISH

Directions:

This instrument is designed for use in connection with a training session on
the diagnosis of learning needs. Tabulate the "grade equivalent score" for
each student as listed on the diagnostic outline sheet (Instrument 6d). Tabulate only the "Mechanics of English" scores, keeping 10th, 11th, and 12th
grade tallies in separate rows.

Reference: A Manual on Diagnosing Learning Difficulties of Student Groups
(Instructional Leadership Training Materials), Series Number 6, by Ben M.
Harris and Kenneth E. McIntyre, 1966.

* * * * *

MECHANICS OF ENGLISH

Test Number 5                                        Advanced Form W
2nd Period English                                   Grades 10, 11, 12

| GRADE OR CLASS | GRADE EQUIVALENT SCORES | | | | | | | TOTAL |
|---|---|---|---|---|---|---|---|---|
|  | 7.0 or below | 7.1 to 8.0 | 8.1 to 9.0 | 9.1 to 10.0 | 10.1 to 11.0 | 11.1 to 12.0 | 12.1 and above |  |
| 10th | // | // | //// | 7HL // | / | //// | / | 21 |
| 11th | ///. | // | // | //// | /// | //// | /// | 21 |
| 12th | / | /// | 0 | // | 7HL | // | //// | 17 |
| TOTAL | 6 | 7 | 6 | 13 | 9 | 10 | 8 | 59 |

Conclusions:

Implications for Teaching:

Suggest that a next logical step would involve analyzing a sub-test within the "Mechanics of English" test to see if a more homogeneous distribution can be achieved on a more specific learning area. Provide a copy of the "Worksheet for Language Sub-test A—Capitalization" to each team (Exhibit 6.7). Ask each team to tabulate the raw scores for each student on the capitalization sub-test. Remind the patricipants that these raw scores are to be found in the upper right-hand corner of the diagnostic outline sheets. Remind them again that they are tabulating "Capitalization" scores separately by grade so that 10th grade student scores are tabulated on the first row, 11th grade on the second, and 12th on the third.

When these tabulations are completed, discuss the results of these as before. Note the approximate grade equivalent scores represented by the raw scores. A score of 32 is about the 10th grade equivalent, while a score of 35 is approximately the 12th grade equivalent. A score of 25 approximates the 7th grade equivalent. Since there appear to be many similarities in strengths and weaknesses in capitalization achievement among grades 10, 11, and 12, suggest the possibility of shifting the approach. (See a sample of this worksheet in Exhibit 6.7 as it will appear when completed.)

*Instruct each team to group students* Have the teams put all the diagnostic sheets of those who are lowest in capitalization into one group, calling it Achievement Group A, those who are strongest in capitalization in Achievement Group C, and the others in a middle group, called Achievement Group B; identify each group of sheets. Recommend the following cutting scores for dividing the students into the three groups:

Achievement Group A—lowest, 25 and below

Achievement Group B—middle, 26 through 33

Achievement Group C—highest, 34 and above

Ask each team member to take one group of diagnostic sheets and think of it as his *teaching group.*

*Distribute the "Worksheet for Diagnosing Learning Needs"* Provide only one sheet for each team (Exhibit 6.8). Suggest to the group that it is now really time to get down to individual diagnosis. Explain to team members, using a sample diagnostic outline sheet, how to identify that category of knowledge within the sub-test of capitalization with which students are having some difficulty. Use category 4, "First words of sentences," as the example. This is a fairly simple category of capitalization, having to do with knowledge that the first words of sentences are capitalized. Call attention to the fact that there are only three items that test this bit of knowledge. If a student misses two or three of the items, as indicated by two or three items being circled, this suggests that the student has not yet come to understand this aspect of capitalization. Ask

## Exhibit 6.7

WORKSHEET FOR LANGUAGE SUB-TEST A--CAPITALIZATION

Directions:

   This instrument is designed for use in connection with a training session on the diagnosis of learning needs. Tabulate the "Capitalization" scores as shown in the upper right-hand corner of each diagnostic outline sheet (Instrument 6d). Tabulate only the raw scores, keeping tallies of 10th, 11th, and 12th grade students in separate rows.

Reference: A Manual on Diagnosing Learning Difficulties of Student Groups (Instructional Leadership Training Materials). Series Number 6. by Ben M. Harris and Kenneth E. McIntyre. 1966.

* * * * *

CAPITALIZATION

Sub-test A                                                        Advanced Form W
2nd Period English                                               Grades 10, 11, 12

| Grade or Class | Lowest Scores (Below 7th ach. level) | | Neither Highest nor Lowest (7th to 9th ach. level) | | Highest Scores (10th to 15th ach. level) | | Total |
|---|---|---|---|---|---|---|---|
| | 0-15 | 16-25 | 26-29 | 30-33 | 34-37 | 38-40 | |
| 10th | 0 | 𝍸𝍸 // | /// | 𝍸𝍸 // | //// | 0 | 21 |
| 11th | 0 | 𝍸𝍸 | 𝍸𝍸 | 𝍸𝍸 | 𝍸𝍸 | / | 21 |
| 12th | / | /// | 0 | 𝍸𝍸 /// | //// | / | 17 |
| TOTAL | / | 15 | 8 | 20 | 13 | 2 | 59 |

Conclusions:

Implications for Teaching:

## Exhibit 6.8

### WORKSHEET FOR DIAGNOSING LEARNING NEEDS

Directions:

This instrument is designed for use in connection with a laboratory session on the diagnosis of learning needs. Students' names are listed below, as shown on diagnostic outline sheets. Students are grouped here according to their scores on "Sub-test A-- Capitalization." You are to item analyze this sub-test to diagnose specific needs for capitalization learning.

In this column headed "4. First words of sentences," place an X opposite the name of each student whose diagnostic outline sheet (Instrument 6d) indicates that two or more of these test items were answered incorrectly. Repeat this process for the other two categories numbered 7 and 9.

\* \* \* \* \*

### DIAGNOSTIC WORKSHEET

Subject: __English__     Period: __2nd__     Grades: __10, 11, and 12__

Problem Area: Capitalization

| Achievement Groups and Student Names | Grade | Sub-test A-- Capitalization Raw Scores | Diagnosed Learning Needs | | |
|---|---|---|---|---|---|
| | | | 4. First words of sentences | 7. Names of rivers, streets, islands, etc. | 9. First words of quotations |
| **Group A--Lowest in Capitalization** | | | | | |
| 1. Baker, Jean | 10 | 25 | | | |
| 2. Brown, Andy | 10 | 21 | X | X | X |
| 3. Bula, David | 11 | 23 | | X | |
| 4. Caffee, Jim | 11 | 17 | X | X | X |
| 5. Crow, Harold | 12 | 2 | X | ? | ? |
| 6. Darwin, Joe | 12 | 24 | | | X |
| 7. Guerra, Juan | 11 | 21 | | X | X |
| 8. Ibsen, Lorraine | 10 | 21 | X | X | X |
| 9. Jones, Agnes | 12 | 16 | X | | X |
| 10. Joslin, Harry | 12 | 25 | X | | X |
| 11. King, Greg | 10 | 17 | | X | X |
| 12. Lawler, Ben | 10 | 25 | | | X |
| 13. Mitchell, Jan | 11 | 23 | | | X |
| 14. Morovsky, Tamara | 10 | 24 | X | | X |
| 15. Morris, Annette | 10 | 16 | X | | X |
| 16. Oliphant, Susan | 11 | 17 | | | X |
| **Group B--Neither Highest nor Lowest in Capitalization** | | | | | |
| 17. Adams, Helen | 11 | 31 | | X | X |
| 18. Arron, John | 11 | 28 | | X | |
| 19. Calhoun, Bill | 11 | 27 | X | X | |
| 20. Cline, Betty | 11 | 27 | X | | X |
| 21. Carter, Dan | 12 | 33 | | | |
| 22. Cortez, Juan | 10 | 33 | | | |
| 23. Cross, Jean | 10 | 26 | X | X | X |

## (Exhibit 6.8 cont.)

| Achievement Groups and Student Names | Grade | Sub-test A-- Capitalization Raw Scores | Diagnosed Learning Needs | | |
|---|---|---|---|---|---|
| | | | 4. First words of sentences | 7. Names of rivers, streets, islands, etc. | 9. First words of quotations |
| **Group B, continued** | | | | | |
| 24. Doyle, Richard | 11 | 32 | | | X |
| 25. Dupree, Mary | 10 | 26 | X | X | X |
| 26. Durham, William | 11 | 33 | | X | |
| 27. Engle, Elaine | 12 | 32 | | | X |
| 28. Escobar, Paul | 12 | 32 | | X | X |
| 29. Escolara, Louise | 12 | 33 | | | X |
| 30. Eubanks, Earl | 11 | 26 | | X | X |
| 31. Fatima, Pat | 10 | 28 | | X | |
| 32. Galbraith, Wayne | 11 | 30 | | | X |
| 33. Gomez, Ricardo | 12 | 31 | | | X |
| 34. Goth, Ralph | 11 | 27 | | | X |
| 35. Haskins, Larry | 10 | 30 | | | X |
| 36. Hawthorne, James | 12 | 32 | | | X |
| 37. Herrera, Maria | 11 | 32 | | | X |
| 38. Hopi, Sue | 10 | 31 | X | X | |
| 39. Johnston, Helen | 10 | 33 | X | X | |
| 40. Lawrence, Lila | 11 | 32 | X | | |
| 41. Massey, Jean | 10 | 30 | X | X | |
| 42. Oliver, Grace | 10 | 33 | | | X |
| 43. Ortiz, Juan | 12 | 31 | X | X | X |
| 44. Osborne, Rex | 10 | 30 | | X | X |
| **Group C--Highest in Capitalization** | | | | | |
| 45. Abbott, Billye Jean | 10 | 35 | | X | |
| 46. Ackerman, Sue | 12 | 37 | | | |
| 47. Agee, Joanne | 10 | 37 | | | |
| 48. Bell, Mary J. | 10 | 37 | | X | |
| 49. Boucher, James | 12 | 38 | | | |
| 50. Boyd, Henry | 11 | 35 | | X | |
| 51. Byler, Randy | 12 | 34 | | X | |
| 52. Cadiz, Hermalinda | 11 | 34 | X | | |
| 53. Dale, Vincent | 11 | 36 | | | |
| 54. Diaz, Tomas | 12 | 36 | | | |
| 55. Dumfey, Marianne | 12 | 37 | | | |
| 56. Harris, Sue | 10 | 35 | | | |
| 57. Hernandez, Joe | 11 | 34 | | | X |
| 58. McIntire, Judy | 11 | 35 | X | | |
| 59. Naboth, Ronald | 11 | 38 | | | |

| TOTALS: | | | | |
|---|---|---|---|---|
| All Grades | | 21 | 24 | 32 |
| 10th only | | 11 | 13 | 11 |
| 11th only | | 6 | 9 | 12 |
| 12th only | | 4 | 2 | 9 |

participants to go through the diagnostic outline sheets and check the names of those who have two or three circles opposite category 4, on the *Diagnostic Worksheet.* Go through each group of diagnostic outline sheets, checking each pupil to see if a capitalization problem of this type seems to exist. Repeat this checking for the next two categories listed on the worksheet. For categories 7 and 9, two or more circled items indicate a possible learning need for any pupil. When checking is complete in each of the three worksheet columns, discuss the results. Note that similar problems are found among pupils in different achievement groups. Suggest that the learning need, specific as it is, might be the best basis for grouping. Discuss the implications of this.

*Direct participants in flexible diagnostic grouping.* Ask each team to begin regrouping students, using the diagnostic outline sheets. The focus *now* is on learning needs. Pull those sheets of pupils checked in category 4. Ask one team member to take these pupils as a diagnostic teaching group. Now pull a third set of diagnostic outline sheets from among those that remain. Pull *only* those sheets of pupils checked in the column headed 9, and suggest to the remaining team member that this be his or her diagnostic teaching group. Keep all the remaining sheets, which are not now in one of the three diagnostic groups, together as a fourth group. These students appear to have none of the three learning needs identified.

Ask each team member to study the information at the top and bottom of each diagnostic outline sheet for his diagnostic group. Note the variety of grade levels and the scores for "Total Language," "Spelling," "Mechanics of English," and "Capitalization" represented in each such group. Emphasize that these pupils are obviously *not* homogeneous in any way, but that they do have at least one learning need in common.

Open a discussion on this approach to grouping. Comment on the necessity for flexibility in such grouping. Note that such groups are formed and call attention to the importance of teaching to specific diagnosed needs when they are formed. Note also that such groups can be formed periodically using teacher initiative and planning without disturbing normal class schedules.

**SEQUENCE OF ACTIVITIES**

| *Time* | *Activities* |
|---|---|
| 5 min. | *Introduction.* Review purposes, type of activity, and time schedule very briefly. |
| 5 min. | *Teaching team formation.* Direct formation of teams with three persons on a team. Describe roles as three high school English teachers, cooperating on work with students during a given period of the school day. |
| 5 min. | *Orientation on test material.* Provide the "Diagnostic Outline— Language Test," to each team. Ask each participant to study one |

sheet. Comment on meanings and sources of information at top
and bottom of the sheet. Appendix VI-B.

13 min.  *Grade grouping using sub-test scores.*  Provide a copy of Exhibit
6.6 to each team. Instruct the teams to prepare frequency tabulations of the one score, "Mechanics of English," keeping tallies separate by assigned grade of student. Briefly discuss results when
tabulations are complete.

7 min.   *Grade grouping using capitalization scores.*  Provide a copy of
Exhibit 6.7 to each team. Instruct the teams to prepare frequency
distributions using only the capitalization score. Comment on results and their similarity to those produced by sub-test scores.

10 min.  *Achievement grouping using capitalization scores.*  Instruct teams
to sort diagnostic outline sheets into three groups—"highest," "lowest," and "neither highest nor lowest"—so each teacher can have
an achievement group to work with. Comment on problem which
remains: What do these individuals most need to learn about
capitalization?

10 min.  *Diagnosing learning needs of individuals.*  Provide the worksheet
for diagnosing learning needs to each team. Instruct team members in checking each individual diagnostic outline sheet to determine existence of the three learning needs to be analyzed. Exhibit 6.8.

10 min.  *Flexible diagnostic grouping.*  Comments on results of checking
individual needs on the worksheet. Direct participants to regroup
students on the basis of these diagnosed needs. Comment on implications of this type of grouping for lesson planning.

20 min.  *Open discussion.*  Ask participants to react, ask questions, or suggest implications.

15 min.  *Summary.*  Summarize key ideas. Caution regarding limitations.
Mention follow-up activities for individuals or subgroups to
consider.

*Adjourn.*

*Total time:* 1 hour and 40 minutes

## CAUTIONS AND LIMITATIONS

The procedures suggested in this laboratory session should not be regarded as a panacea for instructional improvement or an alternative to
individualization of instruction. There is a point beyond which diagnosis
of specific learning needs may not be worth the trouble. Certain learnings
do not seem to lend themselves as well to diagnostic analysis as skill and
knowledge learnings do. Furthermore, flexible diagnostic grouping procedures could destroy continuity and group cohesiveness in the classroom
if used excessively. Experience with this type of grouping suggests that
not more than about 20 percent of class time is profitably used this way.

A final caution can be expressed in the question, "What will you do to
teach more effectively once needs are diagnosed and temporary groups
are formed?" To diagnose is prerequisite, to group accordingly is helpful,

but to teach to a specific learning need is essential. Nothing else will suffice or even make much difference.

SUGGESTED RELATED ACTIVITIES

(1) Use a sample set of test answer sheets to provide a laboratory experience in scoring and item analyzing a sub-test section. By providing each participant with a scoring key and a red pencil, a section of an answer sheet can be scored quickly. A category of knowledge can then be specified for item analysis, and each participant can be directed in checking to see if his test answer sheet reflects such a problem. A second, third, and fourth knowledge category can be selected for item analysis until one or more problems have been identified on each answer sheet.

(2) Develop a diagnostic outline for a section of a test for which diagnostic analysis data have not been provided by the publisher. Provide each member of a faculty group with a copy of the test section to be analyzed. Administer the section to the group members so each person will respond. Provide correct answers so each person can correct his answers. Now, examine each item as a group. Try to agree on a simple statement of the skill or knowledge required to distinguish the correct from the incorrect response. Place the statement for each item on a chalkboard, chart, or transparency so all group members will be able to see it. When a statement has been developed for each item, seek agreement on clusters of items which test identical or closely related skills or knowledge. Prepare diagnostic outline sheets for use in analyzing this sub-test and discuss possible uses of such a form in working with students or planning flexible diagnostic groupings.

(3) Develop master plans and materials kits for *diagnostic* lessons. Work with a small faculty committee to develop a highly refined lesson for teaching a very specific skill or bit of knowledge. The faculty committee should select a teaching purpose that can be diagnosed as important and which needs special attention in teaching certain students. A lesson should be developed to focus upon the diagnosed need with considerable impact. Creative and imaginative procedures to stimulate interest should be identified. Materials for multi-sensory and realistic presentation should be prepared. Practice materials and follow-up tests need to be prepared. The results should be in the form of a packet containing one or more lesson plans worked out in great detail, plus all materials necessary for teaching the lesson and background information for the teacher. If two or three lessons are essential to be assured that a diagnosed learning will be accomplished, these lessons should be developed as a series of packets.

Such master plans can be filed away for repeated use with flexible diagnostic groups as needed.

SUMMARY

This session is designed to help teachers, principals, and supervisors with the practical problems of diagnosing specific learning needs of individuals and dealing with them in a group context. This can be accomplished only when naïve notions about simple ability grouping are abandoned. The problem here is approached from the point of view that small instructional groups can be organized for specific learning needs. When this is accomplished, such a group will be temporary, since no group organized for one diagnosed need is likely to be appropriate for another.

Highly flexible grouping arrangements are required for efficient teaching in terms of diagnosed needs. Such flexibility can be attained using traditional intraclass groupings, as is common in elementary school reading programs. However, two or three teachers can cooperatively plan and implement a program of flexible diagnostic grouping following procedures illustrated here.

## Individualized analysis of achievement

BACKGROUND ON THE PROBLEM

The rise in the use of standardized tests at the elementary, secondary, and collegiate levels has been one of the most striking developments in American education during the past several decades. Standardized instruments of various kinds are being used rather widely from kindergarten through graduate school.

These tests, of course, are of various kinds. Some are achievement tests of the comprehensive, diagnostic, or survey types. Others are aptitude tests, having to do with intellectual, mechanical, musical, and other aptitudes. Interest and personality inventories add still more to the variety of instruments in use.

Standardized instruments are in no sense the only kinds of tests that need to be considered by teacher, administrator, or supervisor as a way of improving instruction. Teacher-made tests and those prepared by local schools for some special purpose are widely used. They have an important place in the development of testing and evaluation programs for instructional improvement. Performance data in the form of anecdotal records are extremely valuable. Although commercially available diagnostic instruments of the nonstandardized kind are available, standardized achievement test data are currently most readily available for diagnostic purposes.

Misuse of standardized achievement test data is common. Among the familiar forms of misuse are practices of evaluating teacher effectiveness, grouping pupils, promoting and awarding pupils, and assigning marks with test scores. While tests may be helpful in accomplishing these tasks, such data are not adequate criteria for a decision requiring consideration of a number of critical factors. Standardized test data are, on the other hand, quite useful for many purposes in the hands of a professionally skilled teacher. In the pages which follow we will consider some practical problems of utilizing test data to guide instructional planning. Our focus will be upon diagnostic use of achievement tests. The procedures described here and the accompanying materials have been developed to assist teachers, administrators, and supervisors in developing understandings and skills in analyzing test data on an individual pupil basis. A sample of data on one pupil—Howard J. Abbe—is used to provide a laboratory experience in data analysis. The activities are initiated with a set of achievement test scores for the sixth grade class in which Howard is enrolled at the Essex Ridge School. Participants are subsequently guided to proceed systematically with various types of analyses to the point of identifying a specific learning need for which the teacher can plan lessons.

**ACTIVITIES**

1. Developing understanding of the practical utility of standardized test scores for individualizing instruction in terms of diagnosed needs.
2. Developing understanding of potential misinterpretations of achievement scores when mental ability and progress factors are not considered.
3. Developing understanding of the need to undertake item analysis of sub-tests and/or sections of sub-tests in order to identify specific learning needs.
4. Developing skill in preparing and interpreting individual pupil test profiles.
5. Developing skill in using answer sheets with other instruments in undertaking item analysis procedures.

**PROCEDURE**

*Introduce the activities of the session.* Employing only a few brief remarks, announce the topic, comment briefly on the importance of making use of standardized achievement test scores for helping individual pupils, and inform participants that they will be asked to run through a series of exercises as a basis for discussion. Emphasize the practical potential of ideas about test data analysis that can be promptly used in lesson planning. Ask each participant to imagine that he is Helen Jones, sixth grade teacher in the Essex Ridge School.

*Ask participants to read the directions and study the "Achievement Test Report" (Exhibit 6.9).* Then they should carefully answer the ques-

## Exhibit 6.9

Directions: A set of achievement test scores is presented below. These test scores are those reported to the teacher of this sixth-grade class in the fall. Study these scores carefully. Make notations as requested on the opposite page.

### ACHIEVEMENT TEST REPORT

| School | Essex Ridge Elem. | Teacher | Helen Jones |
|---|---|---|---|
| Grade | 6th | Test | Achievement Battery |
| Form | A | Level | 6-9 | Year | 196_ to _ |

#### Total Achievement Scores in Grade Equivalents

| Name | Score | | Name | Score |
|---|---|---|---|---|
| 1. Howard Abbe | 9.4 | | 17. Homer Nurca | 5.8 |
| 2. Bill Alpha | 6.5 | | 18. Ted Ordway | 8.1 |
| 3. Sue Brown | 7.5 | | 19. Ann Panola | 6.9 |
| 4. Mike Chappa | 9.1 | | 20. Marjorie Quick | 5.7 |
| 5. John Crown | 7.4 | | 21. John Rogers | 7.9 |
| 6. Jean Drake | 8.7 | | 22. Bill Ralphs | 6.9 |
| 7. Olive Evans | 7.4 | | 23. Orlan Scribner | 5.5 |
| 8. Henry Frank | 6.2 | | 24. Annabelle Todd | 7.8 |
| 9. Bill Golden | 8.4 | | 25. Jan Townley | 6.8 |
| 10. Ben Hanks | 7.2 | | 26. Roy Trot | 5.3 |
| 11. Harold Haynes | 6.0 | | 27. Joyce Williams | 7.8 |
| 12. Orville Hooper | 8.3 | | 28. Hanna Willis | 5.1 |
| 13. Helen James | 7.0 | | 29. Herman Watts | 7.8 |
| 14. Mory King | 6.0 | | 30. Sue Walker | 5.1 |
| 15. Janice Love | 8.3 | | 31. Henry Yoss | 4.9 |
| 16. Tom Manley | 6.9 | | 32. Janine Yuok | 6.9 |
| | | | 33. Ben Zilch | 6.3 |

## Exhibit 6.10

### SAMPLE WORKSHEET FOR TEST REPORT

Directions: Answer the questions below by filling in the blank spaces.

1. Number of students. _33_

2. Range of scores. _49_ to _94_ = _4.5_ grades

3. Median score _69_ Modal score _6.9_ Mean score _6.9 or 7.0_

4. Is this a high I.Q. group? Yes ____ No _We don't know_

5. Have these students had good teaching? Yes ____ No _We don't know_

6. Is this a fast group? _We don't know, too dependent on other meaning of fast group._

7. What information is missing which the teacher needs in order to make these scores meaningful?

  a. _Mental ability data_

  b. _The date when the test was administered_

  c. _The age of the students_

  d. _The socioeconomic background of the students_

  e. _The scores on subtests_

Exhibit 6.10

tions on the "Worksheet" (Exhibit 6.10). When this has been accomplished by most participants, ask for their attention and review the answers to each question. The important outcome at this point is the understanding that total achievement data for a whole class are almost useless.

*Consider the scores of one pupil, using the "Pupil Record Card" for Howard J. Abbe (Exhibit 6.11).* As each participant studies the data, ask for reactions by saying, "What does this tell you about Howard Abbe as a student in *your* class?" Allow a free flow of comments for five or more minutes until several ideas have been expressed. Many comments will suggest the view that Howard is an outstanding student. A few participants may observe that this pupil has not progressed much in the area of "work-study skills." Someone may protest that without knowing the conditions of administration, one cannot be sure about the meaning of these scores. Another participant may observe that without knowing more about Howard one can hardly interpret these scores meaningfully.

*Instruct participants to prepare the "Individual Profile Chart."* Give brief instructions on using an "X" to represent each of the sixth-grade scores. Caution participants not to try to graph all scores, but only those in the last column of the Pupil Record Card. Circulate among participants as they work to assist those having difficulties. Encourage them to work quickly. Instruct them to connect their "X's" with straight lines to complete a line graph. Tell them to ignore, for the time being, the grid lines opposite "Mental Maturity Test" at the bottom of the chart. Exhibit 6.12 shows a completed profile chart.

When all participants have completed their charts, instruct each one to draw a solid vertical line representing actual grade placement (the date of testing is early October). Observe that there appear to be no serious learning problems in Howard's profile.

*Relate mental maturity data to achievement data by turning attention to the "Mental Maturity Record"* (Exhibit 6.13). As participants get a chance to study these mental maturity scores, they will begin to comment on the relationship between Howard's high academic aptitude and his various achievement scores. Ask all participants to draw a wavy vertical line on the individual profile chart to represent total mental ability.

Now, let the participating group discuss this chart and its implications. Some may protest that we cannot expect uniformly high levels of achievement in all areas. Others may wonder about the very high scores in two language arts sub-tests.

*Analyze growth scores for possible problems using the information in Exhibit 6.14.* Explain that these scores represent changes in grade equivalent scores over a two year period from fourth to sixth grade. Ask all participants to prepare a new line graph using the "Growth Profile Chart"

## Exhibit 6.11

Directions:

Study the scores below. Consider yourself Howard's teacher. What do these scores tell you about him? What will be your plans for his instructional program?

PUPIL RECORD CARD

Student: Abbe, Howard J.    School: Essex Ridge

ACHIEVEMENT TESTS

| (Achievement Series Grades 6-9, Form A) | Fourth Grade | Fifth Grade | Sixth Grade |
|---|---|---|---|
| Date of Tests | 10-3-61 | 10-11-62 | 10-1-63 |
| **Work-Study Skills** | | | |
| References | 5.8 | 7.5 | 9.8 |
| Charts | 4.9 | 6.0 | 6.3 |
| **Reading** | | | |
| Comprehension | 7.2 | 6.6 | 9.5 |
| Vocabulary | 6.5 | 6.8 | 7.5 |
| **Language Arts** | | | |
| Punctuation and Capitalization | 9.7 | 9.7 | 12.6 |
| Usage | 7.8 | 8.0 | 12.6 |
| Spelling | 7.0 | 8.8 | 9.5 |
| **Arithmetic** | | | |
| Reasoning | 6.7 | 7.6 | 9.0 |
| Concepts | 7.5 | 8.0 | 9.0 |
| Computation | 6.1 | 6.6 | 7.9 |
| TOTAL ACHIEVEMENT | 6.9 | 7.6 | 9.4 |

## Exhibit 6.12

Directions:

Graph the sixth-grade scores on the grid below. Place an "X" on each horizontal line in the position suggested by each score. Connect the "X's" to form a line graph. Draw a vertical line to represent "actual grade placement." Circle any "X's" which suggest learning problems.

INDIVIDUAL PROFILE CHART

Student _____
Class _____

Teacher _____
Date _____

| TESTS | Grade Equivalents |
|---|---|
| I. Work-Study Skills | |
|   A. References. | |
|   B. Charts. | |
| II. Reading | |
|   A. Comprehension. | |
|   B. Vocabulary. | |
| III. Language Arts | |
|   A. Punctuation and Capitalization | |
|   B. Usage. | |
|   C. Spelling. | |
| IV. Arithmetic | |
|   A. Reasoning. | |
|   B. Concepts. | |
|   C. Computation. | |
| Mental Maturity Test | |
|   Language. | |
|   Nonlanguage. | |

relative weakness in achievement

actual grade placement

expected achievement level

(Exhibit 6.15). Call attention to the numerical designations of the vertical lines. Circulate about to assist those who are experiencing difficulty. Ask participants to draw a wavy vertical line along the dotted line representing three years of growth. Emphasize the reason for expecting more than two years of progress. When this has been accomplished, ask each participant to circle the "X's" that represent areas of learning in which Howard Abbe may not be making appropriate progress. The sub-tests labeled "charts," "vocabulary," and "concepts" will be circled. "Comprehension," "spelling," "reasoning," and "computation" might also be circled, although the growth rate in these measures is not so very slow.

Now allow comments and discussion based on this analysis. Be sure that participants understand that a new type of learning problem has been identified, as well as a new area of weakness. Now, the problem of *rate of learning* as distinguished from *level of achievement* is being identified.

*Summarize the results of these analytical procedures as follows:*

1.  Initially Howard Abbe was simply the student with the highest achievement scores in the class.
2.  Howard's various sub-tests showed scores consistently at the sixth-grade level and above.
3.  Profile analysis in terms of mental ability revealed three *possible* areas of relative underachievement.
4.  Growth profile analysis confirmed the possible problem in achievement in "charts" and "vocabulary," allayed some of our concerns for Howard's achievement in the area of arithmetic "computations," and alerted us to a possible problem in the area of arithmetic "concepts" which was not evident at all in the previous analyses.

*Undertake item analysis in the area of "charts."* The "Item Analysis Worksheet" (Exhibit 6.16), will be used to focus upon only one of Howard Abbe's identified "problems." Since his scores on the section of the test on charts have been consistently low, this section seems worthy of special attention. Emphasize the need to determine the skills or concepts which account for the low scores on the past three tests.

Have participants take the "Answer Sheet—Charts" (Exhibit 6.17), which reveals the way Howard answered the questions on this section of the test. Demonstrate the marking of the item analysis work-sheet using the answer sheet. Ask participants to complete the item analysis sheet as demonstrated, circulating about to offer assistance as needed. Be sure that each participant starts with item number 57 on the answer sheet. Remind them to use a check mark ($\checkmark$) for correct answers and a zero (0) for incorrect answers. Every box should be marked.

When items 57 through 82 have been marked as correct or incorrect on the item analysis sheet, instruct participants in the recording of column totals to show only *incorrect* answers. These totals should be as fol-

MENTAL MATURITY RECORD

Student ____ Abbe, Howard John ____ School ____ Essex Ridge ____

Actual Grade Placement ____ 6. 1 ____ Date ____ October, 19— ____

Chronological Age ____ 11 years 2 months ____

MENTAL MATURITY TEST

(Elementary Form)

Intellectual Grade
Placement

Language . . . . . . . . . . . . . . . . . . . . . . . 9. 3

Nonlanguage . . . . . . . . . . . . . . . . . . . . . 9. 0

Total Mental Ability . . . . . . . . . . . . . . . . . . 9. 1

**Exhibit 6.13**

Directions:

    Study the scores below. These show years of growth in grade equivalents from fourth to sixth grade. Prepare the profile chart on the opposite page. Use "X's" and connecting lines to form a line graph. Circle "X's" falling below two years of growth. What new learning problems are suggested? Draw a wavy vertical line along three year dotted line. Circle any "X's" which fall below this level of growth. What new learning problems are suggested now?

PUPIL GROWTH SCORES

Student ____ Abbe, Howard John ____ School ____ Essex Ridge ____

ACHIEVEMENT TESTS

Dates: October 1961 to
October 1963

Growth Scores
4th-6th
(2 years)

Work-Study Skills

    References . . . . . . . . . . . . . . . . . . 4. 0

    Charts . . . . . . . . . . . . . . . . . . . . 1. 4

Reading

    Comprehension . . . . . . . . . . . . . . . . 2. 3

    Vocabulary . . . . . . . . . . . . . . . . . . 1. 0

Language Arts

    Punctuation and Capitalization. . . . . . . . . . . 2. 9

    Usage . . . . . . . . . . . . . . . . . . . . 4. 8

    Spelling . . . . . . . . . . . . . . . . . . . 2. 5

Arithmetic

    Reasoning . . . . . . . . . . . . . . . . . . 2. 3

    Concepts . . . . . . . . . . . . . . . . . . . 1. 5

    Computation . . . . . . . . . . . . . . . . . 1. 8

TOTAL ACHIEVEMENT . . . . . . . . . . . . . . . 2. 5

**Exhibit 6.14**

lows: I-5, III-2, IV-2, and V-7. Point out the frequent errors in column V. Observe that most errors in column II were associated with errors in columns IV and V.

*Discuss lesson planning that should be considered.* Ask participants to comment on approaches to working with Howard Abbe as his teacher. "How do we help him achieve more fully in this learning area? Will a more careful study of the arithmetic book suffice to help Howard? What materials will be needed? What experiences might be planned?"

*Summarize the main ideas touched upon in this session.* Mention the following briefly:

1. Total achievement scores are almost useless for improving instruction.
2. Data on individuals are more valuable in profile form than as a set of numbers.
3. Profiles that show relative achievement help to identify learning problem areas.
4. Growth profile analysis can reveal learning problems not readily identified by other procedures.
5. Specific learning needs can be diagnosed using item analysis procedures.
6. Lesson planning for an individual or small group can be logically guided by the results of item analysis.

**SEQUENCE OF ACTIVITIES**

| Time | Activities |
|---|---|
| 5 min. | Introduction. |
| 15 min. | Studying "Achievement Test Report" (Exhibit 6.9). Completing and discussing the "Worksheet" (Exhibit 6–10). |
| 10 min. | Studying and discussing Howard Abbe as revealed in "Pupil Record Card" (Exhibit 6.12), followed by the addition of mental maturity data to the profile using Exhibit 6–13. |
| 10 min. | Preparing the "Growth Profile Chart" (Exhibits 6–14 and 6–15). |
| 20 min. | Discussing findings from two profile charts. |
| 20 min. | Analyzing the "Charts" section of Howard Abbe's test using item analysis techniques (Exhibits 6–16 and 6–17). |
| 30 min. | Discussing findings from item analysis and the implications for lesson planning and individualized instructions. Summarizing. |

*Total time:* 1 hour and 50 minutes

**CAUTIONS AND LIMITATIONS**

This approach to improving instruction has limitations like any other. It will not magically solve any of the teacher's problems. It will only assist him or her in dealing with individual needs. Obviously, this use of tests takes a lot of time, and the cost in time must be balanced against the benefits gained.

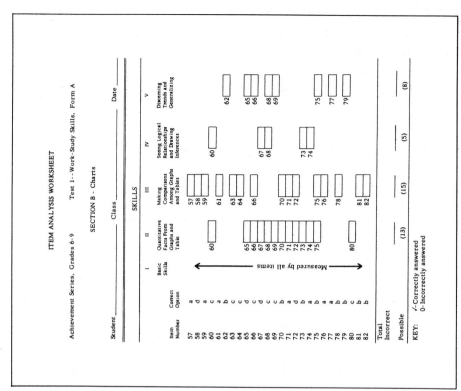

**Exhibit 6.16**

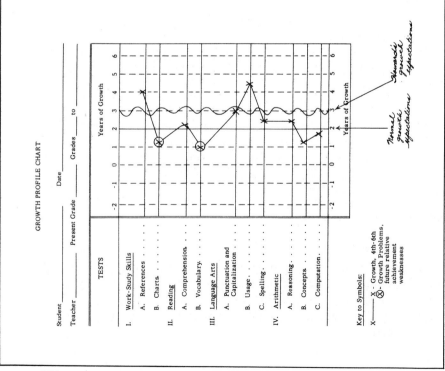

**Exhibit 6.15**

## Exhibit 6.17
## ANSWER SHEET—CHARTS

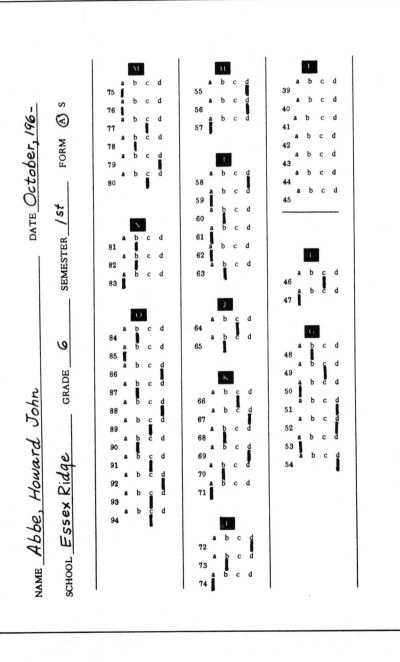

Certain cautions should be exercised. Achievement tests are not usually designed as diagnostic tests. Their usefulness for diagnostic purposes will vary widely, depending upon the specific sub-test or test section being analyzed and the original design of the test. Caution should be exercised at all times against attaching too much significance to a test score. Scores cannot tell us about learning not included among the test items. Many test items are of doubtful significance and hardly merit item analysis efforts. Scores may be highly indicative of the conditions surrounding the test situation, the pupil's physical condition, or his attitudes. We cannot assume that a score is necessarily a valid measure of a certain level of achievement.

Special care must be exercised to discourage the use of item analysis to facilitate "teaching for the test." Teachers must be assisted in planning lessons which focus upon a specific knowledge or skill area, while avoiding any temptation to teach the test items themselves.

One other point deserves mention. It is possible for a child to reach or approach the "top" of the test in certain categories. If this happens, there can be little or no growth subsequently for the child who has already done as well as the test permits.

**SUGGESTED RELATED ACTIVITIES**

A variety of activities will be required to accomplish the purposes listed earlier. Below are a few activities which might be planned as follow-up experiences.

(1) Select another area of learning (spelling, for instance) and prepare an item analysis worksheet for analyzing pupils' answer sheets. Copies of the manuals for a test and copies of the test booklet itself can be used as references by a group constructing such a worksheet. Once it has been produced, it can be reproduced for use as long as that particular test is administered.

(2) Item-analyze a section of a test for an entire class group to suggest intraclass groupings that might be useful. With an item analysis worksheet, have a group of teachers work together at item analysis. Each teacher can handle several answer sheets simultaneously. When all have been analyzed, compare results and plan a series of lessons for individuals or small groups appropriate to their diagnosed needs.

(3) Work with a group of students in helping them prepare their own profiles and item-analyze the section of the test on which most students scored lowest.

**Summary**

Test scores are widely used as the primary basis for interclass grouping of students in efforts to reduce individual differences within each classroom. Standardized achievement test data are not yet widely used by teachers for individualizing instruction, and alternatives to traditional grouping practices are not widely considered. Systematic analytical procedures make it possible to use test data in a variety of ways to facilitate better instruction. An array of test scores without analysis is useless to the teacher and dangerous in the hands of the naïve person.

The sessions described in this chapter, along with other related activities, should provide a basis for better instructional practice. Rigid grouping systems can give way to those that are flexible. Pupil stereotypes can be eliminated gradually in favor of better understanding by teacher, parent, and pupil. Of greatest benefit, perhaps, will be the return of standardized testing to its rightful place as a tool in the kit of the instructional staff for guiding teacher planning and pupil learning.

## Selected references

1. Adams, Georgia S., *Measurement and Evaluation in Education, Psychology, and Guidance.* New York: Holt, Rinehart, and Winston, 1964, Chapters 13 and 14.

2. Adler, M., "Group Flexibility," *Ohio Schools* (March, 1964), p. 26.

3. Bloom, Benjamin S., *Stability and Change in Human Characteristics.* New York: John Wiley & Sons, Inc., 1964.

4. Borg, Walter R., *Ability Grouping in the Public Schools.* Madison, Wisconsin: Dembar Educational Research Service, 1966.

5. Brownell, W. A., *et al., The Measurement of Understanding,* 45th Yearbook, National Society for the Study of Education, Part I. Chicago: The Society, 1946.

6. California Test Bureau, *Test Interpretation Exercises,* Part 2, California Achievement Tests. Monterey, Calif.: The Bureau, 1960.

7. Chauncey, H., and J. E. Dobbin, *Testing: Its Place in Education Today.* New York: Harper and Row, 1963.

8. Cook, Walter, "The Gifted and the Retarded in Historical Perspective," *Phi Delta Kappan* (March, 1958), pp. 249–55.

9. Hammond, Sarah Lou, "A Look at Research on Grouping Practices," *Education Digest* (March, 1962), pp. 22–24.

10. Harris, Chester W., ed., *Encyclopedia of Educational Research.* New York, Macmillan, 1960, pp. 427–28 and 1267.

11. Henry, Nelson B., ed., *Individualizing Instruction.* Chicago: 61st Yearbook of the National Society for the Study of Education, 1962, pp. 177–282.

12. Lyman, Howard B., *Test Scores and What They Mean.* Englewood Cliffs, N.J.: Prentice-Hall, Inc., 1963.

13. *Making the Classroom Test—A Guide for Teachers.* Princeton, New Jersey: Educational Testing Service, 1959.

14. *Manual for Administrators, Supervisors, and Counselors,* Iowa Test of Basic Skills. Boston: Houghton Mifflin Co., 1956.

15. McLaughlin, Kenneth F., *Interpretation of Test Results,* Bulletin OE-25038-1964, No. 7. Washington, D.C.: U.S. Government Printing Office, 1964.

16. *Multiple-Choice Questions: A Close Look.* Princeton, New Jersey: Educational Testing Service, 1963.
17. *N.E.A. Journal* (September, 1959). Special feature on grouping.
18. Otto, Henry J., "Grouping Pupils for Maximum Achievement," *School Review* (Winter, 1959), pp. 387–95.
19. Passow, A. Harry, "The Maze of the Research on Ability Grouping," *The Educational Forum* (March, 1962), pp. 281–88. Condensed in *Education Digest* (September, 1962), pp. 18–20.
20. Peters, H. J., *et al.*, *Guidance in Elementary Schools.* Chicago: Rand McNally and Co., 1965, Chapter 8.
21. Peters, Laurence J., *Prescriptive Teaching.* New York: McGraw-Hill Book Company, 1965, Chapter 4.
22. Pressey, S. L., "Development and Appraisal of Devices Providing Immediate Automatic Scoring of Objective Tests and Concomitant Self-Instruction," *Journal of Psychology*, XXIX (1950), 417–47.
23. Rasmussen, Margaret, ed., *Individualizing Education*, Bulletin 11-A, Association for Childhood Education International (1964).
24. Rasmussen, Margaret, ed., *Toward Effective Grouping*, Bulletin 5-A, Association for Childhood Education International (1962).
25. Shores, J. H., "Ability Grouping by Classes?" *Illinois Education* (December, 1964), pp. 169–72.
26. Stanley, Julian C., *Measurement in Today's Schools*, 4th ed., Englewood Cliffs, N.J.: Prentice-Hall, Inc., 1964.
27. Svensson, Nils Eric, *Ability Grouping and Scholastic Achievement.* Stockholm, Sweden: Almqvist and Wiksell, 1962, especially Chapter 14 (pp. 178–83).
28. Thelen, Herbert A., *Classroom Grouping for Teachability.* New York: John Wiley and Sons, Inc., 1967.
29. Thorpe, Louis P., *et al.*, *Manual for the School Administrator.* Chicago: Science Research Associates, Inc., 1958.
30. Thorpe, Louis P., *et al.*, *Teacher's Handbook: A Guide to the Interpretation and Follow-up of Achievement Scores.* Chicago: Science Research Associates, Inc., 1960.
31. Tiegs, Ernest W., *Education Diagnosis*, Educational Bulletin No. 18 (Revised 1959). Monterey, California: California Test Bureau, 1959.
32. Tillman, R., and J. H. Hull, "Is Ability Grouping Taking Schools in the Wrong Directions?" *Nation's Schools* (April, 1964), pp. 70–71.
33. Tyler, Leona E., *Tests and Measurements.* Englewood Cliffs, N.J.: Prentice-Hall, Inc., 1963.
34. Vergason, G. A., "Critical Review of Grouping," *High School Journal* (April, 1965), pp. 427–33.
35. Woodring, Paul, "Reform Movements from the Point of View of Psychological Theory," *Theories of Learning and Instruction.* Chicago: 63rd Yearbook of the National Society for the Study of Education, 1964, pp. 286–305.
36. Wrightstone, J. Wayne, "The Relation of Testing Programs to Teaching and Learning," Chapter III in *The Impact and Improvement of School Testing Programs*, Part II, 62nd Yearbook of the National Society for the Study of Education, W. G. Findley, ed. Chicago: The University of Chicago Press, 1963.

# Chapter Seven

# OBSERVING AND
# ANALYZING INSTRUCTION

PEOPLE OBSERVE in elementary and secondary school classrooms for a variety of reasons. Sometimes they use observation to study pupil problems and, occasionally they observe out of simple curiosity. Observation of children is a common practice among school nurses, counselors, social workers, psychologists, and others who are concerned primarily with special problems of pupils. Administrators, supervisors, and teachers will sometimes use classroom observation as a "getting acquainted" procedure. Administrators sometimes do a good bit of classroom observation simply to show that they are interested in what the teachers are doing, and that they are doing the job expected of administrators as instructional leaders.

Still another reason for observing has to do with analyzing instruction. The present chapter focuses on observing classroom instruction as a data-gathering activity leading to analytical procedures.

Live observations will be our primary concern although, of course, it is possible to observe indirectly with a sound tape recorder, an 8 or 16 millimeter motion picture camera, or television cameras with live or video tape viewing. Simulated teaching, such as teaching demonstrations, also involves observation and analysis of instruction. However, the most usual approach to observing and analyzing instruction involves one staff member going to a classroom to observe while another is actually teaching. This is the frame of reference for the sessions described in this chapter.

Systematic classroom observation by professional staff members may serve different purposes. At least three purposes may be mentioned because of their frequent use.

*Administrative decision-making*  One purpose has to do with judging individual teacher performance. This usually involves the use of data for some kind of administrative decision-making—merit pay determinations, reprimands, promotions, contract renewals, and so on.

*Program evaluation and planning*  A second purpose has to do with evaluating instructional programs. Here the focus is on the program rather than on the individual teacher. Analyzing the use of materials, equipment, and facilities is not unusual. Analyzing the scope and sequence of content in a given field is another example of observation for program evaluation. Data-gathering for program evaluation is restricted by the kinds of questions posed or the intended development of the in-service program which might follow. Similarly, certain selected teaching practices might be the focus of observation from which data would be used to guide in-service program planning.

*Direct in-service experience*  Classroom observations can be used to provide observers with information with which to help both the observer and the observed staff members develop new insights. For example, a new teacher can learn from those who are more experienced. A staff group can engage in a "round robin" of observations among its members to share ideas and problems. Several staff members can profit from observing and analyzing one member who has developed a new technique or approach. Any of these activities could serve to improve instructional practice.

This chapter will be concerned primarily with this direct in-service purpose since this is the basic concern of the entire volume. It will describe several in-service sessions illustrating ways of improving the classroom observation skills of teachers and other staff members and ways of using observational and analytical procedures for developing insights into teaching practice. The first session described below deals with the nature of systematic professional observation. It is important that those using classroom observation and making analyses of observed data do so with the realization that professional skill is required. The second section of this chapter describes sessions devoted to development of skill in using observation guides with systematic data gathering procedures. The last section describes a variety of observation guides which have proven useful in observing and analyzing various aspects of the teacher-learning process.

Classroom observation for research on instructional practice or child behavior is currently being widely used. It is important to recognize the contributions of a number of educational researchers in providing frames of reference for practitioners to use as they study classroom events. The complex, highly specialized instruments of the researchers are often not the most appropriate for in-service education purposes. They are, however, often adaptable to practitioner uses, and are worthy of study ( 1, 5, 9, 17).

## Discovering observation as professional skill

This in-service session is concerned with the problem of helping staff members gain understanding of the professional nature of classroom observation. Some of the limitations of rather casual approaches to classroom observation are illustrated. An effort is made to develop participant thinking about classroom observation as a set of systematic procedures involving carefully prescribed purposes, the selection of appropriate procedures and instruments, the development of observing and recording skill, and the analysis of data. Attention is given in this session to disabusing staff members of any naïve notions they might have about being able casually to watch a teacher in action if they expect to learn very much about the teaching-learning situation. Attention is also given to the problem of self-discipline required in withholding value judgments and setting aside personal views in order to maximize one's effectiveness as an objective observer.

### BACKGROUND OF THE PROBLEM

When a professional staff member is observing teaching for purposes of improving instruction, it is extremely important to put such observation into a truly professional context. The term *professional* is being used here in two ways. In one sense it refers to objective, constructive efforts based on mutual respect between observer and observed. In another sense, it refers to the high level of skill and understanding required in this situation. Assuming that a professional relationship has been established, the requirements for systematic classroom observation include the following: (1) carefully selected purposes, (2) the development of specific observation skills that are appropriate to the accomplishment of the observation purposes, (3) the development of observation instruments which facilitate the objective viewing and recording of evidence, (4), the development of a set of systematic procedures for observing and (5) the development of methods for analyzing and interpreting the recorded evidence for instructional improvement purposes.

*Purpose selection*    Teaching is a very complex process. It is not possible for an observer to see everything while observing in a classroom. For this reason, it is absolutely essential that a specific purpose or purposes be outlined in order to permit the observer to focus upon those events in a classroom which are most relevant. For instance, the observer who is there to see how a certain teacher handles the problems of inattention and disruption created by an emotionally disturbed student will simply not be concerned with the physical environment of the classroom unless some aspects of it appear to be related to the first problem. On the other hand, an observer who is there to see how a teacher designs bulletin board, chalkboard, and exhibit case displays in such a way as to stimulate interest and impart knowledge will come prepared to look at these aspects of the situation with great care.

*Observation skill*   Specific techniques used in observing teaching will vary depending on the specific purpose and the type of instruments being used. Certain skills are required no matter what the purpose or the instruments. The observer must consciously exclude from his view those events that have no direct relationship to his purpose. On the other hand, he must learn to keep in mind an array of the most relevant events and to be looking and searching consciously for any evidence relating to these, and this requires constant focusing and refocusing upon various events. If the array of events is very broad, then the observer must be very careful to see to it that he does not concentrate on only a limited number of events while others that are also relevant are overlooked or observed only incidentally. On the other hand, when the array of events is very narrow and limited, the need to focus consciously upon that limited array forces the observer to select and record only the relevant bits of evidence.

The observer must learn both to remember notations which can be interpreted and to record them upon leaving the classroom. Written notations, where appropriate, require some kind of shorthand so that the observer does not get involved in extensive note-taking. On the other hand, if written notations are not possible, the observer must concentrate on shifting events so as to be sure to retain the most relevant for later recall and recording. It is important to remember at all times that a person's memory is not to be trusted. Untrained observers retain very few details of observed evidence. Even trained observers tend to retain general impressions better than details. When there is much to see, we resort to generalization even more. Hence, it is important to make written notations while observing whenever this is possible. When recordings must be made from memory, this should be done immediately upon leaving the classroom before anything else intervenes.

*Instruments for observing and recording*   Observation guides of appropriate kinds are developed, have been developed, and need to be developed to serve specific purposes. No one guide will serve all observation purposes, yet without a guide, the kind of careful observation described in the paragraphs above is not possible. Guides may be of various kinds such as the following:

   *1. Free response instruments* requiring the observer to describe in writing what he sees. A series of questions or reminder cues may be provided to guide the observer in focusing on relevant events as he watches. For each cue there is simply a place to record any relevant events. Exhibit 7.1

shows two sections from *The Comprehensive Observation Guide* as an example of this type of instrument. The complete instrument is shown in Appendix VII-A.

## Exhibit 7.1
## SAMPLE ENTRIES ON THE COMPREHENSIVE OBSERVATION GUIDE

---

### II THE TEACHER

What is the evidence that the teacher knows and gives consideration to the socio-economic or cultural difference among children?

*1. Negro girls all sitting together — project groups mixed. When assignments made "Olivia, would you join this group? I think they could use your flair for color to good advantage,"*

*2. Teacher refers to experience with foreign language -- "Pedro, in Spanish they don't use this word 'old' -- How do they say 'age'?"*

*3. Mike asked about measuring tools — father is a carpenter.*

---

### III THE PUPILS

What is the evidence that pupils are actively involved and know what they are doing and why?

*1. Map project ... three assigned ... none working*

*2. Independ. read. gp. ... talking not reading ... teacher scolds ...*

*3. 20 of 28 doing nothing ... 10:40 ... assignments all made.*

*4. John ... works quietly on bull. bd. all alone.*

*5. 10 to 12 crowd around teacher to ask quest. after scolding ....*

2. *Tabulation instruments* have a defined set of categories which require the observer to record by tabulating or coding every event of a particular type. Exhibit 7.6 shows the *Teacher Question Inventory* as an example of a tabulation-type instrument. Such instruments are designed to focus attention upon a fairly limited number of categories in order to permit studying such events by recording the frequency with which they occur.

3. *Checklist instruments* provide a list of relevant events already described, and the observer records by simply checking or coding in some way the occurrence of each of the various events. In order to be more useful than the tabulation or free response types of instruments, the checklist must be quite extensive. It provides an inventory of events but not a count.

4. *Rating instruments* provide a limited number of carefully defined scales calling for some judgment about the degree to which an array of events being observed coincides with a particular point on the scale. Rating scales vary from descriptive scales which require the scaling of a specific act to those which require making sweeping judgments about large clusters or patterns of behavior. In the latter case, observers are asked, for instance, to rate a teacher on "relationships with pupils." Such scales often fail to describe the events to be included when making such a rating, but even when terms are carefully defined, a large array of behaviors is combined into a single rating. Obviously, such ratings tend to lack reliability and are open to question as to their validity. And even when such ratings are reliable, they have limited usefulness for instructional improvement purposes.

On the other hand, descriptive rating scales which ask for a limited judgment with fairly careful criteria for guiding the making of judgments can be quite useful. These judgments need to be bits of evidence, however, if reasonable reliability is to be attained. For instance, a scale asking for a rating on the extent to which pupils were "attending to assigned activities" might be defined to provide reliable data when used in a classroom setting where such pupil behavior was being observed.

Other types of observation guides have been invented and might be useful. The four types described above are most commonly used, however, and can be developed for a variety of purposes.

*Systematic procedures*  Even when purposes have been carefully selected, effective observation still requires systematic procedures of other kinds. Pre-planning is essential not only in order to select purposes, but also in order to insure that teachers and students are anticipating the observer, that the appropriate kind of instructional practices will be visible in terms of the purposes selected, that seating and other physical arrangements in the room are appropriate for observing the events in the classroom, and that time is scheduled for follow-up activities. Systematic procedures also involve the selection of appropriate instruments, securing lesson plans or other advance information about the instructional plan, and having a seating chart with some information about students on hand.

*Analysis and interpretation of data*   An important contribution of systematically recorded data is the possibility of easy analysis and ready interpretation. *The Teacher Question Inventory*, for instance, is an instrument which calls for very simple arithmetic computations in order to provide an easily interpretable pattern of question-asking behavior. On the other hand, *The Comprehensive Observation Guide* (Appendix VII-A) requires more complicated procedures of content analysis and discussion in order to get interpretations that have much usefulness.

**ACTIVITIES**

The discussion until now has emphasized the basic characteristics of professional classroom observation and some of the prerequisites for making such observations of professionally useful caliber. The session described in the following pages is specifically concerned with the problems that occur when such professional procedures are not employed. Many teachers, administrators, and supervisors (to say nothing of laymen) have the impression that one can simply walk into a classroom, casually observe for a few moments, and come out ready to make sound judgments about the teaching-learning process. This session is designed to emphasize the fact that we do not see much with such casual procedures, that we cannot be in agreement about what we have seen, and that only professional skills and systematic procedures can provide reliable and valid classroom observation data that can be helpful in the instructional improvement process.

The specific activities of this session, then, might be described as follows:

1. Demonstrating that casual looking at teaching fails to produce either valid or reliable evidence.
2. Demonstrating that much more is seen when systematic procedures are used than when they are not.
3. Presenting technical knowledge about the procedures required in order to obtain a high degree of reliability among observers.
4. Describing the basic elements of professional observation as contrasted with just "looking."

**PROCEDURE**

The acivities listed above can be accomplished in this session by asking the group to observe some teaching and report immediately what has been seen. A short film clip, a filmstrip, or a bit of video-tape recording taken from a live classroom setting is most useful. If necessary, part of a commercially prepared study film such as the one listed at the end of this chapter, showing realistically staged teaching, may be used (23).

Observers are shown 8 to 12 minutes of this "sample of teaching." They are given only the most limited bit of information about the teaching they are to see and are not instructed as to what to look for. They are provided with no observation instrument. Immediately after viewing the teaching sequence, all participants are given a short test. (See Appendix VII-B for an example of such a test.) This should be a short objective test, asking very specific questions about observable details in the film. Participants are assured that these tests will not be used in any way to embarrass them. In fact, they are asked not to put names upon them. If there is some reason for having any identification, a code system can be employed.

When all participants have competed the test, and before they have a chance to discuss any of the items, the tests are collected for scoring. (If scoring aides are not available, these papers can be folded and held by participants for later self-scoring.) While the papers are being scored, a brief discussion of some of the items which hold the most interest for the participants is carried on. Participants can ask about the right answers to different items, and the leader can discuss these with the participants.

Before giving the participants any information about how well they have done as a group, the same film clip or a similar one is shown. This time, however, the observers are given a guide to use. This guide might be a set of test questions and, in this case, these test questions should be reviewed with the group by the leader so that each member of the group has in mind certain specific questions that are to be answered following the observation. The guide might be only key questions which will focus attention upon certain categories or events. The leader of the group has to emphasize the kinds of events that are not relevant, and urge observers to ignore these while concentrating on others.

After this second viewing, observers are given either the same test or a similar objective test of specific events observable in the film. An answer key is provided so that each participant can score his own paper. These are collected for tabulating.

While the tabulation of both sets of tests is underway, a discussion is started. Now the leader can focus attention not on the specific events that were observed in the film, but on the observers' feeling about the observation process; whether they felt more assured in knowing what they were looking for the second time, and whether they thought they were focusing more upon those events that were relevant.

Once the test scores have been tabulated, they are presented in tabular form, either on a screen with an overhead projector or on a chalkboard. Exhibit 7.2 below shows the results of such a tabulation as they often look for an in-service group. The improved performance is partially the result of practice effect, but a portion of the effect is from "tuning," for when we know what to look for we are more likely to see it.

**Exhibit 7.2**
**SAMPLE OF GROUP TEST RESULTS ON FILM CLIP OBSERVATIONS**

| SCORES | PRE-TEST | POST-TEST | COMMENTS |
|--------|----------|-----------|----------|
| 0-3 | 5 | 0 | |
| 4 | 2 | 0 | |
| 5 | 2 | 1 | |
| 6 | 1 | 0 ◄——————— Chance Score |
| 7 | 0 | 1 | |
| 8 | 3 | 2 | |
| 9 | 0 | 1 | |
| 10 | 0 | 1 | |
| 11 | 0 | 0 | |
| 12 | 1 | 3 | |
| 13 | 0 | 2 | |
| 14 | 1 | 2 ◄——————— 70% Correct |
| 15 or more | 0 | 2 | |
| Range | 3-14 | 5-19 | |
| Mean | 6.0 | 11.4 | |

As the data are presented to the group, the leader needs to highlight the main features of the data on display. He should point out that most of the participants did better the second time than the first, and that on the second test very low scorers tend to be eliminated. He might show participants where "guessing'" and chance factors would have placed them on these two tests. He might also point out that it is possible to get some of the answers correct just by guessing. Finally, he should emphasize that many of the participants would have done just as well on the test if they had never seen the film and had simply guessed.

At this point, it is also useful to take several of the initial test papers and show that on some items every possible answer was selected by someone. This emphasizes the problem of reliability. That is, if several people watching exactly the same events put down three or four quite different answers to the same item, one needs to be concerned about the confidence that can be placed in that kind of observation.

The leader should explore this question of reliability more fully with the group. He should allow for questions and discussion of the data presented. At an appropriate point, he will find it useful to present a graph showing the relationship between frequency of observation and interobserver reliability. Such a graph is shown in Exhibit 7.3 below. It is characteristic of the curves found in most studies of reliability in classroom observation. An important point to emphasize here is that reliability requires a number of different visits to the same classroom before it can be even fairly certain that the observation records will reflect the same kind of teaching on other occasions with the same or different observers. Participants should be cautioned that they cannot generalize on what is being observed from a single period of observation, in the sense of concluding that this is the kind of teaching that regularly goes on in a given classroom. For training purposes, however, observers take what they have observed, accept it for what it is, learn from it, and consider ways of improving on it without being overly concerned with its persistence for most instructional improvement purposes.

On the other hand, if an observer comes too easily to the conclusion that certain kinds of teaching practices do persist and are consistently to

**Exhibit 7.3**
**THE RELIABILITY OF OBSERVATIONS AS A FUNCTION OF NUMBER OF VISITS**

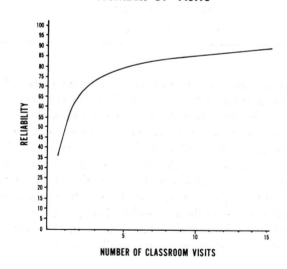

NUMBER OF CLASSROOM VISITS

be found, then it is important for him to make a substantial number of classroom visits over a reasonable period of time, using systematic procedures.

A summary presentation using a diagram such as that shown in Exhibit 7.4 contrasts observations at the unskilled level with those at the professional level. This can be a useful summary presentation. Here the emphasis is on the use of the two senses—visual and auditory—most commonly relied upon for classroom observation. The use of these senses with varying skills and procedures characterizes the level of observation. Observations range from the simple, unsystematic, non-professional to the truly professional level. Terms like *auditing* and *viewing* imply listening and looking with selectivity and interest, while terms like *tuning* and *focusing* imply not only selective observing, but selection on the basis of professional knowledge and defined purposes.

**Exhibit 7.4**
**LEVELS OF OBSERVATION RELATED TO SKILLS EMPLOYED**

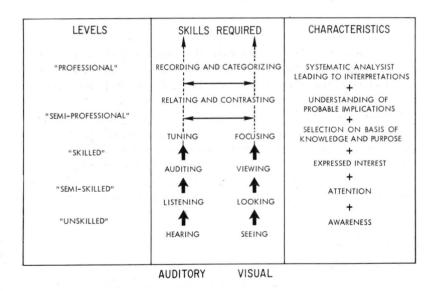

**SEQUENCE OF ACTIVITIES**

The following time schedule and sequence of activities are suggested to direct the planning of the training session and to guide the leader in conducting all activities.

| Time | Activities |
|---|---|
| 3 min. | Introduce topic. |
| 12 min. | Present teaching film clip (initial viewing). |
| 10 min. | Provide test for participants to take. |
| 5 min. | Collect completed tests. Have aide start scoring. |
| 20 min. | Discuss need for focus and ways of looking at teaching; distribute observation guide as focus for discussion. |
| 10 min. | Repeat teaching film clip or show new clip. |
| 10 min. | Present answer key and have participants score their own papers. Collect for tabulation by an aide. |
| 20 min. | Discuss reactions to second observation session as contrasted with first showing. |
| 15 min. | Break for stretch, coffee, relaxation, discussion, and so on. |
| 20 min. | Present and review data contrasting first and second viewing. |
| 15 min. | Open discussion and questions regarding viewing experiences and results presented. Present graph on reliability of observations. |
| 10 min. | Present overview on use of visual and auditory senses at various levels of performance. |

*Total time:* 2 hours and 30 minutes

SPECIAL ARRANGEMENTS

The session just described can be carried on with a group of almost any size. The 16 millimeter motion picture projector is required, and an overhead projector is useful if the group is large. For small groups, a chalkboard will suffice. Since nearly all of these activities are fairly formal and structured, a formal seating arrangement is appropriate. If the group is small enough, a semicircular seating arrangement will facilitate participation in the limited amount of discussion that is provided for.

Tabulators need to be instructed on handling test scoring and tabulation chores. A secretary or a student can serve very nicely in this assignment. About one tabulator for each 20 to 30 participants will be required.

CAUTIONS AND LIMITATIONS

This is not a skill development session, so the leader should avoid getting too much involved in discussing or analyzing the film clips that are used. These materials and the tests which are used following the film showings have served well for this session when the group realizes that just looking will not suffice for either reliable or valid reporting of even simple events. The second film showing with the feedback of the data serves to demonstrate that even slightly more systematic procedures can make a real difference in how much people see and the consistency with which different observers see the same events.

Since much of the content in this session is presented by the leader, he or she should avoid excessive verbalization. This is a fairly highly structured session in which quite a variety of ideas must be presented. The leader should, therefore, try to visualize these ideas as much as possible by using the exhibits provided, either sketching them on the chalkboard or preparing transparencies. The leader should try to present the ideas briefly and directly and then allow participants plenty of opportunity to ask questions.

**SUGGESTED RELATED ACTIVITIES**

The sessions described in subsequent sections of this chapter are appropriate follow-up sessions to this one. Other activities that might be included are suggested below.

(1) Go in groups of four, six or eight persons to classrooms to observe. Have half of each group get together and agree on things to look for while the other half is given no such briefing. Upon leaving the classroom, have each group sit down and maintain twenty minutes of silence while each individual writes his description of "important observed events." Assemble these into a single list of important events for each group. Have these lists read to the combined groups as they reassemble. As the two lists are discussed, guide participants to think about the differences in the listings of those with agreed upon purposes. Several interesting things should be noted about the group that had no specified purpose:

a. Their list is likely to be lengthier and more rambling.

b. Their list is likely to have less specific or vivid descriptions of what was observed.

c. Their list is likely to show more disagreement among group members, or at least, lack of consistency in what they saw.

d. Their list is likely to contain more value judgments.

(2) Some participants would enjoy a bit of action research. Help them plan a field trip or a film-viewing session with their students. In this instance, a preview session will provide the information needed for constructing a test on the trip or on the film. Have the students divided at random before the trip or the film showing. Brief one half of the group on the questions are are going to be asked. They might even be given a copy of the test that has been constructed with the caution not to share it with the others. On returning, the same test can be given to all those who went on the trip or viewed the film. In scoring this test, the results should show:

a. Higher scores for those who were briefed.

b. A smaller variety of errors for that same group.

SUMMARY

This session is designed to alert observers to the problems of effective classroom observation, and to introduce the requirements for professional observation. It is hoped that these procedures will emphasize to participants that observing is not just casually going in and looking around, that two observers do see quite different things depending upon the background and experience of each, and that only a limited amount is really observed unless a set of systematic procedures is used including ways of recording and analyzing data. It is hoped that this session will motivate the group to become familiar with some specific classroom observation procedures and to develop some advanced observation skills.

## Training in the use of observation guides

BACKGROUND ON THE PROBLEM

Live classroom observation is most useful as an activity for analyzing instruction. The requirements for such observational activities have been previously discussed. This session is designed specifically to help professional staff members gain skill as professional observers and analyzers of instructional practices.

The essential elements in which participants must become skillful include the following:

1. Applying specific observational procedures.
2. Defining observation purposes.
3. Selecting and developing appropriate guides.
4. Recording evidence in appropriate forms while withholding judgments.
5. Analyzing recorded evidence.

To see is not necessarily to observe. The recognition of this fact is the first step in developing professionally competent observers. Skilled observation, however, involves more than this. Professional competence is not achieved until staff members, no matter how competent they might be as teachers or administrators, have had an opportunity actually to go into classrooms and get firsthand experience in systematically observing with carefully selected guides for specified purposes.

In the pages which follow, systematic procedures for classroom observation are described with emphasis upon actual training in the use of these procedures. An array of observation guides is introduced to illustrate the different kinds of guides which serve different purposes. Most of the session will focus on the use of a comprehensive observation instrument since the problem of viewing a great variety of complex events in a live classroom setting is most perplexing. However, other guides designed for much more limited and more specific observation purposes will be described. Similar procedures in the use of observation guides would be appropriate no matter which guide is used.

Of special importance is the notion that every new observation instrument requires a careful period of training on the part of even the most skilled observer who has not previously used that particular guide. It is also important to recognize that since no one guide can possibly be used for all purposes, careful selection of guides becomes an important part of the work of professional observers. Furthermore, it is important that observers learn to develop guides for purposes for which none are readily available.

#### ACTIVITIES

This session will focus primarily upon training observers for comprehensive classroom observation. Such training involves a technique that is normally applied whenever the observer wishes to gain as much information as possible about the entire classroom situation. A comprehensive guide is appropriate, for instance, when new teachers are trying to get acquainted with the overall approach of more experienced teachers or when principals and supervisors wish to get acquainted with the general *modus operandi* of new teachers. The use of comprehensive observation procedures is, of course, often a prologue to focusing upon more specific problems which require special guides. The purposes of this training session include the following:

1. Developing attitudes and skill on the part of observers which facilitate objective data-gathering without making value judgments.
2. Developing understanding on the part of observers regarding the vast array of pertinent events that can be observed in a classroom.
3. Developing skill in systematically recording observation data in descriptive form.
4. Developing a broader frame of reference regarding the nature and complexity of classroom practices.

#### PROCEDURE

This session requires approximately two and a half to three hours. It involves a group of about 25 or fewer persons studying the instrument to be used. This group should be further divided into sub-groups of six to ten persons which will go to classrooms by prior arrangements to observe for 30 or 40 minutes, return to separate study areas, record observed evidence, and discuss what was observed.

The main focus of this session is to avoid making judgments about the "goodness" or "badness" of the teaching being observed. The focus is upon such questions as, "What did we observe?" "What did we fail to observe?" "How could we objectively and systematically record the evidence most fully and put it into proper categories for later analysis?"

*Studying the guide*  A set of transparencies or an outline on a chalkboard is used to present the basic form of the *Comprehensive Observation Guide* (see Exhibit 7.5). The four main sections of the guide are

**Exhibit 7.5**
**SAMPLE QUESTIONS FROM EACH SECTION OF**
**THE COMPREHENSIVE OBSERVATION GUIDE**

---

I. The Classroom

"F.  What evidences in the room illustrate orderliness,

good taste, and systematic procedures?"

II. The Teacher

"D.  What indicates that the teacher is sensitive to

the physical well-being of the pupils?"

III. The Pupils

"C.  What indicates that pupils know what they are

doing and why they are doing it?"

IV. The Lesson

"E.  What are the various classroom activities that are

employed to stimulate pupil interest and challenge

different abilities?"

reviewed: I. The Classroom; II. The Teacher; III. The Pupils; IV. The Lesson. The use of a few sample questions illustrates the emphasis being placed on the wording of all questions. Such questions ask about *observable evidence*, they are *positively* worded, and they ask for *no value judgments*.

A copy of the COG Study Form (see Appendix VII-A) is given to each participant. The study form gives illustrations of the kinds of evidence which might be observed and recorded under each question. Participants are asked to skim through the entire guide, reading each question and glancing at some of the "sample" evidences.

When participants have had a chance to familiarize themselves with these guide questions, the session leader should ask for questions and comments. If the following points do not come out via questioning, the session leader should introduce them:

1. While *positive* evidence is called for in each question, the lack of evidence can be objectively recorded.
2. While there are many questions in this guide, they have been selected from among many more that might have been asked. Hence, the guide is not *exhaustive* but *comprehensive* in the sense of covering a broad spectrum of possibly relevant classroom events.
3. While this guide is designed for use in almost any formal classroom setting, its usefulness will vary, depending upon the situation and the nature of the lesson. For instance, a physical education class engaged in game activities might be difficult to observe and some items would not apply. An independent study period in which no presenting, discussing, reporting, or practice activities occurred would leave many questions unused.

*Presenting recording procedures*  Participants should be given a copy of the *recording form* of the COG. This is exactly the same as the *Study Form in Appendix* VII-A except for the omission of all examples to leave spaces for recording purposes.

Recording procedures should be presented as follows:

1. Record notations of any bit of evidence observed in the blank space under the question to which it most directly applies.
2. Keep notations of evidence brief. (See Exhibit 7.1.)
3. Make all notations objective descriptions of what is being observed.
4. Avoid any words like "good," "poor," "weak," "nice," and so on. Just describe what is observed.
5. Proceed through the entire guide from beginning to end in about 15 or 20 minutes *reading every question* and recording any observed evidence.
6. When no evidence is observable in relation to any question, place a check (✔) in that space and go on.

7. When events permit, prepare a sketch showing the physical arrangement of the room and indicate the location of objects and people. (See room diagrams in Appendices VIII-E and F.)

8. Spend another ten minutes reviewing what has been observed up to this point in time. Try to record any additional evidence that comes into focus or is recalled.

9. Spend the last 15 or 20 minutes concentrating on Section IV—*The Lesson*. Reread every question and record any additional evidence while amplifying previous notations.

This set of directions stimulates questions and comments that suggest participants' concerns about using such a voluminous instrument. Participants should be reassured that they can "learn" to use this tool just as hundreds before them have. However, they should realize that hard work is required. Observers must be looking, listening, reading, writing, and consciously shifting focus almost constantly for about 40 minutes. They must be alert and push themselves to function at the highest level of speed, accuracy, and perceptiveness.

*Visiting in classroom*   Participants should go to classrooms to observe a lesson in action. Prior arrangements should be made with teachers being observed. (These arrangements are described below in detail.) Observation groups should ideally consist of 5 to 12 persons. Each such group observes a given teacher for 35 to 50 minutes. Observers sit in the rear or at the side of the classroom and remain as unobtrusive as possible while observing and recording rapidly. A designated group leader selects a moment for departure when all participants have had time for full recording as described above and when their leaving would be least disruptive.

*Recording and studying evidence*   Immediately upon leaving the classroom, the observing group should go to a rather quiet place where, without any discussion, they should spend about twenty minutes completing the recording of evidence. They should be urged to do the following:

1. Add new notations of observed evidence which may have been omitted.

2. Rewrite brief notations under every question to form a descriptive sentence or paragraph of relevant evidence.

3. Where no evidence was observed relative to a question, write "no evidence" in that space. (Previously these spaces had been check (✔) only.)

4. Reread every notation to see if any evaluative terms have been used. Eliminate any words that do not describe. (See Exhibit 7.6 for examples of problems in recording evidence objectively.) The group leader should circulate among participants as they write to help them to avoid value judgments while writing descriptively.

## Exhibit 7.6
## FOUR PROBLEMS IN RECORDING EVIDENCE

Problem No. 1
  Use of value judgments instead of objective description

    Question IA.   How is the physical environment conducive to
                  learning?

    Not:  "Teacher failed to adjust blinds properly."

    But:  "Blinds slanting down, sun shining through and striking
           eight desks."

    Not:  "Teacher had room beautifully decorated."

    But:  "Two bulletin boards designed using photographs, spray
           letters, and colored yarn. Student work mounted on
           colored paper. Green plants growing on window ledges
           with aluminum foil around pots."

Problem No. 2
  Words too vague to describe vividly.

    Question IVA.   What evidence shows progress?

    Not:  "Students seem to be learning."

    But:  "Eight of the ten students at chalkboard completed
           exercises correctly without assistance."

Problem No. 3
  Evidence is inappropriate to the guide question.

    Question IVR.   What efforts are made to help the pupils
                 learn to be self-evaluative?

    Not:  "Tests show many A's earned."

    But:  "Students keep own progress charts."

Problem No. 4
  Negative evidence becomes value judgment.

    Question IIIB.   What indicates that pupils' participation
                 is active and self-initiating?

    Not:  "Students confused, wasting time".

    But:  "Students assigned to map project did not go to work as
           directed. Independent reading group sat and talked until
           teacher scolded them. Twenty out of twenty-eight students
           just sitting when all assignments had been made."

*Discussing and analyzing evidence*   When all participants have completed recording in their guides, the leader should ask for a sharing of
what has been recorded, but should avoid discussion of reactions at this

point. The leader should guide the participants to report what has been recorded. The leader should take note of evidence observed by some and not by others. It may be helpful to those who observed but failed to describe objectively to try rephrasing and rewriting their entries.

After recorded descriptions on a variety of questions have been compared and analyzed for objectivity, encourage free discussion of reactions to this observation session. Discuss problems in seeing what is happening, finding appropriate questions, keeping up with on-going events, avoiding value judgments, and so on. The leader should remind participants that this is for practice in observation. Participants should be urged to form groups among themselves for further group observation practice. Emphasize the need for three to five observation periods before any new guide becomes comfortable in use.

This session requires about three and a half hours, planned somewhat as follows:

| Time | Activities |
|------|-----------|
| 5 min. | Briefing on the purposes and activities of the session. |
| 35 min. | Studying the COG. Overview of structure of the guide, followed by reading of Study Form questions and examples. |
| 20 min. | Presenting recording procedures using the COG Recording Form. |
| 30 min. | Relaxing with a coffee break before going to assigned classrooms for observation. |
| 45 min. | Observing in classrooms in small groups using the COG. |
| 25 min. | Recording and studying evidence in silence, undisturbed. |
| 20 min. | Comparing and contrasting recorded descriptions of observed evidence. |
| 20 min. | Discussing problems, impressions, and next steps in self-directed practice. |

*Total time:* 3 hours and 20 minutes

When a long time period is not available, two shorter periods can be used for these purposes. The first hour of study of the guide can be scheduled before the observation. This permits the last sequence of activities to be scheduled in about two and a half hours.

The introductory activities require no special arrangements. Great care must be exercised in arranging for groups to observe in classrooms, however. The following suggestions should be carefully considered. All arrangements should be made in such a way as to give assurance that the group can see a complete sequence of classroom events in as nearly normal a situation as possible. Arrangements should interfere with or modify daily routine just as little as possible!

*Selecting a classroom*   Select a typical class rather than one which is quite unique to the school or district. Be sure the teacher is one who is reasonably secure and will not be seriously disturbed by the observers. Observing in the classrooms of rather strong or even outstanding teachers is most valuable. Very weak teachers should not be observed at this stage of the game. Emphasize to the teacher being observed that the group will *not* evaluate him or her. The observers are there to learn, not to pass judgment.

*Planning with the teacher*   Give the selected teacher several days to plan the lesson that is to be observed. Too much advance notice may cause undue strain and should be avoided. Ask the teacher to teach the lesson *just as it would normally be taught*, and to avoid any effort to demonstrate "all the things we've been doing." Encourage and help the teacher to plan well for the lesson so things will go well, but try to prevent a "canned" lesson. Normal teaching difficulties should be expected by the observers and should not be artificially eliminated. The teacher should plan a lesson which offers some variety of activity and some pupil-teacher interaction. He should try to avoid lessons that are predominantly independent study, testing, or formal lecture sessions. Let the teacher have a copy of the observation guide to read in advance, but assure him that no one expects to see all the things listed.

*Providing information*   Ask the teacher to provide, in advance, a seating chart, an outline of the overall plan of study, and a brief outline of the plan for the lesson being observed. A few notes about individual pupils on the seating chart are very helpful. Omit last names of pupils when including personal information to avoid any chance of misusing such information and to keep observers from being distracted by identifiable family names.

*Making physical arrangements*   Arrange extra chairs in the most convenient places from the standpoint of the normal functioning of the class. Generally speaking, a row of chairs at the back, or against a side wall, or both, will allow for good viewing with minimum distractions for the teacher and pupils.

*Planning the schedule*   Schedule the observation itself so the group can enter the room with minimum disruption to the class, and so observers can see a fairly complete lesson or sequence of activities in 40 to 45 minutes.

*Other arrangements*   Be sure that there is a place for observers to gather before and after the observation. They need to be able to sit down and write and talk, undisturbed.

## CAUTIONS AND LIMITATIONS

No observation instrument or guide will accomplish everything. This comprehensive guide is designed specifically to broaden the observer's understanding of the significant elements to be observed and to cultivate skill in systematic, thorough observing and recording. When different purposes exist for observing, different observation guides will be required.

Certain items in this guide appear to be repetitious when first employed. An item in one section may be almost identical to an item in another section. The same observed evidence may apply to several questions. Such apparent repetitions are intentional and serve a useful purpose. Certain bits of evidence relating to such ideas as individualization and motivation are pertinent questions in each section of the guide. In each instance, a fundamentally important aspect of the teaching-learning process is brought into focus from a somewhat different point of view.

The presence of a group of observers in a classroom creates an unnatural teaching-learning situation. This is inevitably so, but the observers need not concern themselves with this fact. Regardless of the changes that observers produce in a classroom, the events that do transpire are worthy of study. The purposes of this training session make unimportant the question of whether observed events are the usual ones. Classroom events and objects are being observed, recorded, and analyzed for the value that they can have *for the observer*, not for the conclusions to be drawn about the teacher and his pupils.

Follow-up discussions tend to stray from objective observations to value judgments. The discussion leader must repeatedly emphasize the former and avoid the latter. When the discussants make value judgments or generalized statements, they should be questioned in relation to *evidence* observed. Comments about the absence of certain kinds of evidence should be encouraged as objective evidence without judgments attached or implied.

Discussants who are closely associated with the teacher to be observed will tend to be defensive when observed events are reported that *might* be judged as uncomplimentary. If possible, the principal and co-workers of any teacher being observed should be in another group observing another teacher.

## SUGGESTED RELATED ACTIVITIES

It should not be assumed that these activities leading to the development of observational skills are an end in themselves. These activities will serve in developing better understandings of the significant elements of the teaching-learning process. However, follow-up activities will capitalize upon observing skills in a variety of ways.

(1) The *COG* can be used in connection with a teaching *demonstration*. A teaching demonstration can be arranged in an auditorium using a self-confident and skillful teacher, a small group of children, and a simulated classroom (2, 3, 15). Teachers who have previously studied the guide can observe the demonstration using the recording form. Following the demonstration, the observing teachers can form small groups, complete their notes on the guide sheets, and discuss the implications of what they have observed for improving their own teaching.

(2) The *COG* can also be used with a motion picture of classroom teaching to stimulate thinking about effective instruction. A brief film clip of a teacher in action can be taken from a longer film. A small group can observe and record with a follow-up discussion of the implications for good teaching. This also has possibilities for parent study groups seeking to become more knowledgeable about the nature of effective teaching.

(3) The *COG* can be used effectively as an individualized or small group supervisory technique in connection with *intervisitations*. As a supervisor or principal arranges for one or several teachers to visit and observe another teacher in action, the visiting teachers need guidance in seeing the significant elements in the classroom situation being observed. The supervisor or principal can study the *COG* with the teachers who are to visit. Then they observe together on a prearranged schedule, followed by a three-way conference including the teacher being observed. In this way, the visiting teacher is actively engaged in studying and analyzing teaching.

SUMMARY

This session is designed to help professional staff members gain new skills in systematically observing and analyzing instruction. A comprehensive guide is used to systematize the observing and recording of participants as they watch a teacher at work in the classroom. Small groups of participants observing simultaneously provide the basis for group discussion follow-up and offer an economical approach to in-service education.

### Other observation guides

The session described above for developing skill in observing and recording a comprehensive array of evidence is a useful design for acquainting a group with any of a variety of observation guides. Each of several guides which have been developed to serve special purposes is described below. By familiarizing teachers and other staff members with any one of these guides, a sequence of activities can be employed almost identical to those described for using the *COG*.

One of the most revealing indicators of the learning that is going on in a classroom is the pattern of questions that are being asked. Whether the questions are oral or written, they give the observer some of his most valuable data for studying ways of getting the pupils involved in thinking about subject matter to be learned. The *TQI* is an observation guide designed specifically to gather evidence related to questioning in the teacher-learning process. This guide can be used to serve the following purposes:

1. To develop understanding of the importance of good questions in teaching.
2. To develop skill in analyzing questioning techniques used by teachers in recitations, discussions, or written tests.
3. To identify patterns of questioning which serve as a guide toward improving the questions asked to stimulate better learning.

The basic instrument used for analyzing teachers' questions specifies two major classes of questions. Six cognitive types (4) and two affective types (5) are defined. Each of the eight types of questions is fairly distinctive, although practice is required in categorizing questions before this instrument can serve well. Exhibit 7.7 below shows a completed tabulation of a lesson in an elementary classroom.

Six types of questions are defined below, with examples to help the observer differentiate each category. These represent various types of cognition which such questions stimulate (12).

*1. Recognition*   The student is presented with cues that require only the recognition of the correct option from two or more choices. Examples: "Was the Declaration of Independence signed in 1776 or 1801?" "Was Francis Scott Key a man or a woman?" "Is that correct, Bill?"

*2. Recall*   The student is asked to recall one or more simple facts. Examples: "Who were the authors of *Mutiny on the Bounty*?" "Name the parts of speech." "What is the name of the green matter in plants that is essential to photosynthesis?"

*3. Demonstration of skill*   The question requires the application of knowledge in the performance of a skill, as in arithmetic, reading, or foreign language. Examples: "What does the headline say?" (word recognition). "What does that sentence mean?" (reading for comprehension).

## Exhibit 7.7
## SAMPLE LESSON ANALYSIS USING THE TEACHER QUESTION INVENTORY

Teacher __Mr. "X"__    Grade __8th__    Subject __Social Studies__

Time __9:15__ to __9:45__    Date __January 20__

Topic __"Nations of Southeast Europe"__

| Question Type | Tallies | Total | Percent |
|---|---|---|---|
| A. COGNITIVE | | | |
| 1. Recognition | ||||  ||||| | 10 | 30 |
| 2. Recall | |||| |||| |||| //// | 19 | 58 |
| 3. Demonstration of Skill | | | 1 | 3 |
| 4. Comprehension | /// | 3 | 9 |
| 5. Analysis | | 0 | 0 |
| 6. Synthesis | | 0 | 0 |
| B. AFFECTIVE | | | |
| 7. Opinion | | 0 | 0 |
| 8. Attitude or Value | | 0 | 0 |
| TOTAL - All Types | | 33 | 100 |

Comments:

1. Questions almost all ask for recounting of isolated facts.
2. Nature of topic suggests ample opportunity to ask analysis, opinion, and attitude questions. None asked.
3. Teacher used maps frequently -- pupils did so only once.
4. Five girls and one boy answered nearly all questions.
5. Fifteen girls on left of teacher were never called upon.
6. Teacher followed each pupil response with short "lecturette" elaborating on pupil answer.
7. Comprehension questions answered by teacher. Example: "Why do you think these countries have developed and retained governmental control of their railroads?" Silence! Teacher answers with lecturette on lack of seaports makes rail transportation crucial to economic well-being of some of these countries.

"How many fourths should we borrow from the six?" (basic arithmetic processes). "What is the English translation of that sentence?" (foreign language translation skill).

*4. Comprehension* The student is required to produce evidence that he understands simple relations among facts. Examples: "Can anybody see an example of an abrasive in this room?" "Can you explain in your own words what you just said?" "Show us what you mean by a 'gesture of defiance'."

In the following two categories, it is assumed that the student has not been previously given an analysis or synthesis and cannot answer the question merely by recalling what has been memorized.

*5. Analysis* The student is asked to identify the relationships between elements in a situation or to explain a complex phenomenon. Examples: "Why did the lighted candle go out when we placed it in a closed container?" "What are some similarities between the United States Constitution and that of our own state?" "How could you tell the difference between Jimmy's scarlet king snake and a coral snake?" "Can anybody illustrate, from our own community, what was said in the report on patterns of the urban growth in the U.S.A.?"

*6. Synthesis* The question calls upon the student to combine or reorganize specifics so as to develop a new structure or generalization. Examples: "Knowing about the geographic features that most of the major cities of the world have in common, and recognizing the changing role of geography in man's way of living, where would you predict the development of a new city or industrial complex in the future?" "In view of what we have learned about current trends in education level, modern technology, and salary scales, what would appear to be the high school dropout's vocational opportunities in the future?" "Considering the cost of education, regulations of the Selective Service System, and differences in cultural values as applied to education, what would you predict to be the composition of Army non-commissioned officers serving in Viet Nam in terms of education level, socio-economic status, race, and religion?"

Two categories of questions are defined below, with examples which represent questions calling for *affective* rather than cognitive responses (5).

*7. Opinion* The question requires a response involving expressions of feeling or personal point of view on comparatively simple matters other than facts. Examples: "What do you suppose Dick was thinking when he saw the elephant?" "How would you feel if that happened to you?" "What was the most beautiful sight we saw on our trip?" "What are your opinions on the morality of capital punishment?"

*8. Attitude or value* The student is asked for a response involving deep-seated attitudes or values, and the teacher asks him to defend his position. Examples: "Do you think Eichmann should have been executed?" ("On what premises?") "How do you feel about setting up an official agency to screen the movies, books, magazines, and so on, that the public is permitted to see?" ("Why?")

Following are procedures for observing in a classroom and categorizing questions according to the definitions and examples above.

The observer should listen carefully to all that is being said and, as each question is raised by the teacher, make a tentative judgment as to its type. He should listen to the pupil's response and the teacher's acceptance or nonacceptance of the response to confirm his judgment, and then make his tabulation in the appropriate space on the checksheet.

The observer should be especially alert to questions which appear to be of one type but are actually another type. This is especially important with questions that appear to be of the more complex comprehension, analysis, or synthesis types. For an example, let us consider the following dialogue:

TEACHER: "Doug, what made the lighted candle go out when we placed it in a closed container?"

Up to this point, one would tentatively classify the question under Category 5—Analysis.

DOUG: "It has been extinguished."

TEACHER: "Correct. The oxygen has been exhausted, and the flame goes out."

The teacher's acceptance of Doug's superficial response, which was probably only the simple recall of a term that might or might not have meaning for him, indicated that the question was not one requiring any analysis at all. There was no probing for evidence of Doug's knowledge of causal relationships. The only analysis in evidence was done by the teacher, not the pupil, and even the teacher's explanation was sketchy. This illustrates the importance of listening to the entire question-response-acceptance sequence and not just to the question itself.

### THE PUPIL RESPONSE INVENTORY

The ways in which teachers elicit responses from pupils can be studied and can provide data that will be helpful in assisting teachers to overcome certain kinds of problems. The techniques used in asking questions, for example, can have an important bearing on whether the entire class or just one individual at a time is involved. Systematic observation techniques can provide information concerning how pupil responses are being obtained and the response-evoking patterns that the teacher employs.

This observation guide, the *PRI*, was developed specifically for the following purposes:

1. To develop skills in observing and analyzing the techniques used for eliciting responses from pupils in classroom discussions and recitations.
2. To develop understanding of the relationships between patterns of pupil response and techniques used in leading class discussions and recitations.
3. To develop understanding of the implications of certain response patterns for more efficient learning.

The *PRI* calls for tabulating and categorizing responses of pupils in terms of the procedures used by the teacher to elicit responses. Five categories of response have been defined. They are listed below.

| *Type of Response* | *Description* |
|---|---|
| Type a—*Individual Designated* | The teacher asks a specific pupil to respond by designating the individual *first* and *then* posing the question or giving some cue to guide the response. |
| Type b—*Group Designated* | The teacher asks the group as a whole to consider a question and *then*, after a brief pause, selects a specific pupil to respond. |
| Type c—*No One Designated* | The teacher poses a question or gives a cue to the group as a whole, but allows any pupil to respond by self-selection. |
| Type d—*Spontaneous Response* | A pupil volunteers a comment without a specific question or other cue from the teacher and without being designated. |
| Type e—*Mass Response* | Several pupils respond simultaneously to a question or cue from the teacher. |

Exhibit 7.8 shows the completed tabulation sheet for an elementary class session in social studies.

With practice, the alert observer can learn to categorize each pupil response quite readily. The words and actions of the teacher preceding the pupil response must be carefully observed. When the teacher calls a pupil's name immediately following a question with no time allowed for the group to consider it, the response is categorized as *Type a, Individual Designated*, and a tally is recorded in the appropriate row. When a question is posed with an individual designated, but that pupil responds with only a blank stare, a shake of the head, or an "I don't know," it is still tallied as a response of Type a. When the teacher points to another pupil, or calls another name without restating the question, this consti-

**Exhibit 7.8**
## SAMPLE LESSON ANALYSIS USING THE PUPIL RESPONSE INVENTORY

Teacher _Mrs. "Y"_      Grade _4th_      Subject _Social Studies_

Time _1:15_ to _1:45_   Date _November 20_   Number in Class _33_

Topic _"Trade Routes to the Pacific"._

| RESPONSE TYPES | TALLIES | TOTAL | PERCENT |
|---|---|---|---|
| a. Individual Designated | 7HH 7HH I | 11 | 38 |
| b. Group Designated | II | 2 | 4 |
| c. No one Designated | 7HH 7HH 7HH II | 17 | 58 |
| d. Spontaneous Response | | 0 | 0 |
| e. Mass Response | | 0 | 0 |
| TOTAL --All types | | 30 | 100 |

Notations:

Number of pupils responding _10_      Response rate -- _1 per minute_

Responses per pupil _3.0_      Involvement ratio _1/3_

Comments:

_1. Full use made of types a and c. Little use of type b. Teacher had a habit of pointing to a few individuals while asking a question. Then she allowed those same individuals to respond without being designated when other questions were asked._

_2. Type c most fully used. This suggests efforts to avoid teacher domination and allow freedom of expression. This was restricted to about five individuals._

_3. Heavy use of this type is contradictory to use of types b and c. This may have created uncertainty on the minds of some pupils._

_4. Inconsistent practices by teacher may be producing results shown by no typed responses._

_5. Teacher avoids mass responses even though type c is used substantially._

tutes another *teacher cue* and should be tallied separately. It has now
became a Type b, group designated, response, however, since the first
pupil's failure to respond presumably alerts other pupils to their potential
responsibility for responding.

When the analysis is complete, the types of response eliciting techniques most predominantly used become apparent. The frequency of responses tells us something about the pace of activities in the class. The
ways in which responses are elicited have implications for the quality of
learning being stimulated. When a teacher leads a class so as to get individually designated responses, a type of individual tutoring or testing
is in progress. Such a response pattern encourages pupils to relate to the
topic under discussion only when specifically called upon. On the other
hand, the predominance of group-designated responses tends to encourage attention to the topic under discussion regardless of the individual selected to respond. Type b responses maintain teacher control,
however, and discourage spontaneity required for real discussions. A
predominance of "no one designated" and "spontaneous" responses forming a pattern has special implications. In such a situation, considerable
freedom is conferred upon pupils to volunteer in response to a teacher
cue or even to originate ideas without a cue. Assuming that pupils' comments are serious and not merely diversionary, such response patterns
suggest that the teacher is trying to cultivate a sense of responsibility for
learning and to encourage initiative and creativity with a minimum of
teacher control.

The frequent use of mass responses is especially interesting. Pupils tend
to know, somehow, when a question calls for a mass response. Some
teachers use a key word, or a unique tone of voice, to elicit mass responses. However they are elicited, such responses imply rather restricted
learning expectations. Mass responses nearly always follow a simple recognition or recall type question. Rote memorization is usually involved,
and little depth of learning is likely to be reflected. Mass responses suggest teaching techniques which not only rely heavily upon memorization
of fragments of subject matter, but also encourage overlearning, discourage independent study, and ignore individual differences.

SELECTING AND DEVELOPING OTHER GUIDES

Several other guides are described briefly in Chapter 8 in connection with
protocol analysis activities. These are useful too in observing and analyzing live classroom activities. No guide or combination of guides will
serve all purposes. Sometimes it is necessary to create guides for observing for special purposes.

Research on teacher behavior has been a useful source of ideas for
observation guides. Research instruments generally need to be simplified
and adapted for use by practitioners since purposes are different. Even

so, instruments such as those developed by Medley (17), Coody (7), Flanders (10), and Burnham (6) are but a few of those that can be useful for in-service purposes.

## SUMMARY

The in-service design described in the first part of this chapter can serve for developing basic observation skills and also provide participants with knowledge necessary for using a comprehensive observation guide in a variety of other in-service sessions. The other guides described here briefly illustrate quite different ways of observing to accomplish special purposes. Participants gain insights into the teaching-learning process as they develop skill as observers and learn to view teaching in a variety of ways. Follow-up activities are nonetheless important to gain the in-service outcomes desired. Observation is only a beginning activity which provides the basis for analysis, discussion, or practice sessions which may lead to better teaching.

It is especially important for leaders of in-service programs to be knowledgeable about a variety of observation guides and to provide training in their use for any professional staff group involved in observation for in-service purposes.

## Selected references

1. Anderson, H. H., "Studies in Teachers' Classroom Personalities, II. Effects of Dominative and Integrative Contacts on Children's Classroom Behavior," *Applied Psychology Monograph*, No. 8 (Stanford, California: Stanford University Press, June, 1946).

2. Bartholomew, W., "Place of Demonstration in Supervision," *National Elementary Principal*, XXXV (September, 1960), pp. 189–91.

3. Berger, E. J., "How To Give a Demonstration," *Industrial Arts and Vocational Education*, ed., XXXXIX (September, 1960), pp. 35–36.

4. Bloom, Benjamin S., ed., *Taxonomy of Educational Objectives, Handbook I. Cognitive Domain*. New York: Longmans, Green and Co., 1956.

5. Bloom, Benjamin S., ed., *Taxonomy of Educational Objectives, Handbook II, Affective Domain*. New York: Longmans, Green and Co., 1964.

6. Burnham, Reba M., "An Instrument to Determine the Nature of Learning Opportunities Provided in Elementary School Classrooms," *Journal of Teacher Education* (Dec., 1965), pp. 477–81.

7. Coody, Betty Fay, "A Study of the Impact of Demonstration Teaching on Experienced and Inexperienced Teachers Under Various Supervisory Conditions." Unpublished Doctoral Dissertation, The University of Texas, Austin, 1967.

8. Farley, G. J., and J. J. Santosuosso, "Supervisor and Classroom Visitation," *Educational Administration and Supervision*, XLIII (May, 1957), pp. 311–19.

9. Flanders, Ned A., *Interaction in the Classroom*. Minneapolis, Minnesota: College of Education, University of Minnesota, 1960.
10. Gage, N. L., ed., *Handbook of Research on Teaching*. Chicago: Rand McNally and Co., 1963, Chapter 6.
11. Good, Carter V. and Douglas E. Scates, *Methods of Research, Educational, Psychological, Sociological*. New York: Appleton-Century-Crofts, Inc., 1954, Chapter 6.
12. Harris, Ben M. and Kenneth E. McIntyre, *A Manual for Observing and Analyzing Classroom Instruction*, Series Number One. Instructional Leadership Training Materials. Austin, Texas: Bureau of Extension Teaching and Field Service, The University of Texas, 1964.
13. Harris, Ben M., *A Research Study of the Effects of Demonstration Teaching Upon Experienced and Inexperienced Teachers*, Cooperative Research Project No. S 384. U.S. Office of Education, Austin, Texas: The University of Texas, 1966, pp. 20–23 and 226–53.
14. Harris, Ben M., *Supervisory Behavior in Education*. Englewood Cliffs, N.J.: Prentice-Hall, Inc., 1963, Chapters 3, 5, and 15.
15. Harris, Ben M., "The Teaching Demonstration Model," in *Designs for In-service Education*, ed., E. W. Bessent. Research and Development Center for Teacher Education, Monograph. Austin, Texas: University of Texas Press, 1967.
16, Jahoda, Marie, *et al.*, *Research Methods in Social Relations, Part I, Basic Processes*. New York: The Dryden Press, 1951.
17. Medley, D. M. and H. E. Mitzel, "A Technique for Measuring Classroom Behavior," *Journal of Educational Psychology*, XLIX (April, 1958), 86–92.
18. Neuman, C. E., "In-Service Education Through Demonstration Teaching," *Journal of Secondary Education*, XXXVI (January, 1961), 20–22.
19. Schminke, C. W., "Illustration Lesson: A Technique for In-Service Education," *National Elementary Principal*, XLI (February, 1962), 31–33.
20. Soar, Robert S. and Norman O. Bowers, "Pupil-Teacher Classroom Behavior," *The University of South Carolina Education Report*, IV (April, 1961), 1–4.
21. Trow, William C., "The Learning Process," *What Research Says to the Teacher*, No. 6. Washington, D.C.: National Education Association, December, 1964.
22. Washburne, C. and Louis M. Heil, "What Characteristics of Teachers Affect Children's Growth?" *The School Review*, LXVII (Winter, 1960), 420–28.
23. *Creative Imagination*. 44 min., 16 mm., sound. University Park, Pennsylvania: Pennsylvania State University (rent or purchase).

# Chapter Eight

# ANALYZING LESSON PROTOCOLS

THIS CHAPTER describes sessions using observation instruments for the analysis of classroom instruction when such instruction has been recorded and *lesson protocols* prepared. The term protocol is used here to identify a verbatim record, in typescript form, of classroom events to which detailed descriptions of *non-verbal* communication have been added. The lesson protocol is, then, substantially more than a transcribed record of verbal interaction (4). Added to such a typescript are observer notations regarding the tone of voice, pauses, facial expressions, manipulations of materials, movements about the room, and other observable events that are not available from sound recordings.

The activities described and the materials provided here are intended to help develop understanding of the anatomy of a lesson, to define skills of analysis, and to demonstrate ways in which specific instruments and analytical procedures can be applied. Whether these activities are directed toward the training of supervisors and administrators or used with teachers in an in-service study, the approach is essentially the same. The participants are asked to study a protocol of a lesson or a portion of one. Selected observation instruments are then used to systematically analyze the content of the lesson. The follow-up discussion is guided in an attempt to demonstrate ways of interpreting analytical findings, diagnosing basic problems, and planning for instructional improvement.

As a unique tool for in-service education purposes, the lesson protocol seems useful in several kinds of in-service designs. This chapter describes in considerable detail one training session which is designed to introduce lesson protocols to a group and to develop understanding about the use of various analytical procedures in diagnosing teaching problems. Another section of this chapter describes a variety of analytical systems which might be useful with various protocols.

**Protocol analysis using
special observation guides**

The session described below was designed to familiarize professional staff members with the nature and uses of lesson protocols. Observation guides introduced in Chapter 7 are employed in this session. The group leader is provided with instructions for using instruments and guiding the discussion. A completely analyzed lesson protocol is provided to aid the leader and to illustrate results obtainable. Appendices VIII-D, VIII-E, and VIII-F provide lesson protocols with quite different types of teaching problems, different subject areas, and different levels of instruction represented.

#### BACKGROUND ON THE PROBLEM

Rigorous analysis of lessons has rarely been undertaken except for research purposes. The practice of analyzing a lesson is difficult because of the transitory nature of a lesson. Once taught, it is gone and is no longer available for analysis. Video and sound tape recorders now make it possible to record and retain a lesson for detailed analysis. For the first time, instructional diagnosis based upon rigorous analysis of specific teaching acts is practical. The challenge to teachers, supervisors, and administrators is now one of developing effective procedures for doing just this and of making constructive use of these procedures for improving instructional practice.

The series of activities described here is designed to provide experiences in analyzing and diagnosing teaching using a detailed lesson protocol. The point of view of the authors is implied by the sequence of activities described, but it can be made explicit as follows:

1. Problem identification is not sufficient for instructional improvement.
2. Once a problem area is recognized on the basis of systematic evidence or general impression, the relevant aspects of the teaching-learning situation need to be analyzed in considerable detail.
3. Systematic analytical procedures provide data for diagnosis of specific problems in the sense that certain specified behavior patterns can be isolated.
4. Since most teaching problems of importance are quite complex, different instruments providing various kinds of evidence and requiring different analytical procedures must be used.

5. The diagnosis of specific problems provides the basis for planning in-service efforts, guides the teacher in modifying his behavior, and makes improvement clearly discernible.

#### ACTIVITIES

The intent of this series of activities is to develop fundamental understanding about the dynamics of the teaching-learning process and the relationship of data analysis to diagnoses and alternatives in teaching practice. Session activities are as follows:

1. Demonstrating systematic content analysis as applied to a lesson protocol.
2. Demonstrating the usefulness of a variety of kinds of data analysis in diagnosing teaching problems.
3. Analyzing lessons using multiple approaches to show the influence of each on the diagnosis.
4. Analyzing teaching behavior using selected instruments for skill development.

#### PROCEDURE

Following a brief introduction participants are designated as "observer-analysts" and given a lesson protocol. All participants are instructed to study the protocol material carefully. One or two observation instruments are then provided to each participant with instructions for using these to code the protocol material. The diagnostic summary is prepared independently by each participant showing the results of the coding of the protocol. If time permits, each participant uses several instruments on the same protocol. When time is limited, sub-groups use different instruments simultaneously.

When the analyses have been completed, they are checked against the instructor's key. Then the participants discuss problems of coding and consider interpretations leading to diagnostic decisions. Specific procedures are suggested as follows:

1. Briefly introduce the session by saying that a lesson will be analyzed and then discussed in order to diagnose *fundamental teaching problems.* Each participant should have the protocol "The Russian Revolution" (Forms VIII A through D in *In-Service Education: Materials for Laboratory Sessions*) which provides three columns for coding and making notations.

2. Ask participants to read the material carefully without doing any analysis at this time.

3. Tell the participants that each of them is to work alone in analyzing the lesson. Each participant should have the materials explaining the analytical procedures to be used. Discuss the two systems for analyzing teacher questions and pupil responses before they begin to work. (Refer

to descriptions of the *TQI* and the *PRI* in Chapter 7.) The analytical procedures are described in Appendices VIII-A and VIII A-1.

Instruct participants to try to complete their analyses in twenty-five or thirty minutes. Fifteen minutes will suffice if half of the group uses one set of procedures while another half uses another set.

While participants are studying and analyzing, circulate among them to encourage and assist them in using the analytical procedures described.

4. Participants should tabulate their analyses by tallying questions and responses they have categorized. As individuals complete their analyses, circulate among them to assist them in preparing these summaries.

When twenty-five or thirty minutes (or fifteen minutes) have passed, ask each participant to try to complete his work including the tabular sheet as quickly as possible.

5. Present on a chalkboard or a screen the summaries of teacher and pupil questions provided in Exhibits 8.1 and 8.2, explaining that those are the results of careful analyses by experienced observer-analysts. Discuss variations between the results obtained by participants and those shown in the key. Help participants to understand that it requires not only more time but also more practice and experience to get completely consistent results.

6. Switch attention of the group to specific questions regarding ways of coding various elements of the lesson protocol. Use the *Instructor's Guide* protocol shown below.

Putting the protocols of participants aside, ask participants to consider this question as they study the two summaries on the chalkboard or screen. "What fundamental problem(s), if any, do we see in this teacher's performance?"

7. Brainstorming procedures may be useful here to get a complete list of ideas. As participants suggest problems, list them on the chalkboard under the caption "Problem Diagnosis." As participants repeat the same ideas, add check marks to show the frequency of an expressed idea.

If no new ideas are being expressed, present additional analytical data using Exhibit 8.3. Discuss this new set of analytical categories briefly to give them meaning and emphasize that the *same teaching* has been analyzed in still a different way. If time permits, the new categories presented in Exhibit 8.4 might be used as still another way of viewing this lesson.

8. Now repeat the question "What fundamental problem(s), if any, do we see in this teacher's performance?" List their ideas alongside those previously expressed under the caption "New Diagnosis." When problems that are identical to those previously mentioned are expressed, draw an arrow to show this repetition. When the same idea is repeated, use check marks (✔) to indicate the frequency of mention.

9. When all the ideas seem to have been expressed, circle new ideas that have been repeated several times. Discuss these new problems. How

important are they? What have additional analytical procedures accomplished? What reinforcing evidence about old problems has been provided? What can now be said with some assurance about the most fundamental problem? What are the possible problems for which we have assurance? Why?

10. When these questions have been discussed, shift attention to questions of in-service plans. What kinds of in-service activities might help this teacher? What changes in plans are dictated by the new diagnosis? Buzz groups may be formed to develop "plans."

Exhibit 8.1
SAMPLE PROTOCOL ANALYSIS USING
THE TEACHER QUESTION INVENTORY

Teacher ___Mrs. Oliver___   Grade ___6th___   Subject ___Social Studies___

Time ___9:15___ to ___9:45___   Date ___January 20___   Observer _____

Topic ___"The Russian Revolution"___

| Question Type | Phase: Time: | I 0-8 | II 8-10 | III 10-15 | IV 15-25 | V 25-30 | Total | Percent |
|---|---|---|---|---|---|---|---|---|
| A. COGNITION | | | | | | | | |
| 1. Recognition | | | | | | | 0 | 0 |
| 2. Recall | | 5 | 9 | 4 | 5 | 0 | 23 | 100 |
| 3. Demonstration of Skill | | | | | | | 0 | 0 |
| 4. Comprehension | | | | | | | 0 | 0 |
| 5. Analysis | | | | | | | 0 | 0 |
| 6. Synthesis | | | | | | | 0 | 0 |
| B. AFFECTIVITY | | | | | | | | |
| 7. Opinion | | | | | | | 0 | 0 |
| 8. Attitudes or Values | | | | | | | 0 | 0 |
| TOTAL --ALL TYPES | | 5 | 9 | 4 | 5 | 0 | 23 | 100 |

Comments

1. Questions strictly recall.
2. Most questions asked at the very beginning of the lesson.
3. Flurry of questions in Phase IV before the end of the lesson was entirely recall.
4. Despite the nature of the topic, no genuine effort shown to get opinions or attitudes explored or analyzed.

**168**

ILLUSTRATIVE LABORATORY SESSIONS

## Exhibit 8.2
## SAMPLE PROTOCOL ANALYSIS USING THE PUPIL RESPONSE INVENTORY

Teacher   Mrs. Oliver   Grade   6th         Subject   Social Studies

Time   9:15 to 9:45   Date   January 20   Observer _____

Topic   "The Russian Revolution"

TABULATION WORKSHEET

| Response Types | Tallies | Total | Percent |
|---|---|---|---|
| a. Individual Designated | c,d,g,k,m,q,r,u,aa,cc,dd | 11 | 38 |
| b. Group Designated | e,bb | 2 | 4 |
| c. No One Designated | a,b,f,h,i,j,l,n,o,p,s,t,v,w,x,y,z | 17 | 58 |
| d. Spontaneous Response | | 0 | 0 |
| e. Mass Response | | 0 | 0 |
| TOTAL--ALL TYPES | | 30 | 100 |

Number of pupils         33                Response rate
                                           (in responses
Responses per pupil     0.91               per hour)        100

The following time schedule and sequence of activities are suggested to guide the leader in working with an in-service group. Since a large part of the activity of this session involves discussion, it is difficult to specify the time periods very precisely. The following time sequence is generally feasible although more time could well be used with a group being permitted much more extensive opportunity for discussion.

| *Time* | *Activities* |
|---|---|
| 3 min. | Introduce the topic briefly. |
| 7 min. | Have participants read the protocol entitled "The Russian Revolution." |
| 10 min. | Participants should have materials to guide the analytical procedures and discuss categories as shown in Appendix VIII-A and VIII-A-1. |
| 30 min. | Participants analyze protocols. |
| 25 min. | Present key showing teacher question and pupil response analyses and compare with analyses of participants (Exhibit 8.1 and 8.2). |
| 15 min. | Break. |
| 20 min. | Discuss specific questions raised by participants regarding their own coding of content. |
| 20 min. | Inventory ideas of participants about "Fundamental Problems." |
| 10 min. | Present additional data using new analytical procedures (Exhibits 8.3 and 8.4 if time permits). |
| 10 min. | Inventory "New Diagnosis" ideas. |
| 30 min. | Discuss contrast between diagnosis based on limited data and that based on additional data and implications for in-service activities. |

*Total time:* 3 hours

INSTRUCTOR'S GUIDE PROTOCOL

On the pages which follow all of the materials are presented that would be distributed and used by participants in this session. The material here is different from that distributed to participants in that the analyses have been completed and analytical comments added to aid the leader in discussing the protocol and the analytical results with participants. The analyses completed on this instructor's guide protocol have been carefully reviewed by a number of observer-analysts and represent reasonably expert judgments. Obviously, it is not possible to get perfect agreement on the content analysis of lesson protocol data, and there is room for argument concerning the coding of certain items. Nonetheless, the group leader can use this analyzed protocol with pretty good assurance that sound judgments are reflected in the coding and comments provided. See Appendix VIII-A and VIII-A-1 for information on code designations used in analyzing this protocol. Exhibits 8.1 and 8.2 provide summaries of the code symbols shown in the protocol. A copy of this protocol without coding or comments is included in the volume of materials for participants and is designated as Form 8.5.

## The Russian revolution lesson

**INTRODUCTION**

The following episode was transcribed from a tape recording* (with observer comments) from a classroom with the following characteristics:

A. Sixth grade

B. 33 pupils (16 girls, 17 boys); Mean I.Q. = 112

C. Large, well-lighted, modern building in a middle-class suburban area

D. Individual movable desks set in a semicircle of three rows of eleven facing teacher's desk

The teacher's plan for activity evolved out of a larger unit on Russia. She attempted to cover modern Russian history and geography as a content area with an emphasis upon basic social science concepts. In the episode below, the teacher was attempting to promote the development of one basic concept (revolution) and one basic understanding—stated as follows:

1. The meaning of *revolution* in society.

2. The usefulness of past history for interpreting current events.

Textbook readings on the revolution in Russian history had been previously assigned and discussed by the teacher and class in terms of names, places, and events. The teacher planned to complete the study of Russia (the unit) with a 1918-to-present section in the following days. The only planned-for possibility of further work on the revolution would be the selection of this as a special topic by some youngster. (Each youngster was to identify a special topic to be reported upon during the culminating activities of the unit.)

**THE LESSON**

| Teacher and Pupil Acts | Teacher Questions | Pupil Response | Diagnostic Comments |
|---|---|---|---|
| TEACHER: When you are ready, we will (1) start! (Noise of desks, talk, etc. subsides gradually.) | | | Teacher structures |
| SUSAN: Do we need our books out? (a) | | C | Pupil responds to teacher structuring. |

*This protocol was originally published without coding and analytical comments shown here in *The Nature of Teaching.* Milwaukee, Wisconsin: University of Wisconsin-Milwaukee (1962), pp. 82–85 by Dr. Grace Lund. Reprinted with permission.

| Teacher and Pupil Acts | Teacher Questions | Pupil Response | Diagnostic Comments |
|---|---|---|---|
| TEACHER: Just wait and I will tell you (2) what you need. | | | Teacher regulates and controls behavior. Antagonism is shown. |
| TEACHER: You know, the longer we have (3) to wait, the more time we waste. Do you think it is fair that some of us have to wait for others? | Rhetorical question | | Teacher continues structuring, giving orientation. Question is really just procedural. |
| BILLY: Sh! Sh! (b) | | C | |
| TEACHER: All right. —Now today we are (4) ready to discuss the Russian Revolution. Jack, what is a revolution? | II | | Teacher calls Jack's name before the question is posed. |
| JACK: It is when the people are (c) very unhappy, and they decide to get rid of the king or something. | | A | |
| TEACHER: Then what? Bill? (5) | II | | Bill's name is called without a pause, eliminating all others. |
| BILL: They usually kill the king or (d) czar. | | A | |
| TEACHER: Yes, but what causes a revo- (6) lution? | II | | |
| SUZY: (Raises hand, teacher nods) (e) Well, like Jack said, people are unhappy, and they revolt against the government. | | B | Suzy responds to a non-verbal comment. |
| TEACHER: Oh, then what happens? (7) | II | | Teacher probes, but next question shows it was not for deeper understandings. |
| MARY: There is usually a lot of blood- (f) shed, and then probably the new people get to be the people in power. | | C | Teacher asks for more facts, and Mary obliges by giving what is only a superficial account. Mary apparently selects herself. |
| TEACHER: And? (8) | II | | Line of questioning suggests teacher is not seeking causes, but a recitation of events. |

| Teacher and Pupil Acts | Teacher Questions | Pupil Response | Diagnostic Comments |
|---|---|---|---|
| MARY: They set up their own government. (g) | | A | Somehow Mary seems to know that only she is expected to continue. |
| TEACHER: What revolutions do we know about? (9) | II | | Teacher asks for more recall. |
| TIM: We had one! (h) | | C | |
| BUD: Yeah, we kicked the British out of the colonies! (i) | | C | |
| TEACHER: All right, there was an American Revolution. Do you know about any others? (10) | II | | Teacher accepts simple fact and pushes on to other unrelated facts. |
| FRED: The French cut off a lot of heads. (j) | | C | |
| TEACHER: What was that? (11) | II | | |
| FRED: When they got rid of their king. (k) | | A | |
| TEACHER: O.K., the American, the French, and the Russian revolutions are three examples. Are there any going on now? (12) | II | | |
| MARY: Cuba had a revolution a little while ago. (1) | | C | |
| TEACHER: What about that? (13) | | | Teacher asks open question that could encourage comprehension. |
| MARY: Well, this man Tateeta (teacher corrects—Batista), ah, Batista kept all the money and land and finally there was a revolution. (m) (14) | | A | Mary interprets teacher's question as asking for more recall. |
| TEACHER: Who can tell us more about this? (15) | II | | Teacher asks for more of the same, rather than probing for greater comprehension. |
| JACK: Castro is the dictator now. (n) | | C | |
| BILL: He came out of the hills. (o) | | C | |
| CHARLEY: He looks more like he came out of the trees. (p) | | C | |

| Teacher and Pupil Acts | Teacher Questions | Pupil Response | Diagnostic Comments |
|---|---|---|---|
| TEACHER: (16) That's enough of that (glares at Charley). Now, what happened in Cuba, Mary? | II, II | | Teacher returns to Mary whenever things get out of hand and she wants someone to recite. |
| MARY: (q) The people were poor, and a few men had all the money. So they started a revolution and threw out Batista, and now Castro runs the country and everything is just as bad as it was. | | A | |
| TEACHER: (17) You mean nothing good came of the revolution? | II | | Teacher could be asking for analysis, but the recitation that follows (18) obviates pupil analysis. |
| MARY: (r) Things are worse now, down there. | | A | Student tries to infer causal relations. |
| TEACHER: (18) Well, maybe, but the important thing for us at this point is to realize that there was a revolution. So I think I have been hearing you say that revolutions arise when conditions are bad in a country, that the people or some group arms itself and deliberately sets out to gain control of the government of the country. When this happens we say that there is a revolution. Now what about the Russian Revolution? Who knows some facts? | II | | Teacher casts doubt on students' efforts to get at causes and proceeds to emphasize simple facts. Teacher generalizes. Teacher asks for more facts. |
| TOM: (s) The Russians were fighting against the Turks in World War I, and . . . | | C | |
| TEACHER: (19) It wasn't the Turks, Tom. Who can tell Tom whom the Russians were fighting. | II | | |
| MARY: (t) It was the Germans! | | C | |
| TEACHER: (20) Now, go on Tom . . . | | | |

| Teacher and Pupil Acts | | Teacher Questions | Pupil Response | Diagnostic Comments |
|---|---|---|---|---|
| TOM: (u) | Well, anyway—things were in bad shape, and the Germans were beating the Russians, and the Russian people were hungry and didn't want war, so they had a revolution. | | A | Tom tries to show that he understands relationships between war, defeat, and hunger leading to revolution. |
| TEACHER: (21) | Well, so far, so good, but it wasn't quite so simple. Who can tell us the real story? | II | | But teacher belittles this effort at synthesis. |
| SUSAN: (v) | They shot the czar and his whole family. | | C | |
| BILL: (w) | Yeah, except one small daughter who escaped and is now living in Germany someplace, I think. | | C | |
| FRED: (x) | Aw, that's a bunch of baloney. They were all killed. | | C | Is Fred demonstrating critical thinking ability? Is he presenting an opportunity to discuss the credibility of sources? |
| BILL: (y) | No. they weren't. I . . . | | C | |
| TEACHER: (22) | That's enough. Whether or not what you say is true has very little to do with the revolutions, so let's forget it and stick to what is important. Now, who can tell us what happened? | II | | Teacher cuts off critical thinking and asks students to stick with "important facts." |
| (23) | (There is silence. No hands are raised.) | | | |
| TEACHER: (24) | I don't think you read your textbook very carefully. Oh, well, what happened is this. The Germans sent Lenin to Russia from exile in Switzerland. He was a Marxist or Communist whom the czar had sent away. They wanted Russia out of the war, so they sent Lenin in because they knew he would make trouble. He did. It wasn't long before the Russians got out of the war and a provisional government was set up. | | | Teacher decides to give them the facts. |

| Teacher and Pupil Acts | Teacher Questions | Pupil Response | Diagnostic Comments |
|---|---|---|---|
| TEACHER: (25) This government was quite democratic, and a man named Kerensky was the head of it. But Lenin didn't want a socialist democracy, so he and another man named Trotsky caused so much trouble that the provisional government collapsed. | | | |
| (26) Then the Communists took charge with Lenin at the head of the government and that was the beginning of the present Russian government. | | | |
| (27) Of course, there is much more, but we are basically concerned with the idea, not the facts. | | | What *idea* do you think teacher has in mind? |
| (28) What does this tell us about Russia today? | II | | |
| FRED: (z) Things are better than they were under the czar. | | C | |
| TEACHER: (29) Maybe so, but is that really the important thing? What do you think, Bill? | II | | Is teacher asking Bill to express an opinion? |
| BILL: (aa) Well, I think it says that the Russian people are pretty courageous because they had a revolution and got rid of the czar. | | A | Bill does try to synthesize *his* point of view. |
| TEACHER: (30) Well, yes. I suppose so, but that wasn't what I had in mind. —Jack? | II | | Teacher rejects Bill's efforts at independent thought. |
| JACK: (bb) It certainly helps explain why the Russians are pioneering in space and rockets. They must be a very energetic bunch! | | B | Teacher pauses after posing question before calling on Jack. Jack tries to generalize beyond the facts. |
| TEACHER: (31) Well, I don't quite follow that. —What do you think Mary? | II | | Teacher is skeptical. |
| MARY: (cc) It shows that the Communists are a dictatorship. | | A | Now Mary gives the pat, simple answers desired. |
| TEACHER: (32) Good, what else? | II | | Teacher encourages Mary . . . |

| Teacher and Pupil Acts | | Teacher Questions | Pupil Response | Diagnostic Comments |
|---|---|---|---|---|
| MARY: (dd) | It shows that you can't trust the Russian Communists. If they would do all that to each other, then they wouldn't stop to do worse to us. | | A | . . . so Mary continues with a recitation void of original ideas, an expected recital of facts. |
| TEACHER: (33) | Yes. —So you see, we can learn a lot from the history of a people, and if we study the Russian Revolution carefully, it helps us decide how to deal with Russia today. | | | Teacher is now ready to express her own generalizations. |
| TEACHER: (34) | We can see, for example, that revolution is one way to bring about social change, and that it involved the violent overthrow of the government in power. | | | |
| (35) | We also can see that the Russian Revolution gives us some insight into the ways in which the Communists infiltrate and destroy the governments, and some idea of the kind of tactics we might expect from Russia in relation to us. | | | |
| TEACHER: (36) | Are there any questions you have about revolutions or specifically the Russian Revolution? | | | This is really just a teaching ritual which calls for no response. |
| (37) | (There were about 15–20 seconds of silence. The students moved restlessly in their seats. A few looked as if they had questions, but they apparently decided not to ask them.) | | | |
| TEACHER: (38) | All right. Now, let's work on our projects for the rest of the hour. | | | |
| (39) | Be sure you have checked with me if you haven't picked out your topic. O.K., go ahead. | | | |
| (40) | (Students opened desks, moved into small groups, and a group of five came up to the teacher.) | | | |

SPECIAL ARRANGEMENTS

The only special arrangements required for this training session are (1) a group small enough for free discussion with participation by everyone, (2) seating arrangements which facilitate such discussion, (3) desks or tables which permit working with the protocol materials, and (4) a chalkboard or overhead projector or both.

CAUTIONS AND LIMITATIONS

Lesson protocol analysis can reveal what the contents of the recorded protocol contain and no more. We must recognize that the protocol itself has limitations. The analyst cannot interpret tone of voice, and certain other details are always missing. Any given set of analytical procedures is also necessarily inadequate for complete understanding of anything as complex as a teaching-learning situation.

All the sampling and reliability limitation of live observations are still present in the protocol. One cannot assume that this protocol necessarily reflects the teaching that would have been recorded under any other set of circumstances or at some other time.

The teacher question and pupil response categories used for protocol analysis in this training session are most appropriate when supplemented by a careful consideration of the overall teaching style revealed in the lesson. A full discussion of the lesson itself should be encouraged to assure full consideration of the many aspects of teaching behavior which may not be reflected by the specific analytical procedures being used. Another way of saying the same thing is to emphasize that the data as analyzed must be interpreted in the context of the larger array of teaching events.

The group leader should caution participants against discussing the lesson in speculative or highly generalized terms. Participants should be held to considering the evidence as it exists in the protocol and asked to identify problems in terms of the protocol data. Specific events should be cited whenever participants attempt to draw conclusions or make generalizations.

SUGGESTED RELATED ACTIVITIES

Protocol analysis becomes most stimulating and most valuable when a variety of teaching situations are studied and a variety of analytical procedures are used. The following variations in using this and other lesson protocols might prove valuable.

1. Use analytical procedures developed by other scholars in studying teacher behavior. Interaction analysis categories developed by Bales (3), Hughes (8), Flanders (7), and others might be used to

give participants a chance to see what these categories are like and what insights they might provide.

2. Use a protocol as the basis for role-playing. A brief discussion of a lesson in protocol can lead to role-playing at the point in the protocol where participants are most critical or most concerned about the teacher's behavior. A leader can help participants portray the teacher and develop methods for handling the same situation differently. Participants can play the parts of the students while one person plays that of the teacher.

3. Use other protocols as case material and guide a group in a discussion leading to suggestions for improvement. Have a protocol preanalyzed so the group can begin the discussion of problem diagnosis promptly.

4. Use a filmed or video-taped lesson with a group to stimulate discussion. Lead participants to specify strengths and weaknesses observed on the screen. Then guide the group in analyzing the protocol prepared from the film or tape to verify or modify conclusions.

### Guides for protocol analysis

There is a growing variety of instruments available for selection in observing classroom instruction. Some have been developed for research purposes and may need to be revised for use in in-service education. Others are so specialized in design as to be of little use. The selection of an observation instrument should always be guided by the purpose to be served, but instruments employed in in-service education programs need a large amount of "face validity." They need to produce data that tells the observer something useful with a minimum of analysis.

Instruments which might well be useful are described below; still others which might be adapted for use are described in the references listed at the end of this chapter. At best, however, good instruments to guide observation practices are limited. New and better guides need to be invented by imaginative practitioners.

#### THE TEACHER BEHAVIOR INVENTORY (TBI)

Various studies suggest that teachers tend to develop styles or patterns of classroom behavior which become quite habitual. The relationships between certain teaching styles and teaching effectiveness have become the focus of interest of both researchers and practitioners. The instrument described below permits the analysis of classroom teaching in terms of certain patterns of behavior. Unlike some of the instruments presented on the foregoing pages, this one focuses upon a broad array of teacher behaviors through the following activities:

—Acquainting participants with some major categories of teaching behavior.

—Contrasting the difference between basic teaching behavior patterns and specific teaching acts.

—Stimulating thinking about the effects of various patterns on the learning process.

—Demonstrating specific guidelines for modifying teaching patterns.

An observation instrument shown in Appendix VIII-B is designed for these special purposes, the *TBI* is used to tally teacher acts in terms of six specific categories of behavior. This instrument has been developed from observation systems suggested by Anderson (2), Flanders (7), Hughes (8), and Ryans (10).

Each of the categories of teacher behavior is described below. The illustrations are largely verbal, but non-verbal behavior is also considered.

*Encouraging*  Complimenting, encouraging, praising, showing acceptance, or otherwise expressing self positively and enthusiastically; also interpreting feelings empathetically.

"I think we've had a good session today, class."

"That's a fine idea, Susie!"

"John's been having some difficulties. Perhaps you could help him, Bill."

"I know how you feel . . ."

"Why don't you try it again, Jane?"

Smiling at the class or at an individual.

*Presenting*  Lecturing, visualizing, demonstrating, answering questions, presenting information or ideas, suggesting alternative solutions, or otherwise presenting content to be learned.

"When Columbus made his first voyage, he touched these islands; however, on his second voyage he touched those."

"Now, I am shaking the iron filings vigorously to get them to adhere."

"The formula for salt is NaCl."

"Watch me as I do this one on the board."

"If you advance the spark, combustion occurs when the piston is still in this position." (demonstrates)

"This capital letter looks entirely different in cursive form."

"If you place the compass in this position, like this, you can read it better."

*Assisting*  Guiding, elaborating, clarifying, evaluating, or otherwise assisting with procedures or plans influencing pupil behavior.

"Let me review your assignment for tomorrow."

"When you solder the wire, be sure to hold the iron there long enough for the wire to get hot enough to melt the solder."

"Remember that we go directly to the auditorium tomorrow. We do not come here first."

*Analyzing.* Checking, inquiring, recording, or otherwise securing information regarding the behavior of pupils.

"How many of you missed question number ten on the quiz?"

"Does each of you have an extra pencil?"

Recording scores on a test as pupils report them.

Walking about the room, glancing at tests pupils are taking.

"Did you finish your work all right, John?"

"What was our assignment for today?"

*Directing.* Structuring, regulating, enforcing, controlling, manipulating, or otherwise directing the behavior of pupils.

"Get out your books and turn to page _____."

"We don't do that kind of thing in this room, Bill."

"The one who has the best conduct today will be chairman tomorrow."

"Sit down!"

Grabbing a pupil's arm.

Frowning at a pupil in response to his or her behavior.

"Watch out, Bill, I'll finish that." (collecting papers)

"Careful! You'll cut it the wrong way if you don't look out."

"Don't forget to close that door."

*Discouraging.* Ignoring, threatening, moralizing, accusing, reprimanding, negatively criticizing, or otherwise discouraging pupil behavior.

"You didn't work very hard today, class."

"Those who are late with their papers will have their grades lowered."

"Not now, Bill. Ask me some other time."

The basic approach to the use of the *TBI* involves observing and tallying each specific teacher act, whether verbal or nonverbal, as defined in behavioral terms above. The observer must be actively engaged in interpreting each teacher act. The smallest unit of behavior that can be interpreted should be tallied. For instance, as the chemistry teacher demonstrates a procedure, discusses the procedures being used, and comments upon the chemical reaction to be observed. a variety of tallies should be made. The "presenting" acts are tallied as such. Comments on procedures are tallied as "assisting," while statements of reassurance or smiles are recorded as "encouraging."

The observer must try to tally as frequently as possible in order to

Exhibit 8.3
## SAMPLE TABULATION ON THE TEACHER BEHAVIOR INVENTORY

Teacher _____    Grade  6th   Subject Social Studies _____

Time  9:15 to 9:45          Date  January 20

Topic:  "The Meaning of Revolutions"

| Behavior Categories | Tallies | Total | Per Cent |
|---|---|---|---|
| 1. Encouraging | //// | 4 | 4 |
| 2. Presenting | ҬҬ ҬҬ ҬҬ ҬҬ ҬҬ ҬҬ ҬҬ ҬҬ // | 42 | 36 |
| 3. Assisting | ҬҬ // | 7 | 6 |
| 4. Analyzing | ҬҬ ҬҬ ҬҬ ҬҬ ҬҬ / | 26 | 23 |
| 5. Directing | ҬҬ ҬҬ ҬҬ ҬҬ ҬҬ / | 26 | 23 |
| 6. Discouraging | ҬҬ ҬҬ | 10 | 9 |
| Total - All Categories | | 115 | 101 |

Comments:

1. Discouraging acts exceed encouraging acts.

2. Presenting acts are most frequent.

3. Assisting acts are very infrequent.

4. Present, directing, and discouraging acts combine to total nearly 70% of all acts.

5. Encouraging, assisting combined total only 10% of all acts.

assure recording a tally for each meaningful unit of behavior. A presentation is usually composed of a whole series of physical and verbal acts that have meaning for the pupils. Each such act should be tallied separately. Similarly, a single sentence may include two or more meanings. In an art class, the teacher says: "George, you are making progress, I know, but you must put your things away now." In this way, the teacher encourages and directs, almost simultaneously.

A complete tabulation of teacher acts for one protocol is shown in Exhibit 8.3 above.

### BALES INTERACTION ANALYSIS

Many ways of analyzing interaction among group members have been developed. Borgetta (5) and Bales (5) developed a set of categories and schemes of analysis which have been quite useful in discussion situations. Unlike many classroom observation instruments, this instrument permits analysis of behaviors of both students and teacher.

Four major categories of behavior are used in observing and analyzing groups at work. These categories provide a simple approach to analyzing the teacher as discussion leader and individual students as they work in a group. Both verbal and non-verbal behaviors are observed and categorized. The four major categories include *positive reactions, attempted answers, questions,* and *negative reactions.* Each of these categories includes three specific types of behavior. This scheme with verbal illustrations of each behavior type is shown in Exhibit 8.4 below.

The observer must have studied the behavior categories carefully and be familiar with the illustrations. After a few trial uses of the tabulation sheet shown in Appendix VIII-C, it could be used to analyze interaction in any live group situation. With a lesson protocol, the numbered items can be coded by type of interaction in the margin or a tabulation sheet can be used for recording the item numbers in the appropriate places.

Each distinct verbal and non-verbal unit of behavior should be categorized and recorded on the tabulation sheet. A unit of verbal behavior may be a sentence, a phrase, or even a single word. Each verbal expression that clearly carries enough meaning to be categorized should be recorded separately. Similarly, each frown, laugh, and hand motion that can be clearly interpreted should be categorized and recorded.

Until skill has been developed in recognizing and tabulating responses, the four major categories can be used. As participants become familiar with these major categories, the letter symbols, A, B, C, and so on, may be used to indicate the type of question, answer, or other response. When such designations are used, the analysis of the group processes can be substantially more precise and revealing. Recording teacher, boy, and girl behaviors separately can also provide useful insights.

## Exhibit 8.4
## CATEGORIES AND ILLUSTRATIONS FOR BALES'
## INTERACTION ANALYSIS

Illustrations

I. Positive Reactions

    A.  Shows solidarity         "We certainly handled ourselves well
                                       in the auditorium."

    B.  Shows tension release    "Gee. I'm glad that's out of the way!"
                                       Laughter. Joking.

    C.  Agrees                     "That's correct." "Right."

II. Attempted Answers

    D.  Gives suggestions       "Why not try again at the library
                                       tonight?"

    E.  Gives opinions           "I think your parents would approve
                                         of that."

    F.  Gives orientation        "We try to do our own work on this
                                       kind of assignment, Jane."

III. Questions

    G.  Asks orientation        "What did we agree to do with these
                                       papers today?"

    H.  Asks opinions           "What do you think about John's idea?"

    I.  Asks suggestions        "Have any of you a suggestion of another
                                       way to solve this problem?"

IV. Negative Reactions

    J.  Disagrees                "No, that's not correct." "I don't
                                       believe that's right, Bill."

    K.  Shows tension           "Bill, take your seat." Frowns.
                                       Gestures in reprimanding fashion.

    L.  Shows antagonism        "I'm tired of your disobedience!"

## Other lesson protocols

A variety of kinds of teaching and lesson situations are to be found in the lesson protocols in the Appendices VIII-D through F. These are briefly described here, but should be carefully studied by a group leader before attempting to use them with an in-service group.

### APPENDIX VIII-D. THE ELEMENTARY SCIENCE LESSON

A fifth grade class. The regular classroom teacher leads a discussion aimed at getting students to generalize from their observations of previous days. Despite the fact that the class is conducting experiments and watching demonstrations, questions are predominantly of the recall type, and five or six pupils dominate the discussion.

### APPENDIX VIII-E. THE LEAKING BOTTLE LESSON

A sixth grade class without any special preparation is asked to engage in a discussion to encourage critical thinking. The teacher stimulates interest and verbal responses with a Coke bottle but has real difficulty in releasing control of the discussion and in getting students to go beyond their preconceived ideas.

### APPENDIX VIII-F. A CREATIVE WRITING LESSON

A second grade class engages in creative writing activities. Sub-groups are given quite different kinds of writing tasks planned according to level of difficulty. Within each sub-group, individuals are free to write "creatively." The teacher adopts roles of stimulator, coordinator, encourager, and assister, while minimizing presenting, directing, analyzing, and discouraging behaviors.

## Summary

The twin tools of tape recording and analysis give great flexibility to the study of teaching. The individual teacher or a group can analyze lesson protocols long after the lesson itself has been taught. They can study many different aspects of their teaching, taking time to analyze it in several different ways. Teachers can use many different analytical procedures in studying their own protocols or those of other teachers. In this way, protocol analysis becomes a very direct in-service approach.

Lesson protocol analysis, when applied to a carefully transcribed lesson, has some very specific advantages over live observations in the advancement of instructional practices. In the past, educators have been hampered in their efforts to improve teaching by the fact that a lesson once taught is gone forever. Educators have in the past had little chance to study teaching systematically enough to approach change in terms of carefully diagnosed problems. Now the tool of tape recording gives us a variety of opportunities for analyzing teaching for in-service purposes. As protocols are studied, over-all impressions emerge in the reader's mind. In applying analytical procedures, specific teaching patterns are identified. As several patterns emerge from the use of a variety of analytical approaches, problems can be diagnosed with considerable assurance. It is this process which develops new insights into the dynamics of teaching and can lead to improved practice.

## Selected references

1. Amidon, Edmund J., and Flanders, Ned A., *The Role of the Teacher in the Classroom.* Minneapolis: Paul S. Amidon & Associates, 1963.
2. Anderson, H. H., "Studies in Teachers' Classroom Personalities, II. Effects of Dominative and Integrative Contacts on Children's Classroom Behavior," *Applied Psychology Monograph* No. 8. Stanford, California: Stanford University Press, June, 1946.
3. Bales, Robert F., *Interaction Process Analysis—A Method for the Study of Small Groups.* Addison-Wesley, Cambridge, 1950.
4. Biddle, Bruce J., and Ellena, William J., eds., *Contemporary Research on Teacher Effectiveness.* New York: Holt, Rinehart & Winston, 1964.
5. Borgatta, E. F., and Bales, R. F., "Task and Accumulation Experience as Factors in the Interaction of Small Groups," Sociometry Monographs, No. 34. New York: Beacon House, 1954, p. 240.
6. Brottman, Marvin A., "Typescripts as Observational Experience for Prospective Teachers," *The Journal of Teacher Education.* 16:4 (December, 1965), pp. 466–68.
7. Flanders, Ned A., *Interaction Analysis in the Classroom.* Minneapolis, Minn.: College of Education, University of Minnesota, 1960.
8. Hughes, Marie, *et al.,* A *Research Report—Assessment of the Quality of Teaching in Elementary Schools.* Provo, Utah: University of Utah, 1959 (mimeographed).
9. Nichols, Herb, "Techniques for Recording Behavior With the Video-Tape Recorder," *Lab World/Film World.* Los Angeles, California: Sidale Publishing Co., August, 1966.
10. Ryans, D. G., *Teacher Characteristics.* Washington, D.C.: American Council on Education, 1960.
11. Smith, Louis M., "Group Processes in Elementary and Secondary Schools," *What Research Says to the Teacher,* No. 19. Washington, D.C.: National Education Association, December, 1959.

# Chapter Nine

# STUDYING COMMUNICATION PATTERNS

THIS CHAPTER describes three sessions aimed at the development of concepts and skills of communication in human interactions. In many ways this is the most important aspect of instruction. As we have noted elsewhere in this book, education is a highly "human" activity, and teachers, administrators, and supervisors spend a great deal of time in dealing with people as individuals or in groups. Whether staff members do this skillfully will, in large measure, determine the effectiveness of their professional endeavors.

A great deal has been written about the importance of communication, but little material exists to help train instructional personnel in improving communication skill. The three laboratory exercises presented in this chapter are intended to broaden the awareness of the participant concerning the effects of his behavior on others, and to give him an increased range of "styles" which he may use depending upon his purposes in dealing with others.

In the first session, participants examine the effects of three different interview styles. The second session deals with group discussion-leading technique, and the outcomes of three different patterns of leader-group interactions are demonstrated. In the third session, the effect of feedback is demonstrated by contrasting one-way and two-way communications.

All of these sessions are suitable for groups of from 10 to 30 people, and they are especially suitable for a series of in-service meetings of people who work together: the principal and his faculty, the supervisor and his staff, or the supervisor and a group of principals and teachers.

Most, if not all, of the sessions illustrate ways of working that are equally applicable to teachers when students are involved as individuals or groups. Similarly, these sessions have important implications for training staff members to work with parents, P.T.A. groups, professional associations, or lay committees.

### Three styles of interviewing

The personal interview is one of the basic activities in which professional personnel engage. This one type of activity may well consume the majority of the working hours of many staff members. Whether it is a matter of interviewing students, teachers, parents, or others, the skillful use of appropriate techniques is essential to effective results. This section will describe activities designed to develop interviewing skills. The context for the exercise is a teacher-parent interview, but the principles involved are equally applicable in supervisor-teacher and teacher-pupil interactions.

The point of view advanced in this chapter is that, whatever the content of the interview situation, a positive response from the interviewee is desirable and that this response is dependent on (among other things) the interviewer's style in conducting the interview and the amount and kind of interactions he seeks.

#### BACKGROUND ON THE PROBLEM

Face-to-face communication is such an ordinary activity for teachers that most of them do not really consider many of their interactions as professional activities requiring specific skills and understanding. Even when the situation is a rather formal one, planned to accomplish some purpose, their usual approach may be to do what comes naturally with little thought as to the skills involved or the conduct required in order to achieve the desired response.

One kind of communication is *interviewing*. Interviewing may be thought of as an activity in which one person proposes to exchange information with another person, with some objective in mind. The objective may be some predetermined outcome such as influencing the interviewee's subsequent behavior, or it may be merely to gather information for some future purpose.

One kind of interview is recurrent in professional activities of teachers, principals, and supervisors. This is the supervisory interview, in which a person in a superordinate role seeks to give a subordinate some information about his performance with the hope that the person will understand his own performance better, accept the interviewer's interpretations, and if necessary, change his future behavior in whatever way is indicated. The teacher, for example, might interview a pupil or he might interview a parent in an effort to improve a pupil's home study habits. The way in which this interview is conducted will affect the interviewee's feelings towards the interviewer, his self-confidence, his acceptance of the interviewer's suggestions, and the likelihood of improved future performance. The effect of three interviewing styles on these outcomes is demonstrated in this exercise.

1. Demonstrating three different approaches to interviewing.
2. Analyzing the feelings produced by the different interview styles.
3. Demonstrating the critical importance of interview technique when positive reactions are important.
4. Demonstrating the important role that feelings play in interviewer-interviewee relationships.
5. Practice in critical analysis of interviewing skills.

The basic activities in this session include role-playing three styles of interviews, discussing the role-playing, and analyzing reactions to the interviews. It culminates in the determination of group generalizations about the effects of the interview style on the participant.

A vignette, "Being a Parent Is Too Much Work" (Exhibit 9.1), is used to set up the situation which is the occasion for the interview. The session leader plays the role of the teacher, Roy Greer. Three group members each play the role of Mr. (or Mrs.) Barnes, the parent, in three successive interviews. With no coaching on their roles, they are told to play it as they feel it. They know the situation, having read the vignette, but their reactions are in no way pre-planned. The interviewer's role is defined for him, however. The three interviews are structured to illustrate the directive, critical role; the laissez-faire role; or the non-directive, constructive role.

*Directive, critical role* This role is characterized by the frank, direct approach. The interviewer is an expert. He knows what the problems are and doesn't mind telling the parent straight out. He not only tells the parent what is wrong but gives specific suggestions for improvement. He does not waste time giving compliments. His job is to face the problem squarely and get action for improvement. If the parent resists, he feels quite justified in reiterating his critical views and even uses threats to show that he means business.

*Laissez-faire role* This role is characterized by the easy-going approach. The interviewer wants to see this problem solved but does not want to create a difficult situation. He wants to maintain a cordial relationship

## Exhibit 9.1
## VIGNETTE
## BEING A PARENT IS TOO MUCH WORK

VIGNETTE

BEING A PARENT IS TOO MUCH WORK

Roy Greer, junior high school English teacher, places a great deal of emphasis on independent study and requires pupils to carry out two projects each year. Jeff Barnes, a bright student who does only average work in class, failed to complete his first project on time. At that time, Jeff told Mr. Greer that he had done his library research but didn't get around to writing the report. In a telephone conversation with Mrs. Barnes, Greer learned that she and her husband believe that Jeff's school work is his own responsibility, and they never inquire about it unless he brings up the subject.

Now, at mid-year, Jeff is not making any progress on his second report. Mr. Greer believes that if Jeff had a regular study time, he could complete his project. When this is suggested to Jeff, he responds by saying that his parents like to do things on the spur of the moment and leave him in charge of his younger brother and sister several evenings a week. At other times, the family goes out together. Mr. Greer decides to have a conference with Mr. or Mrs. Barnes to see if a regular study time can be arranged.

with the parent and tries to avoid criticism by keeping comments positive. He compliments the parent, even if only for little things. His general tone implies that there is a problem, but he avoids coming out with it in a direct way.

The interviewer begins with a good bit of conversational small change. He hints that "people" are worried, and he would like to know more about the "situation" from the parent.

If the parent sidetracks the conversation, he follows along. He ends with assurances of his faith in the interviewee's willingness to do a good job.

*Non-directive, constructive role*   This role is characterized by the shared responsibility approach. The interviewer is not taking the role of an expert or the boss. His approach is much like that of a counselor. He acknowledges the existence of a serious problem, but he seeks clarification from the parent about it. He is open to the parent's point of view. He encourages the parent to talk the problem out and encourages him to take remedial action. He offers assistance, but makes it clear that the responsibility for taking the initiative is largely with the parent.

Immediately following each interview, participants are given a copy of the reactionnaire entitled *Reactions to Interview* (see Appendix IX-A). Participants are urged to place themselves in the place of the interviewee, not the interviewer: "Try to feel as you would if *you* had been in the chair of this interviewee." Urge each individual to react as he truly feels and not to be concerned with the reactions of others. As reactionnaires are completed, they are collected by assistants and another interview is role-played without discussion. Have participants fold their reactionnaires as they pass them in, so others will not be influenced. After each round of interviews, reactionnaires are filled out and collected in the same manner.

Assistants tabulate the reactionnaires while the role-playing continues. Following all three interviews, the session leader directs a discussion of the problems posed by the vignette. The discussion should focus upon the problem situation rather than upon interview technique *per se*.

Frequency distributions are prepared for each item on the reactionnaire while the discussion is in progress. Reactions are assigned scale values ranging from 5 for the most positive to 1 for the most negative response. A score for each item thus represents the degree of positiveness or negativeness of the participants toward the interview. An overall reaction score can also be computed. These scores are computed separately for the first, second, and third interviews.

When reported to the participants as a group, their reactions to the styles of interviewing can be seen in the contrasting reaction scores.

*Session plan*   As the session begins, the leader briefs the group on planned activities so that the participants will know what to expect. They are asked to go along with the rapid pace of activities and to try to throw themselves into each role as instructed. The leader then refers participants to the vignette given in Exhibit 9.1: "Being a Parent is Too Much Work."

He may begin by saying, "We will start this session by playing roles of the teacher and the parent in the vignette. I will be the teacher. You will observe an interview between the teacher and the parent. At this point we will ask you to observe carefully and put yourselves in that parent's place as much as you can. We will ask you to give us your reactions to the interview, and then you will observe a second and third interview and react to them. Finally, you will get a chance to discuss all of this." He should avoid giving participants any clues to the specific styles, and just say, "We will be demonstrating different styles."

This first interview is structured, directive, and critical. The interviewer takes just a minute to attend to the amenities and then gets to the point. He is very systematic and thorough. He plays the role of the *expert*. He briefly identifies each of the problems he sees in the parent's attitude towards his child's school work. He mentions the parent's lack of interest and the failure of his child to develop good home study habits. He criticizes the pupil's failure to follow through on the teacher's suggestions. He warns the parent of the consequences of continued failure of the pupil to do acceptable work.

As an afterthought, the interviewer compliments the parent for being well-meaning; assures him that he has faith that an improvement will be seen, and indicates his plan to keep a check on the pupil's progress. At this point, the interview is terminated with a cordial "goodbye" and "thank you" from the interviewer.

Without any pause for comments, the reactionnaires are distributed to all participants. They are asked to express themselves frankly on each of the four questions. After these sheets are completed and collected, a second interview is role-played. This is introduced simply by saying, "Let's see how you react to a different style of interviewing."

In this session, the teacher assumes the laissez-faire role. He begins with a good bit of conversational small change, saying that he wanted to get together with the parent for a chat about his son's school work. He is complimentary about small things, and he hints at the problem but avoids an explicit statement.

The teacher would like to see the problem resolved but does not want to create a difficult situation. If the parent sidetracks the conversation, the teacher goes along with it by expressing the hope that he "will learn more about the situation." He tries to avoid awkward pauses by general comments about the pupil's work.

The interview is concluded with the teacher assuring the parent that things will improve and that both he and the parent want to see the pupil do his best work.

As before, reactionnaires are completed and a third interview is begun. As the parent enters, he is greeted in a friendly way by the interviewer. The amenities are brief as before. The interviewer frankly states his desire to discuss the problem with the parent and asks an open-ended question such as, "How do you feel about your son's school work?" When the parent responds, the interviewer listens thoughtfully. He probes to get the parent to talk about the pupil and his home study habits, but he avoids making direct criticisms. If the parent criticizes himself, the interviewer refrains from either supporting or denying this self-criticism. Instead, he asks the parent to tell him more about it.

The parent will sometimes have difficulty talking about his home situation. At first he may not respond to the probes. The interviewer may simply permit silence to prevail while the parent thinks about the questions raised.

After some exploration, when the parent has come to realize and accept the problems, the teacher may suggest something that could help.

The interview approach throughout this role-playing session emphasizes a cooperative relationship. The parent is encouraged to look at the problem and appraise it himself. The interviewer stands ready to help, but he does not assume *all* responsibility; he is more a counselor and less a critic.

*The Reactionnaires*   While all the reactionnaires are being tabulated, the leader should get the group to discuss the three interviews and try to identify significant differences among them. At this point, he should identify the three interview styles by name. If enough time is available, it is usually effective to get the group to hypothesize about what they think the outcome of the reactionnaires will be. In this way, group members can anticipate the feelings of the parent and the effect of the interview on each of the interview styles. A convenient way to tabulate and examine responses is shown in Exhibit 9.2. Typical responses are shown.

*Discussion*   Experience with this exercise indicates that the following generalizations can usually be made by a group as they analyze their reaction to the three styles of interviewing:

1. Participants tend to react quite differently to distinctly different styles of interviewing. Notice the column totals in Exhibit 9.2.
2. Different individuals tend to react in different ways to the same style of interviewing.
3. Participants tend to be most positive toward the non-directive, constructive style. The total in column three in Exhibit 9.2 is nearly a third larger than in the other columns.
4. Participants tend to be neutral or negative in their reactions to the critical and laissez-faire styles. Mean ratings in Exhibit 9.2 are about 3.0.

## Exhibit 9.2
## SUMMARY FORM FOR GROUP REACTIONS
## TO THREE STYLES OF INTERVIEW

| TYPE OF REACTION | SUM OF RATINGS | | |
|---|---|---|---|
| | DIRECTIVE, CRITICAL | LAISSEZ-FAIRE | NONDIRECTIVE, CONSTRUCTIVE |
| A. Parent's feelings toward interviewer | 62 | 55 | 78 |
| B. Parent's acceptance of suggestions | 70 | 60 | 80 |
| C. Effect on parent's self-confidence | 52 | 65 | 70 |
| D. Effectiveness of interview in improving the situation | 59 | 50 | 74 |
| Total | 243 | 230 | 302 |
| Mean Rating | 3.0 | 2.9 | 3.8 |

5. The directive-critical style tends to discourage verbal interaction.

6. The laissez-faire role tends to encourage verbal interaction but it is not task-oriented or problem-centered. See the low ratings in Item D for the laissez-faire role (col. 2) in Exhibit 9.2.

7. The directive, critical role is economical of time while the non-directive, constructive role takes much more time.

8. Feelings toward the interviewer and his helpfulness tend to be low for the critical, directive style but willingness to accept suggestions tends to be fairly high.

The results of the exercise and the discussion by the group may be summarized by the group leader, if he wishes, in terms of implications for practice such as the following:

1. Directive, critical, and laissez-faire approaches are often less effective as basic styles for interviews if positive responses towards improvement are desired.

2. A directive, critical approach might be effective in getting acceptance of suggestions when negative side effects can be tolerated.

3. A non-directive, constructive approach gives the interviewer insights into the interviewee's perception of the problem, and thus puts him in a better position to be helpful.

4. A directive, critical approach puts the interviewer in the role of expert and thus tends to rule out the use of other resources for improvement.

5. A laissez-faire approach tends to build false confidence on the part of the interviewee and offers no guidelines for improvement.

SEQUENCE OF ACTIVITIES

| Time | Activities |
|---|---|
| 5 min. | Introduction. Short lecture on interviewing purposes. Provide vignette (Exhibit 9.1) and three copies of the reactionnaire (Appendix IX-A) to each participant. |
| 15 min. | First interview. Role-play directive, critical role. Begin scoring reactionnaires. |
| 15 min. | Second interview. Role-play laissez-faire role. Begin scoring reactionnaires. |
| 15 min. | Third interview. Role-play non-directive, constructive role. Begin scoring reactionnaires. |
| 10 min. | Preliminary discussion. Discuss vignette problem, possible alternatives, ramifications, and so forth. Discuss interviewing styles observed; reveal roles demonstrated. |
| 10 min. | Break for coffee while tabulating is being completed. |
| 20 min. | Feedback on reactions and follow-up discussions. Present results of tabulations. Lead group in developing generalizations about effects of interviewing. |

*Total time:* 1 hour and 30 minutes

SPECIAL ARRANGEMENTS

Since these activities are predominantly demonstrations, a fairly large group of staff members can participate. A group of from 20 to not more than 40 participants is quite manageable for all activities except discussions. For very large groups (50 or more), three sets of role-playing sessions can be conducted simultaneously and reactions combined.

Participants should meet in a room which simulates a classroom situation if possible. Space for teaching and demonstration role-playing is required at the front of the group.

A desk for the teacher will help simulate the setting and at least two chairs will be required. The teacher may either sit at the desk with the parent across the desk, or he may place the two chairs together in a more informal arrangement as required by the role being played.

A blackboard or overhead projector will be needed to examine the summary data from the group's reactionnaires.

CAUTIONS AND LIMITATIONS

The most difficult thing about this exercise is that the interviewer must conduct each of the interviews skillfully so that it is a *good* example of the interview style being demonstrated. That is, he should avoid overdrawn caricatures of such styles as the directive, critical role. In general, he should try to maintain the same voice level and general demeanor throughout all three styles. The *content* of the interviews should be changed, but not the feeling tone in any way other than that which would naturally accompany the different styles.

Participants should not be led to see one kind of interview as bad or undesirable under all circumstances. The intent of the session is to demonstrate that the outcome of the interview differs with the approach. There may be times when any one of the three styles is appropriate.

If group members are used as interviewers in the sessions, it will be necessary to coach them carefully beforehand so that the interviews will illustrate the styles intended. In general, it is probably better for the group leader to role-play the interviewer in all three interviews.

SUGGESTED RELATED ACTIVITIES

Further development of skill in interviewing can be developed in a variety of ways. The following are suggestions which can be developed into training sessions:

1. Observe the film "The Conference" (6) and analyze it in terms of the three styles presented above.

2. Develop three-person teams for practice sessions in applying techniques illustrated in the interview styles. Have vignettes available. Assign team members to roles as interviewer, interviewee, and observer. Have the observer watch as the other two role-play. When time is called, rotate roles. Repeat until all have had a chance to interview once or twice.

3. Repeat session described in detail here, using new vignette and new kind of problem. This time use not only reactionnaires but also an "interaction analysis" procedure. Have three or more participants trained to analyze the interviews using the Bales interaction categories (1). These can be combined to report overall pattern to participants as part of the feedback. The Bales categories require tabulations of verbal and non-verbal acts. Each act should be tabulated. The smallest bit of behavior that the observers can categorize should be tabulated.

SUMMARY

Three styles of interviewing are demonstrated in role-playing situations. In each case, the interviewer is a teacher who wishes to have a parent take more responsibility for helping his child develop good home study habits and the interviewee is the parent.

The effects of the three interview styles are contrasted by having the participants express their own responses about the parent's feelings toward the teacher, his acceptance of the teacher's suggestion, his feelings of self-confidence as a parent, and the effectiveness of the interview in achieving its purpose. Generalizations are developed about the appropriate interview style in terms of desired outcomes.

## Three styles of group communication

Instructional personnel find themselves dealing with groups a great deal of the time. It is a commonplace observation that the group leader should be able to communicate effectively with the group, and yet too little attention is typically given to techniques for doing this.

In the laboratory exercise presented in this section, the effects of three different patterns of group communication will be shown. These will be termed the controlling style, the parliamentary style, and the open discussion style. As the designations imply, they represent progressively less structure and control on the part of the discussion leader.

In this exercise, role-playing, buzz groups, and group discussion are the major activities.

### BACKGROUND ON THE PROBLEM

A supervisor is working with a group of teachers to resolve a problem of curriculum sequence; a principal is conducting a faculty meeting to reach consensus on a decision; a teacher is directing a group of pupils in planning a unit of study. What effect will the communication style promoted by the leader have on the group's outcomes?

The answer to this question is of vital concern to instructional personnel because so many important outcomes rest on the quality of group decisions. Let us consider some of the desired outcomes of the group's activity. First, the group leader wants group members to have confidence that the decision reached is the best one possible under the circumstances. This is crucial in education where so many individuals must be expected to act willingly in accord with agreed-upon procedures.

Second, since the problem has been presented to a group for decision, as much individual participation as possible is needed as the group reaches consensus. This is required if group members are to learn from each other and to maintain cooperative relationships for future work.

Third, the decision reached should be the best solution possible. Every effort should be made to explore the nature of the problem, discover all feasible alternatives, and assess the consequences of each suggested course of action.

Finally, the group process should result in a positive feeling about the group's ability to work together. This maintenance of group morale is essential, and is facilitated by shared sentiments that result from pleasurable experiences in working together. The group communication should make it possible for members to enjoy working together.

How these outcomes are affected by the communication pattern set by the leader is demonstrated in the following laboratory exercise:

**ACTIVITIES**

1. Demonstrating the effect of group communication style on participants' evaluation of outcomes.
2. Contrasting satisfaction with decisions reached under different conditions of group communication.
3. Contrasting the extent to which group members express *agreement* with the group decision reached in each style of communication.
4. Contrasting group members' perceptions of the effectiveness of the leader in problem-solving under three styles of communication.
5. Contrasting group members' confidence in the quality of the decision reached working under three different conditions of leadership.
6. Contrasting group members' feelings of responsibility for the decision reached by a group in each of the three styles of group communication.

**PROCEDURE**

The general leader should introduce the exercise by saying that the effects of various styles of communication on group problem-solving are going to be studied. He explains that participants will be divided into groups for the purpose of solving an assigned problem. Each group will have three problems to solve, and, though they are not told this, a different kind of group communication style will be used by the leader each time. Three session leaders are required, one for each communication style.

After introducing the three session leaders and designating three meeting places, the general leader divides the group into three sub-groups. It is best to divide the groups arbitrarily rather than to allow free choice so as to break up groups with similar interests and friendship ties.

After each group has finished its first problem, session leaders rotate to another group and group members prepare their *Group Discussion Reactionnaires* (Appendix IX-B). Reactionnaires are collected and given to scorers and a second problem session is begun. This procedure is repeated for the third session. A suggested schedule for groups, leaders, and problems is shown in Exhibit 9.3 below. "Mary's Reputation," "Bobby's Theme," and "The Old Grouch" are the titles of vignettes which present the problems the groups are to consider (Appendices IX-C through IX-E).

## Exhibit 9.3
## SCHEDULE FOR PROBLEM-SOLVING SESSIONS

|  | FIRST SESSION: "Mary's Reputation" | SECOND SESSION: "Bobby''s Theme" | THIRD SESSION: "The Old Grouch" |
|---|---|---|---|
| CONTROLLING STYLE | Group A | Group B | Group C |
| PARLIAMENTARY STYLE | Group C | Group A | Group B |
| OPEN DISCUSSION STYLE | Group B | Group C | Group A |

Session leaders should follow the same general procedures for conducting the sub-group sessions. In all three styles, the session leader should proceed as follows:

1.  Have participants read vignette.
2.  Record the time each problem is started and ended and enter this on the Tabulation Worksheet shown in Exhibit 9.4. Time begins when the problems are handed out, and ends when group starts writing solutions.
3.  Conduct the session according to the style required until some agreement is reached on ranking of alternatives.
4.  Collect the problems and distribute the *Group Discussion Reactionnaire* shown in Appendix IX-B. The session leader should leave while reactionnaires are being completed. Scorers will collect them at the end of the session.

## Exhibit 9.4
## TABULATION WORKSHEET FOR SUMMARY OF REACTIONNAIRE RESULTS

| QUESTIONS | GROUP COMMUNICATION STYLE | | |
|---|---|---|---|
|  | CONTROLLING | PARLIAMENTARY | OPEN DISCUSSION |
| 1. Satisfaction | 124 | 150 | 165 |
| 2. Agreement | 163 | 184 | 174 |
| 3. Leader effectiveness | 148 | 160 | 172 |
| 4. Quality of decision | 156 | 179 | 197 |
| 5. Sense of responsibility for outcome | 159 | 174 | 188 |
| Average Time Required | 18 | 15 | 25 |

5. Leaders rotate to the next group for the second session.
6. Repeat the above procedures for the second group, using the appropriate problem. While the second group is working on its problem, scorers tabulate the results of the first reactionnaire and enter the data on the Tabulation Worksheet.
7. Repeat again for the third group.
8. After tabulating the data for the last group, compute the averages and enter them in the Summary Analysis form (Exhibit 9.5).

In addition to the above instructions, each session leader should conduct his group by assuming the appropriate role described below.

*Role A: Controlling Style*  The leader arranges the chairs in rows and takes his place at the front of the group. He tries to appear democratic, but has already made up his mind concerning the desired outcome. He tries to influence group members to come around to his point of view. In doing so, he does not hesitate to argue persistently, to ignore those who disagree, and to recognize those who agree with him. In short, his intention is to manipulate the discussion so as to achieve a predetermined outcome.

*Role B: Parliamentary Style*  The parliamentary leader arranges the chairs in rows and stands at the front of the group. He relies on rules and procedures. Unlike the controlling leader, he does not appear to be concerned about the outcome, but is determined to keep an orderly process for reaching it. He dominates the session with procedure, calls for motions, takes a vote, etc. He may begin by saying that he favors an orderly procedure, and by suggesting that the group conduct its discussion with parliamentary procedure, or he may simply appear to assume that a motion, discussion, and vote is the best way to conduct a group meeting.

*Role C: Open Discussion Style*  The session leader assuming this role should arrange the chairs in a circle or some similar arrangement that will permit all members to see each other and communicate freely. In the discussion, he encourages everyone to express his views. He has his own views and expresses them, but does not override or ignore other points of view. He summarizes, makes clarifying comments, promotes compromise in opposing arguments, and seeks consensus in the decision.

After the third session (a coffee break may be appropriate here), the sub-groups are reassembled for a general session. At this session, the design of the demonstration is revealed and the styles of communication set by the leaders are discussed. Results of the Tabulation Worksheets are combined and the scores for each of the five questions on the reactionnaires are displayed to the group. In Exhibit 9.4 above, some results from a typical session are shown.

A group discussion of results such as those shown in Exhibit 9.4 will allow the group to reach an awareness of some of the effects of the leader's style in structuring the communication pattern.

In general, the open discussion and parliamentary styles will produce higher group ratings in all the categories than will the controlling style.

The open discussion style will usually yield superior ratings in the quality of the decision reached by the group and in an individual sense of responsibility for the group decision.

The controlling and parliamentary styles will usually be more efficient in terms of time required to reach some agreement on the solution. Since the sessions have a time limit, time required is not completely free to vary, but it will usually be found that a decision can be forced more readily in the controlled and parliamentary styles.

It may be helpful to look at overall effects by summarizing results over all the questions and showing outcomes for sub-groups as shown in Exhibit 9.5.

**Exhibit 9.5**
**SUMMARY ANALYSIS OF REACTIONNAIRE RESULTS**

| | LEADER STYLES | | |
| --- | --- | --- | --- |
| SUBGROUPS | CONTROLLING | PARLIAMENTARY | OPEN DISCUSSION |
| A | 230 | 265 | 281 |
| B | 262 | 295 | 310 |
| C | 258 | 282 | 305 |
| TOTAL | 750 | 842 | 896 |

The above summary of results will sometimes reveal the over-all effect of the communication pattern, even when results are mixed and ambiguous for individual questions on the reactionnaire. Here it may be seen that, in general, the open discussion and parliamentary styles are clearly superior to the controlling style, with the open discussion style having the edge over the other two.

In addition to demonstrating the feedback of results, the leader should encourage group members to discuss their feelings during the sessions. It will usually be revealed that a higher level of enjoyment, less hostility, and a greater feeling of influence will be reported in the open discussion style.

| Time | Activities |
|---|---|
| 7 min. | Introduction. Set up exercise, introduce topic. Divide into three groups. |
| 5 min. | First decision. Each group discusses "Mary's Reputation" and makes a decision. Groups fill out reactionnaire. Collect and score reactionnaire. |
| 5 min. | Second decision. Leaders rotate and groups discuss "Bobby's Theme." Groups fill out second reactionnaire. Collect and score second reactionnaire. |
| 3 min. | Third decision. Leaders rotate and groups discuss "The Old Grouch." Fill out, collect, and score reactionnaire. |
| 15 min. | Break. |
| 10 min. | Feedback on reactions. Summarize on Tabulation Worksheet after each session. Complete Summary Analysis Form for all sessions. |
| 15 min. | Discussion. Analyze, discuss, and draw conclusions from the data obtained. |

*Total time:* 1 hour

**SPECIAL ARRANGEMENTS**

This laboratory exercise will require a meeting room large enough to accommodate the total group—from 20 to 40 participants. In addition, two rooms will be needed, each large enough for group meetings of one-third of the group. Three session leaders will be required. Each must be trained to lead the group in one of the styles of group communication. One of these leaders may also be the general leader, or he may be a fourth person.

It will be helpful if scorers are available for tabulating results. If the groups are small (five to ten participants), the session leaders can probably handle scoring, otherwise clerical assistance is desirable. An overhead projector or blackboard will be needed to show results to participants.

**CAUTIONS AND LIMITATIONS**

This exercise works best if separate meeting places are available for each group. Rotating group leaders rather than groups reduces the traffic between sessions quite a bit.

The parliamentary style leader may have some difficulty in maintaining a formal communication style with the small groups, especially when they come from the open discussion style previously. He should be prepared for some hostility.

The exercise is more appropriate for people who are preparing to lead groups than it is for those who are usually group members. It seems to be most effective with groups of principals and supervisors.

Some fast, accurate scoring assistance will be needed in order to have the results available for the summary session.

Finally, the exercise is more structured than some others in this book. The leader may reduce the highly structured effect during the final session by encouraging the group to make the generalizations from the data rather than formulating these himself.

### SUGGESTED RELATED ACTIVITIES

(1) Break up into small open discussion groups. Use vignettes to stimulate discussion. Don't try to get quick decisions, but practice getting full expression of ideas. Have observer use the Bales categories (1). After ten minutes, feedback results to leader. Then, rotate leader role and use a new vignette.

(2) Organize discussion group and demonstrate the effect of leader silence once the discussion gets going. Have the leader start the open discussion and then just stop talking gradually while continuing to follow the discussion. Have him gradually stop calling on people—forcing them to respond spontaneously. Finally, discuss what happens *if* enough time is allowed.

### SUMMARY

This laboratory session contrasts three styles of group communication in terms of the effect of each style on the outcomes of group decisions.

A communication process dominated by a leader who is controlling the flow of communication and directing the outcome towards his own preconceived point of view is shown to create barriers to effective relationships among group members and to lessen confidence in the decision reached.

A communication process that is excessively restricted by procedural rules and preoccupation with form is shown to reduce group members' enjoyment and group solidarity although it may result in a relatively quick decision by the group.

Finally, an open discussion, led by a person who is seeking full exploration of a problem and group consensus in its solution is shown to enhance confidence in the decision and satisfaction with the group process.

### The effect of feedback in communications

The foregoing two exercises in this chapter demonstrate the effects of different styles of interviewing in one-to-one relationships and of different styles of communicating in group situations. Basic to both of these, of course, is the flow of communication itself; it may be one-way, going only from the sender to an intended receiver, or it may be two-way communication, allowing some feedback from the intended receiver.

The effect of feedback on the quality of the communication can be dramatically demonstrated by the rather simple exercise presented in this section.

The device for doing this is to have a person describe a geometric figure to a group whose members have the task of reproducing the figure. How well they receive the message with one-way communication is contrasted with the results of two-way communication. In a way, this exercise is a demonstration of the obvious, but the clear-cut results usually obtained have an impact that rescues the principle from the limbo of ideas that we know, but do nothing about.

### BACKGROUND ON THE PROBLEM

If a frequent visitor to schools were to take a problem census by asking teachers what bothers them, he could begin his list before contacting the first school. In every place he visits, someone will report that "communications need to be improved around here."

One of the reasons, of course, is that education is a highly verbal enterprise; people are always tellings things to each other. Too often, we assume that once we have told someone something, he "gets" it. This exercise will demonstrate that, more often than not, he *does not* get it if the communication stops there.

There are other factors that bear on the situation. One is the problem of semantics. Although this is an overworked explanation of differing points of view, it is true that the same words mean different things to different people. This is especially prevalent in situations in which ordinary words have been given special meanings by professional groups such as teachers. For example, the "exceptional child" is most likely to be thought of as gifted by the layman and as retarded by the professional.

Not all communications failures reside in the sender; we do not listen carefully most of the time. Or sometimes we listen not to the content of the message, but to the emotional overtones that burden the message. This "noise" may obscure the content if we are tuned in on how things are said rather than what is being said. A first-grade teacher who is trying to decide about whether or not to recommend retention of a borderline student is not likely to hear the principal's instructions in a faculty meeting as to how to handle the Junior Red Cross fund drive.

One of the most serious communications problems, of course, is in written communications. The flood of ditto fluid from the school office sends out a purple tide of memos, instructions, notices, bulletins, and admonitions ranging from crucial to trivial. The first mistake is to assume that these will be read by all intended receivers, the second mistake is to assume they are understood, if read; and the third mistake is to believe the message is clear and unambiguous enough to be clearly understood. Some of the masterpieces of ambiguity that we have collected over the years emanating from administrative offices in schools and colleges are positively Delphic in style.

One of the most prevalent kinds of communications is that of giving directions and one of the most difficult problems in communicating with people is that of having directions understood. Supervisors, principals, and teachers spend a large part of their days in giving directions. An awareness of factors affecting the extent to which they get their message across is an important topic for in-service meetings.

This exercise demonstrates the advantages to be gained by two-way communication.

Developing an awareness of how feedback in communication affects the accuracy of understanding.

Demonstrating how feedback affects confidence in the accuracy of understanding.

Demonstrating how realistic estimates of accuracy and confidence are with feedback and without feedback.

Contrasting the leader's confidence in how well he is getting his message across with and without feedback.

Contrasting the relative amounts of time required for communication with and without feedback.

PROCEDURE

In this exercise there will be a session leader who directs the sequence of events; a "communicator" whose task is to deliver the "message" under two conditions of feedback; scorers; and participants whose task is to record the "message" as accurately as possible.

Before this session begins, the session leader will need to select some member of the group who is going to be the communicator, and instruct him in his role. The best way to do this is to go over the instructions on directions for communicator shown in Exhibits 9.6 and 9.7.

The leader may begin by telling the group that they are going to take part in a demonstration concerning one of the most difficult problems in communicating with people—that of having directions understood. He may then introduce the communicator and say that there has been no coaching on what the communicator is to say, but that he has been instructed in the rules of the game, and that directions for receivers (see Exhibit 9.8) have been given.

## Exhibit 9.6
## DIRECTIONS FOR COMMUNICATOR

1. Your task is to describe the geometric figure which appears below.  The others will draw what you describe.

2. The following rules will apply:
   a.  You may communicate verbally, but in no other way.
   b.  They may not communicate to you or with each other in any way.

3. Record the time you begin describing the figure and the time you finish in the space provided at the bottom of the page.

4. After you complete your task, estimate the average number of figures your group drew correctly (maximum of six), and place that number in the space at the bottom of the page marked "C-Score."

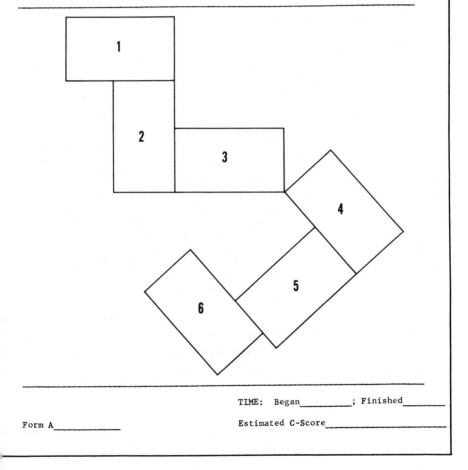

TIME:  Began_____; Finished_____

Form A_____               Estimated C-Score_____

## Exhibit 9.7
## DIRECTIONS FOR COMMUNICATOR

1. Your second task will be to describe another geometric design.  The others will draw what you describe.

2. This time, however, they may ask you as many questions as they wish, and you may answer them.

3. Record the time you begin describing the figure and the time you finish in the spaces provided at the bottom of the page.

4. After you complete your task, estimate the average number of figures your group drew correctly (maximum of six), and place that number in the space at the bottom of the page maked "C-Score."

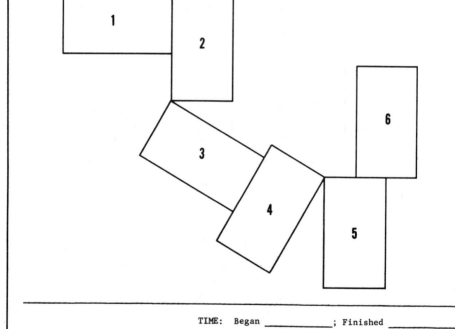

TIME:  Began _____; Finished _____

Form B _____     Estimated C-Score _____

## Exhibit 9.8
## DIRECTIONS FOR RECEIVER

1. The "leader" has a geometric design in his hands. He will describe it to you. Your task is to draw, as accurately as possible, what he describes.

2. The following rules will apply:
   a. You may not communicate with the "leader" in any way.
   b. You may not communicate with your "neighbors" in any way.
   c. The "leader" cannot show you what he has before him.

3. Draw on the space provided below:

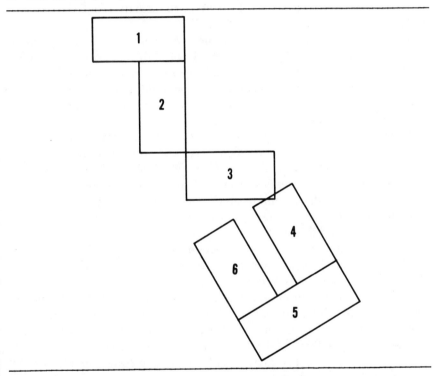

In the space below, marked "C-Score," estimate the number of figures you drew correctly. (The leader described six, so six is the maximum score.)

Form AA __*2*__                                        C-Score __*3*__

The rules are that only the communicator may talk, and that he should not look for visual feedback from the group. In fact, it is better if he is behind a screen or has his back to the group. He will instruct them as carefully and in as much detail as he feels is necessary in how to draw some geometric figures he has before him, and the group is to follow his instructions so that their drawing will look like his.

During the session, group members may not ask any questions of the communicator or each other, and they should not look at each others' drawings. The idea is to have absolutely no feedback from the group to the communicator so that communication is one-way only.

As the communicator begins his instructions, the group leader should remind him to record the time. He will then let the session continue unii.terrupted unless he needs to caution the group about the rules of the game.

When the communicator has finished, participants are instructed to estimate the number of figures they drew correctly and enter the number in the space marked "C-score" (confidence score) on the form shown in Exhibit 9.8. He should also instruct the communicator to fill in the time finished and record his estimate of the average number of figures drawn correctly by the group.

Papers are then collected and scoring is begun. Scorers should have been previously instructed in their task, and the group leader should have had them score several example drawings to check their accuracy. Scoring is simple if directions given in Exhibit 9.10 are followed.

Time required, the communicator's confidence score, the group mean confidence score, and the group mean actual score are recorded on the form shown in Exhibit 9.10.

While scoring is in progress, the session leader should begin the next trial. Participants should have the instruments shown in Exhibit 9.9 in hand as instructions are given.

As before, the communicator remains hidden from the group, but this time they may ask him questions when they fail to understand his directions. The difference, of course, is that verbal feedback is permitted in the second trial. Other feedback, such as gestures, should not be allowed.

When the trial has been completed, the session leader should instruct the group to record their scores as before, and the forms should be collected for scoring.

While scoring and tabulation is in progress, the session leader may conduct a brief discussion of feedback, letting participants voice their reactions to the experience. A typical response is that of frustration experienced in the no-feedback session. The communicator may also tell how he felt as the session progressed.

Participants should be shown what the figures really looked like and how scoring is done. It may be pointed out that the session deals with

**Exhibit 9.9**
## DIRECTIONS FOR RECEIVER

1.  The "leader" has another figure similar to the one you have just completed.
    Your task again is to draw, as accurately as possible, what he describes.

2.  This time, however, you may ask the "leader" as many questions as you wish,
    and he may answer them.

3.  Draw on the space provided below.

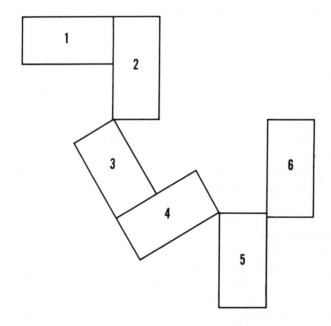

In the space below, marked "C-Score," again estimate the number of figures you
drew correctly.  (The leader described six, so six is the maximum score.)

Form BB____4____                                    C-Score____5____

## Exhibit 9.10
## DIRECTIONS FOR SCORING FEEDBACK EXERCISE

|  | TIME REQUIRED | SUPERIOR'S CONFIDENCE SCORE | SUBORDINATES' CONFIDENCE SCORE | ACTUAL SCORE |
|---|---|---|---|---|
| NO-FEEDBACK | 5 min | 3.0 | 3.25 | 2.37 |
| FREE-FEEDBACK | 14 min | 4.0 | 4.34 | 4.19 |
| DIFFERENCE | 9 min | 1.0 | .89 | 1.82 |

only one of many relevant variables in communication: that of feedback. The central question, of course, is how transmission from the communicator to receiver is affected by return transmission. An assumption is made in such things as lectures and "one-way" announcements that communication is effective without feedback.

The group may be led to develop several hypotheses about the experience that can be checked when the scoring is completed. Typical results from a session using this exercise are shown in Exhibit 9.10.

Results like those shown in Exhibit 9.10 support several generalizations that the leader may want to develop with the group. They are as follows:

1.  Feedback takes more time than no-feedback.
2.  Feedback increases the accuracy with which a message is received.
3.  Feedback increases the communicator's confidence in the accuracy of his communication. This is not always the case, however. There may be times when numerous questions raised at what he thinks are clear instructions shake the communicator's confidence.
4.  Feedback increases the receiver's confidence in the accuracy of his comprehension. There is less frustration and hostility with feedback.
5.  Both communicator and receiver overestimate the accuracy of the communication, but the receivers are closer to actual results.

SEQUENCE OF ACTIVITIES

| Time | Activity |
|---|---|
| 5 min. | Introduction. |
| 10 min. | Appoint communicator, distribute the instrument shown in Exhibit 9.8, and instruct group for no-feedback trial. |
| 10 min. | Conduct trial 1 and collect results. |

| 5 min. | Distribute the instrument shown in Exhibit 9.9 and give instructions for feedback trial. |
| 10 min. | Conduct trial 2 and collect results. |
| 20 min. | Group discussion of feedback while results are being tabulated. |
| 30 min. | Discussion of results of exercise. |

*Total time:* 1 hour and 30 minutes

### SPECIAL ARRANGEMENTS

This is one exercise that can be used with large groups. We have used it successfully with as many as 350 people, although this makes tabulation a greater problem. It can be done by sampling results, however. Groups of 15 to 35 are better because discussion is easier to manage.

There needs to be some provision for screening off the view between the communicator and the group. He may be behind a screen or outside the door, or in the back of the room. It is as important that *he* cannot see the group as that they cannot see him since he will get many visual clues if he sees puzzled looks, gestures of frustration, and so on.

If enough room is available, it is probably better to seat group members in such a way as to minimize their looking at each others' progress, although this did not seem to make a lot of difference on occasions when we have used this in large groups where people were obviously comparing results. A blackboard or overhead projector will be needed to feedback results to the group.

### CAUTIONS AND LIMITATIONS

This exercise is not intended to be the whole story on communications. It is limited to the effect of verbal feedback in a communication in which instructions are being given. One-way communication is unsuitable in many instances and necessary in others, but it is important to know something about its relative effectiveness under the conditions demonstrated.

The session leader should be prepared for some hostility to develop in the session, particularly if the communicator is a status person in the group and he feels his "ability to communicate" is being revealed as weak. This may occur if repeated feedback shows a lot of uncertainty about his instructions. This, of course, can be turned to good effect as a learning experience in the discussion period if it should occur.

The success of the exercise depends on accurate scoring of responses. The scoring is not difficult, but the session leader should check a few papers to make sure it is being done correctly.

A lot also depends on the communicator. It is best to pick someone who is recognized as being good at giving directions, since the task is difficult enough even under the best circumstances.

Finally, this is one of the exercises in which time is usually available for a lot of group involvement in the discussion. The session leader should avoid "telling them what they found out," and should take the time necessary to let the group explore the results, develop the generalizations, and suggest ways in which the results can be utilized in practice.

SUGGESTED RELATED ACTIVITIES

1. Take some school bulletins and analyze the contents for items that require feedback for understanding.
2. Repeat the feedback session allowing gestures to be used. The addition of visual communication should improve accuracy considerably. This can be used as a basis for a discussion of face-to-face communication as contrasted with telephone messages.
3. Teachers may find this exercise useful with their classes. The principles being demonstrated are useful for everyone and are especially relevant in language arts classes.

### Summary

This chapter has presented three laboratory exercises suitable for leading instructional groups in developing insight into communications and human interactions. In the first exercise, dyadic relationships were considered in the context of the supervisory interview and the effects of different interview styles were observed. In the second exercise, the effects of the group leader's communication style on problem solution were shown. This was done by role-playing three different group leadership styles and recording the effect of these on individual response to the groups. The last exercise was a demonstration of the effect of feedback when instructions are being given. The accuracy with which instructions are followed, the communicator's confidence in the interaction, and the difference in time required were examined with and without feedback.

These three exercises do not, of course, comprise any suggested sequence of activities although the order in which they are given is probably a satisfactory one. They are intended to be used in conjunction with more comprehensively planned in-service designs and are appropriate for initiating more thorough involvement in a study of human interactions.

*Selected references*

1. Bales, Robert F., *Interaction Process Analysis. A Method for the Study of Small Groups.* Cambridge, Mass.: Addison-Wesley, 1950.
2. Harris, Ben M., "Attitudes Toward Two Types of Supervisory Interviews," Chapter 13 in *Supervisory Behavior in Education.* Englewood Cliffs, N.J.: Prentice-Hall, Inc., 1963.
3. _____, "Interview Technique in Education," Austin, Texas: Department of Educational Administration, The University of Texas, 1962 (mimeographed).
4. Klein, A. F., *How to Use Role-Playing Effectively.* New York: Association Press, 1959.
5. Leavitt, Harold J., and Ronald Muellar, "Three Effects of Feedback on Communications," *Human Relations.* 4:40–10, 1951.
6. University Council for Educational Administration, *The Conference,* 16 mm. sound film (b&w). 65 Oral Drive, Columbus, Ohio.

# Chapter Ten

# SETTING INSTRUCTIONAL OBJECTIVES

IT IS probably advisable for teachers to reconsider their practices from time to time on the more fundamental aspects of teaching—planning instruction, selecting instructional activities, and evaluating instruction. Since these become the workaday decisions of teaching, they are likely to fall victim to the law of entropy and become less organized, less sharply defined as time goes on.

This chapter presents a laboratory exercise designed to help teachers take a new look at one of the most crucial single decisions the teacher must make in teaching—this is the decision regarding what learning is being sought as a direct outcome of teaching.

Objectives for instruction are not usually stated with enough clarity and precision to serve as effective guides to the teacher as he attempts to plan the most effective instructional procedures or as he tries to evaluate the effectiveness of that instruction. This training session demonstrates a procedure for developing statements of instructional objectives that can serve as functional guides to selecting and evaluating instruction. The approach used as a basis for this in-service activity was developed by Robert F. Mager. For a full exposition of the method, see his extremely lucid book, *Preparing Objectives for Programmed Instruction*.

### BACKGROUND ON THE PROBLEM

Stating instructional objectives with enough precision to permit unambiguous interpretations by those who use them is an ubiquitous problem

**214**

in education. The monumental work contained in the two volumes of *Taxonomy of Educational Objectives* represents an important step forward in making possible a classification of educational goals (1, 3). The *Taxonomy* provides curriculum workers and teachers with a comprehensive means of classifying objectives and of developing test exercises for evaluation of objectives. In addition to the taxonomic problem, the teacher's task in planning lessons with specific outcomes in mind is to get unambiguous statements of the outcomes desired. It would be helpful to have available a form that permits the precise statement of the instructional intent.

Clearly stated objectives are necessary for several reasons.

1. Such statements are essential in communicating from teacher to pupil and parent, from curriculum worker to teacher, from principal to teacher, and from teacher to materials producer.
2. Such statements are essential for guiding the selection of material and activities of instruction.
3. Such statements are essential in providing evaluative criteria.
4. Such statements permit the learner to be more self-directed.

Greatest precision of statement of educational objectives requires that at least three components be specified, unless some of these are so clearly implied in the statement that there is little chance of misunderstanding. The three criteria of a well-stated objective are:

1. The anticipated behaviors are specified.
2. The conditions under which anticipated behaviors are to be demonstrated are specified.
3. The standard of minimum acceptable performance is specified.

Such specific statements are not intended to fractionate the educational program into small bits, and it must be realized that an objective might meet the demanding criteria suggested above and yet result in planning, teaching, and evaluating inconsequential content. The concern for the "so what" question is of critical importance and belongs properly in the domain of curriculum development and determination of *goals* too long-range for individual lesson planning.

Assuming that a satisfactory goal structure has been developed for the school, this exercise is intended to provide teachers with a means for making daily operational interpretations of these in a precise, clear, and unambiguous way.

**Exhibit 10.1**
## CONTENT, ACTIVITIES, OBJECTIVES, AND GOALS

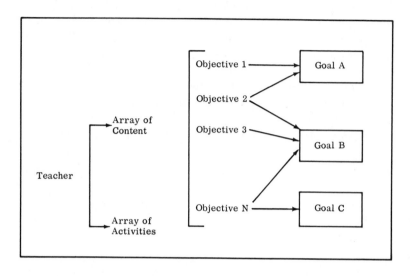

Exhibit 10.1 above is presented to illustrate the relationships between objectives, goals, content, and activities in the instructional context. The figure is intended to show that the teacher selects from an array of content and teaching-learning activities those that are appropriate to specific objectives which are linked together to reach more comprehensive goals. This exercise is concerned with the statement of specific objectives.

##### ACTIVITIES

Since this exercise is designed to teach a specific approach to the statement of instructional objectives, it is important that the objectives of the exercise itself be stated in the suggested form. Specifically, the objectives of this demonstration are such that the successful participant will be able to do the following:

1. Select all the statements that are instructional objectives when given a list that includes some statements of objectives and some statements that are not objectives.
2. Select all the objectives that are stated in performance terms when given a list of statements, some of which are not stated as behavioral outcomes.
3. Identify every objective that states the conditions under which learning is to be demonstrated when given a list that contains some such items.
4. Identify all the instructional objectives that define a criterion of

acceptable performance from a set of objectives, some of which do not contain criterion statements.

It will be readily seen from the above list that the intent of this exercise is to bring about some *behavioral* change in the participant. That is, he will be able to demonstrate when he successfully completes the exercise that he has learned what the in-service exercise has been designed to produce. This object lesson itself, should be a powerful reinforcement to the teacher as to the utility of clearly stated objectives. In this sense, this exercise is in the spirit of the laboratory demonstration method in that the points to be made are *demonstrated* by the outcomes of the experience, and the teacher generates his own data upon which the generalizations are based.

**PROCEDURE**

Since this exercise follows a sharply defined line of development, the demonstrator should have a good grasp of both the content and the procedure. As he develops the sequence of ideas, he may find it helpful to follow the procedure suggested below.

*Introducing the exercise* The emphasis in the demonstration is on good *statements* of objectives, not on statements of *good* objectives. The difference, of course, is that an objective may be well stated and still not be a significant outcome. The latter question depends upon other important considerations that are outside the intent of the present exercise.

It should also be made clear to participants from the outset that the procedures presented have to do with stating of objectives from the viewpoint of the teacher who is planning specific lessons or units of study. Broader educational objectives under which these instructional objectives may be subsumed may be subject to somewhat different principles. The statement of broad educational goals of the school is also outside the scope of the exercise.

Finally, it should be made clear in the introductory statement that this is by no means the final procedure for stating instructional objectives. It happens to be the most clearly developed of any available at present and hence is worthy of the teacher's attention as he concerns himself with this extremely important step in teaching—having clearly in mind what the objective of the teaching is. Participants should be referred to the books by Robert F. Mager (2), Bloom, *et al.* (1), and Krathwohl, *et al.* (3) for more depth of insight into this problem.

The session leader should inform the participants that he is assuming the role of an instructor who is presenting a lesson. This is done not to impress them with his expertise, but to establish a realistic frame of reference for the "lesson" that is to follow. He should let them know what his objectives are because he will later evaluate the learning in terms of these objectives.

*Pretesting beliefs* Participants should be given the material shown in Exhibit 10.2 and asked to fill it out before the lesson begins in order to give them an opportunity to state their beliefs about what constitutes a good statement of instructional objectives. One member of the group will be needed to collect and score results. In scoring, he will need to record the number who checked each item. Since none of the items can be considered to be good statements of objectives, all the numbers tallied represent "wrong" answers to items.

*Stating outcomes* It is a good idea to inform participants that they will not hand in answers to items shown in Exhibits 10.3 to 10.6. These will

### Exhibit 10.2
### PREPARING INSTRUCTIONAL OBJECTIVES

Check the ones of the following that are good statements of instructional objectives.

| | |
|---|---|
| 33[a] | 1. Review pages 15-23 in <u>Working with Numbers</u> and answer odd numbered questions at the end of the section. |
| 38 | 2. An overview of the theories, principles, and issues in curriculum construction for modern education. Designed for Master's degree students with majors outside curriculum and instruction and for doctoral students needing to update preparation. |
| 72 | 3. An appreciation of the American way of like. |
| 96 | 4. To really appreciate the freedoms guaranteed in the Bill of Rights. |
| 91 | 5. The student must be able to identify the opera and the name of the character singing the aria. |
| 142 | 6. In Homemaking II, the student must be able to prepare a nutritious meal. |
| 131 | 7. The student must be able to spell words from the third grade basic spelling list when they are used in writing assignments. |
| 146 | 8. The student must be able to name leaf specimens when shown leaves previously identified. |

[a]These numbers represent the number of persons (out of 216) who marked each item wrong in one in-service group.

be used only as a kind of self-test of the ideas to be presented. This will help to relieve any tension about wrong answers.

With the material shown in Exhibit 10.3, the point is made that an objective is a statement of *outcomes*, not processes or procedures. The intent in this phase of the session is to get the participants to be able to distinguish between objectives and other kinds of statements relating to instruction. Some examples will probably help in this. The leader may want to refer back to statement number 1 of Exhibit 10.2 to make ·the point that this is a typical assignment for a lesson, not a statement of what learning the assignment is supposed to produce.

Statement number 2 in Exhibit 10.2 is a college catalog description of a graduate course in curriculum. It is not an objective because it does not specify an outcome. The leader will probably think of many similar examples of assignments, unit titles, and courses that should not be thought of as objectives.

When this point has been accepted, participants respond to items shown in Exhibit 10.3. This form is a self-test of their ability to distinguish a statement of an objective (outcome) from a description of a course.

### Exhibit 10.3
### SPECIFYING OUTCOMES

1. Look at the following statement and then answer the question below it.

   "A survey of American history with emphasis on the colonial period includes a study of the revolution, the Constitution, and the Declaration of Independence."

   What does the above statement represent? Does the statement appear to be an <u>objective</u> of a course, or does it look more like a <u>description</u> of a course?

   _____ An objective of a course.

   _____ A description of a course.

2. Which of the statements below seem most like an objective?

   _____ a. To be able to spell the list of basic vocabulary words.

   _____ b. A study of spelling with emphasis on a list of basic vocabulary words.

   _____ c. To know basic English vocabulary.

In Exhibit 10.3, the second alternative of question number 1 should be checked since the statement in question number 1 is a description of a course. The second question has three alternatives. The first should be checked because "to spell" is an outcome, not a process. The second should not be checked since "a study of" is a description of a course, not an end or product of learning. The third alternative may be checked since it is stated in terms of an outcome, but it has another difficulty which helps make a transition from this to the next major point. That is, "to know . . ." does not tell very much about what the expected outcome is to be. What is a person doing when he is "knowing"? This point will be clarified in the following section.

*Stating objectives in performance terms*   A major point which the discussion leader will want to make is that objectives, to be functional, must be stated in performance terms. That is, they must state what the learner is to be able to do when he demonstrates that he has reached the objective.

It will help clarify this point to mention some of the key words that are useful in making behavioral descriptions. Some words that are descriptive of performance are: to say, to write, to list, to name, to recognize, to contrast, to discriminate, to identify, and so forth. These phrases state what the learner does in contrast to unseen, inner states such as understanding, appreciating, enjoying, knowing, believing, and so forth.

This is a point at which the leader should encourage some discussion in order to deal with the problem that some will express: that to *appreciate*, for example, is an important outcome for learning, but that it is usually expressed in such ambiguous terms that no teacher can be sure of when the objective has been reached. Such outcomes should be stated in behavorial terms. To *appreciate* music, for example, might become to *select* music from a list of things when asked to identify what one enjoys.

To reinforce the point, it may be helpful to call to the attention of the group many instances in which an attempt has been made to reduce the ambiguity of "to enjoy . . ." by adding "really to enjoy . . ." Such attempts add only emotion, not clarity, to the objective.

Items 3 and 4 in Exhibit 10.2 were designed to illustrate this point. What does "an appreciation of the American way of life" mean? How will the teacher ever know when a pupil really appreciates "the freedoms guaranteed in the Bill of Rights"?

Exhibit 10.3 may be used to illustrate the points above. Alternative 2a is stated in performance terms because it tells what the learner is able to do. Alternative 2c, while it is stated as an outcome, is not stated in performance terms. What is the person supposed to *do* when he is demonstrating that he "knows basic English vocabulary"? Is he to write it, say it, use it in everyday English, use it on a test, or what?

When the concept has been accepted by the group, the instructor should make available the items shown in Exhibit 10.4 for their responses. This is a self-test of ability to select objectives which contain performance statements of objectives. Participants should score their own responses as follows:

Item *a* is not stated in performance terms. To enjoy poetry does not describe what the learner does to demonstrate that he enjoys poetry.

Items *b* and *c* are stated in performance terms.

Item *d* is not stated in performance terms. How can we tell when the learner *knows how* to repair a bell circuit?

Item *e* is stated in performance terms.

Items *f* and *g* are not stated in performance terms for reasons that should be clear by now.

Item *h* is stated in performance terms.

By the end of this portion of the exercise, all of the group members should have a clear grasp of what an objective is and what it means to state an objective in performance terms. Two more major points are to be made.

**Exhibit 10.4**
**STATING OBJECTIVES IN PERFORMANCE TERMS**

Which of the following objectives are stated in performance terms?

_____ a. To enjoy poetry.

_____ b. To be able to divide fractional positive numbers.

_____ c. To be able to repair a bell circuit.

_____ d. To know how a bell circuit works.

_____ e. To be able to write a summary of reasons for the failure of the League of Nations.

_____ f. To really appreciate music.

_____ g. To know the rules of parliamentary procedure.

_____ h. To be able to outline the plot of The Rime of the Ancient Mariner.

*Clarifying Conditions for Objectives*   Sometimes an objective does not clearly communicate the desired outcome because it is not clear under what conditions the desired behavior is to occur. For example, Item 6 in Exhibit 10.2 states that the student must be able to prepare a nutritious meal. It is not clear whether he is to do this at home or in class, whether he is to use a recipe or not, or whether it is to be a simple meal or a formal dinner. The student could even warm a TV dinner and meet the literal requirements of the objective.

Some objectives, of course, do not require this additional clarification. To be able to do ten pull-ups on a bar is probably clear enough without having to specify wind conditions, or whether barefooted or wearing shoes. Most instructional objectives, however, are complex enough to need additional clarification in the form of conditions stated in the objective. For example, Item 5 in Exhibit 10.2 should specify what the stimulus is to be for the student to identify. Is he to listen to a record, read the words, remember a story line, or simply recall a previous list from which he is to "identify the opera and the name of the character singing the aria"?

The discussion leader will need to invent other examples to make this point clear. It may be helpful to suggest that (1) the objective may contain a statement of what the student has to work with, such as, "Given a slide rule, the student . . ."; (2) the objective may contain a statement of sources of the learning, such as, "To list the principles of good composition stated in . . ."; (3) the objective may specify the stimulus to which the student must respond, such as, "When shown flash cards with words from the basic sight reading vocabulary . . .".

The items in Exhibit 10.5 are designed as a self-test of ability to identify objectives which contain clarifying conditions. Item 2 is the only one which does so. A transparency may be useful in discussing the items in Exhibit 10.5. By underlining the phrase, "Given a list of basic sight reading words from the pre-primer," the session leader can emphasize the way in which this states the conditions for the objective.

Item 1 should not be missed by anyone since this is an item that was discussed earlier (it is the same as Item 6 in Exhibit 10.2). In Item 3, it is not clear whether this typing is to be done on an electric or a manual typewriter, or how difficult the test material is. Item 4 does not clarify whether the student is to outline his own theme or another, or whether the outline follows the writing of a theme or precedes it. The final item, of course, does not say whether the equations are to be linear, quadratic. or simultaneous equations, or where this is to be demonstrated (on a test in class, or in homework, and so forth).

*Stating criteria*   The final point to be made in this exercise is that in order to be stated with the maximum degree of clarity, an objective

## Exhibit 10.5
## CLARIFYING CONDITIONS FOR OBJECTIVES

Which of the objectives stated below describe the conditions under which
the desired behavior is to occur?

_____ 1.  In Homemaking II, the student must be able to
prepare a nutritious meal.

_____ 2.  Given the list of basic sight reading words from the
pre-primer, the pupil must be able to recognize and
pronounce them correctly.

_____ 3.  To be able to type 40 words a minute.

_____ 4.  To be able to outline an English theme.

_____ 5.  To be able to solve Algebra equations.

should not only state the conditions for the desired performance, but should include a statement of minimum acceptable performance.

The inclusion of a criterion statement in an objective provides the teacher with the information needed to evaluate learning, and makes it possible for the teacher to plan the required depth or scope of instruction necessary to meet the objective.

To illustrate this point, it might be well to refer to Items 7 and 8 in Exhibit 10.2. Both these items could be stated more clearly by the inclusion of a criterion. Item 7, for example, should specify how many errors, if any, are acceptable in spelling words from the third grade basic spelling list. In the last item, it should be made clear whether the identification of the leaf specimens should be error-free, one error allowed, or whatever.

This concept is usually easily understood by participants. When the leader feels that the point has been accepted, he should ask participants to respond to items shown in Exhibit 10.6. This form, like the preceding ones, is a self-test on the point just made.

Only the second objective in Exhibit 10.6 contains a criterion statement (15 out of 20 named correctly). The first objective does not say how many errors are to be located in the sentences. In fact, if the statement were taken literally, locating two errors would satisfy the objective. The same thing is true for the third item: if a student were to spell _any_ words right, he would meet the objective. Both of these statements could

## Exhibit 10.6
## STATING CRITERIA

In each of the following objectives, indicate by checking "YES" if the objective gives the criterion of acceptable performance. Check "NO" if it does not.

1. Objective:

> The learner must be able to locate and correct errors in the sentences when given a list of English sentences containing punctuation errors.

> _____a. Yes, it does indicate the criterion.

> _____b. No, it does not.

2. Objective:

> The student must be able to name at least 15 leaf specimens correctly when given a frame containing 20 previously identified leaves.

> _____a. Yes, it does indicate the criterion.

> _____b. No, it does not.

3. Objective:

> The student must be able to spell words from the third grade basic spelling list when they are used in writing assignments.

> _____a. Yes, it does indicate the criterion.

> _____b. No, it does not.

be improved by specifying the error level to be permitted for acceptable performance.

*Post-test on objectives*   Implicit in the design of this exercise is the notion that well-stated objectives provide an effective tool for evaluating the outcomes of teaching. To that end, participants are asked to respond to Exhibit 10.7. If everyone has reached all the objectives of the exercise, there should be no errors.

When participants have completed Exhibit 10.7, this is a good place to take a break for ten minutes. During this time, items in Exhibit 10.7 can be scored. If the group is large, several scoring keys should be constructed so that several people can score at once. Items 1, 4, 5, 6, 11, and 13 (Exhibit 10.7) should be answered *no* and the remainder of the items should be answered *yes*. The responses on this test can be contrasted with those on the pretest (Exhibit 10.2).

*Feedback on outcomes*   It will be remembered that none of the items in Exhibit 10.2 could qualify as good statements of instructional objectives according to all the qualifications set in this exercise. For that reason, all items checked represent wrong answers. On a previous page, Exhibit 10.2 is shown with the number of people who checked each item in one use that was made of this exercise in a group of 216 teachers. It may be seen in the example that as the items included more of the characteristics of good objectives, more people checked them as being *good* statements of objectives, but it may also be noted that nearly 20 per cent of the participants checked items 1 and 2 which are not objectives at all. Nearly half checked items 3 and 4, although these are not stated in performance terms. Over half considered items 5 and 6 to be good statements although neither states any of the conditions necessary to clarify the objectives. Over two thirds of the group checked items 7 and 8 despite the fact that there is no indication of any criterion of minimum acceptable performance.

In the feedback of results on the post-test, Exhibit 10.7 should be used. Items 1 through 5 are tests of how well objective 2 of this exercise has been met. It was assumed that everyone can distinguish an objective from other types of statements by this time so that no items relating to objective 1 are included. Some typical results of the post-test are shown in Exhibit 10.7. This group of 216 teachers was able to identify objectives stated in performance terms in the first five items with errors ranging from about 5 per cent to about 10 per cent. Another way of putting it is that all but ten people met this objective as measured by Item 2 and all but 28 met this objective as measured by Item 4. It is convenient to score Exhibit 10.7 in terms of each item missed in order to use this form for teaching purposes, although a strict evaluation of the objective would call for recording the number of participants who missed none of the first five items.

## Exhibit 10.7
## EVALUATING OUTCOMES

| No. Right | No. Wrong | |
|---|---|---|
| | | In the following items, check the item number if the objective is stated in at least performance terms. That is, it specifies the behavior of the learner if he is demonstrating that he has achieved the objective. |
| 188 | 28 | 1. To understand the rules of parliamentary procedure. |
| 206 | 10 | 2. To be able to identify the location of the continents of the earth when given a map with names omitted. |
| 183 | 13 | 3. To be able to list the forms of regular Spanish verbs. |
| 188 | 28 | 4. To have an appreciation of the American way of life. |
| 192 | 24 | 5. To really appreciate the freedoms guaranteed in the Bill of Rights. |
| | | In the following items, check the item number if the objective includes a statement of the conditions under which the desired behavior is to occur. |
| 200 | 16 | 6. To be able to solve a linear equation. |
| 192 | 22 | 7. To be able to write complete sentences using words from the new vocabulary list when given the assignment in class. |
| 189 | 19 | 8. Using a slide rule, the student must be able to find the square root of numbers correct to three significant digits. |
| 196 | 26 | 9. The student must be able to correctly identify the opera and the name of the character singing the aria when a record of arias from familiar operas is played. |
| | | In the following items, check the item number if the objective indicates a standard or criterion of minumum acceptable performance. |
| 188 | 18 | 10. The student must be able to correctly identify all the organs in the human digestive system on an unlabeled diagram. No errors are permitted. |
| 187 | 29 | 11. The student must be able to understand the responsibilities of citizens in a democracy. Evidence of understanding will be obtained from an essay on the subject. |
| 201 | 15 | 12. The student must be able to select 80 per cent of the pictures identified by the teacher as being good composition when presented with a series of pictures illustrating good and bad composition. |
| 204 | 12 | 13. The student will know the rules of good health. |

Since Item 3 in Exhibit 10.2 is the same as Item 4 in Exhibit 10.7, it is also possible to point out to participants that some of them thought this was a good statement of an objective before the exercise began, but only a few typically consider it to be a satisfactory objective at the end of the exercise.

The third objective of the exercise is tested by items 6 through 9 in Exhibit 10.7. An assessment of the number of participants who missed these items will be an indication of how well they are able to identify objectives which include a statement of the conditions under which the desired behavior is to occur. It may also be noted that Item 9 is the same as pretest Item 5 so that a comparison of pre-post-test change can be made. In the example data shown in Exhibit 10.7, 91 participants missed this item in the pretest and 26 missed it on the post-test.

The last objective is tested by Items 10–13 of Exhibit 10.7. The same general comparison should be made with the results of these items as those above.

The feedback of results from the post-test has been suggested for two reasons. First, the participants get one more opportunity to learn the procedure presented in the exercise in the event that they have failed to do so up to this point. Secondly, the leader can use this as a way of demonstrating that well-written objectives can be used in evaluating the effectiveness of the instruction. Only by having clearly stated objectives, however, can they function effectively in the evaluation stage.

SEQUENCE OF ACTIVITIES

The following brief sequence of activities may help the demonstrator plan for time required and also serve as a brief overview of the more detailed procedures described above.

| Time | Activity |
|------|----------|
| 7 min. | Introduce laboratory exercise; state objectives. |
| 24 min. | Make available material shown in Exhibit 10.2 and have participants respond to items. Collect and begin scoring (scorer required) and refer participants to material shown in Exhibits 10.3–10.7. |
| 10 min. | Discuss objectives as outcomes. Participants fill out self-test in Exhibit 10.3, score, and discuss. |
| 12 min. | Discuss statement of objectives in performance terms. Participants respond to items in Exhibit 10.4, and discuss. |
| 7 min. | Discuss communication clarity gained by stating conditions under which learning is to be demonstrated. Participants respond to items in Exhibit 10.5. Participants score and discuss items. |
| 12 min. | Discuss statement of minimum acceptable performance in objec- |

tives. Participants respond to item in Exhibit 10.6. Participants score and discuss items.

10 min.    Summarize points made. Participants respond to items in Exhibit 10.7.

8 min.     Break.

15 min.    Score and discuss items on post-test. Summarize and evaluate exercise in terms of the objectives set forth at the beginning.

*Total time:* 1 hour and 45 minutes

SPECIAL ARRANGEMENTS

The setting for this exercise can be almost any room that will seat 20 to 30 people comfortably. The leader will need a chalkboard or an overhead projector. Participants will need some surface for writing on the various forms. Although it is not essential, seating around a conference table with the leader at the head of the table would be a very good arrangement.

In the sample data given, it can be seen that over 200 teachers participated. Large groups of this kind can be treated satisfactorily, but only at the sacrifice of the discussion that is necessary to get real commitment to the ideas suggested.

It would appear to be a better idea to limit the number of participants to a group of not more than 20, and allow for plenty of discussion. They need not all be of the same subject or grade level. In fact, something is to be gained by having cross-sectional groups such as might be found in the faculty of an elementary school.

CAUTIONS AND LIMITATIONS

This exercise is highly structured and leader-dominated. For this reason, the leader should be aware of the need to allow for objections or disagreements to be raised for discussion. He should emphasize throughout that he is presenting procedure based on a highly consistent point of view, but that this is not the only point of view. He may find it helpful, however, to try to get participants who do not agree with this procedure to face the consequences of their own views. For example, someone who believes that "To appreciate . . ." is a good way to state an objective may want to explain how he will evaluate an objective stated in this way. What does it mean when an objective is stated in such a way that we can never know when it has been reached?

Some participants may raise the point that they do not have to state objectives with any formal procedure, because *they* know what they are trying to teach and why. The thing to be emphasized here, of course, is that teaching is not a private matter, but a school-wide concern, and that instructional objectives have to be organized into some meaningful sequence of learning steps through grade and content levels.

This exercise should not be expected by itself to result in any great changes in the way in which teachers actually state their objectives. They should be able to do so at the conclusion of the exercise, but whether they do so or not will depend upon the efficiency of the follow-up exercises mentioned above.

### SUGGESTED RELATED ACTIVITIES

Several follow-up activities should be used in conjunction with this exercise. First, since it deals with the statement of instructional objectives, it would be instructive to have teachers bring examples of some of their own instructional objectives to later meetings and for the group to try to restate them in performance terms, specifying conditions and stating criteria.

Secondly, individuals or groups may want to examine objectives listed in instructional materials and curriculum guides to see if they have the required rigor of statement.

Thirdly, teachers may want to use the methods described to get pupils to help set their own objectives for learning. The discipline of specifying performance terms and setting minimum acceptable performance could be a highly motivating device for some pupils.

## Selected references

1. Bloom, Benjamin S., ed., *Taxonomy of Educational Objectives, Handbook I: Cognitive Domain*. New York: McKay, 1956, 207 pp.
2. Mager, Robert F., *Preparing Objectives for Programmed Instruction*. San Francisco: Fearon, 1962.
3. Krathwohl, David R., Benjamin S. Bloom, and Bertram B. Masia, *Taxonomy of Educational Objectives, Handbook II: Affective Domain*. New York: McKay, 1964, 196 pp.

# PART THREE

# Descriptions of Basic Activities

A substantial array of basic supervisory activities has been identified. Some 26 reasonably distinctive activities might be regarded as *basic* in the sense that they can serve rather fundamental purposes of promoting human growth and development. These have previously been identified by Harris (53). A limited number of these activities will here be described and analyzed with respect to their use in in-service programs.

An activity is properly designated as basic when it is defined in such a way as to clearly delineate the kind of endeavors in which the leader and participants are engaged when that activity is being employed. Hence the term *interview* usually brings to mind an image of two people, one asking questions or at least giving general direction to the activity and the other responding to him. Of course, the term also suggests verbal interaction in a relatively private environment, as contrasted with other kinds of activities in which two people might be engaged. In this sense, then, interviewing is a basic activity characterized by a distinctive set of behaviors and situational factors.

Similarly, the term *group discussion* is relatively descriptive of a distinct set of behaviors and situational factors. This term generally brings to mind the image of a small group sitting around a table or in a circle, engaging in behavior that is largely verbal, with interaction between leader and group as well as among group members.

On the other hand, terms such as *conference* do not tend to be so clearly descriptive. This term is used in a variety of ways. It may be a synonym for interview. It may mean a large professional gathering. Even when this term is used to mean an organized series of group activities involving a large number of participants, it provides very little in the way of clues as to the kinds of behavior involved. Even if the term *conference* brings familiar experiences to mind, it still does not describe a basic activity because a distinctive set of behaviors and situational factors cannot be associated with it. Accordingly, it is much more useful to think of a term in which several activities such as those mentioned above are brought together and used by a single large group.

232

Although terms like *brainstorming, group discussion, role-playing,* and *demonstration* do tend to identify rather distinctive sets of behaviors in reasonably specific situations, they do not indicate the problems towards which these activities are directed or the purposes they are supposed to serve. This is another way in which these activities are truly basic. That is, they may be applicable to a variety of problems, serving a variety of purposes in a number of different educational contexts. As such, they are basic tools with which to work upon an array of problems.

In this chapter, a few useful basic activities are described and analyzed. This is not an exhaustive list, and in certain instances an activity is described singularly when several variations or alternate forms actually exist. The purpose of the authors in Part III is to describe a good selection of basic activities to serve any leader seeking to organize in-service programs for nearly any purpose in nearly any school situation. Some of these activities will be familiar to the reader from other professional sources or from first-hand experience. When this is true, the reader might find it valuable to check his previous impressions of those activities against the descriptions presented here. In other instances, the reader may find a new or strange activity being described. Where this is the case, we would advise that the description be studied carefully and that this type of activity be selected for use in in-service training programs with some caution and with careful planning and preparation.

Each of the activities is presented so as to give the practitioner a brief, practical guide to its use. To maintain this part of the book as a ready reference, the authors have made as brief a presentation of each basic activity as is consistent with its clear and adequate description. When the reader is somewhat familiar with an activity, this abbreviated description will suffice as a reminder and will provide helpful hints on planning and making in-service arrangements. Selected references for further study of each activity are also provided.

In Part II, entire laboratory sessions using various activities were described in some detail. The differences between laboratory sessions and the activities described here are several. A single activity rarely provides the kinds of impact required for in-service growth to occur. On the other hand, an in-service design could conceivably consist of a single activity repeated several times. The relationship of a basic activity to a laboratory session or other in-service session is that basic activities are components carefully put together for a desired effect in a larger design—the laboratory session. Hence, the session on interview styles in Chapter 9 involves role-playing, demonstrating, and discussing. The first session on classroom observation in Chapter 7 involves film viewing, testing, visualized lecturing, and group discussion.

Each basic activity described and analyzed has a place in one or more of the laboratory sessions presented in Part II. These are also useful, of course, as basic building blocks for constructing other in-service programs.

# Section One

# BRAINSTORMING*

DEFINITION

Brainstorming is an activity in a group session in which ideas held by participants are orally expressed with special procedures employed to *avoid* any discussion, criticism, or analysis. Some record or report of all ideas is maintained for later use. It is essentially an oral inventory of ideas.

PURPOSES

—To inform all participants of ideas held by others.

—To stimulate the development of ideas.

—To provide an inventory of ideas for later use.

—To suggest a variety of alternative approaches to problems.

—To influence opinions or attitudes regarding the state of thinking of the group.

—To cultivate positive attitudes towards alternative approaches to problems.

PROCEDURE

*Orientation is given to the group of participants* on brainstorming. A problem, topic, or issue is selected as the focus for the brainstorming activity. The selected focus is clearly described to the group to assure

---

*A. F. Osborn is generally credited with having originated this term and formalized the activity itself.

unity in the frame of reference employed by each brainstormer. The "ground rules" or special procedures are made explicit, as follows:

1. All ideas related to the focus in any direct way are desired.
2. A maximum number of related ideas is desired.
3. One idea may be modified or adapted and expressed as another idea. (This is sometimes called "hitch hiking" on ideas.)
4. Ideas should be expressed as clearly and concisely as possible.
5. No discussion of ideas should be attempted.
6. No criticism of ideas should be attempted.

*A time period is established for the brainstorming* to fit the situation, type of problem in focus, size of group, and so on. Ordinarily, 20 to 30 minutes is minimal. Often, brainstorming can continue effectively for an hour or more. When ideas run out and interest seems to wane, the leader should terminate the session.

*Ideas are permitted to "flow" without formality.* In a large group, the leader may recognize individuals. In a small group, spontaneous expressions may be more desirable without formal recognition.

*Each idea is recorded* by a person designated as recorder. The ideas may be slightly abbreviated but should *not* be changed in context or terminology any more than absolutely necessary. Ideas are recorded on a chalkboard, transparency, or large chart so that participants can refer to them during the brainstorming session.

*The group leader might want to repeat ideas* as expressed to indicate acceptance of each and to make sure others hear each idea. In very large groups, the leader can use a microphone on a long cord, and move around among participants to assure that every contribution is heard. The leader encourages rapid-fire expression of ideas, restricts his comments, repeats ideas if necessary, and avoids any criticism by word, facial expression, or tone of voice. He receives every idea with enthusiasm and acceptance as something worthy of expression and future consideration. If ideas begin to flow which are distinctly irrelevant, the leader should briefly restate the focus and ask for ideas related to it without being critical of specific ideas.

*The leader allows silence to prevail* after a round of expressions. Silent periods provide time for thought. New ideas may be generating. A period of silence lasting thirty seconds seems long, but it is often essential to idea production. When silence is no longer productive of new ideas, when the same ideas are being repeated, when interest seems to wane, or when available time has been exhausted, the leader terminates the session.

*A brief feedback session* on the many ideas recorded should be provided to let participants see how productive they have been.

*Recorded ideas, slightly edited,* should be made available for whatever follow-up uses have been planned.

1. Buzz sessions for analysis and criticism of ideas
2. Group discussion for analysis, criticism, assigning priorities, proposing revisions, combining ideas, and so on
3. Committee sessions for editing, revising, and suggesting ways of implementing ideas
4. Panel discussion of ideas for the purpose of suggesting combinations, challenging, or suggesting implementation procedures

ARRANGEMENTS

*Group size*  Two or more people can do brainstorming. Ordinarily ten or more will produce good results. A large group of 60 to 70 people tends to work quite well. When larger groups are involved, special facilities are almost essential, and two or three leaders may be needed to receive ideas simultaneously and record them as they flow from the group.

*Facilities*  Formal seating can be used if necessary. Chalkboard, overhead projector with transparent sheets or acetate roll, or large sheets of newsprint or butcher paper on the wall can be used for recording ideas. Microphones may be required as the size of the group and the acoustics demand. The "man in the audience" technique with a microphone on a long extension cord can be very effective in securing maximum idea flow in minimum time.

*Personnel*  A group leader can handle all responsibilities for conducting the activity of a small group. With larger groups, recorders and assistant leaders need to be added. The leader must be able to encourage and stimulate while avoiding directiveness.

ILLUSTRATION

A new video-tape recorder had been purchased by the West Valley Schools in connection with an in-service training project and a demonstration center. As the in-service project was nearing completion, the superintendent felt the need for ideas about future uses for the recorder. He wanted ideas for use by a planning committee, and he wanted to get his school principals and supervisory staff as much involved as possible.

A dinner meeting was planned, and all principals and supervisors were invited. After dinner, the superintendent briefly described his purpose in bringing the group together. He then introduced a college consultant who had been working in the West Valley schools. The consultant reviewed the procedures for brainstorming, set a time limit of 40 minutes, and assured the group that follow-up on their ideas was planned by the special committee. He then asked for all ideas.

The ideas came slowly at first. The consultant used a chalkboard to record ideas himself while asking an elementary supervisor in the group to act as "official recorder." Soon, the ideas began to flow more rapidly:

"We should involve other grade levels."

"Can we get beyond Language Arts into other subject areas?"

"Let's turn attention to Special Education."

"Video-taping in real classroom situations would be worthwhile."

"Can you get video-tape presentations of units, for example, physical education?"

"How about using tapes to inform the public of plans?"

"How much of this can be assumed by our own staff? What additional staff is needed?"

As several of the ideas seemed somewhat irrelevant, the consultant reviewed the focus: "Remember, we're trying to get any and every idea on how we might use the video-tape recorder for in-service purposes." The group resumed without further interruption:

"Let's get teachers involved in planning for demonstrations."

"Develop narrowly focused demonstrations involving specific skills."

"Homogeneous groups of observers should be tried."

"Can't we involve certain teachers according to their needs or interests?"

"Use the recorder for demonstrations of model faculty meetings."

"Let's plan for specific needs of teachers—beginning teachers as well as experienced teachers."

"Use the tapes to help the teacher see her own progress."

"Explore possibilities of bringing in specialists to demonstrate."

"A mobile unit to operate in classrooms would be helpful."

"Teachers need to have information on what to look for in demonstrations."

After the 40 minutes came to an end, the consultant asked the recorder to report. "Tell us how many ideas you have listed, and read them in abbreviated form for our review." The elementary supervisor took about five minutes to read some 60 ideas. The consultant turned the meeting back to the superintendent, suggesting that he comment on next steps in making use of these very interesting ideas.

## CAUTIONS AND LIMITATIONS

Brainstorming should not be used without follow-up. Participants enjoy brainstorming, *but* they also expect something to be done with their ideas.

Brainstorming should not be used unless there is a real need for a look at all available ideas or the production of new ideas, or both, by a group. Obviously, this implies that the group has some knowledge about, or interest in, the topic or problem in focus. It would be useless to brainstorm with a group lacking either knowledge or interest. On the other hand, when a problem can be solved by consultation with an expert, brainstorming is hardly in order despite the group's interest. When only one or two alternative solutions are feasible, brainstorming is inappropriate.

Participants should be cautioned that not all ideas can be implemented, that critical analysis must follow, and that not all ideas should be expected to survive the process.

SUMMARY

Brainstorming is an activity for stimulating idea expression and production. It can be used to inform, stimulate, and develop understanding and attitudes relating to a problem and a group. The special procedures that are employed make this activity unique, and it is usable with a wide range of group sizes. Extra precautions should be observed to plan appropriate follow-up activities and to avoid use of brainstorming for inappropriate purposes.

# Section Two

# BUZZ SESSIONS

DEFINITION

The buzz session is a small-group activity in which groups are temporarily formed to discuss a specific topic with minimum structure, maximum emphasis upon interaction, and full opportunity to express ideas related to the topic. An optimum amount of critical analysis of ideas related to the topic is encouraged in a permissive topic-centered situation.

**PURPOSES**

—To facilitate maximum verbal interaction among participants.
—To promote understanding of all points of view held by participants.
—To determine the possibility of arriving at consensus on certain points.
—To identify points of view that are distinctly at issue.
—To stimulate interest in and commitment to working on a project or problem.

**PROCEDURE**

A group which has focused its attention upon a topic or problem issue is divided into sub-groups referred to as "buzz groups."

*Each buzz group is assigned a specific location* in which it is to work. Usually this is around a table, but in a large auditorium setting it may be simply an identified section of the available space or a cluster of chairs.

*Buzz groups are asked to focus very specifically upon a given topic.* This topic is identified, defined, and described in advance by the leader so that all will be tuned in on it.

*Buzz groups are given a definite time limit* during which they are expected to discuss, analyze, and maximize their expression of ideas about the topic. Ordinarily, a minimum of 10 to 15 minutes is provided. A topic of some complexity may require 40 minutes to an hour and a half.

A *"recorder" is designated for each buzz group*, with instructions to record the highlights of ideas expressed including main points of view, agreements, disagreements, and suggestions.

*Buzz groups are informed that completely free interaction* with full expression of all ideas is being sought. In buzz sessions, unlike in brainstorming, participants should feel free to discuss, agree, disagree, or suggest alternatives. The interaction should be spirited, free-flowing, and unrestricted. On the other hand, participants should be cautioned against making long-winded speeches or dominating the discussion.

A *"discussion leader" is usually appointed*, simply to facilitate interaction. Leaders should be selected who will not dominate or overstructure but simply encourage full, fair, and well-distributed participation. Sometimes no discussion leader is appointed, in which case the groups are clearly informed that there will be none. In such instances, each buzz group may be instructed to select its own leader, or a leaderless group-discussion procedure may be followed in which each individual is expected not only to be a fully participating discussant but also to facilitate the participation of others.

*Recorders are asked to keep their notes brief* and central to the discussion topic. They should report orally, but very briefly, to the group at the end of the buzz session.

*Recorders should turn notes over to appropriate officials* for follow-up activity planning.

*Leaders should circulate among buzz groups*, "eavesdropping" but *not* verbally participating in the interaction. This gives the leaders a feel for the quality of thinking and the ideas emerging. It also eliminates any notion on the part of participants that they have been abandoned by their leaders.

SUGGESTED FOLLOW-UP ACTIVITIES

1. A panel or symposium of recorders or selected participants and consultants analyze ideas expressed.
2. Recorders' notes are analyzed, and study groups, committees, lectures, or discussion groups are organized.
3. A tentative draft of a written document may be developed by a representative committee to synthesize ideas as a policy statement or in other appropriate form for review by all participants.

ARRANGEMENTS

*Group size*    It takes at least five participants to have an effective spontaneous buzz session. When total groups vary from ten to 40 participants, buzz groups of five to eight persons work quite well. When large total groups are involved, buzz groups can be a bit larger to avoid the need for so many separate locations.

*Facilities*   A buzz group can work most effectively about a round table. A rectangular table works well *if* it is not too long and narrow. When tables are not available or the buzz groups are too large (tables seating more than ten persons rarely facilitate interaction), a small circle of chairs is quite satisfactory. When a circle is used, it should be as small as is consistent with the size of the group and the comfort of the participants.

No "head" position should be designated—neither a round table nor circle has a head. If a rectangular table is used, the leader should avoid sitting at either end, as this is associated with the "seat of authority" in the minds of many persons.

Each buzz group should be separated from all others far enough to avoid interference with one another. Buzz groups can be assigned to separate rooms if any are available *close at hand.* If such facilities are not available, large spaces such as a library reading room, an auditorium, a cafeteria, or a gymnasium can be used by designating a corner for each buzz group.

*Personnel*   Leaders and recorders are needed. The recorders should be persons who can screen ideas, digest, synthesize, and analyze. They should not be "stenographers." The leaders of buzz groups have only nominal leadership responsibilities. They must be coached in advance to avoid any unnecessary structuring, formal procedures, or controlling efforts. They should act as facilitators and stimulators. A brief training session is very desirable for leaders and recorders. Such a session might consist of a buzz session in which skilled personnel demonstrate how to lead and record.

*Name Tags*   Buzz groups work better when the participants know the names and something about the persons in the group. Name tags are advisable when even a few persons do not know each other. Color coding of name tags to show position, affiliation, or interest can help.

ILLUSTRATION

The Georgetown High School building was a shining new monument to educational progress. It was the first school building constructed in Georgetown in many years, and it served the people on "the other side of the tracks." Superintendent James Ramey took real pride in promoting this new building for the "poor kiddoes." His assistant, Bill Holdsworth, had worked closely with the architect and selected staff members to be sure that instructional facilities were designed for flexibility and modern methods.

As the fall semester began in the new building, painters and electricians were still finishing their work. Trouble with the air-conditioning system caused some difficulty in September, and projection screens were still not installed in October. Despite these inconveniences, the staff members carried on as best they could. Everyone was enthusiastic about the new building. The students seemed to reflect their pride in both conduct and appearance.

By late October, Bill Holdsworth was able to turn from mechanical details to instructional concerns. He was commissioned by the superintendent to work with the high school principal and staff in developing an outstanding instructional program. Here was a fine facility, an eager and able teaching staff, and a waiting community. The new language lab could accommodate foreign language, drama, speech, and regular English classes. Some classrooms had folding walls for large group instruction. Windowless construction made extensive use of visual aids practical. A beautiful library was available, and no study halls cluttered the facility. Bill decided to move before the holiday season to stimulate the faculty group and to get plans developed for improving instructional practices.

In consultation with the principal, Holdsworth arranged for school to be dismissed a bit early on the following Wednesday, October 27. The principal announced to his faculty that a special program planning meeting would be held on that day, in the library, from 2:45 until 4:30. Holdsworth got in touch with a university professor who was familiar with the building and willing to serve as a consultant to the faculty. He agreed to attend this meeting and make a few introductory remarks.

As the faculty group assembled at about 2:40, coffee and cookies were served. The principal called the meeting to order at 2:50, introduced the visiting consultant, and briefly stated the purpose of the meeting. Holdsworth then reviewed the plan of action.

"We want to begin thinking seriously about ways of using this building so as to provide the best possible instructional program. Superintendent Ramey has assured me that we can have just as much freedom as we need to try new ideas. We've had a couple of months now to get school started and become familiar with the building. These have been trying months for all of you, but things are now under control. We'd like to move with you in the direction of identifying *promising new ways of working at teaching*. If you can come up with some promising ideas, we'll work with you in developing project plans and trying these ideas this spring and next year.

"Now, to get to work today, we'd like to have you break into buzz groups. We will break into four groups of eight and nine persons each. The purpose of all of the groups will be the same. You are to concentrate on suggesting new teaching practices which might be worth trying in this school. Each group should try to identify a few practices which someone in that group finds promising. Each practice suggested should be discussed and analyzed freely. When the session is over in about 40 minutes, you should have one or more new teaching practices to propose in fairly well developed form. Your group does not need to agree upon the value of the practice. You are not committing yourself or anyone else to adopting any practices. You are simply developing some promising ideas for further serious consideration.

"Now are you ready to go to work?"

At this point, Holdsworth made quick buzz group assignments, getting clusters of teachers into four corners of the library where large tables had already been arranged. Group leaders were not designated, but a recorder had been assigned to each buzz group and instructed in note-taking procedures.

Holdsworth, the visiting consultant, and the principal circulated from group to group. They did not enter into the discussion. Instead, they listened for a few moments, sitting at the edge of the circle of participants. After about five minutes of "eavesdropping," the three men changed buzz groups. This was repeated at intervals until all three had listened to each group twice and had a "feeling" for the thinking in progress.

After 35 minutes, Holdsworth interrupted with an announcement. "Will you try to pull your thoughts together in the next five minutes, please? Your recorder has been taking notes. Let that person review the highlights of those notes, and then spend the remaining time getting your suggestions formalized. We'll ask recorders to report suggestions of each buzz group to the total group at 3:45."

As Bill stopped talking, the buzz of interaction reached a high pitch. Each group was now under pressure to pull its diverse ideas together. By 3:40, three groups were breaking up. By 3:45, the recorder in the last group made final notes, and Bill called for attention, directing all participants to be seated again in the center of the library. Recorders reported their suggestions after being cautioned to take only one minute each. The visiting consultant wrote brief phrases on a transparency as the recorders mentioned each major suggestion. When the reporting was over, Holdsworth asked the visiting consultant to discuss the suggestions that were made. He did so, using the visual he had prepared based on the reports. He focused attention upon similarities in suggestions, commenting on uses of facilities for implementing suggestions, and emphasizing the need for attention to what is known about good teaching before any suggestions are selected for development into project plans.

The principal concluded the meeting with a request: "I hope each of you will give some further thought to these teaching ideas in the next week. We will be asking for volunteer groups to do further planning on some of these ideas with the expectation that several new things will be in progress by early spring. Meeting adjourned."

### CAUTIONS AND LIMITATIONS

Buzz sessions, like most other in-service activities, do not suffice without follow-up activities. Unlike brainstorming, buzz sessions are rarely used as introductory activities; they presume some prior events. For each session to be effective, participants must have a concern for the problem or an interest in the topic, some knowledge about the problem or topic, and opinions, attitudes, or feelings to express.

Buzz sessions should be avoided when attitudes, opinions, and feelings of the participants are not of crucial importance in approaching the problem. Teachers might appropriately engage in a buzz session when the topic is how to allocate library funds to various categories of instructional materials. A buzz session on the format of the purchase order, on the other hand, is probably not worthwhile.

Similarly, when a problem is such that expert advice is required, this should either precede or substitute for a buzz session. When a problem has only one feasible solution, a buzz session is inappropriate, except as a way of testing the hypothesis that no other solution is feasible.

### SUMMARY

The buzz session is an activity which permits maximum face-to-face interaction in small groups even when large numbers of participants need to be involved. This activity has been used for a variety of purposes. It serves especially well when interest, stimulation and consideration of diverse points of view are required. As temporary groups, buzz groups can be organized with maximum flexibility and can function with a minimum of structure. Lead-up activities are important to the success of a buzz session, and follow-up activities are essential.

# Section Three

# DEMONSTRATIONS

The demonstration is an activity in which participants observe planned, carefully presented examples of real or simulated behavior illustrating certain techniques, materials, equipment, and procedures as they might realistically be employed. Techniques, materials, and other elements are presented in as nearly natural a context as possible to give observing participants the illusion of reality. Departures from reality are planned where necessary to focus attention upon those selected elements being demonstrated.

**PURPOSES**

—To inform observing participants of the materials, equipment, skills, procedures, and other elements involved.

—To develop understanding about the time and space relationships between the various elements being demonstrated.

—To stimulate interest in the use of the techniques, materials, and procedures being demonstrated.

**PROCEDURE**

Specific procedures will vary with the particular bit of reality being demonstrated. The demonstration might focus upon a number of behaviors involved in conducting a certain lesson. Another demonstration might focus upon a minute series of finger movements required for threading a motion-picture projector. In any instance, basic procedures will include:

**245**

(1) defining the focus of the demonstration, (2) selecting a person or persons to demonstrate, (3) planning the demonstration itself, (4) arranging for observers to view effectively, and (5) conducting follow-up activities of appropriate kinds.

*Define the focus of the demonstration* just as specifically as possible. Expect one demonstration to accomplish only a limited purpose. If a series of different purposes is intended, define each and plan a series of demonstrations. For instance, a single demonstration planned "to show how to use the 16mm projector" is not feasible because many techniques and procedures are implied by the term "to use." "To show the correct threading and rewinding of the 16mm projector" suggests limiting the demonstration to mechanical operations, procedures, and techniques. Even with such a specific purpose, a carefully planned sequence is necessary to bring each element into focus in a meaningful way. Hence, the focus might shift from "properly unwinding the leader" to "placing the film reel on the spindle," to "accurately adjusting the film in its channel," and then to some other procedure.

*Select a person (or persons) for a demonstrator* who has considerable skill and knowledge of the specifics being demonstrated. Avoid selecting someone "who makes a pleasing appearance" but has little to offer otherwise. When a demonstrator is being asked to present something new in his or her experience, a person's flexibility and interest in new practices may be crucial.

*Demonstration planning should be very detailed.* One or more supervisory staff members should consult with the demonstrator in developing the plans. A sequence like the one below is often useful:

1. Ask the demonstrator to outline the sequence of events which might be followed in the demonstration.
2. Review the demonstrator's outline and revise it by eliminating any elements that are unnecessary and by adding any necessary new elements.
3. Develop a revised demonstration plan, giving a detailed description of each event in sequence and all the materials and/or equipment required.
4. Stage a "dry run" of the demonstration with only a few persons present to suggest refinements.
5. Revise the demonstration plan and work out a carefully developed time schedule with briefing and follow-up plans included.
6. Prepare materials for observers to use before, during, or after the demonstration. These should include an agenda for the entire session, orientation materials which would provide background information, sketches to assist with interpretations, and an observation instrument which encourages notetaking.

*Design the demonstration to make maximum use of viewing,* using listening as a supporting element. This means that realism might have to be sacrificed in part to facilitate a clear view. Dialogue should be of a kind that would be natural to the situation being demonstrated. Explanatory comments should be avoided if they sacrifice realism and should be very limited in any event.

*Select participants carefully,* using criteria that give assurance of having the people there who can and will profit from the demonstration. Participants may be selected on the basis of interest, expressed need, or diagnosed need. Avoid selecting participants on the basis of "the more the merrier," or "anybody could get something out of it," or "all new teachers should go." Include status persons who could assist with follow-up activities, including principals, deans, supervisors, or department heads.

*Introduce the demonstration briefly,* giving any information necessary for meaningful viewing. Encourage the use of orientation materials during the demonstration. Withhold explanations, analysis, and discussion for follow-up activities *after* the demonstration.

*Plan some immediate follow-up* for the demonstration while impressions are vivid and interest is high. Use the demonstrator as one resource person in follow-up activities, but do not expect this person to take heavy follow-up responsibilities! The demonstrator may be handicapped in a variety of ways, such as fatigue, emotional involvement, or the need to shift his role.

SUGGESTED FOLLOW-UP ACTIVITIES

1.  Discussion of techniques, procedures, and materials observed.
2.  Laboratory session in which observers in a group attempt to do what they have seen demonstrated.
3.  Directed practice sessions in which the individual observer is guided in his efforts to do what has been demonstrated.
4.  Interview for planning ways of using demonstrated procedures or techniques in a real situation.

ARRANGEMENTS

*Group size*   The size of the group is restricted only by the need for each individual to see and hear. Very large group situations tend to produce difficulties in viewing, listening, and follow-up. On the other hand, the staff time and expense involved in producing a good demonstration may be excessive when observed only by very small groups.* Demonstrations

---

*However, video-taping of demonstrations permits use with many people in nearly any group size.

involving large objects and movements and clearly audible sounds can easily serve a group of 40 to 50 observers. Demonstrations involving small objects and movements may require groups of only five to ten observers.

*Facilities*    Essential facilities include good lighting and acoustics, sitting or standing room for good viewing, and a physical setting that can be "staged" to approximate reality. An auditorium offers a sloped floor and good lighting to insure good viewing. A classroom offers ideal physical surroundings for some types of teaching demonstrations. A cafeteria or gymnasium often serves well where space is an important requirement or where "central staging" is advantageous. Microphones suspended over the demonstration area assist with the sound problem. If necessary, the demonstrator should have a microphone with a long cord about his neck facilitating movement and leaving his hands free.

*Personnel*    The selection and use of the demonstrator has previously been discussed. In addition, an in-service session leader or chairman should be designated to introduce the demonstration, give directions to observer participants, and direct the transition to follow-up activities. Follow-up activity group leaders who are familiar with the purposes of the demonstration should be selected, trained, and briefed in advance. It may or may not be appropriate for the viewing session leader to lead follow-up activities as well. The special skills and knowledge required for follow-up activities will indicate appropriate leaders.

*Special note*    The use of closed-circuit television as a medium for viewing demonstrations and producing taped recordings has been gaining interest and is being used. Such approaches to the use of demonstrations involve a host of special arrangements, additional skilled leaders, and some special procedures (13).

ILLUSTRATION

Carson Creek school officials were trying to get their elementary school teachers to adopt demonstration and laboratory approaches to the teaching of science. Strong criticisms had been expressed by visiting team members when they wrote their evaluation report for regional accreditation. The report said, "The science program appears to be textbook bound. Few experiences which would stimulate curiosity, discovery, or analytical thinking are included in science lessons beyond the kindergarten level. Demonstrations, experiments, and projects are needed in this program."

With this problem in mind, the curriculum director arranged for a specialist in elementary school science to assist with the planning of an in-service program for fifth and sixth grade teachers. A demonstration was planned with follow-up discussion sessions. The specific purposes of the demonstration were agreed upon as follows:

1. To demonstrate the use of a simple demonstration technique in elementary science.
2. To illustrate the use of a simple demonstration for stimulating analytical thinking.
3. To demonstrate the role of the teacher as a stimulator and a guide in the discovery process rather than as an information giver.

A science education specialist from a nearby college had been invited to assist in improving the science program. He had observed in a number of Carson Creek classrooms and spent the morning before the demonstration in Mrs. Gilbert's fifth grade room. Preplanning involved Mrs. Gilbert, the principal, the curriculum director, and the science specialist. This is how the demonstration progressed:

*2:40* Teachers began to arrive in the selected classroom. The science specialist had already assembled a small group of students from Mrs. Gilbert's room in front of a table. Pupil desks were pushed aside and 40 chairs were arranged in three semi-circles.

*2:45* The curriculum director called the group to order and introduced the demonstrator. He referred to the children as "a volunteer group from Mrs. Gilbert's fifth grade room." With brief reference to the materials given each teacher as he or she entered the room, the demonstration began.

*2:50* "Boys and girls, you and I are really on the spot with all these teachers watching us, aren't we? Well, let's try to forget them and just relax and act natural. Actually, I think you'll find this fun as we get going. We're going to play a game. It's a brain-teasing kind of game. Are you ready?"

A few said "yes," "um-huh," and "ok."

The demonstrator reached under the table, opened a box, and brought out a Coke bottle. The children made remarks reflecting interest, wonder, and anticipation.

*2:55* "No. We are not going to drink this Coke. I have only the one bottle. That's not enough to go around. Besides we have a more important job for that bottle."

He placed the bottle on the table where children and audience could see it well.

"Now, watch that bottle while I put a few things on this board." He walked to the chalk board and wrote at the top, "Testing a Theory."

He returned to the table, looked at the bottle, and asked, "Now, what do you observe?" Moisture was collecting on the bottle. Someone said so. "Good. Let's write that down. Scientists need to record their observations." He went to the chalkboard and placed a new heading at one side: "Observed Evidence." Under this he wrote: "1. Moisture is forming on the bottle."

*2:58* Staying near the board, he asked, "What else do you observe?" Someone said, "It's cold." The demonstrator asked, "How do you observe that? Can you see it?" Many students quickly responded, "No!"

"Well, how do you observe coldness? I've a hunch that it is cold, but we should have some tangible evidence. We *infer* that it is cold, but how can we secure evidence?"

A boy waved his hand vigorously. The demonstrator pointed to him and said, "What evidence would you like to offer?" The boy said, "You can feel it to see if it's cold."

"Good! Come up and do that." The boy came forward eagerly, touched the bottle, and said, "Yep, it's cold and wet." The demonstrator turned to the board and wrote: "2. The bottle feels wet. 3. The bottle feels cold."

He then turned to the students again. "All right, do you observe anything else?" There was silence.

*3:03* "Well, let me ask you a question. Where does the moisture come from?" Many hands went up and the demonstrator led a little discussion, giving the students a chance to show their knowledge about condensation, air, humidity, dew point, and so on. The demonstrator did not judge the statements of the students. He simply encouraged full participation in the discussion. Nearly everyone had some information to offer. Disagreements were resolved by the students themselves.

*3:10* Finally, the demonstrator interrupted. "You know, I have another theory about this moisture formation on the bottle. I believe it comes from inside the bottle!" The students giggled. "Seriously, now. Consider my theory. The bottle is cold. As the room is not cold, the liquid inside must be getting warmer. As it becomes warmer it expands. The pressure inside the bottle increases, and under pressure the moisture seeps through the slightly porous glass of the bottle. What do you think about that?"

The students responded excitedly. Each student was eager to deny this theory and state his own ideas. The demonstrator said nothing. He let them express themselves quite fully.

*3:18* Finally, he said, "Well, you may be correct, but you haven't offered any new evidence to support your theory nor any evidence casting doubt on my theory! All you've been saying is that your theory is correct. It may be, but then, mine may be correct. The evidence we have supports my theory just as well as it does yours. How can we gather evidence regarding my theory?"

There was utter silence. The students frowned. The demonstrator said not a word. Several students looked again at the bottle as if the answer might be written upon it. Silence continued for nearly 30 seconds.

*3:20*  Finally, one girl blurted out in a frustrated tone, "Well, the Coke's not going down in the bottle!" The demonstrator argued, "Well, it may be too soon to tell. Your observation is a fine one though." He went to the board and put up a new heading. "Tests to Consider."

"This young lady tells us that we could logically test my theory." He wrote: "1. Observe whether the liquid level changes."

"Can anyone suggest another test? This one will take some time." A boy waved his hand and then blurted out, "You could weigh it!" The demonstrator wrote: "2. Weigh the Coke bottle."

"What would you expect to find by weighing it?" The boy explained his test. Another student objected. "The moisture would still be there whether on the inside or on the outside. It would weigh the same." The demonstrator nodded. Another student volunteered a suggestion, "Well, you could wipe the bottle dry, and then weigh it. Then wipe it dry again and weigh it. That way, it should have less weight *if* your theory is correct."

## CAUTIONS AND LIMITATIONS

Status leaders are generally better advised to arrange demonstrations than to become demonstrators. The time of such leaders is scarce and a number of demonstrations could be arranged in the time required to prepare a single demonstration. Demonstrations by peers seem better accepted in many instances, and those working regularly with students, materials, and subject matter can demonstrate with greater economy of time.

Don't expect demonstrations to develop skills. Knowledge and understanding may come from watching a demonstration, but skill development is another matter.

Selection of observers in terms of their needs and interests is important. Those who know what is to be demonstrated but lack the skill, interest, or willingness to adopt the practices will not gain much from the demonstration. On the other hand, those struggling and frustrated by simple problems of educational practice should be exposed to demonstrations with caution to prevent further frustration. Finally, a demonstration should be geared to offering observers something new or different, or at least a more highly refined practice.

Avoid demonstrations which are so staged and rehearsed that all semblance of realism is lost. Careful, detailed planning with a trial run should *not* involve rehearsal in the theatrical sense. If students are involved, they should know the plan in sufficient detail to know what to expect, but their behavior should be *real*, spontaneous, and natural.

SUMMARY

The demonstration is one of the truly promising in-service activities for acquainting a group with practices, procedures, and techniques of a wide variety. Demonstrators try to retain verisimilitude while structuring the presentation to focus on very specific things to be learned by observers.

In making demonstrations truly effective, a skilled demonstrator is assisted by developing a very detailed plan. A trial run of the demonstration is undertaken so that revisions of the plan can be made. Selected observers are provided with a briefing and materials so that they know why they are observing, what to look for, and how to look, and they are actively, analytically involved.

Follow-up activities are planned to emphasize the demonstration's purposes, and also to facilitate adoption and adaptation of demonstrated practices.

# Section Four

# GROUP DISCUSSIONS

**DEFINITION**

A group discussion is a small group activity usually extending over a prolonged period of time in which systematic verbal interaction on a given topic (or problem) leads to consensus, decisions, recommendations, or clearly recognized disagreement. An extended lifespan assures the development of a genuine group with clearly defined group purposes, as distinguished from an aggregation of individuals sharing independent ideas.

**PURPOSES**

—To share the knowledge of individuals with others in the group.
—To develop understanding about complex problems.
—To analyze proposals for dealing with problems.
—To stimulate the development of new attitudes and opinions.
—To arrive at carefully considered decisions for dealing with complex problems.

**PROCEDURES**

Group discussion activities of a variety of kinds have been developed in recent years. The buzz session is a striking variation described earlier in this chapter. Case analysis and leaderless group discussion are briefly described as well. The procedures described here are those which apply to most discussion situations as defined. They would be modified somewhat, of course, as variations are employed.

*Analyze the selected problem (or topic)* to be sure that it is one which is important enough to justify the time required and is suitable for discussion as contrasted with the use of the lecture, buzz session, or other activity.

*Check to see that an appropriate group of discussants* is available. Discussants are appropriate when they have:

1. a real interest in the topic or problem,
2. a need to discuss the topic or problem, and
3. some pertinent information, opinions, or feelings concerning the topic or problem.

*Select an appropriate discussion leader.* It is not essential that the leader be an expert on the topic or problem in focus. In fact, expertness of that kind can complicate efforts towards efficient group action. The leader *must* have other characteristics, however. He should be interested in the problem, be reasonably knowledgeable about the various ramifications of the problem, have the respect of the group members, be open-minded regarding approaches to the problem, and have skill in discussion leading techniques.

*Provide training in discussion leading techniques for the leader.* Unless the person is already highly skilled, he usually welcomes an opportunity to receive training. Brief discussion sessions focusing upon vignettes of problem situations serve as effective training experiences when followed by critical analysis by a skilled discussion leader. Tape recordings of brief discussion sessions can be analyzed to help leaders employ techniques more skillfully.

*Organize the initial discussion session by informing prospective discussants of the problem and the nature of the group* being formed, suggest a tentative schedule and specify possible outcomes.

*Conduct the initial discussion sessions with emphasis on getting acquainted,* exploring the problem area, and reviewing and revising plans. It is not necessary or even desirable that procedural decisions be made at this point. Too much eagerness to "decide what to do and get it done" can lead to confusion and frustrate group cohesion.

*Conduct subsequent sessions with a focus upon the identification of the basic elements or specific problems* within the larger problem area. Relevant questions include: (1) What concerns participants most? (2) What is most important? (3) What may be resolved?

A group may have to wander verbally about the problem area without much semblance of direction for several sessions before basic elements or specific problems can be identified. Don't get discouraged with the group. Don't let the group get discouraged with itself. Expect some anxiety and discontent to be expressed, and accept it.

*Provide resources for gaining more knowledge relevant to the problem area.* This may involve use of films, books, pamphlets, visiting consultants, tape recordings, and similar resources. These should not be imposed on the group, but made available and their use encouraged by individuals and the group as a whole when appropriate.

*Encourage the group to make decisions or otherwise achieve benchmarks of its progress by consensus.* (These may be agreements, conclusions, disagreements, suggestions, and so forth.) Avoid formalities like voting or recording conclusions in very carefully worded language, but stimulate participants to consider progress and then move on.

*Encourage openmindedness in considering all ideas relevant to the basic problem or topic.* Encourage participants to assume the attitude of the trial judge who withholds judgment and considers all relevant evidence before rendering a verdict. In promoting this attitude among participants, the discussion leader sets the example and uses a variety of techniques:

1. Ask open-ended questions which stimulate a variety of responses.
2. Restate unpopular points of view with the suggestion that discussants might want to react.
3. Encourage the less active discussants to express themselves.
4. Encourage discussants to search out new information and report it to the group at appropriate times.
5. Invite resource persons to share relevant information with the group at appropriate times.
6. Accept all ideas expressed as worthy of consideration by the group.
7. Avoid ignoring or criticizing ideas that seem least acceptable.
8. Avoid promoting certain ideas over others.
9. Summarize main ideas, information, or points of view relevant to a basic element in the discussion to encourage full consideration.
10. Suggest postponement of decisions when consensus has not really been achieved or information is lacking.
11. Encourage the decision to agree, or to disagree when consensus does not seem possible.

*Encourage the group to project its own plan and timetable* for accomplishing its purposes and dissolving itself.

*Arrange for the recording of group outcomes.* This should not be a stenographic record but an abstract of ideas, agreements, disagreements, decisions, and plans. These notes should be maintained by one or more designated persons. The responsibility can be a rotating assignment among discussants or an assistant to the group can serve as permanent recorder. A copy of the recorder's notes should go to each discussant prior to the session.

CASE DISCUSSION

The case method in group discussion has been developed to provide for a more highly structured discussion situation. In this form a carefully developed case is presented to all discussants. A case is an objective report of a real situation in which many aspects of a complex problem are presented as information. This is usually a narrative description of a real situation which illustrates in very specific terms a problem or problems worthy of discussion. The case, then, not only stimulates meaningful participation, but also contains much relevant information for use by discussants.

In case discussions, the basic style and most techniques of discussion leading still apply. Certain procedures are significantly different.

Since the case is not the actual problem of the participants, and available information is readily available, less time is required for analysis and the interest span of the participants is likely to be relatively short. Such discussions are rarely extended over more than two or three sessions. Often a single two-hour session is the limit of time profitably spent.

Since the problem situation is described in narrative form with a minimum of irrelevant information included, discussants are led to analysis with a minimum of exploratory discussion.

A certain amount of interpretation has entered into the case writing as the writer selected information to include or omit. This places the leader in the position of one who stimulates participants to "discover" the interpretations which are possible. This places him in the role of one who already knows many of the alternatives. This may or may not be true in real problem-centered discussion groups. The case discussion leader, therefore, structures the discussion to some degree. It can be quite structured when used to illustrate only a specific theory, concept or pattern of events, but leaders should take care not to over-structure the discussion and lose spontaneity. Furthermore, a well-written case has potential for illustrating a variety of concepts, and speculation can be freely stimulated regarding the consequences that might follow from alternative events to those reported in the case. For such uses, the discussion technique must be much less structured.

LEADERLESS DISCUSSION

This variation of group discussion activity calls upon participants to share the leadership responsibilities described previously. The advantage offered by having no designated leader derives from the greater feeling of responsibility and involvement on the part of the discussants. Disadvantages include the possibility that leadership responsibilities will not be adequately assumed by participants. When leadership development and group assumption of responsibility are more important outcomes than problem-solving, leaderless discussions have much to offer.

Leaderless group discussions tend to require the following procedures:

1. The group is oriented regarding the absence of an assigned leader and the reasons for this unless the situation requires no such explanation. Each group member is encouraged to exercise responsibilities as both discussant and leader. Formal selection of a leader is discouraged, and the group is urged to guard against letting any one person exercise leadership for an extended period.

2. Leaderless groups are carefully observed by those responsible for organizing them. Should a group completely fall apart, a skilled leader may be assigned to the group just long enough to assist discussants in analyzing progress, setting new directions, and overcoming obstacles. This provides each group member with an opportunity to try his hand again at exercising leadership.

### SUGGESTED FOLLOW-UP ACTIVITIES

Frequently, a discussion group will have purposes which can be relatively well accomplished in the group without other follow-up activities. This is likely to be the case when development of attitudes, opinions, and understanding are the purposes selected. When decisions, suggestions, or recommendations for action come from a discussion group, the follow-up activities are important.

1. Publish a brief report on the conclusions of the group for dissemination to others interested in the same problem or topic.

2. Organize a committee or study group to formulate plans and make arrangements as suggested by the discussion group.

3. Undertake an action research or pilot project to develop and evaluate ideas generated in the group.

### ARRANGEMENTS

*Group size* A discussion group requires a sufficient number of participants to produce a working unit as contrasted with a very small number of individuals. On the other hand, a group requires few enough participants so that full interaction involving face-to-face contact is possible. Ordinarily a discussion group should be no smaller than seven or eight persons and no larger than 15.

*Facilities* Discussions should be held in a quiet, comfortable room. Chairs should be arranged in a circle, or oval, or around a table. The furniture should be arranged so that each individual can easily look at each other member of the group. A "head" position should be avoided. The leader should be designated by his behavior rather than his position in the circle. Chairs should be comfortable for fairly prolonged sitting.

*Personnel*    The need for a leader and a recorder has been discussed. Resource persons are important to the success of many discussion groups. Budgetary and other arrangements should be made for such persons to be available as needed by the group.

ILLUSTRATION *

The Austin schools, like many, were confronted with the problem of securing public acceptance and support for changes in the mathematics program under the label of "The New Math." Teacher attitudes posed a problem in some instances, too, but interest was highest in meeting the need for a program of parent information.

The mathematics supervisor developed plans for a discussion group to face this problem. Each junior and senior high school was asked to send one mathematics teacher—this made a total of 15 teachers. Most of these people were acquainted with one another and with the supervisor.

The discussions were scheduled in the conference room of School A, a new and modern school which was centrally located in the city. In the conference room, a large round table was available to seat up to 20 people.

A series of four sessions was tentatively planned. The sessions lasted from 3:00 p.m. to 5:00 p.m. with the teachers released from teaching duties during the last period of the school day. Coffee was served at the beginning of each session, and 10 to 15 minutes were used for social interaction at this time.

Since the group was formed for a special problem, the leader initiated the first session by a brief statement of the purpose and suggested that discussants share their experiences related to the problem. Several discussants began to ask about their responsibilities as related to the problem. The leader suggested that they might be able to clarify the problem and attempt to develop some recommendations for improving public relations in this field. The leader asked that each of the participants discuss the problem with his colleagues.

As a stimulus for the first discussion period, the leader used a tape recording obtained when a parent came to him for an interview. In the recording, the parent told about a back-to-school night experience with his child's math teacher. The child was taking geometry, and the teacher left the parent feeling that modern mathematics would make this course completely obsolete. Consequently, the parent felt that the child was wasting his time. The interview graphically illustrated a misunderstanding and the need for better public information.

The discussion followed from this in a free and spontaneous manner with the leader acting almost as a participant.

*This illustration was provided by Mr. Elgin Schilhab, mathematics supervisor, Austin Independent School District, Austin, Texas.

Sometimes group members engaged in side conversations in their eagerness to express views or feelings. These continued briefly but the leader encouraged all members to share their thoughts with the total group when such a side conversation continued. The leader interrupted occasionally to ask for clarification of some point or to summarize briefly. This usually stimulated still more discussion.

The discussion was scheduled to stop at 5:00 p.m., and the schedule was followed. In terminating the discussion, the supervisory leader briefly summarized major points and promised to provide a written review which discussants could refer to at the beginning of the next discusison period. The leader suggested some possible next steps for the group to consider, including an attempt to identify several of the more serious public relations problems. With that the session was adjourned.

### CAUTIONS AND LIMITATIONS

Do not assume that any informed, personable, or eager person can lead a group discussion effectively. The most highly informed person may inhibit discussion, and specific skills are required for discussion leading in any case. Training of a discussion leader is essential in most situations.

Avoid a discussion group in which opinions, attitudes, and knowledge of participants are highly similar. Diversity among group members is important.

Avoid the temptation to make critical decisions for the group when consensus cannot be reached. Similarly, avoid "taking a vote." If consensus has not been reached and the decision is really critical, the group is not ready for decision-making.

Avoid letting a discussion become a recitation in which the leaders ask questions and responds to everything that is said. The leader should generally be silent, and make his few questions as open-ended as possible to stimulate a variety of responses.

Avoid the tendency to get everyone participating by calling upon each participant in some systematic way. A good discussion leader gets everyone involved by stimulating free interaction, being sparing with his own remarks, and keeping others from dominating the discussion.

Do not be afraid of silence. Sometimes a group needs a chance just to sit and contemplate an idea or a problem. The silence will be broken when someone feels the need. In fact, most adults feel so uncomfortable with silence that a group discussion leader might have to encourage it occasionally.

Do not involve a discussion group in your problem unless it is also the group's problem in some significant way. Most people are too busy to deal with a problem for the time required in a discussion group unless they are interested and concerned. Leaders who organize discussion groups to make themselves feel less insecure with a problem are not likely to meet with success.

Do not organize a discussion group to support what you or some authority have already decided. Participants are very quick to sense that they are discussing a problem that the leader has already solved (in his own mind). A reasonably intelligent group sees through manipulation by the leader very quickly. Even the most skilled manipulator is less than successful in that his discussion group senses that something is not quite right and hence functions inefficiently and tends to lack creativity.

## SUMMARY

The group discussion is an activity facilitating extended group interaction with focus upon a problem or idea of common interest and concern. Such an activity under skillful leadership serves well in stimulating ideas, sharing information, developing understanding, and influencing attitudes and opinions. Discussion groups are not usually action groups except in that they can make decisions, recommendations, or express consensus and disagreement. They often provide the basis of understanding upon which action groups can operate.

In several modified forms, group discussions serve special purposes. The case method of discussion provides a unique approach to stimulating thinking about complex situations. The leaderless group discussion provides for maximum involvement and is a valuable approach to leader identification and training.

# Section Five

# ROLE-PLAYING

DEFINITION

Role-playing may be defined as a spontaneous dramatization involving one or more persons assuming designated roles in relation to a specified problem in a given situation. The drama is structured by the problem and the situation, but is unrehearsed and not preplanned. The objective is to encourage the fullest possible assumption of roles by the players so that they "act" and "feel" as they might in a real situation.

**PURPOSES**

—To provide concrete examples of behavior as a basis for discussion.

—To stimulate new attitude formation.

—To develop skill in interviewing and questioning, or others skills needed in spontaneous verbal interaction.

—To develop understanding of feelings and attitudes of other people.

**PROCEDURES**

Role-playing has been widely used to stimulate learning associated with problems of human interaction. The terms sociodrama and psychodrama have been used in describing role-playing activities of various kinds. The specific procedures vary depending upon the purposes, the size of the group, and the extent of involvement required. Essential procedures for role-playing under nearly any conditions seem to include establishing rapport, identifying a specific problem, assigning roles, adhering to roles, and terminating the activity at an appropriate time.

**261**

*Participants should feel comfortable* with each other if role-playing is to be "for real." Initial experiences with role-playing are often resisted, but a group readily learns to accept this kind of activity once it comes into use. Often a group leader can start role-playing by assuming roles and inviting one or more self-assured individuals to join him. Role-playing can be more comfortably experienced by some participants if two or three people are all involved and no audience is observing. Above all, leaders need to display a friendly, permissive, and constructive attitude towards all role-players as they get involved for the first few times.

*Role-players must be directed towards a very specific problem* to which all participants can relate. Roles must be played in terms of individuals interacting with others in a very concrete situation. A critical incident, a case, a lesson can be the basis for role-playing, but the players must act in terms of a specific time and place as well as having the problem clearly in mind. A lesson protocol such as the one in Chapter 8 might be used for this purpose, with the role-playing built upon this lesson involving this teacher, class, and period. However, each role-playing session should begin with a specific instance in the lesson with the leader suggesting, for instance, "Let's role-play that portion that starts with item number 68 and see how we would try to get expressions of pupil attitudes."

*Roles need to be specifically assigned* so each person knows what is expected of him. It is not wise to tell participants how to act, for spontaneity is essential. However, teacher, parent, pupil, principal, and other persons involved in the specific situation should be designated in advance. When one role is not too complimentary or flattering, it may be wise to ask a very well-liked participant to assume it. Roles do not need to *match* the people playing them. One of the characteristics that makes role-playing a very useful activity is the ease with which participants can assume a role and then return to reality and discuss it objectively.

*Role-players should be urged to adhere to assigned roles.* This is not always possible, but when roles are abandoned, the action should stop. If role-players find themselves unable to adhere to the role assigned, this may be the result of anxiety. However, participants can learn to adhere to roles with a bit of coaching and encouragement. Leaders should be alert to keep participants from getting into the habit of dropping out of a role when it becomes a bit awkward. Some self-discipline can be cultivated.

*Leaders should terminate* role-playing sessions at an appropriate time. Ordinarily, a few minutes of involvement in a role provides a lot of experience for discussion. If a role-player remains in his role too long, he may get emotionally involved to the point of embarrassment.

### SUGGESTED FOLLOW-UP ACTIVITIES

1. Ask observers to react to the role-playing they saw.
2. Ask each role-player to describe his feelings as he became involved.

3. Discuss alternative ways of dealing with the situation.
4. Have an observer-analyst report on his analysis of the interaction.
5. Switch roles among the role-players and have the same situation played again.

#### ARRANGEMENTS

*Group size* Role-playing can be used with nearly any number of participants. Two people can role-play in a very private and personal situation. Small groups (10 to 15 participants) facilitate optimum use of this activity since all can watch, all can discuss, and all can be role-players. Large groups generally require an audience situation, and buzz groups may have to be used to get follow-up discussion.

#### ILLUSTRATION

Role-playing is involved in most of the laboratory sessions discussed in Part II of this book. In Chaper 9, the session on interview styles illustrates structured role-playing which also serves by way of demonstration.

An interesting illustration of role-playing involved Dr. Laurine Johnson, the new Director of Special Education in the Wakeville City Schools. As she met for the second time with the new "screening committee," she decided to role-play a situation in which a pupil had been designated for possible placement in a special class for the "brain injured." In a previous meeting with the committee she was concerned that they seemed to want her to make the decisions for them to accept. Their discussion of the responsibilities of the committee to "review all relevant information and make the best educational placement" seemed to worry several of the committee members. One elementary school principal had said to her following the meeting, "I don't know too much about this kind of problem, but I'll go along with what you recommend." A sixth-grade teacher had asked, "Are there some materials we should read to guide our decisions?" A counselor had been overheard commenting to a supervisor during the last committee meeting, "I hope we can get a lot of new classes organized for these kids who can't make it in the seventh and eighth grades."

With these comments and questions in mind, Dr. Johnson carefully planned her second meeting of the committee as an in-service session. On their arrival, she briefly introduced her plan to have "a practice session". She distributed folders containing information on a single pupil. "Now, this is not for real. We don't need to make a decision on this boy at this time. It is a real case, however, and we could well have this or another just like it at our next meeting; let's role-play our approach to this problem. This boy is not doing at all well in school."

After this introduction, each committee member read the material carefully. Finally, when all seemed to have finished, Dr. Johnson asked, "Well, what do you think?" A discussion followed. Opinions were given, additional information was requested, suggestions were made. When specific kinds of additional information were requested, Dr. Johnson provided it, since she had a much more complete case record than had been provided for the committee members.

After nearly 40 minutes, one member said, "Let's make a decision. We have other cases to review today!" Dr. Johnson said, "All right. Will you make a specific recommendation?" Another committee member volunteered, "I move we ask the parents for permission to place him in a special class for the emotionally disturbed." A flurry of discussion followed this motion. Some agreed strongly. Others were not sure. Some thought a class for minimally brain-injured would be better.

After a while, Dr. Johnson asked, "Do we have a second to this motion for placement?" Several volunteered to second the motion. "Are we ready for a decision?" (Heads nod.) "All in favor?" (Most assent). "Those opposed?" (One or two weak negative responses are heard.)

At this point the hour was 5:05 p.m. Dr. Johnson glanced at her watch and acknowledged the lateness of the hour. "I know we must leave promptly. Before we go, however, I want to share some additional information with you about this boy and set a date for another meeting." As she talked, Dr. Johnson distributed a mimeographed sheet. "This contains physical examination data, a report from the school social worker on a home visit, and a quotation from the psychologist. Most of this is new information in the sense that you did not ask for it so I did not give it to you."

As the participants glanced at the new information, there was a flurry of comments. They saw almost immediately that some of this information might have changed their decision. Some complained, "Why didn't you give us this information, even without our asking?" Dr. Johnson replied, "I wanted to dramatize the importance of information from various sources. Also, I wanted us to realize how easily a poor decision can be made in good conscience and good faith."

"Would you like to meet again soon to role-play this and other cases?" Most seemed eager to do so and a date was set.

CAUTIONS AND LIMITATIONS

Many of the cautions in using role-playing have already been mentioned. Players must be encouraged to get involved for the first time, and then be protected from embarrassment. Leaders must be alert to terminate role-playing before emotional involvement becomes excessive.

Role-playing, like most activities providing stimulating and spontaneous involvement, requires analysis. Some kind of follow-up is needed to help participants interpret and make applications.

SUMMARY

Role-playing is an activity uniquely suited for in-service education sessions designed to deal with human relations problems. The depth of involvement in simulated reality provides high experience impact for attitude and insight development as well as for building certain verbal interaction skills. While groups may need some coaching and encouragement in the use of role-playing, it is readily accepted by most people in a comfortable group situation and stimulates much interest.

*Selected references*

**BRAINSTORMING**

1. Bass, Bernard M., *Leadership, Psychology and Organizational Behavior*, New York: Harper and Brothers, 1960 pp. 125–27.
2. Coon, Arthur M., "Brainstorming: A Creative Problem-Solving Technique," *Journal of Communication*: 7 (Autumn, 1957).
3. Osborn, A. F., *Applied Imagination: Principles and Procedures of Creative Thinking*. New York: Charles Scribner's Sons, 1957.
4. Taylor, Donald W., Paul C. Berry, and C. H. Block, "Does Group Participation When Using Brainstorming Facilitate or Inhibit Creative Thinking?" *Administrative Science Quarterly*, 3:23–47 (June, 1958 ).

**BUZZ SESSIONS**

5. Bass, B. M. and F. T. M. Norton, "Group Size and Leaderless Discussions," *Journal of Applied Psychology*, 35: 397–400 (1951).
6. Cook, Lloyd, and Elaine Cook, *School Problems in Human Relations*. New York: McGraw-Hill Book Company, 1957, p. 87.
7. Gibb, J. R., G. N. Platts, and L. E. Miller, *Dynamics of Participative Groups*. St. Louis: J. S. Swift, 1961.

**DEMONSTRATION**

8. Algood, Mary B., *Demonstration Techniques*. Englewood Cliffs, N.J.: Prentice-Hall, Inc., 1947.
9. Angrilli, Albert, O. Bernard Liebman, and Cecily Cross, "Observations of Semi-Structured Play in Teacher Education," *Journal of Teacher Education*, 15:415–20.
10. Bartholomew, W., "The Place of Demonstration in Supervision," *National Elementary Principal*, 35: 189–91 (September, 1955).
11. Bessent, E. W., *et al.*, *Designs for In-Service Education*. Austin, Texas: Research and Development Center for Teacher Education, 1967.
12. Bradfield, Luther E., *Supervision for Modern Elementary Schools*. Columbus, Ohio: Charles E. Merrill Books, Inc., 1964, pp. 33–36.
13. Harris, Ben M., *A Research Study of the Effects of Demonstration Teaching Upon Experienced and Inexperienced Teachers*. Austin, Texas: Research and Development Center for Teacher Education, 1966.
14. Kersh, Bert, "The Classroom Simulator," *Journal of Teacher Education*, 13: No. 1 (March, 1962).

15. Lazarsfeld, Paul F., and Sam D. Sieber, *Organizing Educational Research—An Exploration*. Englewood Cliffs, N.J.: Prentice-Hall, Inc., 1964, pp. 69–73.

16. Melchior, William T., *Instructional Supervision, A Guide to Modern Practice*. Boston: D. C. Heath & Company, 1950, pp. 52–54, 95–99.

17. Newman, Charles, "In-Service Education Through Demonstration Teaching," *Journal of Secondary Education*, 36:20–22 (January, 1961).

18. "The Supervisor at Work," *Educational Leadership*, 19:82–114 (November, 1961).

19. Wiles, Kimball, Camille Brown, and Rosalind Cassidy, *Supervision in Physical Education*, Englewood Cliffs, N.J.: Prentice-Hall, Inc., 1955, chapter 12.

**GROUP DISCUSSION**

20. Anderson, R. C., "Learning in Discussions: A Resume of the Authoritarian-Democratic Studies," *Harvard Education Review*, 29:201–15 (Summer, 1959).

21. Bion, W. R., *Experiences in Groups*. New York: Basic Books, Inc., 1961.

22. Bales, Robert F., *Interaction Process Analysis—A Method for the Study of Small Groups*. Cambridge, Mass.: Addison-Wesley, 1950.

23. Bonner, Herbert, *Group Dynamics, Principles and Applications*. New York: The Ronald Press Company, 1959.

24. Bonney, Merle E., *Friends and Leaders*. Austin, Texas: Hogg Foundation for Mental Health, 1949.

25. Bradford, Leland P., and Dorothy Mial, "When is a Group?", *Educational Leadership*, 21:147 (December, 1963).

26. Cantor, Nathaniel Freeman, *Learning Through Discussion*. Buffalo, New York: Human Relations for Industry, 1951.

27. Chevens, Frank, *Leading Group Discussions*. Austin, Texas: Hogg Foundation for Mental Health, 1962.

28. Corey, S. M., P. M. Halverson, and Elizabeth Lowe, *Teachers Prepare for Discussion Group Leadership*. New York: Bureau of Publications, Teachers College, Columbia University, 1953.

29. Donovan, Helen M., and Irene Conlon, "Group Discussion in the School Program," *Strengthening Democracy*, 14:4–5 (January, 1962). Board of Education in the City of New York.

30. Glanz, Edward C., *Groups in Guidance*. Boston: Allyn and Bacon, Inc., 1962.

31. Gullahorn, I. J., "Teaching by the Case Method," *School Review*, 67:448–60 (Winter, 1959).

32. Gulley, Halbert E., *Discussion, Conference and Group Process*. New York: Henry Holt and Company, 1960, especially chapters 1 to 12.

33. Hall, D. M., *Dynamics of Group Discussion*. Danville, Ill.: The Interstate Printers and Publishers, Inc., 1963.

34. Hereford, Carl F., *Organizing Group Discussion*. Austin, Texas: The Hogg Foundation for Mental Health, 1961.

35. Hill, R. J., *A Comparative Study of Lecture and Discussion Methods*. New York: The Fund for Adult Education, 1960.

36. Kaess, W. A., "Leadership Group Discussion Techniques," *Journal of Applied Psychology*, 45:345–50 (October, 1961).
37. Kaplan, A. A., *Study-Discussion in the Liberal Arts*. New York: The Fund for Adult Education, 1960.
38. Kemp, C. Gratton, *Perspectives on the Group Process. A Foundation for Counseling with Groups*. Boston: Houghton, Mifflin Company, 1964.
39. Strang, Ruth M., *Group Work in Education*. New York: Harper and Brothers, 1958.
40. Swearingen, Mildred E., *Supervision of Instruction: Foundations and Dimensions*. Boston: Allyn and Bacon, Inc., 1962.
41. Thelen, Herbert A., "Purpose and Process in Groups," *Educational Leadership* (December, 1963).
42. Thomas, Michael P., Jr., *Strategies in the Preparation of School Administrators*. A report of the 17th Annual Meeting, National Conference of Professors of Educational Administration, Albuquerque, New Mexico (August, 1964), pp. 15–21.
43. Utterbault, W. H., *Decision Through Discussion*. New York: Rinehart and Company, Inc., 1960.
44. Wasterlund, Gunnor, *Group Leadership, A Field Experiment*. Stockholm, Sweden: Nondisk Rotogravayr, 1952.

ROLE-PLAYING

45. Balinsky, B., and A. Dispenzieri, "Evaluation of the Lecture Role-Playing Methods in the Development of Interviewing Skills," *Personnel and Guidance Journal*, 39:583–85 (March, 1961).
46. Bradford, L. P., "The Use of Psychodrama for Group Consultants," *Sociatry*, 1:192–97 (June, 1947).
47. Cook, Lloyd, and Elaine Cook, *School Problems in Human Relations*. New York: McGraw-Hill Book Company, 1957, pp. 39–42.
48. Graham, G., "Sociodrama as a Teaching Technique," *Social Studies*, 51:257–59 (December, 1960).
49. Hendry, C. E., R. Lippitt, and A. Zander, "Reality Practice as Educational Method," *Psychodrama Monographs, No. 9*. New York: Beacon House, 1944.
50. Miles, Matthew B., *Learning to Work in Groups*. New York: Bureau of Publications, Teachers College, Columbia University, 1959, pp. 191–93.
51. Shaftel, Fannie, and George R. Shaftel, *Role-Playing for Social Values: Decision-Making in the Social Studies*. Englewood Cliffs, N.J.: Prentice-Hall, Inc., 1967.
52. Solem, Allen R., "An Experimental Test of Two Theories of Involvement in Role-Playing," *International Journal of Sociometry*, 1:163–70 (December, 1957).

GENERAL

53. Harris, Ben M., *Supervisory Behavior in Education*. Englewood Cliffs, N.J.: Prentice-Hall, Inc., 1963, pp. 78–97.

Appendix I

GLOSSARY OF TERMS

1. **Feedback** — a term used to describe an event in which a person receives some information from a prior action or event that concerned him.

2. **Flexible diagnostic grouping** — a set of procedures for assigning pupils to groups for instructional purposes in which assignments are temporary on the basis of specific learning needs.

3. **In-service design** — a plan for conducting an in-service education effort including specifying outcomes and selecting appropriate activities for reaching those outcomes.

4. **In-service program** — a planned sequence of in-service sessions which may extend as long as a year and may involve different groups, arrangements, participants and leaders.

5. **In-service session** — a continuous series of activities directed toward specific outcomes that takes place with the same group in a single block of time.

6. **Instructional goal** — a statement of broad educational outcomes which may include multiple objectives.

7. **Instructional objective** — a specification of an intended outcome of a lesson or sequence of learning activities planned by a teacher.

8. **Instructional staff** — an inclusive term used in this book to refer to staff members who are involved in direct teaching or in instruction-related supporting activities such as supervisors, coordinators, principals, directors, and superintendants.

9. **Laboratory approach** — an approach to teaching that involves simulation of problem situations and calls for participants to generate the data that are used as a basis for study.

10. **Lesson protocols** — a typescript of a teaching incident or lesson in which verbal and non-verbal interactions have been recorded.

11. **Observation guide** — an instrument used to identify relevant instructional data and facilitate the recording made by an observer.

12. **Planned change** — any change brought about as a result of a conscious effort or intervention in the on-going course of events.

13. **Vignette** — a brief account of some event or episode which usually depicts a problem situation; a short case.

14. **Interviewing** — a two-person oral communication in which one person seeks to transmit and receive information from another.

Appendix II

SOURCES OF OTHER MATERIALS


Cases

The University Council for Educational Administration; 65 29 West Woodruff
Avenue, Columbus, Ohio.


Films

Kinescopes of "Teaching Strategies," South Park Schools, Beaumont, Texas.


In-Basket Simulation Materials

Madison Township Simulation, The University Council for Educational Administration, 65 Oval Drive, Columbus, Ohio.


Laboratory Exercises

Harris, Ben M., Kenneth E. McIntyre, and Wailand Bessent, In-service Education
—Materials for Laboratory Sessions, Englewood Cliffs, N.J.: Prentice-Hall, Inc.
1968.

Instructional Leadership Training Materials, Extension Teaching and Field
Service Bureau, The University of Texas, Austin, Texas.

Appendix III

## LOCATOR FOR LABORATORY SESSIONS AND MATERIALS

Since in-service group leaders will not necessarily be calling for the use of materials in the same sequence that they appear in this volume, and since materials for use by participants have been scrambled in the companion volume, *In-Service Education—Materials for Laboratory Sessions* by Bessent, Harris, and McIntyre, the listing below is provided as a cross reference to all materials which participants will use. Materials identified by Arabic numerals (e. g., 6.6) refer to items that appear as exhibits in this book. Materials numbered in Roman numerals (e. g., VI-A) refer to items that appear in the appendix of this book. Materials identified by either Arabic or Roman numerals are listed below in sequence.

Participants can locate materials they will need by referring to the "locator" in the volume mentioned above. All materials in the companion volume are designated as "Forms" but carry the same numerical designation as shown below. Hence, the leader can refer to any item as "Form number     " with assurance that participants will be using the appropriate piece of material whether in the body or appendix of this volume.

| Exhibit, Form or Appendix Number* | Title | Location in In-Service Education: A Guide to Better Practice | Materials for Laboratory Sessions |
|---|---|---|---|
| VIII-A | Description of Teacher | 348 | 235 |
| VIII-A1 | Description of Pupil Response Categories | 348 | 241 |
| VIII-B | Tabulation Worksheet for Teacher Behavior Analysis | 349 | 271 |
| VIII-C | Tabulation Worksheet for Bales' Interaction Analysis | 350 | 293 |
| VIII-D | Lesson Protocol—The Elementary Science Lesson | 352-378 | 245-269 |
| VIII-E | Lesson Protocol—The Leaking Bottle | 380-398 | ·273-288 |
| VIII-F | Lesson Protocol—Creative Writing | 399-420 | 295-313 |
| VIII-G | Analytical Summary for Questions | Not Included | 233 |
| 9.1 | Vignette - Being a Parent Is Too Much Work | 189 | 315 |
| 9.2 | Summary Forms for Reactions to Three Styles of Interviews | 193 | Not Included |
| 9.3 | Schedule for Problem-Solving Sessions | 198 | Not Included |
| 9.4 | Tabulation Worksheet for Summary of Reactionnaire Results | 198 | Not Included |
| 9.5 | Summary Analysis of Reactionnaire Results | 200 | Not Included |
| 9.6 | Directions for Communicator (Form A) | 205 | Not Included |
| 9.7 | Directions for Cummunicator (Form B) | 206 | Not Included |
| 9.8 | Directions for Receivers | 207 | 327 |
| 9.9 | Directions for Receivers | 209 | 329 |
| 9.10 | Directions for Scoring Feedback Exercise | 210 | Not Included |

Note: Exhibits and appendices for chapters 2, 3, and 4 are not included.

| Exhibit, Form or Appendix Number* | Title | Location in In-Service Education: A Guide to Better Practice | Materials for Laboratory Sessions |
|---|---|---|---|
| IX-A | Reaction to Interview | 421 | 317 (3 copies) |
| IX-B | Group Discussion Reactionnaire | 422 | 325 (3 copies) |
| IX-C | First Session: Mary's Reputation | 423 | 319 |
| IX-D | Second Session: Bobby's Theme | 424 | 321 |
| IX-E | Third Session: The Old Grouch | 425 | 323 |
| 10.1 | Content, Activities, Objectives, and Goals | 216 | Not Included |
| 10.2 | Preparing Instructional Objectives | 218 | 331 |
| 10.3 | Specifying Outcomes | 219 | 333 |
| 10.4 | Stating Objectives in Performance Terms | 221 | 335 |
| 10.5 | Clarifying Conditions for Objectives | 223 | 337 |
| 10.6 | Stating Criteria | 224 | 339 |
| 10.7 | Evaluating Outcomes | 226 | 341 |
| 5.1 | The Best Teacher I Have Ever Had | 68 | 179–180 |
| 5.2a | Equality of Man (theme) | 69 | 181–182 |
| 5.2b | Equality of Man (theme) | 70 | 193–194 |
| 5.3a | The Job I Would Like To Have Ten Years From Now (theme) | 71 | 183–184 |
| 5.3b | The Job I Would Like To Have Ten Years From Now (theme) | 72 | 195–196 |
| 5.4a | The Day Pedro Met Tiny (theme-low I. Q.) | 73 | 185–186 |
| 5.4b | The Day Pedro Met Tiny (theme-high I. Q.) | 73 | 197–198 |
| 5.5 | Arithmetic Test | 74 | 187–188 |
| 5.6a | Test Over Selected Spelling Demons | 75 | 189–190 |
| 5.6b | Key to Spelling Demons Test | 76 | 191 |
| 5.6c | Spelling Demons Test-Percentage and Letter Marks | 76 | 199 |
| 5.6d | Spelling Demons Test-Janice's Class | 77 | 205 |
| 5.6e | Spelling Demons Test-Nine Classes | 77 | 209 |
| V-A | Collection of Items From Teacher- | 274 | 1– 6 |
| 6.1 | Sample Data of One Pupil | 97 | Not Included |
| 6.2 | Instructions for Grouping | 98-100 | Not Included |
| 6.3 | Worksheet for Analyzing Individual Differences | 102 | 37 |
| 6.4 | Worksheet for Analyzing Individual Differences (Four Class Sections) | 105 | Not Included |
| 6.5 | Sample Sheet Diagnostic Outline - Language Test | 109 | Not Included |
| 6.6 | Worksheet for Mechanics of English | 110 | 219 |
| 6.7 | Worksheet for Language Sub-Test A - Capitalization | 112 | 221 |
| 6.8 | Worksheet for Diagnosing Learning Needs | 113-114 | 159–161 |
| 6.9 | Achievement Test Report | 120 | 163 |
| 6.10 | Sample Worksheet for Test Report | 120 | 165 |
| 6.11 | Pupil Report Card (Howard J. Abbe) Achievement Record | 122 | 201 |
| 6.12 | Individual Profile Chart | 122 | 203 |
| 6.13 | Mental Maturity Record | 124 | 207 |
| 6.14 | Pupil Growth Scores | 124 | 211 |

| Exhibit, Form or Appendix Number | Title | Location in In-Service Education: A Guide to Better Practice | Materials for Laboratory Sessions |
|---|---|---|---|
| 6.15 | Growth Profile Chart | 126 | 213 |
| 6.16 | Item Analysis Worksheet | 126 | 215 |
| 6.17 | Answer Sheet–Charts | 127 | 217 |
| VI-A | Data on One Hundred Pupils | 281-295 | 7– 35 |
| VI-B | Diagnostic Outline Sheets-Language Test; A Set of Data on Fifty-Nine Pupils | 297-327 | 39–157 |
| 7.1 | Sample Entries on the *Comprehensive Observation Guide* | 135 | Not Included |
| 7.2 | Sample of Group Test Results on Film Clip Observations | 139 | Not Included |
| 7.3 | The Reliability of Observations as a Function of Number of Visits | 140 | Not Included |
| 7.4 | Levels of Observation Related to Skills Employed | 141 | Not Included |
| 7.5 | Sample Questions from Each Section of the Comprehensive Observation Guide | 146 | Not Included |
| 7.6 | Four Problems in Recording Evidence | 149 | 177 |
| 7.7 | Sample Lesson Analysis Using the *Teacher Question Inventory* | 155 | 237 |
| 7.7a | *Teacher Question Inventory* | Not Included | 239 |
| 7.8 | Sample Lesson Analysis Using the *Pupil Response Inventory* | 159 | 242 |
| 7.8a | *Pupil Response Inventory* | Not Included | 243 |
| VII-A | *Comprehensive Observation Guide* | 329-344 | 167–175 |
| VII-B | Sample Test - Observing for Details | 345-347 | Not Included |
| 8.1 | Sample Protocol Analysis Using the *Teacher Question Inventory* | 167 | Not Included |
| 8.2 | Sample Protocol Analysis Using the *Pupil Response Inventory* | 168 | Not Included |
| 8.3 | Sample Tabulation in the *Teacher Behavior Inventory* | 181 | Not Included |
| 8.4 | Categories & Illustrations of Bales' Interaction Analysis & Teacher Behavior Analysis | 183 | Not Included |
| 8.5 | Lesson Protocol – The Russian Revolution | 170-176 (No exhibit no.) | 223–231 |
| 8.6 | Categories & Illustrations for Teacher Behavior Analysis | 179-180 (No exhibit no.) | 291–292 |

# Appendix IV

## ACTIVITIES ASSOCIATED WITH LABORATORY SESSIONS

| Sessions Described by Chapters | Types of Activities | | | | | | | | |
|---|---|---|---|---|---|---|---|---|---|
| | 1. Brainstorming* | 2. Buzz Sessions* | 3. Demonstrations* | 4. Group Discussions | 5. Role-Playing* | 6. Directed Practice** | 7. Film Presentations** | 8. Lecture Presentations** | 9. Testing** |
| **Chapter V   Evaluating Pupil Performance** | | | | | | | | | |
| "Marking Pupils' Work" | | | | X | | X | | X | X |
| "Analyzing Teacher-Made Tests" | | | X | X | | X | | X | |
| **Chapter VI   Indiv. and Grouping for Instruction** | | | | | | | | | |
| "Grouping for Effective Instruction" | | | | X | X | X | | X | |
| "Diagnostic Flexible Grouping" | | | X | X | X | X | | | |
| "Individualized Analysis of Achievement" | | | X | X | X | X | | | |
| **Chapter VII   Observing and Analyzing Instruction** | | | | | | | | | |
| "Discovering Observation as Professional Skill" | | | | | X | | X | X | X |
| "Training in the Use of Observation Guides" | | | X | X | | X | X | | |
| **Chapter VIII   Analyzing Lesson Protocols** | X | X | X | X | | X | | | |
| **Chapter IX   Studying Communication Patterns** | | | | | | | | | |
| "Three Styles of Interviewing" | | | X | X | X | | | | X |
| "Three Styles of Group Communication" | | X | | X | X | | | | X |
| "The Effect of Feedback in Communications" | | | X | X | | X | | | |
| **Chapter X   Setting Instructional Objectives** | | | X | X | | X | | X | X |

\* See Part III - Basic Activities for descriptions and suggestions for using these activities.

\*\* These activities are briefly defined and described by Ben M. Harris in Supervisory Behavior in Education. Englewood Cliffs, N.J.: Prentice-Hall, Inc., 1963. Chapter 3.

COLLECTION OF ITEMS FROM TEACHER-MADE TESTS

INSTRUCTIONS

Following is a collection of items taken from teacher-made tests. You will find various subject areas represented, and it will be obvious that items from both the elementary school and the secondary school are represented; in fact, two of the objective items were selected from tests given in a graduate school.

For the next few minutes you are to assume the role of a student and answer these items as if they constituted a test. After you have completed the objective items in Part I, study the essay items and essay tests in Part II, but do not attempt to answer the essay items.

Since this exercise is for discussion purposes only, you will not be asked to hand in your paper.

As you study each item, indicate not only what you think the correct response is, but also note what you consider to be the good or bad features of the item. For example, look for clues that give the answers away or ambiguities that make it difficult to ascertain what is wanted.

Be ready to contribute your ideas to the discussion that will begin in a few minutes.

PART I

OBJECTIVE ITEMS

Answer the following questions to the best of your ability.

A. Multiple-choice

1. The Battle of Chattanooga ended
   (a) December 9, 1935
   (b) November 25, 1863
   (c) July 4, 1923
   (d) February 30, 1492

2. Man differs from birds in that man has a

(a) four-chambered heart
(b) hair
(c) warm blood
(d) eyes

3. The Frenchman who developed a cure for rabies was

(a) Harvey
(b) Banting
(c) Pasteur
(d) Leeuwenhoek

4. The person who made the first American flag was
(a) Samuel Adams
(b) Paul Revere
(c) John Hancock
(d) Betsy Ross

5. An 8-sided polygon is an
(a) octagon
(b) pentagon
(c) hexagon
(d) decagon

6. Which of the following state aid systems would favor school districts in which few pupils reside?

(a) a uniform grant per census pupil
(b) a uniform grant per pupil in average daily attendance
(c) a uniform grant per enrolled pupil
(d) a uniform grant per teacher

7. Because of the time in which each of the following men lived, which one could have been present during the Battle of the Alamo?

(a) Daniel Boone
(b) Kit Carson
(c) George Rogers Clark
(d) George Armstrong Custer

8. Adding the same number to the numerator and denominator of a fraction

(a) decreases it
(b) increases it
(c) may either increase or decrease it
(d) leaves it the same

B. True-False

   1. The Battle of Lexington was fought in 1775 B.C.
   2. The most famous American general in World War I was John James Pershing.
   3. The value of pi is 3.14.
   4. A child with a weak heart may be given aspirin.
   5. All dogs have a keen sense of smell.
   6. No mammals fly.
   7. All squares are rectangles.
   8. A married high school student may be expelled from school.

C. Matching

| 1. First battle of the civil war took place here | A. John Wilkes Booth |
|---|---|
| 2. Made the famous march through Georgia | B. Emancipation Proclama- |
| 3. Set the slaves free | tion |
| 4. Assasinated (sic) Abraham Lincoln. | C. Fourteenth Amendment |
| 5. Term applied to freed slaves | D. Freedmen |
| 6. Used to discourage Negro voting | E. Carpetbaggers |
| 7. Was set up to help the Negro who was free | F. Military governors |
|     and did not know where to go or what to do | G. Fort Sumpter (sic) |
| 8. Are heads of the military districts under | H. General Sherman |
|     the Congressional plan of Reconstruction | I. Poll tax |
| 9. Persons who came from the North to make | J. Freedmens Bureau |
|     a profit on Reconstruction events | |
| 10. Made the Negro (sic) citizens of the U.S. | |
|     with full citizenship rights | |

D. Completion

   1. The force of gravity causes water to flow _____ .
   2. The Battle of New Orleans was fought in _____ .
   3. The Nile River is _____ miles long.
   4. A child who is 10 years old should _____ _____ _____ every night.
   5. The Continental Congress chose well when it made George Washington
      _____ ____ _____ of the army.
   6. Match these proper nouns with a common noun:
      a. Canada _____
      b. July     _____
      c. Easter _____
      d. Arizona_____
   7. When Washington became commander in chief, the British held_____ .

PART II

ESSAY ITEMS

A. General (Selected Items)

1. Discuss what is needed for good health.
2. What did Edison do?
3. Give a brief sketch of Lincoln, telling where and when he was born, offices he held, and how and when he died.
4. List the four causes of the depression of the 1930's.
5. Tell me briefly why you do or do not appreciate our American heritage.

B. American History, 1789-1860 (A Complete Test)

Copy the question on your own paper. Skip a line and begin your answer. Turn in your question sheet with your test papers.

1. List the four parts of Hamilton's financial program. Explain why he felt each part was necessary. Explain why Jefferson and his followers opposed each part of the plan.
2. Discuss the "Jeffersonian Era." In doing this, explain why it is often called a "social revolution." Give and explain Jefferson's political philosophy as applied to "democracy" and to "purpose of government."
3. Discuss the "Jacksonian Era." Bring out points about his philosophy of government, his attitude towards the federal union, the "spoils system," his opinion about the presidency, the inventions and social reforms.
4. Discuss Chief Justice John Marshall's influence on our history. Give his political philosophy and his reasons for assuming the power of judicial review. Give at least (3) of his major decisions and show how each one expressed Marshall's ideal of the federal union.
5. State Calhoun's theory of the federal union. State Webster's theory.
6. Discuss the economic reasons for the rise of sectionalism: 1815-1860.
7. Give the theory of "Manifest Destiny" and list political events which occurred from 1840-1860 which were an expression by our nation of belief in this theory.
8. Discuss the Lincoln-Douglass debates and the 1860 presidential election.

C. Comparison of Two Essay Examinations

Compare the two essay examinations that follow. Each is on the Wilson administration. What kinds of teaching objectives are revealed in each? What kinds of study will students do in preparation for each examination?

## Teacher Perkins' Examination

1. List the names of the men in Wilson's first cabinet and give the departments that they headed.
2. Name the three important pieces of legislation that were passed in Wilson's first administration.
3. Give the sequence of events leading up to the declaration of war by Germany on France, beginning with the formation of the Triple Entente.
4. What was the Schlieffen Plan?
5. How did Germany get Russia out of the War?
6. What event caused America's declaration of war on Germany?
7. List Woodrow Wilson's Fourteen Points.

## Teacher Brown's Examination

1. Why was it necessary for Wilson to appoint William Jennings Bryan as Secretary of State? In your answer tell what you think this reveals about American political parties. In your opinion was this appointment justified? (Give reasons why or why not.)
2. Why was Woodrow Wilson's legislative program called the New Freedom and how did this program take advantage of changes in the economic and social pattern that had begun in this country?
3. Discuss the effect of imperialism, nationalism, secret alliances, and arms races on the nations which engaged in World War I.
4. Woodrow Wilson went to Paris to the Peace Conference at the end of World War I to make "the world safe for democracy." Why was this objective not achieved?
5. Can you see any reason for the often heard statement, "The first World War contained the seeds of the second World War?" Explain.

D. What Do You Think of These Questions?

Assuming that the students had been taught the subject matter involved but had never been confronted with these specific questions, evaluate the following with respect to the kind of thinking required of the students:

1. Generally speaking, what do these periods of history have in common: Athens under Pericles; Rome under Augustus; India under the Guptas; China under the Tangs?
2. In what respects was Athenian democracy similar to that in the United States today? In what respects different?
3. In what ways was the life of an American teen-ager at the time of the Mexican War different from your life today, assuming comparable family circumstances?

4. According to scientists, certain criteria must be met before an area can become a "cradle of civilization." On the basis of these factors, could the area around Austin (the home city of the students) have been a "cradle"? Explain.

5. Following are some phrases that we have not studied, but from your knowledge of etymology see if you can construct the words that these phrases define:

(a) a hater of mankind (answer: misanthrope)
(b) the study of religion and religious ideas (answer: theology)
(c) a lover of books (answer: bibliophile)
(d) a mental disorder characterized by a persistent desire to burn property (answer: pyromania)

6. Assume that you are contemplating a visit to Planet X, where the force of gravity is twice what it is on earth, the amount of light is half of what it is on earth, the temperature ranges from -50 degrees to +10 degrees, and other factors are similar to those on the earth, what might the plant and animal life on Planet X be like? Explain each point that you make.

7. If the Rocky Mountains were located where the Mississippi Valley now is, what differences would it make to the people in Western Iowa?

8. Explain why the symbol "11" could not be used for the number eleven in the base twelve number system.

9. From your study of winds and ocean currents, would you expect the coast of Peru to be cooler or warmer than the coast of Brazil in the same latitude? Explain.

## NOTES AND COMMENTS

What are fundamental weaknesses in this collection of items?

a. From the student's point of view?

b. From the point of view of use of teacher time?

c. From the point of view of effective teaching?

Other comments:

# Appendix VI—A

## DATA ON ONE HUNDRED PUPILS

# Stanine Numbering Cards
## (cut into nine cards)

| | | |
|---|---|---|
| Stanine 1 | Stanine 2 | Stanine 3 |
| Stanine 4 | Stanine 5 | Stanine 6 |
| Stanine 7 | Stanine 8 | Stanine 9 |

SLOW SECTION

MIDDLE SECTION

FAST SECTION

| | | | |
|---|---|---|---|
| 4 Grade-point average | Divergent thinking 3 | 4 Grade-point average | Divergent thinking 3 |
| 3 Science | Convergent thinking 3 | 2 Science | Convergent thinking 3 |
| 3 Social studies | Mental maturity 3 | 3 Social studies | Mental maturity 3 |
| 1 Total arithmetic | Achievement drive 5 | 2 Total arithmetic | Achievement drive 6 |
| 2 Arith. fundamentals | Peer status 8 | 3 Arith. fundamentals | Peer status 6 |
| 2 Arith. reasoning | Social status 6 | 2 Arith. reasoning | Social status 6 |
| 2 Total language | Social inadequacy 4 | 3 Total language | Social inadequacy 4 |
| 2 Spelling | Personal adjustment 3 | 4 Spelling | Personal adjustment 4 |
| 2 Mechanics of English | Study habits 4 | 3 Mechanics of English | Study habits 7 |
| 3 Total reading | Schol. motivation 5 | 3 Total reading | Schol. motivation 6 |
| 3 Reading comprehension | Self confidence 6 | 3 Reading comprehension | Self confidence 6 |
| 3 Vocabulary | Procrastination or. 5 | 4 Vocabulary | Procrastination or. 6 |
| Boy | | Girl | |
| S6 | Card # 1 | S8 | Card # 2 |
| 4 Grade-point average | Divergent thinking 4 | 6 Grade-point average | Divergent thinking 3 |
| 3 Science | Convergent thinking 3 | 5 Science | Convergent thinking 2 |
| 4 Social studies | Mental maturity 2 | 4 Social studies | Mental maturity 2 |
| 3 Total arithmetic | Achievement drive 7 | 3 Total arithmetic | Achievement drive 6 |
| 3 Arith. fundamentals | Peer status 3 | 3 Arith. fundamentals | Peer status 8 |
| 4 Arith. reasoning | Social status 6 | 4 Arith. reasoning | Social status 7 |
| 3 Total language | Social inadequacy 5 | 3 Total language | Social inadequacy 5 |
| 4 Spelling | Personal adjustment 6 | 5 Spelling | Personal adjustment 5 |
| 3 Mechanics of English | Study habits 8 | 2 Mechanics of English | Study habits 6 |
| 3 Total reading | Schol. motivation 6 | 4 Total reading | Schol. motivation 6 |
| 4 Reading comprehension | Self confidence 6 | 4 Reading comprehension | Self confidence 4 |
| 3 Vocabulary | Procrastination or. | 3 Vocabulary | Procrastination or. 6 |
| Girl | | Boy | |
| S8 | Card # 3 | S8 | Card # 4 |

## Card # 5 — Girl S9

| | | |
|---|---|---|
| 4 | Grade-point average | Divergent thinking 4 |
| 3 | Science | Convergent thinking 4 |
| 3 | Social studies | Mental maturity 3 |
| 4 | Total arithmetic | Achievement drive 6 |
| 5 | Arith. fundamentals | Peer status 8 |
| 3 | Arith. reasoning | Social status 8 |
| 2 | Total language | Social inadequacy 6 |
| 3 | Spelling | Personal adjustment 6 |
| 2 | Mechanics of English | Study habits 7 |
| 3 | Total reading | Schol. motivation 6 |
| 3 | Reading comprehension | Self confidence 3 |
| 3 | Vocabulary | Procrastination or. 4 |

## Card # 6 — Girl S10

| | | |
|---|---|---|
| 4 | Grade-point average | Divergent thinking 3 |
| 3 | Science | Convergent thinking 2 |
| 4 | Social studies | Mental maturity 3 |
| 4 | Total arithmetic | Achievement drive 5 |
| 5 | Arith. fundamentals | Peer status 4 |
| 4 | Arith. reasoning | Social status 6 |
| 3 | Total language | Social inadequacy 5 |
| 3 | Spelling | Personal adjustment 6 |
| 2 | Mechanics of English | Study habits 6 |
| 3 | Total reading | Schol. motivation 3 |
| 4 | Reading comprehension | Self confidence 4 |
| 3 | Vocabulary | Procrastination or. 5 |

## Card # 7 — Girl S10

| | | |
|---|---|---|
| 4 | Grade-point average | Divergent thinking 3 |
| 3 | Science | Convergent thinking 3 |
| 3 | Social studies | Mental maturity 4 |
| 3 | Total arithmetic | Achievement drive 3 |
| 3 | Arith. fundamentals | Peer status 3 |
| 4 | Arith. reasoning | Social status 6 |
| 3 | Total language | Social inadequacy 6 |
| 3 | Spelling | Personal adjustment 8 |
| 2 | Mechanics of English | Study habits 5 |
| 3 | Total reading | Schol. motivation 3 |
| 3 | Reading comprehension | Self confidence 6 |
| 2 | Vocabulary | Procrastination or. 7 |

## Card # 8 — Boy S10

| | | |
|---|---|---|
| 4 | Grade-point average | Divergent thinking 4 |
| 4 | Science | Convergent thinking 4 |
| 3 | Social studies | Mental maturity 4 |
| 3 | Total arithmetic | Achievement drive 5 |
| 3 | Arith. fundamentals | Peer status 8 |
| 4 | Arith. reasoning | Social status 4 |
| 3 | Total language | Social inadequacy 5 |
| 4 | Spelling | Personal adjustment 4 |
| 3 | Mechanics of English | Study habits 4 |
| 3 | Total reading | Schol. motivation 6 |
| 4 | Reading comprehension | Self confidence 6 |
| 3 | Vocabulary | Procrastination or. 5 |

## Card # 10 — Girl S9

| | | |
|---|---|---|
| 5 | Grade-point average | Divergent thinking 3 |
| 7 | Science | Convergent thinking 2 |
| 5 | Social studies | Mental maturity 2 |
| 4 | Total arithmetic | Achievement drive 5 |
| 5 | Arith. fundamentals | Peer status 8 |
| 5 | Arith. reasoning | Social status 7 |
| 4 | Total language | Social inadequacy 6 |
| 5 | Spelling | Personal adjustment 7 |
| 3 | Mechanics of English | Study habits 5 |
| 5 | Total reading | Schol. motivation 5 |
| 5 | Reading comprehension | Self confidence 6 |
| 5 | Vocabulary | Procrastination or. 6 |

## Card # 10 — Girl S11

| | | |
|---|---|---|
| 4 | Grade-point average | Divergent thinking 3 |
| 3 | Science | Convergent thinking 2 |
| 3 | Social studies | Mental maturity 2 |
| 4 | Total arithmetic | Achievement drive 4 |
| 4 | Arith. fundamentals | Peer status 6 |
| 4 | Arith. reasoning | Social status 7 |
| 5 | Total language | Social inadequacy 4 |
| 5 | Spelling | Personal adjustment 4 |
| 4 | Mechanics of English | Study habits 3 |
| 4 | Total reading | Schol. motivation 4 |
| 4 | Reading comprehension | Self confidence 6 |
| 3 | Vocabulary | Procrastination or. 5 |

## Card # 11 — Boy S11

| | | |
|---|---|---|
| 4 | Grade-point average | Divergent thinking 4 |
| 5 | Science | Convergent thinking 5 |
| 5 | Social studies | Mental maturity 4 |
| 3 | Total arithmetic | Achievement drive 6 |
| 3 | Arith. fundamentals | Peer status 8 |
| 4 | Arith. reasoning | Social status 1 |
| 4 | Total language | Social inadequacy 8 |
| 5 | Spelling | Personal adjustment 6 |
| 4 | Mechanics of English | Study habits 7 |
| 3 | Total reading | Schol. motivation 7 |
| 3 | Reading comprehension | Self confidence 6 |
| 3 | Vocabulary | Procrastination or. 7 |

## Card # 12 — Boy S11

| | | |
|---|---|---|
| 5 | Grade-point average | Divergent thinking 6 |
| 6 | Science | Convergent thinking 5 |
| 6 | Social studies | Mental maturity 5 |
| 3 | Total arithmetic | Achievement drive 6 |
| 3 | Arith. fundamentals | Peer status 2 |
| 4 | Arith. reasoning | Social status 5 |
| 3 | Total language | Social inadequacy 4 |
| 4 | Spelling | Personal adjustment 5 |
| 3 | Mechanics of English | Study habits 4 |
| 4 | Total reading | Schol. motivation 5 |
| 4 | Reading comprehension | Self confidence 5 |
| 3 | Vocabulary | Procrastination or. 5 |

| 3 | Grade-point average | Divergent thinking | 4 |
|---|---|---|---|
| 3 | Science | Convergent thinking | 3 |
| 3 | Social studies | Mental maturity | 4 |
| 4 | Total arithmetic | Achievement drive | 2 |
| 4 | Arith. fundamentals | Peer status | 1 |
| 4 | Arith. reasoning | Social status | 7 |
| 4 | Total language | Social inadequacy | 6 |
| 4 | Spelling | Personal adjustment | 8 |
| 4 | Mechanics of English | Study habits | 3 |
| 4 | Total reading | Schol. motivation | 3 |
| 3 | Reading comprehension | Self confidence | 4 |
| 4 | Vocabulary | Procrastination or. | 4 |

Girl
S12     Card # 13

| 5 | Grade-point average | Divergent thinking | 2 |
|---|---|---|---|
| 5 | Science | Convergent thinking | 5 |
| 4 | Social studies | Mental maturity | 6 |
| 3 | Total arithmetic | Achievement drive | 3 |
| 3 | Arith. fundamentals | Peer status | 6 |
| 3 | Arith. reasoning | Social status | 3 |
| 3 | Total language | Social inadequacy | 6 |
| 4 | Spelling | Personal adjustment | 6 |
| 2 | Mechanics of English | Study habits | 4 |
| 4 | Total reading | Schol. motivation | 3 |
| 4 | Reading comprehension | Self confidence | 2 |
| 4 | Vocabulary | Procrastination or. | 2 |

Boy
S12     Card # 14

| 5 | Grade-point average | Divergent thinking | 4 |
|---|---|---|---|
| 4 | Science | Convergent thinking | 3 |
| 4 | Social studies | Mental maturity | 4 |
| 4 | Total arithmetic | Achievement drive | 4 |
| 4 | Arith. fundamentals | Peer status | 1 |
| 5 | Arith. reasoning | Social status | 6 |
| 4 | Total language | Social inadequacy | 5 |
| 6 | Spelling | Personal adjustment | 5 |
| 2 | Mechanics of English | Study habits | 5 |
| 4 | Total reading | Schol. motivation | 5 |
| 5 | Reading comprehension | Self confidence | 5 |
| 4 | Vocabulary | Procrastination or. | 4 |

Boy
S12     Card # 15

| 5 | Grade-point average | Divergent thinking | 5 |
|---|---|---|---|
| 3 | Science | Convergent thinking | 4 |
| 3 | Social studies | Mental maturity | 3 |
| 4 | Total arithmetic | Achievement drive | 4 |
| 4 | Arith. fundamentals | Peer status | 4 |
| 4 | Arith. reasoning | Social status | 4 |
| 5 | Total language | Social inadequacy | 6 |
| 4 | Spelling | Personal adjustment | 6 |
| 5 | Mechanics of English | Study habits | 3 |
| 3 | Total reading | Schol. motivation | 5 |
| 3 | Reading comprehension | Self confidence | 5 |
| 3 | Vocabulary | Procrastination or. | 5 |

Boy
S12     Card # 16

| 5 | Grade-point average | Divergent thinking | 5 |
|---|---|---|---|
| 4 | Science | Convergent thinking | 5 |
| 3 | Social studies | Mental maturity | 6 |
| 2 | Total arithmetic | Achievement drive | 6 |
| 2 | Arith. fundamentals | Peer status | 9 |
| 2 | Arith. reasoning | Social status | 7 |
| 4 | Total language | Social inadequacy | 6 |
| 4 | Spelling | Personal adjustment | 5 |
| 5 | Mechanics of English | Study habits | 4 |
| 5 | Total reading | Schol. motivation | 6 |
| 4 | Reading comprehension | Self confidence | 5 |
| 6 | Vocabulary | Procrastination or. | 5 |

Boy
S12     Card # 17

| 5 | Grade-point average | Divergent thinking | 6 |
|---|---|---|---|
| 5 | Science | Convergent thinking | 3 |
| 4 | Social studies | Mental maturity | 3 |
| 4 | Total arithmetic | Achievement drive | 6 |
| 5 | Arith. fundamentals | Peer status | 9 |
| 4 | Arith. reasoning | Social status | 6 |
| 5 | Total language | Social inadequacy | 4 |
| 4 | Spelling | Personal adjustment | 3 |
| 6 | Mechanics of English | Study habits | 4 |
| 4 | Total reading | Schol. motivation | 6 |
| 4 | Reading comprehension | Self confidence | 6 |
| 4 | Vocabulary | Procrastination or. | 7 |

Girl
S12     Card # 18

| 4 | Grade-point average | Divergent thinking | 4 |
|---|---|---|---|
| 4 | Science | Convergent thinking | 5 |
| 5 | Social studies | Mental maturity | 5 |
| 4 | Total arithmetic | Achievement drive | 6 |
| 4 | Arith. fundamentals | Peer status | 6 |
| 5 | Arith. reasoning | Social status | 7 |
| 4 | Total language | Social inadequacy | 3 |
| 5 | Spelling | Personal adjustment | 5 |
| 4 | Mechanics of English | Study habits | 7 |
| 4 | Total reading | Schol. motivation | 7 |
| 4 | Reading comprehension | Self confidence | 6 |
| 5 | Vocabulary | Procrastination or. | 7 |

Girl
S13     Card # 19

| 5 | Grade-point average | Divergent thinking | 3 |
|---|---|---|---|
| 3 | Science | Convergent thinking | 3 |
| 4 | Social studies | Mental maturity | 4 |
| 4 | Total arithmetic | Achievement drive | 3 |
| 4 | Arith. fundamentals | Peer status | 0 |
| 4 | Arith. reasoning | Social status | 5 |
| 5 | Total language | Social inadequacy | 5 |
| 5 | Spelling | Personal adjustment | 4 |
| 4 | Mechanics of English | Study habits | 2 |
| 4 | Total reading | Schol. motivation | 3 |
| 4 | Reading comprehension | Self confidence | 3 |
| 4 | Vocabulary | Procrastination or. | 4 |

Boy
S13     Card # 20

285

## Card # 21 — Boy S13

| | | | |
|---|---|---|---|
| 5 | Grade-point average | Divergent thinking | 3 |
| 5 | Science | Convergent thinking | 4 |
| 5 | Social studies | Mental maturity | 4 |
| 4 | Total arithmetic | Achievement drive | 7 |
| 4 | Arith. fundamentals | Peer status | 5 |
| 3 | Arith. reasoning | Social status | 7 |
| 5 | Total language | Social inadequacy | 5 |
| 5 | Spelling | Personal adjustment | 4 |
| 5 | Mechanics of English | Study habits | 6 |
| 5 | Total reading | Schol. motivation | 8 |
| 5 | Reading comprehension | Self confidence | 6 |
| 5 | Vocabulary | Procrastination or. | 7 |

## Card # 22 — Girl S13

| | | | |
|---|---|---|---|
| 5 | Grade-point average | Divergent thinking | 4 |
| 5 | Science | Convergent thinking | 4 |
| 6 | Social studies | Mental maturity | 5 |
| 4 | Total arithmetic | Achievement drive | 6 |
| 5 | Arith. fundamentals | Peer status | 6 |
| 4 | Arith. reasoning | Social status | 6 |
| 4 | Total language | Social inadequacy | 4 |
| 3 | Spelling | Personal adjustment | 4 |
| 5 | Mechanics of English | Study habits | 6 |
| 4 | Total reading | Schol. motivation | 6 |
| 4 | Reading comprehension | Self confidence | 4 |
| 5 | Vocabulary | Procrastination or. | 7 |

## Card # 23 — Girl S13

| | | | |
|---|---|---|---|
| 5 | Grade-point average | Divergent thinking | 4 |
| 3 | Science | Convergent thinking | 4 |
| 5 | Social studies | Mental maturity | 4 |
| 5 | Total arithmetic | Achievement drive | 2 |
| 5 | Arith. fundamentals | Peer status | 7 |
| 5 | Arith. reasoning | Social status | 7 |
| 4 | Total language | Social inadequacy | 4 |
| 4 | Spelling | Personal adjustment | 3 |
| 5 | Mechanics of English | Study habits | 2 |
| 5 | Total reading | Schol. motivation | 3 |
| 4 | Reading comprehension | Self confidence | 4 |
| 5 | Vocabulary | Procrastination or. | 4 |

## Card # 24 — Boy S13

| | | | |
|---|---|---|---|
| 5 | Grade-point average | Divergent thinking | 5 |
| 3 | Science | Convergent thinking | 5 |
| 4 | Social studies | Mental maturity | 5 |
| 4 | Total arithmetic | Achievement drive | 3 |
| 4 | Arith. fundamentals | Peer status | 6 |
| 5 | Arith. reasoning | Social status | 4 |
| 4 | Total language | Social inadequacy | 4 |
| 3 | Spelling | Personal adjustment | 4 |
| 5 | Mechanics of English | Study habits | 4 |
| 4 | Total reading | Schol. motivation | 5 |
| 4 | Reading comprehension | Self confidence | 5 |
| 5 | Vocabulary | Procrastination or. | 4 |

## Card # 25 — Boy S13

| | | | |
|---|---|---|---|
| 6 | Grade-point average | Divergent thinking | 4 |
| 2 | Science | Convergent thinking | 4 |
| 3 | Social studies | Mental maturity | 5 |
| 4 | Total arithmetic | Achievement drive | 2 |
| 4 | Arith. fundamentals | Peer status | 3 |
| 5 | Arith. reasoning | Social status | 6 |
| 4 | Total language | Social inadequacy | 7 |
| 3 | Spelling | Personal adjustment | 7 |
| 5 | Mechanics of English | Study habits | 3 |
| 4 | Total reading | Schol. motivation | 2 |
| 4 | Reading comprehension | Self confidence | 2 |
| 5 | Vocabulary | Procrastination or. | 4 |

## Card # 26 — Girl S13

| | | | |
|---|---|---|---|
| 6 | Grade-point average | Divergent thinking | 5 |
| 6 | Science | Convergent thinking | 5 |
| 7 | Social studies | Mental maturity | 5 |
| 3 | Total arithmetic | Achievement drive | 5 |
| 3 | Arith. fundamentals | Peer status | 4 |
| 4 | Arith. reasoning | Social status | 4 |
| 5 | Total language | Social inadequacy | 9 |
| 5 | Spelling | Personal adjustment | 7 |
| 6 | Mechanics of English | Study habits | 4 |
| 5 | Total reading | Schol. motivation | 4 |
| 5 | Reading comprehension | Self confidence | 5 |
| 5 | Vocabulary | Procrastination or. | 5 |

## Card # 27 — Girl S13

| | | | |
|---|---|---|---|
| 5 | Grade-point average | Divergent thinking | 7 |
| 4 | Science | Convergent thinking | 5 |
| 4 | Social studies | Mental maturity | 3 |
| 5 | Total arithmetic | Achievement drive | 7 |
| 5 | Arith. fundamentals | Peer status | 4 |
| 4 | Arith. reasoning | Social status | 3 |
| 5 | Total language | Social inadequacy | 6 |
| 4 | Spelling | Personal adjustment | 7 |
| 5 | Mechanics of English | Study habits | 9 |
| 4 | Total reading | Schol. motivation | 7 |
| 4 | Reading comprehension | Self confidence | 6 |
| 4 | Vocabulary | Procrastination or. | 8 |

## Card # 28 — Boy S13

| | | | |
|---|---|---|---|
| 5 | Grade-point average | Divergent thinking | 8 |
| 7 | Science | Convergent thinking | 6 |
| 5 | Social studies | Mental maturity | 4 |
| 4 | Total arithmetic | Achievement drive | 4 |
| 5 | Arith. fundamentals | Peer status | 3 |
| 5 | Arith. reasoning | Social status | 6 |
| 5 | Total language | Social inadequacy | 3 |
| 5 | Spelling | Personal adjustment | 4 |
| 5 | Mechanics of English | Study habits | 7 |
| 5 | Total reading | Schol. motivation | 4 |
| 5 | Reading comprehension | Self confidence | 3 |
| 5 | Vocabulary | Procrastination or. | 4 |

| | | | |
|---|---|---|---|
| 7 | Grade-point average | Divergent thinking | 3 |
| 5 | Science | Convergent thinking | 4 |
| 6 | Social studies | Mental maturity | 4 |
| 4 | Total arithmetic | Achievement drive | 7 |
| 4 | Arith. fundamentals | Peer status | 7 |
| 5 | Arith. reasoning | Social status | 7 |
| 5 | Total language | Social inadequacy | 3 |
| 6 | Spelling | Personal adjustment | 4 |
| 4 | Mechanics of English | Study habits | 6 |
| 4 | Total reading | Schol. motivation | 7 |
| 4 | Reading comprehension | Self confidence | 7 |
| 3 | Vocabulary | Procrastination or. | 6 |

Girl
S13 — Card # 29

| | | | |
|---|---|---|---|
| 7 | Grade-point average | Divergent thinking | 4 |
| 6 | Science | Convergent thinking | 5 |
| 6 | Social studies | Mental maturity | 4 |
| 3 | Total arithmetic | Achievement drive | 7 |
| 5 | Arith. fundamentals | Peer status | 8 |
| 2 | Arith. reasoning | Social status | 5 |
| 6 | Total language | Social inadequacy | 3 |
| 5 | Spelling | Personal adjustment | 3 |
| 7 | Mechanics of English | Study habits | 8 |
| 5 | Total reading | Schol. motivation | 7 |
| 6 | Reading comprehension | Self confidence | 6 |
| 5 | Vocabulary | Procrastination or. | 8 |

Girl
S13 — Card # 30

| | | | |
|---|---|---|---|
| 4 | Grade-point average | Divergent thinking | 4 |
| 5 | Science | Convergent thinking | 4 |
| 3 | Social studies | Mental maturity | 6 |
| 4 | Total arithmetic | Achievement drive | 3 |
| 4 | Arith. fundamentals | Peer status | 9 |
| 5 | Arith. reasoning | Social status | 6 |
| 4 | Total language | Social inadequacy | 2 |
| 4 | Spelling | Personal adjustment | 4 |
| 5 | Mechanics of English | Study habits | 3 |
| 3 | Total reading | Schol. motivation | 4 |
| 3 | Reading comprehension | Self confidence | 5 |
| 4 | Vocabulary | Procrastination or. | 4 |

Boy
S14 — Card # 31

| | | | |
|---|---|---|---|
| 4 | Grade-point average | Divergent thinking | 4 |
| 6 | Science | Convergent thinking | 5 |
| 5 | Social studies | Mental maturity | 4 |
| 4 | Total arithmetic | Achievement drive | 2 |
| 4 | Arith. fundamentals | Peer status | 3 |
| 5 | Arith. reasoning | Social status | 6 |
| 6 | Total language | Social inadequacy | 5 |
| 5 | Spelling | Personal adjustment | 8 |
| 7 | Mechanics of English | Study habits | 3 |
| 5 | Total reading | Schol. motivation | 3 |
| 6 | Reading comprehension | Self confidence | 4 |
| 5 | Vocabulary | Procrastination or. | 2 |

Girl
S14 — Card # 32

| | | | |
|---|---|---|---|
| 4 | Grade-point average | Divergent thinking | 7 |
| 5 | Science | Convergent thinking | 5 |
| 5 | Social studies | Mental maturity | 6 |
| 4 | Total arithmetic | Achievement drive | 3 |
| 4 | Arith. fundamentals | Peer status | 4 |
| 4 | Arith. reasoning | Social status | 6 |
| 4 | Total language | Social inadequacy | 3 |
| 3 | Spelling | Personal adjustment | 4 |
| 5 | Mechanics of English | Study habits | 3 |
| 5 | Total reading | Schol. motivation | 4 |
| 4 | Reading comprehension | Self confidence | 5 |
| 5 | Vocabulary | Procrastination or. | 4 |

Boy
S14 — Card # 33

| | | | |
|---|---|---|---|
| 5 | Grade-point average | Divergent thinking | 6 |
| 5 | Science | Convergent thinking | 3 |
| 4 | Social studies | Mental maturity | 4 |
| 4 | Total arithmetic | Achievement drive | 6 |
| 4 | Arith. fundamentals | Peer status | 6 |
| 5 | Arith. reasoning | Social status | 6 |
| 6 | Total language | Social inadequacy | 6 |
| 7 | Spelling | Personal adjustment | 7 |
| 5 | Mechanics of English | Study habits | 9 |
| 4 | Total reading | Schol. motivation | 6 |
| 4 | Reading comprehension | Self confidence | 6 |
| 4 | Vocabulary | Procrastination or. | 6 |

Girl
S14 — Card # 34

| | | | |
|---|---|---|---|
| 6 | Grade-point average | Divergent thinking | 4 |
| 5 | Science | Convergent thinking | 3 |
| 4 | Social studies | Mental maturity | 3 |
| 6 | Total arithmetic | Achievement drive | 5 |
| 5 | Arith. fundamentals | Peer status | 7 |
| 7 | Arith. reasoning | Social status | 5 |
| 5 | Total language | Social inadequacy | 5 |
| 6 | Spelling | Personal adjustment | 6 |
| 4 | Mechanics of English | Study habits | 4 |
| 4 | Total reading | Schol. motivation | 6 |
| 5 | Reading comprehension | Self confidence | 5 |
| 3 | Vocabulary | Procrastination or. | 5 |

Girl
M14 — Card # 35

| | | | |
|---|---|---|---|
| 6 | Grade-point average | Divergent thinking | 6 |
| 4 | Science | Convergent thinking | 3 |
| 4 | Social studies | Mental maturity | 4 |
| 5 | Total arithmetic | Achievement drive | 7 |
| 5 | Arith. fundamentals | Peer status | 7 |
| 5 | Arith. reasoning | Social status | 8 |
| 5 | Total language | Social inadequacy | 5 |
| 6 | Spelling | Personal adjustment | 5 |
| 5 | Mechanics of English | Study habits | 8 |
| 4 | Total reading | Schol. motivation | 6 |
| 5 | Reading comprehension | Self confidence | 6 |
| 3 | Vocabulary | Procrastination or. | 6 |

Girl
M14 — Card # 36

| | | | |
|---|---|---|---|
| 6 | Grade-point average | Divergent thinking | 6 |
| 4 | Science | Convergent thinking | 5 |
| 5 | Social studies | Mental maturity | 4 |
| 4 | Total arithmetic | Achievement drive | 4 |
| 4 | Arith. fundamentals | Peer status | 6 |
| 5 | Arith. reasoning | Social status | 4 |
| 6 | Total language | Social inadequacy | 6 |
| 5 | Spelling | Personal adjustment | 6 |
| 6 | Mechanics of English | Study habits | 5 |
| 5 | Total reading | Schol. motivation | 3 |
| 5 | Reading comprehension | Self confidence | 2 |
| 5 | Vocabulary | Procrastination or. | 4 |

Girl
M14 — Card # 37

| | | | |
|---|---|---|---|
| 6 | Grade-point average | Divergent thinking | 6 |
| 4 | Science | Convergent thinking | 5 |
| 5 | Social studies | Mental maturity | 4 |
| 4 | Total arithmetic | Achievement drive | 5 |
| 4 | Arith. fundamentals | Peer status | 3 |
| 5 | Arith. reasoning | Social status | 6 |
| 6 | Total language | Social inadequacy | 3 |
| 6 | Spelling | Personal adjustment | 9 |
| 5 | Mechanics of English | Study habits | 3 |
| 5 | Total reading | Schol. motivation | 3 |
| 5 | Reading comprehension | Self confidence | 4 |
| 5 | Vocabulary | Procrastination or. | 4 |

Girl
M14 — Card # 38

| | | | |
|---|---|---|---|
| 7 | Grade-point average | Divergent thinking | 3 |
| 3 | Science | Convergent thinking | 4 |
| 4 | Social studies | Mental maturity | 4 |
| 5 | Total arithmetic | Achievement drive | 4 |
| 5 | Arith. fundamentals | Peer status | 6 |
| 5 | Arith. reasoning | Social status | 5 |
| 5 | Total language | Social inadequacy | 3 |
| 3 | Spelling | Personal adjustment | 3 |
| 6 | Mechanics of English | Study habits | 4 |
| 4 | Total reading | Schol. motivation | 4 |
| 4 | Reading comprehension | Self confidence | 5 |
| 4 | Vocabulary | Procrastination or. | 5 |

Girl
M14 — Card # 39

| | | | |
|---|---|---|---|
| 7 | Grade-point average | Divergent thinking | 6 |
| 6 | Science | Convergent thinking | 5 |
| 6 | Social studies | Mental maturity | 6 |
| 3 | Total arithmetic | Achievement drive | 7 |
| 3 | Arith. fundamentals | Peer status | 7 |
| 4 | Arith. reasoning | Social status | 8 |
| 5 | Total language | Social inadequacy | - |
| 5 | Spelling | Personal adjustment | 7 |
| 5 | Mechanics of English | Study habits | 6 |
| 6 | Total reading | Schol. motivation | 7 |
| 5 | Reading comprehension | Self confidence | 6 |
| 6 | Vocabulary | Procrastination or. | 6 |

Girl
M14 — Card # 40

| | | | |
|---|---|---|---|
| 4 | Grade-point average | Divergent thinking | 7 |
| 4 | Science | Convergent thinking | 4 |
| 5 | Social studies | Mental maturity | 6 |
| 4 | Total arithmetic | Achievement drive | 7 |
| 4 | Arith. fundamentals | Peer status | 4 |
| 4 | Arith. reasoning | Social status | 5 |
| 5 | Total language | Social inadequacy | 4 |
| 4 | Spelling | Personal adjustment | 7 |
| 5 | Mechanics of English | Study habits | 6 |
| 5 | Total reading | Schol. motivation | 4 |
| 5 | Reading comprehension | Self confidence | 3 |
| 5 | Vocabulary | Procrastination or. | 6 |

Girl
M15 — Card # 41

| | | | |
|---|---|---|---|
| 4 | Grade-point average | Divergent thinking | 6 |
| 6 | Science | Convergent thinking | 5 |
| 5 | Social studies | Mental maturity | 4 |
| 4 | Total arithmetic | Achievement drive | 6 |
| 3 | Arith. fundamentals | Peer status | 1 |
| 6 | Arith. reasoning | Social status | 5 |
| 7 | Total language | Social inadequacy | 4 |
| 7 | Spelling | Personal adjustment | 7 |
| 6 | Mechanics of English | Study habits | 9 |
| 4 | Total reading | Schol. motivation | 4 |
| 6 | Reading comprehension | Self confidence | 3 |
| 3 | Vocabulary | Procrastination or. | 4 |

Boy
M15 — Card # 42

| | | | |
|---|---|---|---|
| 5 | Grade-point average | Divergent thinking | 3 |
| 5 | Science | Convergent thinking | 5 |
| 7 | Social studies | Mental maturity | 5 |
| 4 | Total arithmetic | Achievement drive | 7 |
| 4 | Arith. fundamentals | Peer status | 4 |
| 5 | Arith. reasoning | Social status | 6 |
| 6 | Total language | Social inadequacy | 6 |
| 6 | Spelling | Personal adjustment | 7 |
| 6 | Mechanics of English | Study habits | 6 |
| 4 | Total reading | Schol. motivation | 6 |
| 5 | Reading comprehension | Self confidence | 6 |
| 3 | Vocabulary | Procrastination or. | 6 |

Girl
M15 — Card # 43

| | | | |
|---|---|---|---|
| 5 | Grade-point average | Divergent thinking | 5 |
| 6 | Science | Convergent thinking | 4 |
| 5 | Social studies | Mental maturity | 5 |
| 4 | Total arithmetic | Achievement drive | 6 |
| 4 | Arith. fundamentals | Peer status | 6 |
| 4 | Arith. reasoning | Social status | 5 |
| 6 | Total language | Social inadequacy | 6 |
| 6 | Spelling | Personal adjustment | 6 |
| 6 | Mechanics of English | Study habits | 5 |
| 5 | Total reading | Schol. motivation | 6 |
| 5 | Reading comprehension | Self confidence | 6 |
| 4 | Vocabulary | Procrastination or. | 6 |

Girl
M15 — Card # 44

288

| | | | |
|---|---|---|---|
| 5 | Grade-point average | Divergent thinking | 4 |
| 2 | Science | Convergent thinking | 5 |
| 4 | Social studies | Mental maturity | 5 |
| 5 | Total arithmetic | Achievement drive | 3 |
| 5 | Arith. fundamentals | Peer status | 5 |
| 5 | Arith. reasoning | Social status | 5 |
| 5 | Total language | Social inadequacy | 3 |
| 5 | Spelling | Personal adjustment | 4 |
| 5 | Mechanics of English | Study habits | 4 |
| 5 | Total reading | Schol. motivation | 4 |
| 4 | Reading comprehension | Self confidence | 4 |
| 6 | Vocabulary | Procrastination or. | 5 |

Boy
M15      Card # 45

| | | | |
|---|---|---|---|
| 6 | Grade-point average | Divergent thinking | 4 |
| 4 | Science | Convergent thinking | 5 |
| 4 | Social studies | Mental maturity | 6 |
| 5 | Total arithmetic | Achievement drive | 4 |
| 5 | Arith. fundamentals | Peer status | 1 |
| 5 | Arith. reasoning | Social status | 3 |
| 4 | Total language | Social inadequacy | 6 |
| 5 | Spelling | Personal adjustment | 7 |
| 4 | Mechanics of English | Study habits | 4 |
| 4 | Total reading | Schol. motivation | 4 |
| 4 | Reading comprehension | Self confidence | 3 |
| 5 | Vocabulary | Procrastination or. | 3 |

Boy
M15      Card # 46

| | | | |
|---|---|---|---|
| 6 | Grade-point average | Divergent thinking | 5 |
| 6 | Science | Convergent thinking | 5 |
| 6 | Social studies | Mental maturity | 5 |
| 5 | Total arithmetic | Achievement drive | 8 |
| 5 | Arith. fundamentals | Peer status | 3 |
| 5 | Arith. reasoning | Social status | 4 |
| 5 | Total language | Social inadequacy | 8 |
| 5 | Spelling | Personal adjustment | 8 |
| 6 | Mechanics of English | Study habits | 7 |
| 5 | Total reading | Schol. motivation | 7 |
| 5 | Reading comprehension | Self confidence | 5 |
| 5 | Vocabulary | Procrastination or. | 7 |

Girl
M15      Card # 47

| | | | |
|---|---|---|---|
| 6 | Grade-point average | Divergent thinking | 6 |
| 5 | Science | Convergent thinking | 5 |
| 5 | Social studies | Mental maturity | 6 |
| 4 | Total arithmetic | Achievement drive | 5 |
| 5 | Arith. fundamentals | Peer status | 3 |
| 4 | Arith. reasoning | Social status | 5 |
| 5 | Total language | Social inadequacy | 6 |
| 5 | Spelling | Personal adjustment | 7 |
| 5 | Mechanics of English | Study habits | 4 |
| 5 | Total reading | Schol. motivation | 4 |
| 4 | Reading comprehension | Self confidence | 5 |
| 5 | Vocabulary | Procrastination or. | 5 |

Girl
M15      Card # 48

| | | | |
|---|---|---|---|
| 6 | Grade-point average | Divergent thinking | 6 |
| 8 | Science | Convergent thinking | 6 |
| 7 | Social studies | Mental maturity | 6 |
| 5 | Total arithmetic | Achievement drive | 4 |
| 5 | Arith. fundamentals | Peer status | 6 |
| 5 | Arith. reasoning | Social status | 4 |
| 4 | Total language | Social inadequacy | 6 |
| 5 | Spelling | Personal adjustment | 5 |
| 4 | Mechanics of English | Study habits | 5 |
| 7 | Total reading | Schol. motivation | 4 |
| 8 | Reading comprehension | Self confidence | 5 |
| 6 | Vocabulary | Procrastination or. | 4 |

Boy
M15      Card # 49

| | | | |
|---|---|---|---|
| 6 | Grade-point average | Divergent thinking | 7 |
| 6 | Science | Convergent thinking | 5 |
| 6 | Social studies | Mental maturity | 5 |
| 5 | Total arithmetic | Achievement drive | 5 |
| 5 | Arith. fundamentals | Peer status | 1 |
| 5 | Arith. reasoning | Social status | 3 |
| 5 | Total language | Social inadequacy | 4 |
| 3 | Spelling | Personal adjustment | 3 |
| 6 | Mechanics of English | Study habits | 4 |
| 5 | Total reading | Schol. motivation | 5 |
| 5 | Reading comprehension | Self confidence | 4 |
| 5 | Vocabulary | Procrastination or. | 5 |

Boy
M15      Card # 50

| | | | |
|---|---|---|---|
| 6 | Grade-point average | Divergent thinking | 4 |
| 5 | Science | Convergent thinking | 4 |
| 5 | Social studies | Mental maturity | 3 |
| 5 | Total arithmetic | Achievement drive | 4 |
| 5 | Arith. fundamentals | Peer status | 8 |
| 5 | Arith. reasoning | Social status | 6 |
| 7 | Total language | Social inadequacy | 6 |
| 7 | Spelling | Personal adjustment | 5 |
| 6 | Mechanics of English | Study habits | 4 |
| 4 | Total reading | Schol. motivation | 5 |
| 4 | Reading comprehension | Self confidence | 5 |
| 5 | Vocabulary | Procrastination or. | 5 |

Girl
M15      Card # 51

| | | | |
|---|---|---|---|
| 7 | Grade-point average | Divergent thinking | 5 |
| 7 | Science | Convergent thinking | 5 |
| 7 | Social studies | Mental maturity | 4 |
| 4 | Total arithmetic | Achievement drive | 6 |
| 5 | Arith. fundamentals | Peer status | 9 |
| 4 | Arith. reasoning | Social status | 3 |
| 7 | Total language | Social inadequacy | 8 |
| 6 | Spelling | Personal adjustment | 6 |
| 7 | Mechanics of English | Study habits | 6 |
| 6 | Total reading | Schol. motivation | 6 |
| 6 | Reading comprehension | Self confidence | 6 |
| 5 | Vocabulary | Procrastination or. | 6 |

Girl
M15      Card # 52

289

| | Card # 53 | | |
|---|---|---|---|
| 7 | Grade-point average | Divergent thinking | 6 |
| 5 | Science | Convergent thinking | 5 |
| 7 | Social studies | Mental maturity | 4 |
| 6 | Total arithmetic | Achievement drive | 6 |
| 6 | Arith. fundamentals | Peer status | 7 |
| 6 | Arith. reasoning | Social status | 5 |
| 5 | Total language | Social inadequacy | 5 |
| 5 | Spelling | Personal adjustment | 5 |
| 5 | Mechanics of English | Study habits | 7 |
| 6 | Total reading | Schol. motivation | 7 |
| 6 | Reading comprehension | Self confidence | 6 |
| 5 | Vocabulary | Procrastination or. | 7 |

Girl
M15

| | Card # 54 | | |
|---|---|---|---|
| 7 | Grade-point average | Divergent thinking | 9 |
| 7 | Science | Convergent thinking | 5 |
| 6 | Social studies | Mental maturity | 5 |
| 4 | Total arithmetic | Achievement drive | 6 |
| 4 | Arith. fundamentals | Peer status | 6 |
| 5 | Arith. reasoning | Social status | 3 |
| 6 | Total language | Social inadequacy | 2 |
| 5 | Spelling | Personal adjustment | 2 |
| 7 | Mechanics of English | Study habits | 7 |
| 6 | Total reading | Schol. motivation | 7 |
| 6 | Reading comprehension | Self confidence | 7 |
| 6 | Vocabulary | Procrastination or. | 6 |

Girl
M15

| | Card # 55 | | |
|---|---|---|---|
| 5 | Grade-point average | Divergent thinking | 4 |
| 6 | Science | Convergent thinking | 5 |
| 5 | Social studies | Mental maturity | 6 |
| 4 | Total arithmetic | Achievement drive | 6 |
| 4 | Arith. fundamentals | Peer status | 7 |
| 4 | Arith. reasoning | Social status | 6 |
| 6 | Total language | Social inadequacy | 4 |
| 5 | Spelling | Personal adjustment | 5 |
| 6 | Mechanics of English | Study habits | 6 |
| 5 | Total reading | Schol. motivation | 7 |
| 5 | Reading comprehension | Self confidence | 7 |
| 5 | Vocabulary | Procrastination or. | 6 |

Boy
M16

| | Card # 56 | | |
|---|---|---|---|
| 5 | Grade-point average | Divergent thinking | 4 |
| 5 | Science | Convergent thinking | 5 |
| 4 | Social studies | Mental maturity | 6 |
| 5 | Total arithmetic | Achievement drive | 6 |
| 5 | Arith. fundamentals | Peer status | 6 |
| 5 | Arith. reasoning | Social status | 6 |
| 5 | Total language | Social inadequacy | 6 |
| 6 | Spelling | Personal adjustment | 5 |
| 5 | Mechanics of English | Study habits | 4 |
| 5 | Total reading | Schol. motivation | 6 |
| 5 | Reading comprehension | Self confidence | 5 |
| 5 | Vocabulary | Procrastination or. | 5 |

Girl
M16

| | Card # 57 | | |
|---|---|---|---|
| 6 | Grade-point average | Divergent thinking | 4 |
| 6 | Science | Convergent thinking | 6 |
| 7 | Social studies | Mental maturity | 6 |
| 4 | Total arithmetic | Achievement drive | 4 |
| 5 | Arith. fundamentals | Peer status | 6 |
| 5 | Arith. reasoning | Social status | 3 |
| 6 | Total language | Social inadequacy | 7 |
| 6 | Spelling | Personal adjustment | 5 |
| 6 | Mechanics of English | Study habits | 2 |
| 6 | Total reading | Schol. motivation | 5 |
| 6 | Reading comprehension | Self confidence | 5 |
| 6 | Vocabulary | Procrastination or. | 4 |

Girl
M16

| | Card # 58 | | |
|---|---|---|---|
| 6 | Grade-point average | Divergent thinking | 4 |
| 6 | Science | Convergent thinking | 7 |
| 6 | Social studies | Mental maturity | 6 |
| 4 | Total arithmetic | Achievement drive | 4 |
| 4 | Arith. fundamentals | Peer status | 4 |
| 4 | Arith. reasoning | Social status | 5 |
| 6 | Total language | Social inadequacy | 3 |
| 6 | Spelling | Personal adjustment | 5 |
| 6 | Mechanics of English | Study habits | 6 |
| 6 | Total reading | Schol. motivation | 4 |
| 6 | Reading comprehension | Self confidence | 5 |
| 6 | Vocabulary | Procrastination or. | 4 |

Girl
M16

| | Card # 59 | | |
|---|---|---|---|
| 6 | Grade-point average | Divergent thinking | 5 |
| 7 | Science | Convergent thinking | 5 |
| 6 | Social studies | Mental maturity | 4 |
| 5 | Total arithmetic | Achievement drive | 6 |
| 5 | Arith. fundamentals | Peer status | 1 |
| 5 | Arith. reasoning | Social status | 1 |
| 7 | Total language | Social inadequacy | 2 |
| 5 | Spelling | Personal adjustment | 5 |
| 8 | Mechanics of English | Study habits | 8 |
| 5 | Total reading | Schol. motivation | 7 |
| 5 | Reading comprehension | Self confidence | 7 |
| 4 | Vocabulary | Procrastination or. | 7 |

Girl
M16

| | Card # 60 | | |
|---|---|---|---|
| 6 | Grade-point average | Divergent thinking | 6 |
| 5 | Science | Convergent thinking | 5 |
| 5 | Social studies | Mental maturity | 5 |
| 4 | Total arithmetic | Achievement drive | 3 |
| 4 | Arith. fundamentals | Peer status | 6 |
| 4 | Arith. reasoning | Social status | 7 |
| 7 | Total language | Social inadequacy | 3 |
| 9 | Spelling | Personal adjustment | 4 |
| 6 | Mechanics of English | Study habits | 3 |
| 5 | Total reading | Schol. motivation | 4 |
| 5 | Reading comprehension | Self confidence | 6 |
| 5 | Vocabulary | Procrastination or. | 4 |

Girl
M16

| | | | |
|---|---|---|---|
| 6 | Grade-point average | Divergent thinking | 6 |
| 5 | Science | Convergent thinking | 7 |
| 5 | Social studies | Mental maturity | 6 |
| 5 | Total arithmetic | Achievement drive | 5 |
| 6 | Arith. fundamentals | Peer status | 8 |
| 5 | Arith. reasoning | Social status | 4 |
| 5 | Total language | Social inadequacy | 4 |
| 5 | Spelling | Persqnal adjustment | 3 |
| 6 | Mechanics of English | Study habits _ | 4 |
| 6 | Total reading | Schol. motivation | 7 |
| 6 | Reading comprehension | Self confidence | 7 |
| 5 | Vocabulary | Procrastination or. | 5 |

Boy
M16     Card # 61

| | | | |
|---|---|---|---|
| 6 | Grade-point average | Divergent thinking | 9 |
| 7 | Science | Convergent thinking | 6 |
| 7 | Social studies | Mental maturity | 7 |
| 5 | Total arithmetic | Achievement drive | 4 |
| 5 | Arith. fundamentals | Peer status | 8 |
| 6 | Arith. reasoning | Social status | 3 |
| 4 | Total language | Social inadequacy | 4 |
| 3 | Spelling | Personal adjustment | 3 |
| 6 | Mechanics of English | Study habits | 4' |
| 6 | Total reading | Schol. motivation | 5 |
| 5 | Reading comprehension | Self confidence | 4 |
| 6 | Vocabulary | Procrastination or. | 5 |

Boy
M16     Card # 62

| | | | |
|---|---|---|---|
| 7 | Grade-point average | Divergent thinking | 4 |
| 5 | Science | Convergent thinking | 6 |
| 6 | Social studies | Mental maturity | 6 |
| 5 | Total arithmetic | Achievement drive | 5 |
| 5 | Arith. fundamentals | Peer status | 0 |
| 5 | Arith. reasoning | Social status | 7 |
| 5 | Total language | Social inadequacy | 9 |
| 5 | Spelling | Personal adjustment | 7 |
| 5 | Mechanics of English | Study habits | 4 |
| 5 | Total reading | Schol. motivation | 6 |
| 5 | Reading comprehension | Self confidence | 6 |
| 5 | Vocabulary | Procrastination or. | 6 |

Boy
M16     Card # 63

| | | | |
|---|---|---|---|
| 7 | Grade-point average | Divergent thinking | 5 |
| 6 | Science | Convergent thinking | 7 |
| 5 | Social studies | Mental maturity | 6 |
| 5 | Total arithmetic | Achievement drive | 6 |
| 5 | Arith. fundamentals | Peer status | 9 |
| 5 | Arith. reasoning | Social status | 3 |
| 5 | Total language | Social inadequacy | 5 |
| 5 | Spelling | Personal adjustment | 3 |
| 5 | Mechanics of English | Study habits | 5 |
| 5 | Total reading | Schol. motivation | 7 |
| 5 | Reading comprehension | Self confidence | 7 |
| 5 | Vocabulary | Procrastination or. | 8 |

Boy
M16     Card # 64

| | | | |
|---|---|---|---|
| 4 | Grade-point average | Divergent thinking | 5 |
| 4 | Science | Convergent thinking | 6 |
| 5 | Social studies | Mental maturity | 6 |
| 5 | Total arithmetic | Achievement drive | 5 |
| 5 | Arith. fundamentals | Peer status | 3 |
| 6 | Arith. reasoning | Social status | 6 |
| 6 | Total language | Social inadequacy | 5 |
| 6 | Spelling | Personal adjustment | 4 |
| 6 | Mechanics of English | Study habits | 3 |
| 5 | Total reading | Schol. motivation | 5 |
| 4 | Reading comprehension | Self confidence | 7 |
| 5 | Vocabulary | Procrastination or. | 3 |

Boy
M17     Card # 65

| | | | |
|---|---|---|---|
| 5 | Grade-point average | Divergent thinking | 6 |
| 4 | Science | Convergent thinking | 5 |
| 5 | Social studies | Mental maturity | 6 |
| 6 | Total arithmetic | Achievement drive | 6 |
| 5 | Arith. fundamentals | Peer status | 3 |
| 6 | Arith. reasoning | Social status | 7 |
| 5 | Total language | Social inadequacy | 2 |
| 4 | Spelling | Personal adjustment | 3 |
| 5 | Mechanics of English | Study habits | 4 |
| 5 | Total reading | Schol. motivation | 4 |
| 5 | Reading comprehension | Self confidence | 4 |
| 5 | Vocabulary | Procrastination or. | 5 |

Boy
M17     Card # 66

| | | | |
|---|---|---|---|
| 6 | Grade-point average | Divergent thinking | 4 |
| 4 | Science | Convergent thinking | 4 |
| 6 | Social studies | Mental maturity | 5 |
| 6 | Total arithmetic | Achievement drive | 6 |
| 6 | Arith. fundamentals | Peer status | 0 |
| 6 | Arith. reasoning | Social status | 4 |
| 6 | Total language | Social inadequacy | 5 |
| 5 | Spelling | Personal adjustment | 5 |
| 6 | Mechanics of English | Study habits | 5 |
| 5 | Total reading | Schol. motivation | 7 |
| 4 | Reading comprehension | Self confidence | 6 |
| 5 | Vocabulary | Procrastination or. | 7 |

Girl
M17     Card # 67

| | | | |
|---|---|---|---|
| 6 | Grade-point average | Divergent thinking | 6 |
| 6 | Science | Convergent thinking | 5 |
| 5 | Social studies | Mental maturity | 6 |
| 5 | Total arithmetic | Achievement drive | 5 |
| 5 | Arith. fundamentals | Peer status | 5 |
| 5 | Arith. reasoning | Social status | 4 |
| 6 | Total language | Social inadequacy | 6 |
| 5 | Spelling | Personal adjustment | 7 |
| 7 | Mechanics of English | Study habits | 3 |
| 6 | Total reading | Schol. motivation | 3 |
| 5 | Reading comprehension | Self confidence | 4 |
| 6 | Vocabulary | Procrastination or. | 4 |

Girl
F17     Card # 68

| | | | |
|---|---|---|---|
| 6 | Grade-point average | Divergent thinking | 6 |
| 8 | Science | Convergent thinking | 6 |
| 6 | Social studies | Mental maturity | 6 |
| 6 | Total arithmetic | Achievement drive | 5 |
| 5 | Arith. fundamentals | Peer status | 6 |
| 7 | Arith. reasoning | Social status | 6 |
| 5 | Total language | Social inadequacy | 5 |
| 5 | Spelling | Personal adjustment | 6 |
| 5 | Mechanics of English | Study habits | 4 |
| 6 | Total reading | Schol. motivation | 4 |
| 5 | Reading comprehension | Self confidence | 4 |
| 6 | Vocabulary | Procrastination or. | 4 |

Girl
F17  Card # 69

| | | | |
|---|---|---|---|
| 6 | Grade-point average | Divergent thinking | 7 |
| 5 | Science | Convergent thinking | 6 |
| 5 | Social studies | Mental maturity | 6 |
| 5 | Total arithmetic | Achievement drive | 7 |
| 6 | Arith. fundamentals | Peer status | 7 |
| 5 | Arith. reasoning | Social status | 7 |
| 6 | Total language | Social inadequacy | 4 |
| 5 | Spelling | Personal adjustment | 5 |
| 6 | Mechanics of English | Study habits | 5 |
| 5 | Total reading | Schol. motivation | 6 |
| 5 | Reading comprehension | Self confidence | 6 |
| 5 | Vocabulary | Procrastination or. | 6 |

Girl
F17  Card # 70

| | | | |
|---|---|---|---|
| 6 | Grade-point average | Divergent thinking | 8 |
| 6 | Science | Convergent thinking | 5 |
| 4 | Social studies | Mental maturity | 6 |
| 5 | Total arithmetic | Achievement drive | 7 |
| 4 | Arith. fundamentals | Peer status | 6 |
| 5 | Arith. reasoning | Social status | 3 |
| 6 | Total language | Social inadequacy | 5 |
| 6 | Spelling | Personal adjustment | 5 |
| 6 | Mechanics of English | Study habits | 8 |
| 5 | Total reading | Schol. motivation | 7 |
| 5 | Reading comprehension | Self confidence | 7 |
| 5 | Vocabulary | Procrastination or. | 7 |

Girl
F17  Card # 71

| | | | |
|---|---|---|---|
| 7 | Grade-point average | Divergent thinking | 4 |
| 6 | Science | Convergent thinking | 7 |
| 6 | Social studies | Mental maturity | 6 |
| 5 | Total arithmetic | Achievement drive | 8 |
| 5 | Arith. fundamentals | Peer status | 5 |
| 6 | Arith. reasoning | Social status | 5 |
| 6 | Total language | Social inadequacy | 6 |
| 5 | Spelling | Personal adjustment | 6 |
| 6 | Mechanics of English | Study habits | 7 |
| 5 | Total reading | Schol. motivation | 7 |
| 5 | Reading comprehension | Self confidence | 7 |
| 5 | Vocabulary | Procrastination or. | 8 |

Girl
F17  Card # 72

| | | | |
|---|---|---|---|
| 7 | Grade-point average | Divergent thinking | 6 |
| 4 | Science | Convergent thinking | 5 |
| 7 | Social studies | Mental maturity | 6 |
| 5 | Total arithmetic | Achievement drive | 6 |
| 4 | Arith. fundamentals | Peer status | 2 |
| 6 | Arith. reasoning | Social status | 5 |
| 6 | Total language | Social inadequacy | 8 |
| 4 | Spelling | Personal adjustment | 6 |
| 7 | Mechanics of English | Study habits | 6 |
| 6 | Total reading | Schol. motivation | 6 |
| 6 | Reading comprehension | Self confidence | 6 |
| 6 | Vocabulary | Procrastination or. | 5 |

Girl
F17  Card # 73

| | | | |
|---|---|---|---|
| 7 | Grade-point average | Divergent thinking | 7 |
| 6 | Science | Convergent thinking | 7 |
| 6 | Social studies | Mental maturity | 5 |
| 6 | Total arithmetic | Achievement drive | 7 |
| 5 | Arith. fundamentals | Peer status | 9 |
| 6 | Arith. reasoning | Social status | 4 |
| 6 | Total language | Social inadequacy | 4 |
| 6 | Spelling | Personal adjustment | 5 |
| 7 | Mechanics of English | Study habits | 7 |
| 6 | Total reading | Schol. motivation | 4 |
| 6 | Reading comprehension | Self confidence | 7 |
| 5 | Vocabulary | Procrastination or. | 5 |

Girl
F17  Card # 74

| | | | |
|---|---|---|---|
| 7 | Grade-point average | Divergent thinking | 8 |
| 5 | Science | Convergent thinking | 5 |
| 6 | Social studies | Mental maturity | 5 |
| 5 | Total arithmetic | Achievement drive | 7 |
| 4 | Arith. fundamentals | Peer status | 7 |
| 6 | Arith. reasoning | Social status | 4 |
| 7 | Total language | Social inadequacy | 5 |
| 7 | Spelling | Personal adjustment | 6 |
| 7 | Mechanics of English | Study habits | 6 |
| 5 | Total reading | Schol. motivation | 7 |
| 5 | Reading comprehension | Self confidence | 8 |
| 5 | Vocabulary | Procrastination or. | 7 |

Girl
F17  Card # 75

| | | | |
|---|---|---|---|
| 6 | Grade-point average | Divergent thinking | 5 |
| 5 | Science | Convergent thinking | 6 |
| 6 | Social studies | Mental maturity | 6 |
| 6 | Total arithmetic | Achievement drive | 4 |
| 6 | Arith. fundamentals | Peer status | 2 |
| 7 | Arith. reasoning | Social status | 5 |
| 6 | Total language | Social inadequacy | 3 |
| 5 | Spelling | Personal adjustment | 4 |
| 7 | Mechanics of English | Study habits | 3 |
| 6 | Total reading | Schol. motivation | 4 |
| 6 | Reading comprehension | Self confidence | 6 |
| 6 | Vocabulary | Procrastination or. | 4 |

Boy
F18  Card # 76

| | | | |
|---|---|---|---|
| 7 | Grade-point average | Divergent thinking | 4 |
| 5 | Science | Convergent thinking | 6 |
| 6 | Social studies | Mental maturity | 7 |
| 5 | Total arithmetic | Achievement drive | 6 |
| 5 | Arith. fundamentals | Peer status | 6 |
| 5 | Arith. reasoning | Social status | 4 |
| 6 | Total language | Social inadequacy | 6 |
| 6 | Spelling | Personal adjustment | 5 |
| 6 | Mechanics of English | Study habits | 4 |
| 5 | Total reading | Schol. motivation | 4 |
| 5 | Reading comprehension | Self confidence | 4 |
| 5 | Vocabulary | Procrastination or. | 6 |

Girl
F18                    Card # 77

| | | | |
|---|---|---|---|
| 7 | Grade-point average | Divergent thinking | 4 |
| 5 | Science | Convergent thinking | 6 |
| 7 | Social studies | Mental maturity | 6 |
| 5 | Total arithmetic | Achievement drive | 3 |
| 5 | Arith. fundamentals | Peer status | 3 |
| 6 | Arith. reasoning | Social status | 6 |
| 7 | Total language | Social inadequacy | 2 |
| 7 | Spelling | Personal adjustment | 4 |
| 7 | Mechanics of English | Study habits | 4 |
| 6 | Total reading | Schol. motivation | 4 |
| 6 | Reading comprehension | Self confidence | 4 |
| 7 | Vocabulary | Procrastination or. | 5 |

Girl
F18                    Card # 78

| | | | |
|---|---|---|---|
| 7 | Grade-point average | Divergent thinking | 5 |
| 7 | Science | Convergent thinking | 7 |
| 7 | Social studies | Mental maturity | 6 |
| 5 | Total arithmetic | Achievement drive | 7 |
| 5 | Arith. fundamentals | Peer status | 1 |
| 6 | Arith. reasoning | Social status | 4 |
| 7 | Total language | Social inadequacy | 6 |
| 5 | Spelling | Personal adjustment | 4 |
| 7 | Mechanics of English | Study habits | 7 |
| 7 | Total reading | Schol. motivation | 7 |
| 7 | Reading comprehension | Self confidence | 7 |
| 7 | Vocabulary | Procrastination or. | 7 |

Girl
F18                    Card # 79

| | | | |
|---|---|---|---|
| 7 | Grade-point average | Divergent thinking | 5 |
| 6 | Science | Convergent thinking | 8 |
| 7 | Social studies | Mental maturity | 7 |
| 5 | Total arithmetic | Achievement drive | 5 |
| 5 | Arith. fundamentals | Peer status | 8 |
| 6 | Arith. reasoning | Social status | 2 |
| 6 | Total language | Social inadequacy | 7 |
| 5 | Spelling | Personal adjustment | 5 |
| 7 | Mechanics of English | Study habits | 5 |
| 6 | Total reading | Schol. motivation | 6 |
| 6 | Reading comprehension | Self confidence | 5 |
| 5 | Vocabulary | Procrastination or. | 3 |

Boy
F18                    Card # 80

| | | | |
|---|---|---|---|
| 7 | Grade-point average | Divergent thinking | 6 |
| 6 | Science | Convergent thinking | 7 |
| 6 | Social studies | Mental maturity | 7 |
| 6 | Total arithmetic | Achievement drive | 6 |
| 5 | Arith. fundamentals | Peer status | 8 |
| 7 | Arith. reasoning | Social status | 4 |
| 5 | Total language | Social inadequacy | 5 |
| 5 | Spelling | Personal adjustment | 3 |
| 5 | Mechanics of English | Study habits | 6 |
| 4 | Total reading | Schol. motivation | 8 |
| 4 | Reading comprehension | Self confidence | 8 |
| 5 | Vocabulary | Procrastination or. | 6 |

Boy
F18                    Card # 81

| | | | |
|---|---|---|---|
| 7 | Grade-point average | Divergent thinking | 7 |
| 5 | Science | Convergent thinking | 6 |
| 6 | Social studies | Mental maturity | 7 |
| 6 | Total arithmetic | Achievement drive | 5 |
| 6 | Arith. fundamentals | Peer status | 7 |
| 5 | Arith. reasoning | Social status | 5 |
| 5 | Total language | Social inadequacy | 6 |
| 5 | Spelling | Personal adjustment | 5 |
| 6 | Mechanics of English | Study habits | 5 |
| 6 | Total reading | Schol. motivation | 4 |
| 5 | Reading comprehension | Self confidence | 4 |
| 7 | Vocabulary | Procrastination or. | 5 |

Girl
F18                    Card # 82

| | | | |
|---|---|---|---|
| 7 | Grade-point average | Divergent thinking | 7 |
| 7 | Science | Convergent thinking | 7 |
| 8 | Social studies | Mental maturity | 5 |
| 7 | Total arithmetic | Achievement drive | 5 |
| 6 | Arith. fundamentals | Peer status | 9 |
| 5 | Arith. reasoning | Social status | 3 |
| 8 | Total language | Social inadequacy | 7 |
| 8 | Spelling | Personal adjustment | 5 |
| 7 | Mechanics of English | Study habits | 5 |
| 6 | Total reading | Schol. motivation | 6 |
| 7 | Reading comprehension | Self confidence | 6 |
| 5 | Vocabulary | Procrastination or. | 5 |

Girl
F18                    Card # 83

| | | | |
|---|---|---|---|
| 6 | Grade-point average | Divergent thinking | 7 |
| 5 | Science | Convergent thinking | 6 |
| 6 | Social studies | Mental maturity | 7 |
| 5 | Total arithmetic | Achievement drive | 4 |
| 5 | Arith. fundamentals | Peer status | 7 |
| 6 | Arith. reasoning | Social status | 2 |
| 7 | Total language | Social inadequacy | 6 |
| 6 | Spelling | Personal adjustment | 7 |
| 7 | Mechanics of English | Study habits | 4 |
| 6 | Total reading | Schol. motivation | 5 |
| 5 | Reading comprehension | Self confidence | 4 |
| 6 | Vocabulary | Procrastination or. | 3 |

Boy
F19                    Card # 84

293

## Card # 85 — Girl F19

| | | | |
|---|---|---|---|
| 7 | Grade-point average | Divergent thinking | 5 |
| 6 | Science | Convergent thinking | 6 |
| 8 | Social studies | Mental maturity | 6 |
| 6 | Total arithmetic | Achievement drive | 8 |
| 6 | Arith. fundamentals | Peer status | 4 |
| 6 | Arith. reasoning | Social status | 6 |
| 7 | Total language | Social inadequacy | 3 |
| 7 | Spelling | Personal adjustment | 3 |
| 7 | Mechanics of English | Study habits | 8 |
| 8 | Total reading | Schol. motivation | 8 |
| 8 | Reading comprehension | Self confidence | 9 |
| 8 | Vocabulary | Procrastination or. | 8 |

## Card # 86 — Girl F19

| | | | |
|---|---|---|---|
| 7 | Grade-point average | Divergent thinking | 5 |
| 8 | Science | Convergent thinking | 8 |
| 7 | Social studies | Mental maturity | 6 |
| 6 | Total arithmetic | Achievement drive | 4 |
| 5 | Arith. fundamentals | Peer status | 7 |
| 7 | Arith. reasoning | Social status | 4 |
| 7 | Total language | Social inadequacy | 6 |
| 5 | Spelling | Personal adjustment | 8 |
| 8 | Mechanics of English | Study habits | 3 |
| 7 | Total reading | Schol. motivation | 3 |
| 7 | Reading comprehension | Self confidence | 5 |
| 7 | Vocabulary | Procrastination or. | 4 |

## Card # 87 — Girl F19

| | | | |
|---|---|---|---|
| 7 | Grade-point average | Divergent thinking | 6 |
| 6 | Science | Convergent thinking | 7 |
| 6 | Social studies | Mental maturity | 6 |
| 6 | Total arithmetic | Achievement drive | 7 |
| 5 | Arith. fundamentals | Peer status | 4 |
| 6 | Arith. reasoning | Social status | 3 |
| 7 | Total language | Social inadequacy | 2 |
| 6 | Spelling | Personal adjustment | 2 |
| 7 | Mechanics of English | Study habits | 5 |
| 7 | Total reading | Schol. motivation | 7 |
| 5 | Reading comprehension | Self confidence | 8 |
| 8 | Vocabulary | Procrastination or. | 8 |

## Card # 88 — Girl F19

| | | | |
|---|---|---|---|
| 7 | Grade-point average | Divergent thinking | 6 |
| 8 | Science | Convergent thinking | 7 |
| 8 | Social studies | Mental maturity | 6 |
| 6 | Total arithmetic | Achievement drive | 8 |
| 5 | Arith. fundamentals | Peer status | 8 |
| 7 | Arith. reasoning | Social status | 4 |
| 7 | Total language | Social inadequacy | 2 |
| 7 | Spelling | Personal adjustment | 1 |
| 6 | Mechanics of English | Study habits | 7 |
| 7 | Total reading | Schol. motivation | 8 |
| 7 | Reading comprehension | Self confidence | 7 |
| 7 | Vocabulary | Procrastination or. | 8 |

## Card # 89 — Girl F19

| | | | |
|---|---|---|---|
| 7 | Grade-point average | Divergent thinking | 8 |
| 6 | Science | Convergent thinking | 6 |
| 5 | Social studies | Mental maturity | 6 |
| 6 | Total arithmetic | Achievement drive | 6 |
| 5 | Arith. fundamentals | Peer status | 0 |
| 6 | Arith. reasoning | Social status | 5 |
| 7 | Total language | Social inadequacy | 8 |
| 7 | Spelling | Personal adjustment | 8 |
| 7 | Mechanics of English | Study habits | 4 |
| 6 | Total reading | Schol. motivation | 6 |
| 6 | Reading comprehension | Self confidence | 3 |
| 6 | Vocabulary | Procrastination or. | 5 |

## Card # 90 — Girl F20

| | | | |
|---|---|---|---|
| 7 | Grade-point average | Divergent thinking | 7 |
| 7 | Science | Convergent thinking | 6 |
| 7 | Social studies | Mental maturity | 7 |
| 6 | Total arithmetic | Achievement drive | 6 |
| 6 | Arith. fundamentals | Peer status | 3 |
| 7 | Arith. reasoning | Social status | 0 |
| 7 | Total language | Social inadequacy | 5 |
| 6 | Spelling | Personal adjustment | 4 |
| 7 | Mechanics of English | Study habits | 6 |
| 7 | Total reading | Schol. motivation | 6 |
| 7 | Reading comprehension | Self confidence | 7 |
| 6 | Vocabulary | Procrastination or. | 6 |

## Card # 91 — Boy F20

| | | | |
|---|---|---|---|
| 8 | Grade-point average | Divergent thinking | 4 |
| 9 | Science | Convergent thinking | 8 |
| 8 | Social studies | Mental maturity | 7 |
| 6 | Total arithmetic | Achievement drive | 7 |
| 5 | Arith. fundamentals | Peer status | 1 |
| 7 | Arith. reasoning | Social status | 4 |
| 7 | Total language | Social inadequacy | 3 |
| 8 | Spelling | Personal adjustment | 3 |
| 7 | Mechanics of English | Study habits | 5 |
| 9 | Total reading | Schol. motivation | 8 |
| 9 | Reading comprehension | Self confidence | 8 |
| 8 | Vocabulary | Procrastination or. | 8 |

## Card # 92 — Girl F20

| | | | |
|---|---|---|---|
| 8 | Grade-point average | Divergent thinking | 5 |
| 8 | Science | Convergent thinking | 8 |
| 7 | Social studies | Mental maturity | 6 |
| 6 | Total arithmetic | Achievement drive | 8 |
| 5 | Arith. fundamentals | Peer status | 4 |
| 7 | Arith. reasoning | Social status | 5 |
| 8 | Total language | Social inadequacy | 6 |
| 7 | Spelling | Personal adjustment | 5 |
| 8 | Mechanics of English | Study habits | 7 |
| 9 | Total reading | Schol. motivation | 7 |
| 9 | Reading comprehension | Self confidence | 6 |
| 9 | Vocabulary | Procrastination or. | 8 |

| | | | |
|---|---|---|---|
| 7 | Grade-point average | Divergent thinking | 6 |
| 8 | Science | Convergent thinking | 7 |
| 6 | Social studies | Mental maturity | 7 |
| 6 | Total arithmetic | Achievement drive | 6 |
| 6 | Arith. fundamentals | Peer status | 1 |
| 7 | Arith. reasoning | Social status | 4 |
| 8 | Total language | Social inadequacy | 5 |
| 8 | Spelling | Personal adjustment | 5 |
| 8 | Mechanics of English | Study habits | 6 |
| 8 | Total reading | Schol. motivation | 7 |
| 8 | Reading comprehension | Self confidence | 6 |
| 9 | Vocabulary | Procrastination or. | 8 |

Girl
F21                    Card # 93

| | | | |
|---|---|---|---|
| 7 | Grade-point average | Divergent thinking | 6 |
| 6 | Science | Convergent thinking | 8 |
| 7 | Social studies | Mental maturity | 8 |
| 6 | Total arithmetic | Achievement drive | 7 |
| 6 | Arith. fundamentals | Peer status | 8 |
| 7 | Arith. reasoning | Social status | 3 |
| 7 | Total language | Social inadequacy | 3 |
| 6 | Spelling | Personal adjustment | 3 |
| 7 | Mechanics of English | Study habits | 8 |
| 6 | Total reading | Schol. motivation | 8 |
| 6 | Reading comprehension | Self confidence | 8 |
| 6 | Vocabulary | Procrastination or. | 8 |

Girl
F21                    Card # 94

| | | | |
|---|---|---|---|
| 7 | Grade-point average | Divergent thinking | 8 |
| 9 | Science | Convergent thinking | 8 |
| 8 | Social studies | Mental maturity | 8 |
| 7 | Total arithmetic | Achievement drive | 4 |
| 6 | Arith. fundamentals | Peer status | 3 |
| 7 | Arith. reasoning | Social status | 2 |
| 6 | Total language | Social inadequacy | 5 |
| 5 | Spelling | Personal adjustment | 5 |
| 7 | Mechanics of English | Study habits | 6 |
| 9 | Total reading | Schol. motivation | 6 |
| 9 | Reading comprehension | Self confidence | 6 |
| 8 | Vocabulary | Procrastination or. | 5 |

Boy
F21                    Card # 95

| | | | |
|---|---|---|---|
| 8 | Grade-point average | Divergent thinking | 6 |
| 7 | Science | Convergent thinking | 7 |
| 7 | Social studies | Mental maturity | 6 |
| 7 | Total arithmetic | Achievement drive | 6 |
| 9 | Arith. fundamentals | Peer status | 1 |
| 5 | Arith. reasoning | Social status | 3 |
| 8 | Total language | Social inadequacy | 6 |
| 7 | Spelling | Personal adjustment | 6 |
| 8 | Mechanics of English | Study habits | 6 |
| 8 | Total reading | Schol. motivation | 5 |
| 9 | Reading comprehension | Self confidence | 5 |
| 6 | Vocabulary | Procrastination or. | 7 |

Girl
F21                    Card # 96

| | | | |
|---|---|---|---|
| 7 | Grade-point average | Divergent thinking | 4 |
| 6 | Science | Convergent thinking | 8 |
| 7 | Social studies | Mental maturity | 7 |
| 8 | Total arithmetic | Achievement drive | 7 |
| 8 | Arith. fundamentals | Peer status | 2 |
| 7 | Arith. reasoning | Social status | 4 |
| 8 | Total language | Social inadequacy | 6 |
| 8 | Spelling | Personal adjustment | 8 |
| 8 | Mechanics of English | Study habits | 8 |
| 7 | Total reading | Schol. motivation | 8 |
| 7 | Reading comprehension | Self confidence | 7 |
| 7 | Vocabulary | Procrastination or. | 8 |

Girl
F23                    Card # 97

| | | | |
|---|---|---|---|
| 7 | Grade-point average | Divergent thinking | 7 |
| 8 | Science | Convergent thinking | 8 |
| 7 | Social studies | Mental maturity | 8 |
| 6 | Total arithmetic | Achievement drive | 6 |
| 6 | Arith. fundamentals | Peer status | 7 |
| 7 | Arith. reasoning | Social status | 4 |
| 9 | Total language | Social inadequacy | 5 |
| 8 | Spelling | Personal adjustment | 7 |
| 9 | Mechanics of English | Study habits | 6 |
| 8 | Total reading | Schol. motivation | 6 |
| 7 | Reading comprehension | Self confidence | 8 |
| 8 | Vocabulary | Procrastination or. | 6 |

Girl
F23                    Card # 98

| | | | |
|---|---|---|---|
| 7 | Grade-point average | Divergent thinking | 5 |
| 9 | Science | Convergent thinking | 8 |
| 7 | Social studies | Mental maturity | 8 |
| 8 | Total arithmetic | Achievement drive | 6 |
| 8 | Arith. fundamentals | Peer status | 1 |
| 7 | Arith. reasoning | Social status | 3 |
| 8 | Total language | Social inadequacy | 5 |
| 7 | Spelling | Personal adjustment | 6 |
| 8 | Mechanics of English | Study habits | 7 |
| 7 | Total reading | Schol. motivation | 7 |
| 8 | Reading comprehension | Self confidence | 8 |
| 5 | Vocabulary | Procrastination or. | 8 |

Girl
F24                    Card # 99

| | | | |
|---|---|---|---|
| 8 | Grade-point average | Divergent thinking | 7 |
| 7 | Science | Convergent thinking | 8 |
| 8 | Social studies | Mental maturity | 7 |
| 9 | Total arithmetic | Achievement drive | 8 |
| 9 | Arith. fundamentals | Peer status | 8 |
| 8 | Arith. reasoning | Social status | 4 |
| 8 | Total language | Social inadequacy | 3 |
| 7 | Spelling | Personal adjustment | 4 |
| 8 | Mechanics of English | Study habits | 7 |
| 8 | Total reading | Schol. motivation | 7 |
| 8 | Reading comprehension | Self confidence | 6 |
| 8 | Vocabulary | Procrastination or. | 7 |

Girl
F24                    Card# 100

Appendix VI-B

DIAGNOSTIC OUTLINE – LANGUAGE TEST

A Set of Data on Fifty-Nine Pupils

## DIAGNOSTIC OUTLINE--LANGUAGE TEST

Test 5--Mechanics of English   Advanced Form   Grades 9 to 14

| Battery Summary | Raw Scores | Grade Placement Scores | Sub-test A-- Capitalization |
|---|---|---|---|
| Total Language | 52 | 6.3 | 28 correct |
| Mechanics of English | 42 | 6.3 | out of 40 |
| Spelling | 10 | 9.0 | |

### Item Analysis for Capitalization

1. Names of institutions and organizations · · · (2)(19) 23 27 38 39
2. Titles of persons · · · 3 18 24
3. Titles of literature and drama · · · 4 (14) 32 (35)
4. First words of sentences · · · 5 15 (28)
5. Names of persons · · · 6 (22) 36
6. Names of cities · · · 7 10 (13)
7. Names of rivers, streets, islands, etc. · · · (20)(25)(37)
8. Days and months · · · 9 16 30
9. First words of quotations · · · 11 21 33 40
10. Names of languages · · · (31)
11. Over-capitalization · · · 1 8 12 17 (26) 29 34

Student's Name *Fatima, Pat*    Grade 9 (10) 11 12

---

## DIAGNOSTIC OUTLINE--LANGUAGE TEST

Test 5--Mechanics of English   Advanced Form   Grades 9 to 14

| Battery Summary | Raw Scores | Grade Placement Scores | Sub-test A-- Capitalization |
|---|---|---|---|
| Total Language | 153 | 14.6 | 36 correct |
| Mechanics of English | 131 | 14.9 | out of 40 |
| Spelling | 22 | 14.3 | |

### Item Analysis for Capitalization

1. Names of institutions and organizations · · · 2 19 23 27 38 39
2. Titles of persons · · · 3 18 24
3. Titles of literature and drama · · · 4 14 32 35
4. First words of sentences · · · 5 (15) 28
5. Names of persons · · · 6 22 36
6. Names of cities · · · 7 10 13
7. Names of rivers, streets, islands, etc. · · · 20 25 37
8. Days and months · · · 9 (16)(30)
9. First words of quotations · · · 11 21 33 40
10. Names of languages · · · 31
11. Over-capitalization · · · 1 8 12 (17)(26) (29)(34)

Student's Name *Dale, Vincent*    Grade 9 10 (11) 12

# DIAGNOSTIC OUTLINE--LANGUAGE TEST

Test 5--Mechanics of English    Advanced Form    Grades 9 to 14

| Battery Summary | Raw Scores | Grade Placement Scores | Sub-test A -- Capitalization |
|---|---|---|---|
| Total Language | 144 | 13.7 | 37 correct out of 40 |
| Mechanics of English | 126 | 14.3 | |
| Spelling | 18 | 12.9 | |

## Item Analysis for Capitalization

| | | | | | |
|---|---|---|---|---|---|
| 1. Names of institutions and organizations | 2 | 19 | 23 | 27 (38) | 39 |
| 2. Titles of persons | 3 | 18 | 24 | | |
| 3. Titles of literature and drama | 4 | 14 | 32 | 35 | |
| 4. First words of sentences | 5 | 15 | 28 | | |
| 5. Names of persons | 6 | 22 | 36 | | |
| 6. Names of cities | 7 | 10 | 13 | | |
| 7. Names of rivers, streets, islands, etc. | 20 | 25 | 37 | | |
| 8. Days and months | 9 | 16 | 30 | | |
| 9. First words of quotations | 11 | 21 | 33 | 40 | |
| 10. Names of languages | 31 | | | | |
| 11. Over-capitalization | 1 | 8 | 12 | 17 | 26 |
| | | | | (29) | (34) |

Student's Name _Ackerman, Sue_    Grade    9    10    11    (12)

---

# DIAGNOSTIC OUTLINE--LANGUAGE TEST

Test 5--Mechanics of English    Advanced Form    Grades 9 to 14

| Battery Summary | Raw Scores | Grade Placement Scores | Sub-test A -- Capitalization |
|---|---|---|---|
| Total Language | 125 | 11.8 | 35 correct out of 40 |
| Mechanics of English | 107 | 11.9 | |
| Spelling | 18 | 12.9 | |

## Item Analysis for Capitalization

| | | | | | |
|---|---|---|---|---|---|
| 1. Names of institutions and organizations | (2) | 19 | 23 | 27 | 38 (39) |
| 2. Titles of persons | 3 | 18 | 24 | | |
| 3. Titles of literature and drama | 4 | 14 | 32 | 35 | |
| 4. First words of sentences | 5 | (15) | 28 | | |
| 5. Names of persons | 6 | 22 | 36 | | |
| 6. Names of cities | 7 | 10 | 13 | | |
| 7. Names of rivers, streets, islands, etc. | 20 | (25) | 37 | | |
| 8. Days and months | 9 | 16 | 30 | | |
| 9. First words of quotations | 11 | 21 | 33 | 40 | |
| 10. Names of languages | 31 | | | | |
| 11. Over-capitalization | 1 | 8 | 12 | 17 | 26 |
| | | | | 29 | (34) |

Student's Name _Harris, Sue_    Grade    9    (10)    11    12

299

## DIAGNOSTIC OUTLINE--LANGUAGE TEST
### Test 5--Mechanics of English    Advanced Form    Grades 9 to 14

| Battery Summary | Raw Scores | Grade Placement Scores | Sub-test A-- Capitalization |
|---|---|---|---|
| Total Language | 116 | 11.0 | 36 correct out of 40 |
| Mechanics of English | 100 | 11.0 | |
| Spelling | 16 | 12.0 | |

Item Analysis for Capitalization

1. Names of institutions and organizations . . . . . . 2 19 23 27 38 39
2. Titles of persons . . . . . . . . . . . . . . . 3 18 24
3. Titles of literature and drama . . . . . . . . . 4 14 32 35
4. First words of sentences . . . . . . . . . . . 5 15 28
5. Names of persons . . . . . . . . . . . . . . 6 22 36
6. Names of cities . . . . . . . . . . . . . . . 7 10 13
7. Names of rivers, streets, islands, etc. . . . . . 20 25 37
8. Days and months . . . . . . . . . . . . . . (9) 16 30
9. First words of quotations . . . . . . . . . . . 11 21 33 40
10. Names of languages . . . . . . . . . . . . . 31
11. Over-capitalization . . . . . . . . . . . . . (1) (8) 12 17 26 29 (34)

Student's Name _Diaz, Tomás_     Grade 9 10 11 (12)

---

## DIAGNOSTIC OUTLINE--LANGUAGE TEST
### Test 5--Mechanics of English    Advanced Form    Grades 9 to 14

| Battery Summary | Raw Scores | Grade Placement Scores | Sub-test A-- Capitalization |
|---|---|---|---|
| Total Language | 143 | 13.6 | 37 correct out of 40 |
| Mechanics of English | 126 | 14.3 | |
| Spelling | 17 | 12.5 | |

Item Analysis for Capitalization

1. Names of institutions and organizations . . . . . . 2 19 23 27 38 39
2. Titles of persons . . . . . . . . . . . . . . . (3) 18 (24)
3. Titles of literature and drama . . . . . . . . . 4 14 32 35
4. First words of sentences . . . . . . . . . . . 5 (15) 28
5. Names of persons . . . . . . . . . . . . . . 6 22 36
6. Names of cities . . . . . . . . . . . . . . . 7 10 13
7. Names of rivers, streets, islands, etc. . . . . . 20 25 37
8. Days and months . . . . . . . . . . . . . . 9 16 30
9. First words of quotations . . . . . . . . . . . 11 21 33 40
10. Names of languages . . . . . . . . . . . . . 31
11. Over-capitalization . . . . . . . . . . . . . 1 8 12 17 26 29 34

Student's Name _Dumfey, Marianne_ Grade 9 10 11 (12)

## DIAGNOSTIC OUTLINE--LANGUAGE TEST

### Test 5--Mechanics of English    Advanced Form    Grades 9 to 14

| Battery Summary | Raw Scores | Grade Placement Scores | Sub-test A-- Capitalization |
|---|---|---|---|
| Total Language | 131 | 12.4 | 38 correct out of 40 |
| Mechanics of English | 118 | 13.3 | |
| Spelling | 13 | 10.5 | |

#### Item Analysis for Capitalization

| | | | | |
|---|---|---|---|---|
| 1. Names of institutions and organizations | 2 | 19 | 23 | 27 38 39 |
| 2. Titles of persons | 3 | 18 | 24 | |
| 3. Titles of literature and drama | 4 | 14 | 32 | 35 |
| 4. First words of sentences | 5 | 15 | 28 | |
| 5. Names of persons | 6 | 22 | 36 | |
| 6. Names of cities | 7 | 10 | 13 | |
| 7. Names of rivers, streets, islands, etc. | 20 | 25 | 37 | |
| 8. Days and months | 9 | 16 | 30 | |
| 9. First words of quotations | (11) | 21 | 33 | 40 |
| 10. Names of languages | 31 | | | |
| 11. Over-capitalization | 1 | 8 | 12 17 26 | 29 (34) |

Student's Name _Boucher, James_    Grade   9   10   11 (12)

---

## DIAGNOSTIC OUTLINE--LANGUAGE TEST

### Test 5--Mechanics of English    Advanced Form    Grades 9 to 14

| Battery Summary | Raw Scores | Grade Placement Scores | Sub-test A-- Capitalization |
|---|---|---|---|
| Total Language | 119 | 11.3 | 37 correct out of 40 |
| Mechanics of English | 104 | 11.6 | |
| Spelling | 15 | 11.5 | |

#### Item Analysis for Capitalization

| | | | | |
|---|---|---|---|---|
| 1. Names of institutions and organizations | 2 | 19 | 23 | 27 38 39 |
| 2. Titles of persons | 3 | 18 | 24 | |
| 3. Titles of literature and drama | 4 | 14 | 32 | 35 |
| 4. First words of sentences | 5 | 15 | 28 | |
| 5. Names of persons | 6 | 22 | 36 | |
| 6. Names of cities | 7 | 10 | 13 | |
| 7. Names of rivers, streets, islands, etc. | (20) | 25 | 37 | |
| 8. Days and months | 9 | 16 | 30 | |
| 9. First words of quotations | 11 | 21 | 33 | 40 |
| 10. Names of languages | 31 | | | |
| 11. Over-capitalization | 1 | 8 (12) 17 26 | 29 (34) | |

Student's Name _Agee, Joanne_    Grade   9 (10) 11 12

DIAGNOSTIC OUTLINE--LANGUAGE TEST   Advanced Form   Grades 9 to 14

Test 5--Mechanics of English

| Battery Summary | Raw Scores | Grade Placement Scores | Sub-test A-- Capitalization |
|---|---|---|---|
| Total Language | 135 | 12.8 | 33 correct out of 40 |
| Mechanics of English | 115 | 13.0 | |
| Spelling | 20 | 13.5 | |

Item Analysis for Capitalization

1. Names of institutions and organizations . . . . . . . . . . . . . 2 (19) 23 27 38 39
2. Titles of persons . . . . . . . . . . . . . . . . . . . . . . . . . . . 3 18 (24)
3. Titles of literature and drama . . . . . . . . . . . . . . . . . . 4 (14) 32 (35)
4. First words of sentences . . . . . . . . . . . . . . . . . . . . . 5 15 28
5. Names of persons . . . . . . . . . . . . . . . . . . . . . . . . . . 6 22 36
6. Names of cities . . . . . . . . . . . . . . . . . . . . . . . . . . . . 7 10 13
7. Names of rivers, streets, islands, etc. . . . . . . . . . . . . . 20 (25) 37
8. Days and months . . . . . . . . . . . . . . . . . . . . . . . . . . . 9 (16) 30
9. First words of quotations . . . . . . . . . . . . . . . . . . . . . 11 21 33 40
10. Names of languages . . . . . . . . . . . . . . . . . . . . . . . . . 31
11. Over-capitalization . . . . . . . . . . . . . . . . . . . . . . . . . 1 8 12 17 26 29 (34)

Student's Name *Carter, Dax*   Grade   9   10   11 (12)

---

DIAGNOSTIC OUTLINE--LANGUAGE TEST   Advanced Form   Grades 9 to 14

Test 5--Mechanics of English

| Battery Summary | Raw Scores | Grade Placement Scores | Sub-test A-- Capitalization |
|---|---|---|---|
| Total Language | 142 | 13.5 | 38 correct out of 40 |
| Mechanics of English | 123 | 14.0 | |
| Spelling | 19 | 13.2 | |

Item Analysis for Capitalization

1. Names of institutions and organizations . . . . . . . . . . . . . 2 19 23 27 38 39
2. Titles of persons . . . . . . . . . . . . . . . . . . . . . . . . . . . 3 18 24
3. Titles of literature and drama . . . . . . . . . . . . . . . . . . 4 14 32 35
4. First words of sentences . . . . . . . . . . . . . . . . . . . . . 5 15 28
5. Names of persons . . . . . . . . . . . . . . . . . . . . . . . . . . 6 22 36
6. Names of cities . . . . . . . . . . . . . . . . . . . . . . . . . . . . 7 10 (13)
7. Names of rivers, streets, islands, etc. . . . . . . . . . . . . . (20) 25 37
8. Days and months . . . . . . . . . . . . . . . . . . . . . . . . . . . 9 16 30
9. First words of quotations . . . . . . . . . . . . . . . . . . . . . 11 21 33 40
10. Names of languages . . . . . . . . . . . . . . . . . . . . . . . . . 31
11. Over-capitalization . . . . . . . . . . . . . . . . . . . . . . . . . 1 8 12 17 26 29 34

Student's Name *Naboth, Ronald*   Grade   9   10 (11) 12

# DIAGNOSTIC OUTLINE--LANGUAGE TEST

Test 5--Mechanics of English    Advanced Form    Grades 9 to 14

| Battery Summary | Raw Scores | Grade Placement Scores | Sub-test A-- Capitalization |
|---|---|---|---|
| Total Language . . . . | 93 | 9.1 | |
| Mechanics of English . . . | 86 | 9.3 | 25 correct |
| Spelling . . . . . . . | 7 | 7.5 | out of 40 |

## Item Analysis for Capitalization

1. Names of institutions and organizations . . . . . . .  2 (19) (23) (27) (38) (39)
2. Titles of persons . . . . . . . . . . . . . . .  3 (18) (24)
3. Titles of literature and drama . . . . . . . . .  4  14  32  35
4. First words of sentences . . . . . . . . . . .  5  15 (28)
5. Names of persons . . . . . . . . . . . . . .  6 (22)  36
6. Names of cities . . . . . . . . . . . . . . . .  7  10  13
7. Names of rivers,  streets,  islands, etc. . . . . . .  (20)  25  37
8. Days and months . . . . . . . . . . . . . .  (9)  16  30
9. First words of quotations . . . . . . . . . . .  11  21  33  40
10. Names of languages . . . . . . . . . . . . .  (31)
11. Over-capitalization . . . . . . . . . . . . .  1  8  12 (17) (26)  29 (34)

Student's Name _Baker, Jean_    Grade  9 (10)  11  12

# DIAGNOSTIC OUTLINE--LANGUAGE TEST

Test 5--Mechanics of English    Advanced Form    Grades 9 to 14

| Battery Summary | Raw Scores | Grade Placement Scores | Sub-test A-- Capitalization |
|---|---|---|---|
| Total Language . . . . | 94 | 9.2 | |
| Mechanics of English . . . | 84 | 9.1 | 33 correct |
| Spelling . . . . . . . | 10 | 9.0 | out of 40 |

## Item Analysis for Capitalization

1. Names of institutions and organizations . . . . . . .  2  19  23 (27)  38 (39)
2. Titles of persons . . . . . . . . . . . . . . .  3  18  24
3. Titles of literature and drama . . . . . . . . .  4  14  32  35
4. First words of sentences . . . . . . . . . . .  5  15  28
5. Names of persons . . . . . . . . . . . . . .  6  22  36
6. Names of cities . . . . . . . . . . . . . . . .  7  10 (13)
7. Names of rivers,  streets,  islands, etc. . . . . . .  (20)  25  37
8. Days and months . . . . . . . . . . . . . .  9  16  30
9. First words of quotations . . . . . . . . . . .  11  21  33  40
10. Names of languages . . . . . . . . . . . . .  31
11. Over-capitalization . . . . . . . . . . . . .  1  8  12 (17) (26)  29 (34)

Student's Name _Cortez, Juan_    Grade  9 (10)  11  12

303

## DIAGNOSTIC OUTLINE--LANGUAGE TEST

Test 5--Mechanics of English    Advanced Form    Grades 9 to 14

| Battery Summary | Raw Scores | Grade Placement Scores | Sub-test A--Capitalization |
|---|---|---|---|
| Total Language | 128 | 12.1 | 34 correct out of 40 |
| Mechanics of English | 117 | 13.2 | |
| Spelling | 11 | 9.5 | |

### Item Analysis for Capitalization

1. Names of institutions and organizations .... 2  19  23  27  38  39
2. Titles of persons .... 3  18  (24)
3. Titles of literature and drama .... 4  14  32  35
4. First words of sentences .... 5  15  28
5. Names of persons .... 6  22  36
6. Names of cities .... 7  10  13
7. Names of rivers, streets, islands, etc. .... 20  25  (37)
8. Days and months .... 9  16  30
9. First words of quotations .... (11)  21  (33)  40
10. Names of languages .... 31
11. Over-capitalization .... 1  8  12  17  26  29  (34)

Student's Name Hernandez, Joe    Grade  9  10  (11)  12

---

## DIAGNOSTIC OUTLINE--LANGUAGE TEST

Test 5--Mechanics of English    Advanced Form    Grades 9 to 14

| Battery Summary | Raw Scores | Grade Placement Scores | Sub-test A--Capitalization |
|---|---|---|---|
| Total Language | 82 | 8.0 | 17 correct out of 40 |
| Mechanics of English | 71 | 7.7 | |
| Spelling | 11 | 9.5 | |

### Item Analysis for Capitalization

1. Names of institutions and organizations .... 2  (19)  23  27  (38)  39
2. Titles of persons .... (3)(18)(24)
3. Titles of literature and drama .... (4)(14)  32  (35)
4. First words of sentences .... 5  15  (28)
5. Names of persons .... 6  22  36
6. Names of cities .... 7  10  13
7. Names of rivers, streets, islands, etc. .... (20)  25  37
8. Days and months .... 9  16  30
9. First words of quotations .... (11)(21)(33)(40)
10. Names of languages .... (31)
11. Over-capitalization .... 1  8  (12)(17)  26  (29)(34)

Student's Name Oliphant, Susan    Grade  9  10  (11)  12

304

## (Top form)

# DIAGNOSTIC OUTLINE--LANGUAGE TEST

### Test 5--Mechanics of English  Advanced Form  Grades 9 to 14

| Battery Summary | Raw Scores | Grade Placement Scores | Sub-test A-- Capitalization |
|---|---|---|---|
| Total Language | 105 | 10.1 | 32 correct out of 40 |
| Mechanics of English | 95 | 10.2 | |
| Spelling | 10 | 9.0 | |

### Item Analysis for Capitalization

1. Names of institutions and organizations . . . . . . 2 19 23 27 38 39
2. Titles of persons . . . . . . . . . . . . . . . . 3 18 24
3. Titles of literature and drama . . . . . . . . . 4 14 32 35
4. First words of sentences . . . . . . . . . . . . 5 15 (28)
5. Names of persons . . . . . . . . . . . . . . . . 6 22 (36)
6. Names of cities . . . . . . . . . . . . . . . . 7 10 13
7. Names of rivers, streets, islands, etc. . . . . . 20 25 (37)
8. Days and months . . . . . . . . . . . . . . . . 9 16 30
9. First words of quotations . . . . . . . . . . . . (11) (21) (33) (40)
10. Names of languages . . . . . . . . . . . . . . 31
11. Over-capitalization . . . . . . . . . . . . . . 1 8 12 17 26 29 (34)

Student's Name *Herrera, Maria*  Grade 9 10 (11) 12

---

## (Bottom form)

# DIAGNOSTIC OUTLINE--LANGUAGE TEST

### Test 5--Mechanics of English  Advanced Form  Grades 9 to 14

| Battery Summary | Raw Scores | Grade Placement Scores | Sub-test A-- Capitalization |
|---|---|---|---|
| Total Language | 94 | 9.2 | 27 correct out of 40 |
| Mechanics of English | 85 | 9.2 | |
| Spelling | 9 | 8.5 | |

### Item Analysis for Capitalization

1. Names of institutions and organizations . . . . . . 2 19 23 27 38 39
2. Titles of persons . . . . . . . . . . . . . . . . 3 18 (24)
3. Titles of literature and drama . . . . . . . . . 4 (14) 32 35
4. First words of sentences . . . . . . . . . . . . 5 15 28
5. Names of persons . . . . . . . . . . . . . . . . 6 22 36
6. Names of cities . . . . . . . . . . . . . . . . 7 (10)(13)
7. Names of rivers, streets, islands, etc. . . . . . (20) 25 37
8. Days and months . . . . . . . . . . . . . . . . 9 16 30
9. First words of quotations . . . . . . . . . . . . (11) (21) (33) (40)
10. Names of languages . . . . . . . . . . . . . . (31)
11. Over-capitalization . . . . . . . . . . . . . . 1 8 12 17 26 29 (34)

Student's Name *Goth, Ralph*  Grade 9 10 (11) 12

## DIAGNOSTIC OUTLINE--LANGUAGE TEST

Test 5--Mechanics of English     Advanced Form     Grades 9 to 14

| Battery Summary | Raw Scores | Grade Placement Scores | Sub-test A-- Capitalization |
|---|---|---|---|
| Total Language . . . . . . . | 94 | 9.2 | 32 correct out of 40 |
| Mechanics of English . . . | 85 | 9.2 | |
| Spelling . . . . . . . . . . | 9 | 8.5 | |

### Item Analysis for Capitalization

| | | | | | |
|---|---|---|---|---|---|
| 1. Names of institutions and organizations . . . . . . | 2 | 19 | 23 | 27 | 38  39 |
| 2. Titles of persons . . . . . . . . . . . . . . . . | 3 | 18 | 24 | | |
| 3. Titles of literature and drama . . . . . . . . . | 4 | (14) | (32) | 35 | |
| 4. First words of sentences . . . . . . . . . . . | 5 | 15 | (28) | | |
| 5. Names of persons . . . . . . . . . . . . . . . | 6 | 22 | 36 | | |
| 6. Names of cities . . . . . . . . . . . . . . . | 7 | 10 | 13 | | |
| 7. Names of rivers, streets, islands, etc. . . | 20 | 25 | 37 | | |
| 8. Days and months . . . . . . . . . . . . . | (9) | 16 | 30 | | |
| 9. First words of quotations . . . . . . . . . | (11) | (21) | (33) | (40) | |
| 10. Names of languages . . . . . . . . . . . | 31 | | | | |
| 11. Over-capitalization . . . . . . . . . . . . | 1 | 8 | 12 | 17 | 26  29  34 |

Student's Name *Doyle, Richard*     Grade   9   10  (11)  12

---

## DIAGNOSTIC OUTLINE--LANGUAGE TEST

Test 5--Mechanics of English     Advanced Form     Grades 9 to 14

| Battery Summary | Raw Scores | Grade Placement Scores | Sub-test A-- Capitalization |
|---|---|---|---|
| Total Language . . . . . . . | 88 | 8.6 | 30 correct out of 40 |
| Mechanics of English . . . | 79 | 8.4 | |
| Spelling . . . . . . . . . . | 9 | 8.5 | |

### Item Analysis for Capitalization

| | | | | | |
|---|---|---|---|---|---|
| 1. Names of institutions and organizations . . . . . . | 2 | (19) | 23 | 27 | 38  39 |
| 2. Titles of persons . . . . . . . . . . . . . . . . | 3 | 18 | (24) | | |
| 3. Titles of literature and drama . . . . . . . . . | 4 | 14 | 32 | 35 | |
| 4. First words of sentences . . . . . . . . . . . | 5 | 15 | (28) | | |
| 5. Names of persons . . . . . . . . . . . . . . . | 6 | 22 | 36 | | |
| 6. Names of cities . . . . . . . . . . . . . . . | 7 | 10 | 13 | | |
| 7. Names of rivers, streets, islands, etc. . . | 20 | 25 | (37) | | |
| 8. Days and months . . . . . . . . . . . . . | (9) | 16 | 30 | | |
| 9. First words of quotations . . . . . . . . . | (11) | (21) | (33) | (40) | |
| 10. Names of languages . . . . . . . . . . . | 31 | | | | |
| 11. Over-capitalization . . . . . . . . . . . . | 1 | 8 | 12 | 17 | 26  29  (34) |

Student's Name *Galbraith, Wayne*     Grade   9   10  (11)  12

# DIAGNOSTIC OUTLINE--LANGUAGE TEST

Test 5--Mechanics of English    Advanced Form    Grades 9 to 14

| Battery Summary | Raw Scores | Grade Placement Scores | Sub-test A--Capitalization |
|---|---|---|---|
| Total Language . . . . . . | 111 | 10.6 | |
| Mechanics of English . . . | 99 | 10.8 | 31 correct out of 40 |
| Spelling . . . . . . . . . | 12 | 10.0 | |

## Item Analysis for Capitalization

1. Names of institutions and organizations . . . . (2) 19 (23) 27 38 39
2. Titles of persons . . . . . . . . . . . . (3) 18 (24)
3. Titles of literature and drama . . . . . . . . 4 14 32 35
4. First words of sentences . . . . . . . . . 5 15 28
5. Names of persons . . . . . . . . . . . . 6 22 36
6. Names of cities . . . . . . . . . . . . 7 10 13
7. Names of rivers, streets, islands, etc. . . . . . 20 25 37
8. Days and months . . . . . . . . . . . . 9 16 30
9. First words of quotations . . . . . . . . . (11) (21) (33) (40)
10. Names of languages . . . . . . . . . . . 31
11. Over-capitalization . . . . . . . . . . . 1 8 12 17 26 29 (34)

Student's Name Gomez, Ricardo    Grade 9 10 11 (12)

---

# DIAGNOSTIC OUTLINE--LANGUAGE TEST

Test 5--Mechanics of English    Advanced Form    Grades 9 to 14

| Battery Summary | Raw Scores | Grade Placement Scores | Sub-test A--Capitalization |
|---|---|---|---|
| Total Language . . . . . . | 111 | 10.6 | |
| Mechanics of English . . . | 96 | 10.3 | 33 correct out of 40 |
| Spelling . . . . . . . . . | 15 | 11.5 | |

## Item Analysis for Capitalization

1. Names of institutions and organizations . . . . 2 19 23 27 38 39
2. Titles of persons . . . . . . . . . . . . 3 18 (24)
3. Titles of literature and drama . . . . . . . . 4 14 32 35
4. First words of sentences . . . . . . . . . 5 15 28
5. Names of persons . . . . . . . . . . . . 6 22 36
6. Names of cities . . . . . . . . . . . . 7 10 13
7. Names of rivers, streets, islands, etc. . . . . . 20 25 37
8. Days and months . . . . . . . . . . . . (9) 16 30
9. First words of quotations . . . . . . . . . (11) (21) (33) (40)
10. Names of languages . . . . . . . . . . . 31
11. Over-capitalization . . . . . . . . . . . 1 8 12 17 26 29 (34)

Student's Name Escolara, Louise    Grade 9 10 11 (12)

## DIAGNOSTIC OUTLINE--LANGUAGE TEST

Test 5--Mechanics of English  Advanced Form  Grades 9 to 14

| Battery Summary | Raw Scores | Grade Placement Scores | Sub-test A-- Capitalization |
|---|---|---|---|
| Total Language . . . . . | 107 | 10.2 | 32 correct out of 40 |
| Mechanics of English . . . | 98 | 10.6 | |
| Spelling . . . . . . . . | 9 | 8.5 | |

### Item Analysis for Capitalization

1. Names of institutions and organizations . . . . . . 2 (19) 23 27 38 39
2. Titles of persons . . . . . . . . . . . . . . 3 18 (24)
3. Titles of literature and drama . . . . . . . . . 4 14 32 35
4. First words of sentences . . . . . . . . . . . 5 15 28
5. Names of persons . . . . . . . . . . . . . . 6 22 36
6. Names of cities . . . . . . . . . . . . . . (7) 10 13
7. Names of rivers, streets, islands, etc. . . . . . 20 25 37
8. Days and months . . . . . . . . . . . . . . 9 16 30
9. First words of quotations . . . . . . . . . . 11 (21) (33) (40)
10. Names of languages . . . . . . . . . . . . . 31
11. Over-capitalization . . . . . . . . . . . . . 1 8 12 17 26 29 (34)

Student's Name *Engle, Elaine*  Grade  9 10 11 (12)

---

## DIAGNOSTIC OUTLINE--LANGUAGE TEST

Test 5--Mechanics of English  Advanced Form  Grades 9 to 14

| Battery Summary | Raw Scores | Grade Placement Scores | Sub-test A-- Capitalization |
|---|---|---|---|
| Total Language . . . . . | 99 | 9.6 | 32 correct out of 40 |
| Mechanics of English . . . | 90 | 9.7 | |
| Spelling . . . . . . . . | 9 | 8.5 | |

### Item Analysis for Capitalization

1. Names of institutions and organizations . . . . . . 2 (19) (23) 27 38 39
2. Titles of persons . . . . . . . . . . . . . . 3 18 24
3. Titles of literature and drama . . . . . . . . . 4 14 32 35
4. First words of sentences . . . . . . . . . . . 5 15 (28)
5. Names of persons . . . . . . . . . . . . . . 6 22 36
6. Names of cities . . . . . . . . . . . . . . 7 10 13
7. Names of rivers, streets, islands, etc. . . . . . 20 (25) 37
8. Days and months . . . . . . . . . . . . . . 9 16 30
9. First words of quotations . . . . . . . . . . 11 (21) 33 (40)
10. Names of languages . . . . . . . . . . . . . 31
11. Over-capitalization . . . . . . . . . . . . . 1 8 12 17 26 (29) (34)

Student's Name *Hawthorne, James*  Grade  9 10 11 (12)

308

## DIAGNOSTIC OUTLINE--LANGUAGE TEST

Test 5--Mechanics of English     Advanced Form     Grades 9 to 14

| Battery Summary | Raw Scores | Grade Placement Scores | Sub-test A-- Capitalization |
|---|---|---|---|
| Total Language . . . . . . | 64 | 6.8 | |
| Mechanics of English . . . | 53 | 6.6 | 23 correct out of 40 |
| Spelling . . . . . . . . | 11 | 9.5 | |

### Item Analysis for Capitalization

1. Names of institutions and organizations . . . . . . (2) 19 23 27 (38) (39)
2. Titles of persons . . . . . 3 (18) 24
3. Titles of literature and drama . . . . 4 (14) (32) (35)
4. First words of sentences . . . . 5 15 28
5. Names of persons . . . . 6 22 (36)
6. Names of cities . . . . 7 10 13
7. Names of rivers, streets, islands, etc. . . . 20 25 (37)
8. Days and months . . . . 9 16 30
9. First words of quotations . . . 11 21 (33) (40)
10. Names of languages . . . . 31
11. Over-capitalization. . . . 1 (8) (12) (17) (26) (29) (34)

Student's Name *Mitchell, Jan*     Grade 9 10 (11) 12

---

## DIAGNOSTIC OUTLINE--LANGUAGE TEST

Test 5--Mechanics of English     Advanced Form     Grades 9 to 14

| Battery Summary | Raw Scores | Grade Placement Scores | Sub-test A-- Capitalization |
|---|---|---|---|
| Total Language . . . . . . | 96 | 9.3 | |
| Mechanics of English . . . | 84 | 9.1 | 30 correct out of 40 |
| Spelling . . . . . . . . | 12 | 10.0 | |

### Item Analysis for Capitalization

1. Names of institutions and organizations . . . . . . 2 19 23 (27) 38 (39)
2. Titles of persons . . . . . 3 18 (24)
3. Titles of literature and drama . . . . 4 14 32 35
4. First words of sentences . . . . (5) 15 28
5. Names of persons . . . . 6 22 36
6. Names of cities . . . . 7 10 (13)
7. Names of rivers, streets, islands, etc. . . . 20 (25) 37
8. Days and months . . . . 9 16 30
9. First words of quotations . . . (11) (21) 33 (40)
10. Names of languages . . . . 31
11. Over-capitalization. . . . 1 8 12 17 (26) 29 34

Student's Name *Haskins, Larry*     Grade 9 (10) 11 12

309

## DIAGNOSTIC OUTLINE--LANGUAGE TEST

### Test 5--Mechanics of English    Advanced Form    Grades 9 to 14

| Battery Summary | Raw Scores | Grade Placement Scores | Sub-test A-- Capitalization |
|---|---|---|---|
| Total Language . . . . . . | 87 | 8.5 | 16 correct out of 40 |
| Mechanics of English . . . | 78 | 8.3 | |
| Spelling . . . . . . . . . | 9 | 8.5 | |

#### Item Analysis for Capitalization

1. Names of institutions and organizations    2 (19) 23 (27) 38 (39)
2. Titles of persons    3 (18) (24)
3. Titles of literature and drama    4 (14) 32 35
4. First words of sentences    5 (15) 28
5. Names of persons    6 22 36
6. Names of cities    7 (10) (13)
7. Names of rivers, streets, islands, etc.    20 (25) 37
8. Days and months    9 (16) 30
9. First words of quotations    11 (21) (33) (40)
10. Names of languages    (31)
11. Over-capitalization    1 (8) (12) (17) (26) 29 34

Student's Name *Morris, Annette*    Grade    9 (10) 11 12

---

## DIAGNOSTIC OUTLINE--LANGUAGE TEST

### Test 5--Mechanics of English    Advanced Form    Grades 9 to 14

| Battery Summary | Raw Scores | Grade Placement Scores | Sub-test A-- Capitalization |
|---|---|---|---|
| Total Language . . . . . . | 83 | 8.1 | 24 correct out of 40 |
| Mechanics of English . . . | 75 | 8.0 | |
| Spelling . . . . . . . . . | 8 | 8.0 | |

#### Item Analysis for Capitalization

1. Names of institutions and organizations    (2) (19) 23 27 (38) (39)
2. Titles of persons    3 18 (24)
3. Titles of literature and drama    4 14 32 (35)
4. First words of sentences    5 15 28
5. Names of persons    (6) 22 (36)
6. Names of cities    7 10 (13)
7. Names of rivers, streets, islands, etc.    20 25 (37)
8. Days and months    9 16 30
9. First words of quotations    (11) 21 (33) (40)
10. Names of languages    31
11. Over-capitalization    1 8 (12) 17 26 (29) (34)

Student's Name *Darwin, Joe*    Grade    9 10 11 (12)

# DIAGNOSTIC OUTLINE--LANGUAGE TEST

Test 5--Mechanics of English    Advanced Form    Grades 9 to 14

| Battery Summary | Raw Scores | Grade Placement Scores | Sub-test A-- Capitalization |
|---|---|---|---|
| Total Language . . . . | 86 | 8.4 | 16 correct out of 40 |
| Mechanics of English . . | 74 | 7.9 | |
| Spelling . . . . . . . | 12 | 10.0 | |

## Item Analysis for Capitalization

1. Names of institutions and organizations . . . . . . . .   2 (19) 23 27 38 (39)
2. Titles of persons   . . . . . . . . . . . . . . . .   (3) 18 (24)
3. Titles of literature and drama . . . . . . . . . . . .   4 (14) (32) (35)
4. First words of sentences . . . . . . . . . . . . . .   5 (15) (28)
5. Names of persons . . . . . . . . . . . . . . . . . .   (6) (22) 36
6. Names of cities . . . . . . . . . . . . . . . . . .   7 10 13
7. Names of rivers, streets, islands, etc. . . . . . . .   (20) 25 37
8. Days and months . . . . . . . . . . . . . . . . . .   (9) (16) (30)
9. First words of quotations . . . . . . . . . . . . .   (11) (21) (33) (40)
10. Names of languages . . . . . . . . . . . . . . . .   (31)
11. Over-capitalization . . . . . . . . . . . . . . . .   1 8 12 (17) 26 29 (34)

Student's Name _Jones, Agnes_    Grade 9 10 11 (12)

---

# DIAGNOSTIC OUTLINE--LANGUAGE TEST

Test 5--Mechanics of English    Advanced Form    Grades 9 to 14

| Battery Summary | Raw Scores | Grade Placement Scores | Sub-test A-- Capitalization |
|---|---|---|---|
| Total Language . . . . | 88 | 8.6 | 25 correct out of 40 |
| Mechanics of English . . | 75 | 8.0 | |
| Spelling . . . . . . . | 13 | 10.5 | |

## Item Analysis for Capitalization

1. Names of institutions and organizations . . . . . . . .   2 19 (23) 27 (38) 39
2. Titles of persons   . . . . . . . . . . . . . . . .   3 18 24
3. Titles of literature and drama . . . . . . . . . . . .   4 (14) 32 35
4. First words of sentences . . . . . . . . . . . . . .   (5) (15) (28)
5. Names of persons . . . . . . . . . . . . . . . . . .   6 22 36
6. Names of cities . . . . . . . . . . . . . . . . . .   7 10 13
7. Names of rivers, streets, islands, etc. . . . . . . .   20 25 (37)
8. Days and months . . . . . . . . . . . . . . . . . .   (9) (16) 30
9. First words of quotations . . . . . . . . . . . . .   (11) (21) (33) (40)
10. Names of languages . . . . . . . . . . . . . . . .   31
11. Over-capitalization . . . . . . . . . . . . . . . .   1 8 12 (17) 26 29 (34)

Student's Name _Joslin, Harry_    Grade 9 10 11 (12)

311

DIAGNOSTIC OUTLINE--LANGUAGE TEST

Test 5--Mechanics of English   Advanced Form   Grades 9 to 14

| Battery Summary | Raw Scores | Grade Placement Scores | Sub-test A-- Capitalization |
|---|---|---|---|
| Total Language . . . | 72 | 7.2 | |
| Mechanics of English . . | 67 | 7.4 | 25 correct out of 40 |
| Spelling . . . . . . . | 5 | 6.6 | |

### Item Analysis for Capitalization

1. Names of institutions and organizations . . . . 2 (19) 23 27 38 (39)
2. Titles of persons . . . . . . 3 18 24
3. Titles of literature and drama . . . 4 (14) 32 35
4. First words of sentences . . . . 5 (15) (28)
5. Names of persons . . . . 6 22 36
6. Names of cities . . . . 7 10 13
7. Names of rivers, streets, islands, etc. . . 7. (20) 25 37
8. Days and months . . . . 9 16 30
9. First words of quotations . . . 11 (21) (33) (40)
10. Names of languages . . . . 31
11. Over-capitalization . . . . 1 8 12 (17) (26) 29 (34)

Student's Name *Lawler, Ben*    Grade 9 (10) 11 12

---

DIAGNOSTIC OUTLINE--LANGUAGE TEST

Test 5--Mechanics of English   Advanced Form   Grades 9 to 14

| Battery Summary | Raw Scores | Grade Placement Scores | Sub-test A-- Capitalization |
|---|---|---|---|
| Total Language . . . | 61 | 6.6 | |
| Mechanics of English . . | 53 | 6.6 | 17 correct out of 40 |
| Spelling . . . . . . . | 8 | 8.0 | |

### Item Analysis for Capitalization

1. Names of institutions and organizations . . . . 2 (19) 23 27 38 (39)
2. Titles of persons . . . . . . (3) 18 24
3. Titles of literature and drama . . . 4 (4) (32) 35
4. First words of sentences . . . . 5 15 (28)
5. Names of persons . . . . 6 22 (36)
6. Names of cities . . . . 7 10 13
7. Names of rivers, streets, islands, etc. . . (20) (25) (37)
8. Days and months . . . . 9 16 30
9. First words of quotations . . . 11 (21) (33) (40)
10. Names of languages . . . . 31
11. Over-capitalization . . . . 1 8 (12) (17) 26 (29) (34)

Student's Name *Caffee, Jim*    Grade 9 10 (11) 12

312

## DIAGNOSTIC OUTLINE--LANGUAGE TEST

Test 5--Mechanics of English    Advanced Form    Grades 9 to 14

| Battery Summary | Raw Scores | Grade Placement Scores | Sub-test A--Capitalization |
|---|---|---|---|
| Total Language | 97 | 9.4 | |
| Mechanics of English | 84 | 9.1 | 21 correct out of 40 |
| Spelling | 13 | 10.5 | |

### Item Analysis for Capitalization

1. Names of institutions and organizations . . . 2 (19) 23 (27) 38 (39)
2. Titles of persons . . . 3 (18) 24
3. Titles of literature and drama . . . 4 14 32 35
4. First words of sentences . . . 5 (15)(28)
5. Names of persons . . . 6 22 36
6. Names of cities . . . 7 (10)(13)
7. Names of rivers, streets, islands, etc. . . . (20)(25) 37
8. Days and months . . . (9)16 30
9. First words of quotations . . . (11)(21)(33)(40)
10. Names of languages . . . 31
11. Over-capitalization . . . 1 8 12 (17) 26   29 (34)

Student's Name *Ibsen, Lorraine*    Grade 9 (10) 11 12

## DIAGNOSTIC OUTLINE--LANGUAGE TEST

Test 5--Mechanics of English    Advanced Form    Grades 9 to 14

| Battery Summary | Raw Scores | Grade Placement Scores | Sub-test A--Capitalization |
|---|---|---|---|
| Total Language | 59 | 6.5 | |
| Mechanics of English | 49 | 6.5 | 17 correct out of 40 |
| Spelling | 10 | 9.0 | |

### Item Analysis for Capitalization

1. Names of institutions and organizations . . . 2 (19) 23 (27) 38 (39)
2. Titles of persons . . . 3 18 (24)
3. Titles of literature and drama . . . 4 14 32 (35)
4. First words of sentences . . . (5)(15) 28
5. Names of persons . . . (6) 22 36
6. Names of cities . . . (7)(10)(13)
7. Names of rivers, streets, islands, etc. . . . (20)(25) 37
8. Days and months . . . (9)(16) 30
9. First words of quotations . . . (11)(21) 33 (40)
10. Names of languages . . . (31)
11. Over-capitalization . . . 1 8 12 (17) 26   29 34

Student's Name *King, Greg*    Grade 9 (10) 11 12

313

# DIAGNOSTIC OUTLINE--LANGUAGE TEST

## Test 5--Mechanics of English    Advanced Form    Grades 9 to 14

| Battery Summary | Raw Scores | Grade Placement Scores | Sub-test A-- Capitalization |
|---|---|---|---|
| Total Language . . . . . | 88 | 8.6 | 26 correct out of 40 |
| Mechanics of English . . | 77 | 8.2 | |
| Spelling . . . . . . . . | 11 | 9.5 | |

### Item Analysis for Capitalization

1. Names of institutions and organizations . . . . .   2   19   (23)   27   (38)   (39)
2. Titles of persons . . . . . . . . . . . . . . . . .   3   (18)   24
3. Titles of literature and drama . . . . . . . . . .   4   14   32   35
4. First words of sentences . . . . . . . . . . . . .   5   (15)   (28)
5. Names of persons . . . . . . . . . . . . . . . . .   6   22   36
6. Names of cities . . . . . . . . . . . . . . . . . .   7   10   (13)
7. Names of rivers, streets, islands, etc. . . . . . .   (20)   (25)   37
8. Days and months . . . . . . . . . . . . . . . . . .   9   16   30
9. First words of quotations . . . . . . . . . . . . .   (11)   (21)   (33)   (40)
10. Names of languages . . . . . . . . . . . . . . . .   31
11. Over-capitalization . . . . . . . . . . . . . . . .   1   8   (12)   17   26   29   (34)

Student's Name _Dupree, Mary_    Grade   9   (10)   11   12

---

# DIAGNOSTIC OUTLINE--LANGUAGE TEST

## Test 5--Mechanics of English    Advanced Form    Grades 9 to 14

| Battery Summary | Raw Scores | Grade Placement Scores | Sub-test A-- Capitalization |
|---|---|---|---|
| Total Language . . . . . | 90 | 8.8 | 21 correct out of 40 |
| Mechanics of English . . | 76 | 8.1 | |
| Spelling . . . . . . . . | 14 | 11.0 | |

### Item Analysis for Capitalization

1. Names of institutions and organizations . . . . .   2   (19)   23   27   38   (39)
2. Titles of persons . . . . . . . . . . . . . . . . .   3   (18)   (24)
3. Titles of literature and drama . . . . . . . . . .   (4)   14   32   35
4. First words of sentences . . . . . . . . . . . . .   (5)   (15)   28
5. Names of persons . . . . . . . . . . . . . . . . .   6   (22)   36
6. Names of cities . . . . . . . . . . . . . . . . . .   7   10   13
7. Names of rivers, streets, islands, etc. . . . . . .   (20)   (25)   (37)
8. Days and months . . . . . . . . . . . . . . . . . .   (9)   (16)   30
9. First words of quotations . . . . . . . . . . . . .   (11)   (21)   (33)   (40)
10. Names of languages . . . . . . . . . . . . . . . .   31
11. Over-capitalization . . . . . . . . . . . . . . . .   1   8   12   (17)   (26)   29   (34)

Student's Name _Brown, Andy_    Grade   9   (10)   11   12

314

DIAGNOSTIC OUTLINE--LANGUAGE TEST

Test 5--Mechanics of English    Advanced Form    Grades 9 to 14

| Battery Summary | Raw Scores | Grade Placement Scores | Sub-test A--Capitalization |
|---|---|---|---|
| Total Language . . . . . . | 95 | 9.2 | |
| Mechanics of English . . . | 90 | 9.7 | 27 correct out of 40 |
| Spelling . . . . . . . . | 5 | 6.6 | |

## Item Analysis for Capitalization

1. Names of institutions and organizations . . . . . . 2  19  23  27  38  (39)
2. Titles of persons . . . . . . . (3)  18  24
3. Titles of literature and drama . . . 4  14  32  (35)
4. First words of sentences . . . . (5)  (15)  28
5. Names of persons . . . . . . 6  22  36
6. Names of cities . . . . . . (7)  10  13
7. Names of rivers, streets, islands, etc. . . (20)  (25)  37
8. Days and months . . . . . 9  (16)  30
9. First words of quotations . . . 11  21  33  40
10. Names of languages . . . . . (31)
11. Over-capitalization . . . . (1)  8  12  (17)  26  29  (34)

Student's Name Calhoun, Bill    Grade  9  10  (11)  12

---

DIAGNOSTIC OUTLINE--LANGUAGE TEST

Test 5--Mechanics of English    Advanced Form    Grades 9 to 14

| Battery Summary | Raw Scores | Grade Placement Scores | Sub-test A--Capitalization |
|---|---|---|---|
| Total Language . . . . . . | 94 | 9.2 | |
| Mechanics of English . . . | 84 | 9.1 | 26 correct out of 40 |
| Spelling . . . . . . . . | 10 | 9.0 | |

## Item Analysis for Capitalization

1. Names of institutions and organizations . . . . . . 2  (19)  (23)  27  (38)  (39)
2. Titles of persons . . . . . . . 3  18  24
3. Titles of literature and drama . . . 4  14  32  35
4. First words of sentences . . . . (5)  15  (28)
5. Names of persons . . . . . . 6  22  36
6. Names of cities . . . . . . 7  10  13
7. Names of rivers, streets, islands, etc. . . (20)  (25)  37
8. Days and months . . . . . 9  (16)  30
9. First words of quotations . . . (11)  (21)  (33)  (40)
10. Names of languages . . . . . (31)
11. Over-capitalization . . . . 1  8  12  17  26  29  34

Student's Name Cross, Jean    Grade  9  (10)  11  12

315

# DIAGNOSTIC OUTLINE--LANGUAGE TEST

Test 5--Mechanics of English    Advanced Form    Grades 9 to 14

| Battery Summary | Raw Scores | Grade Placement Scores | Sub-test A-- Capitalization |
|---|---|---|---|
| Total Language | 97 | 9.4 | 31 correct out of 40 |
| Mechanics of English | 86 | 9.3 | |
| Spelling | 11 | 9.5 | |

## Item Analysis for Capitalization

1. Names of institutions and organizations . . . 2 19 23 27 38 39
2. Titles of persons . . . 3 18 24
3. Titles of literature and drama . . . 4 (14) 32 35
4. First words of sentences . . . 5 (15)(28)
5. Names of persons . . . 6 22 36
6. Names of cities . . . 7 10 13
7. Names of rivers, streets, islands, etc. . . . (20)(25) 37
8. Days and months . . . 9 (16) 30
9. First words of quotations . . . (11) 21 33 40
10. Names of languages . . . (31)
11. Over-capitalization . . . 1 8 12 17 26 / 29 34

Student's Name Hopi, Sue    Grade 9 (10) 11 12

---

# DIAGNOSTIC OUTLINE--LANGUAGE TEST

Test 5--Mechanics of English    Advanced Form    Grades 9 to 14

| Battery Summary | Raw Scores | Grade Placement Scores | Sub-test A-- Capitalization |
|---|---|---|---|
| Total Language | 124 | 11.7 | 33 correct out of 40 |
| Mechanics of English | 105 | 11.7 | |
| Spelling | 19 | 13.2 | |

## Item Analysis for Capitalization

1. Names of institutions and organizations . . . 2 19 23 27 38 39
2. Titles of persons . . . 3 18 24
3. Titles of literature and drama . . . 4 14 32 35
4. First words of sentences . . . 5 15 (28)
5. Names of persons . . . 6 (22) 36
6. Names of cities . . . 7 10 13
7. Names of rivers, streets, islands, etc. . . . (20)(25) 37
8. Days and months . . . 9 16 30
9. First words of quotations . . . 11 21 33 40
10. Names of languages . . . 31
11. Over-capitalization . . . 1 8 12 17 (26) / 29 (34)

Student's Name Johnston, Helen    Grade 9 (10) 11 12

## DIAGNOSTIC OUTLINE--LANGUAGE TEST

Test 5--Mechanics of English    Advanced Form    Grades 9 to 14

| Battery Summary | Raw Scores | Grade Placement Scores | Sub-test A-- Capitalization |
|---|---|---|---|
| Total Language | 114 | 10.8 | 31 correct out of 40 |
| Mechanics of English | 103 | 11.4 | |
| Spelling | 11 | 9.5 | |

### Item Analysis for Capitalization

| | |
|---|---|
| 1. Names of institutions and organizations | 2   19   23   27   38   39 |
| 2. Titles of persons | 3   18   24 |
| 3. Titles of literature and drama | 4   14   32   35 |
| 4. First words of sentences | 5   15   (28) |
| 5. Names of persons | 6   22   36 |
| 6. Names of cities | 7   10   13 |
| 7. Names of rivers, streets, islands, etc. | 20   (25)   37 |
| 8. Days and months | 9   (16)   30 |
| 9. First words of quotations | (11)   (21)(33)(40) |
| 10. Names of languages | 31 |
| 11. Over-capitalization | 1   8   12   17   26   /   29   (34) |

Student's Name _Ortiz, Juan_    Grade  9  10  11  (12)

---

## DIAGNOSTIC OUTLINE--LANGUAGE TEST

Test 5--Mechanics of English    Advanced Form    Grades 9 to 14

| Battery Summary | Raw Scores | Grade Placement Scores | Sub-test A-- Capitalization |
|---|---|---|---|
| Total Language | 110 | 10.5 | 30 correct out of 40 |
| Mechanics of English | 100 | 11.0 | |
| Spelling | 10 | 9.0 | |

### Item Analysis for Capitalization

| | |
|---|---|
| 1. Names of institutions and organizations | 2   (19)(23)   27   38   39 |
| 2. Titles of persons | 3   18   24 |
| 3. Titles of literature and drama | 4   (14)   32   35 |
| 4. First words of sentences | (5)(15)   28 |
| 5. Names of persons | 6   (22)   36 |
| 6. Names of cities | 7   10   (13) |
| 7. Names of rivers, streets, islands, etc. | (20)(25)   37 |
| 8. Days and months | 9   16   30 |
| 9. First words of quotations | 11   (21)   33   40 |
| 10. Names of languages | 31 |
| 11. Over-capitalization | 1   8   (12)   17   (26)   /   29   (34) |

Student's Name _Massey, Jean_    Grade  9  (10)  11  12

317

## DIAGNOSTIC OUTLINE--LANGUAGE TEST

### Test 5--Mechanics of English    Advanced Form    Grades 9 to 14

| Battery Summary | Raw Scores | Grade Placement Scores | Sub-test A-- Capitalization |
|---|---|---|---|
| Total Language . . . . . | 122 | 11.5 | 35 correct out of 40 |
| Mechanics of English . . | 107 | 11.9 | |
| Spelling . . . . . . . | 15 | 11.5 | |

#### Item Analysis for Capitalization

| | | | | |
|---|---|---|---|---|
| 1. Names of institutions and organizations . . . . | 2 | (19) | 23 | 27   38   39 |
| 2. Titles of persons . . . . . . . . . . . . . . | 3 | 18 | (24) | |
| 3. Titles of literature and drama . . . . . . . . | 4 | 14 | 32 | 35 |
| 4. First words of sentences . . . . . . . . . . | 5 | 15 | (28) | |
| 5. Names of persons . . . . . . . . . . . . . | 6 | 22 | 36 | |
| 6. Names of cities . . . . . . . . . . . . . . | 7 | 10 | 13 | |
| 7. Names of rivers, streets, islands, etc. . . . . | (20) | (25) | 37 | |
| 8. Days and months . . . . . . . . . . . . . | 9 | 16 | 30 | |
| 9. First words of quotations . . . . . . . . . . | 11 | 21 | 33 | 40 |
| 10. Names of languages . . . . . . . . . . . | 31 | | | |
| 11. Over-capitalization . . . . . . . . . | 1 | 8 | 12   17   26 | 29   34 |

Student's Name *Abbott, Billye, Jean* Grade 9 (10) 11   12

---

## DIAGNOSTIC OUTLINE--LANGUAGE TEST

### Test 5--Mechanics of English    Advanced Form    Grades 9 to 14

| Battery Summary | Raw Scores | Grade Placement Scores | Sub-test A-- Capitalization |
|---|---|---|---|
| Total Language . . . . . | 106 | 10.2 | 21 correct out of 40 |
| Mechanics of English . . | 96 | 10.3 | |
| Spelling . . . . . . . | 10 | 9.0 | |

#### Item Analysis for Capitalization

| | | | | |
|---|---|---|---|---|
| 1. Names of institutions and organizations . . . . | 2 | 19 | 23   27   (38) | (39) |
| 2. Titles of persons . . . . . . . . . . . . . . | 3 | (18) | (24) | |
| 3. Titles of literature and drama . . . . . . . . | 4 | (14) | 32   (35) | |
| 4. First words of sentences . . . . . . . . . . | 5 | (15) | 28 | |
| 5. Names of persons . . . . . . . . . . . . . | 6 | 22 | (36) | |
| 6. Names of cities . . . . . . . . . . . . . . | 7 | (10) | (13) | |
| 7. Names of rivers, streets, islands, etc. . . . . | (20) | (25) | (37) | |
| 8. Days and months . . . . . . . . . . . . . | 9 | 16 | 30 | |
| 9. First words of quotations . . . . . . . . . . | (11) | (21) | (33)   (40) | |
| 10. Names of languages . . . . . . . . . . . | 31 | | | |
| 11. Over-capitalization . . . . . . . . . | 1 | 8 | (12)   17   26 | 29   (34) |

Student's Name *Guerra, Juan* Grade 9   10 (11) 12

# DIAGNOSTIC OUTLINE--LANGUAGE TEST

Test 5--Mechanics of English    Advanced Form    Grades 9 to 14

| Battery Summary | Raw Scores | Grade Placement Scores | Sub-test A-- Capitalization |
|---|---|---|---|
| Total Language | 114 | 10.8 | 35 correct out of 40 |
| Mechanics of English | 100 | 11.0 | |
| Spelling | 14 | 11.0 | |

## Item Analysis for Capitalization

1. Names of institutions and organizations . . . . . . . 2 19 23 27 38 39
2. Titles of persons . . . . . . . . . . . . . . . . . . . 3 18 (24)
3. Titles of literature and drama . . . . . . . . . . . . 4 14 32 35
4. First words of sentences . . . . . . . . . . . . . . . 5 15 28
5. Names of persons . . . . . . . . . . . . . . . . . . . 6 22 36
6. Names of cities . . . . . . . . . . . . . . . . . . . . 7 10 13
7. Names of rivers, streets, islands, etc. . . . . . . . (20)(25) 37
8. Days and months . . . . . . . . . . . . . . . . . . . 9 16 30
9. First words of quotations . . . . . . . . . . . . . . 11 21 33 40
10. Names of languages . . . . . . . . . . . . . . . . . 31
11. Over-capitalization . . . . . . . . . . . . . . . . . 1 8 12 17 26  29 (34)

Student's Name Boyd, Henry    Grade 9 10 (11) 12

---

# DIAGNOSTIC OUTLINE--LANGUAGE TEST

Test 5--Mechanics of English    Advanced Form    Grades 9 to 14

| Battery Summary | Raw Scores | Grade Placement Scores | Sub-test A-- Capitalization |
|---|---|---|---|
| Total Language | 146 | 13.9 | 37 correct out of 40 |
| Mechanics of English | 125 | 14.2 | |
| Spelling | 21 | 13.8 | |

## Item Analysis for Capitalization

1. Names of institutions and organizations . . . . . . . 2 19 23 27 38 39
2. Titles of persons . . . . . . . . . . . . . . . . . . . 3 18 24
3. Titles of literature and drama . . . . . . . . . . . . 4 14 32 35
4. First words of sentences . . . . . . . . . . . . . . . 5 15 28
5. Names of persons . . . . . . . . . . . . . . . . . . . 6 22 36
6. Names of cities . . . . . . . . . . . . . . . . . . . . 7 10 13
7. Names of rivers, streets, islands, etc. . . . . . . . (20) 25 (37)
8. Days and months . . . . . . . . . . . . . . . . . . . 9 16 30
9. First words of quotations . . . . . . . . . . . . . . 11 21 33 40
10. Names of languages . . . . . . . . . . . . . . . . . 31
11. Over-capitalization . . . . . . . . . . . . . . . . . 1 8 12 17 (26)  29 34

Student's Name Bell, Mary J.    Grade 9 (10) 11 12

## DIAGNOSTIC OUTLINE--LANGUAGE TEST

Test 5--Mechanics of English    Advanced Form    Grades 9 to 14

| Battery Summary | Raw Scores | Grade Placement Scores | Sub-test A-- Capitalization |
|---|---|---|---|
| Total Language . . . . . . | 71 | 7.1 | 24 correct out of 40 |
| Mechanics of English . . | 56 | 7.7 | |
| Spelling . . . . . . . . | 15 | 11.5 | |

### Item Analysis for Capitalization

1. Names of institutions and organizations . . . . . . .   2   (19)   (23)   (27)   (38)   (39)
2. Titles of persons . . . . . . . . . . .   3   18   (24)
3. Titles of literature and drama . . . . . . .   4   14   (32)   (35)
4. First words of sentences . . . . . . . .   (5)   15   (28)
5. Names of persons . . . . . . . . . .   6   22   36
6. Names of cities . . . . . . . .   7   10   13
7. Names of rivers, streets, islands, etc. . . . . .   20   25   37
8. Days and months . . . . . . . . .   9   (16)   30
9. First words of quotations . . . . . .   (11)   (21)   33   (40)
10. Names of languages . . . . . . . .   (31)
11. Over-capitalization . . . . . . . . .   1   8   (12)   17   26   29   34

Student's Name _Morovsky, Tamara_ Grade   9   (10)   11   12

---

## DIAGNOSTIC OUTLINE--LANGUAGE TEST

Test 5--Mechanics of English    Advanced Form    Grades 9 to 14

| Battery Summary | Raw Scores | Grade Placement Scores | Sub-test A-- Capitalization |
|---|---|---|---|
| Total Language . . . . . . | 116 | 11.0 | 34 correct out of 40 |
| Mechanics of English . . | 104 | 11.6 | |
| Spelling . . . . . . . . | 12 | 10.0 | |

### Item Analysis for Capitalization

1. Names of institutions and organizations . . . . . . .   2   (19)   23   27   38   39
2. Titles of persons . . . . . . . . . . .   3   (18)   24
3. Titles of literature and drama . . . . . . .   4   14   32   35
4. First words of sentences . . . . . . . .   5   15   28
5. Names of persons . . . . . . . . . .   6   22   36
6. Names of cities . . . . . . . .   7   10   13
7. Names of rivers, streets, islands, etc. . . . . .   20   (25)   (37)
8. Days and months . . . . . . . . .   9   16   30
9. First words of quotations . . . . . .   11   21   33   (40)
10. Names of languages . . . . . . . .   31
11. Over-capitalization . . . . . . . . .   1   8   12   17   26   29   (34)

Student's Name _Byler, Randy_ Grade   9   10   11   (12)

## DIAGNOSTIC OUTLINE--LANGUAGE TEST

Test 5--Mechanics of English    Advanced Form    Grades 9 to 14

| Battery Summary | Raw Scores | Grade Placement Scores | Sub-test A-- Capitalization |
|---|---|---|---|
| Total Language . . . . . . | 148 | 14.1 | |
| Mechanics of English . . . | 124 | 11.7 | 34 correct out of 40 |
| Spelling . . . . . . . . . | 24 | 15.2 | |

### Item Analysis for Capitalization

1. Names of institutions and organizations . . . . . 2 19 23 (27) 38 39
2. Titles of persons . . . . . . . . . . . . . 3 18 24
3. Titles of literature and drama . . . . . . . . 4 14 32 35
4. First words of sentences . . . . . . . . . 5 (15) (28)
5. Names of persons . . . . . . . . . . . . 6 22 36
6. Names of cities . . . . . . . . . . . . . 7 10 (13)
7. Names of rivers, streets, islands, etc. . . . . . (20) 25 37
8. Days and months . . . . . . . . . . . . 9 16 30
9. First words of quotations . . . . . . . . . (11) 21 33 40
10. Names of languages . . . . . . . . . . . 31
11. Over-capitalization . . . . . . . . . . . . 1 8 12 17 26 / 29 34

Student's Name _Cadiz, Hermalinda_ Grade 9 10 (11) 12

---

## DIAGNOSTIC OUTLINE--LANGUAGE TEST

Test 5--Mechanics of English    Advanced Form    Grades 9 to 14

| Battery Summary | Raw Scores | Grade Placement Scores | Sub-test A-- Capitalization |
|---|---|---|---|
| Total Language . . . . . . | 98 | 9.5 | |
| Mechanics of English . . . | 85 | 9.2 | 27 correct out of 40 |
| Spelling . . . . . . . . . | 13 | 10.5 | |

### Item Analysis for Capitalization

1. Names of institutions and organizations . . . . . 2 19 23 27 (38) 39
2. Titles of persons . . . . . . . . . . . . . 3 18 24
3. Titles of literature and drama . . . . . . . . 4 (14) 32 35
4. First words of sentences . . . . . . . . . (5) (15) 28
5. Names of persons . . . . . . . . . . . . 6 22 36
6. Names of cities . . . . . . . . . . . . . (7) 10 13
7. Names of rivers, streets, islands, etc. . . . . . 20 (25) 37
8. Days and months . . . . . . . . . . . . (9) (16) 30
9. First words of quotations . . . . . . . . . (11) (21) (33) (40)
10. Names of languages . . . . . . . . . . . 31
11. Over-capitalization . . . . . . . . . . . . 1 8 12 (17) 26 / 29 (34)

Student's Name _Cline, Betty_ Grade 9 10 (11) 12

## DIAGNOSTIC OUTLINE--LANGUAGE TEST

### Test 5--Mechanics of English    Advanced Form    Grades 9 to 14

| Battery Summary | Raw Scores | Grade Placement Scores | Sub-test A -- Capitalization |
|---|---|---|---|
| Total Language | 123 | 11.6 | 35 correct out of 40 |
| Mechanics of English | 106 | 11.8 | |
| Spelling | 17 | 12.5 | |

#### Item Analysis for Capitalization

1. Names of institutions and organizations . . . . . . . 2 19 23 27 38 39
2. Titles of persons . . . . . . . 3 18 24
3. Titles of literature and drama . . . . . . . 4 14 32 (35)
4. First words of sentences . . . . . . . (5)(15)(28)
5. Names of persons . . . . . . . 6 22 36
6. Names of cities . . . . . . . 7 10 13
7. Names of rivers, streets, islands, etc. . . . . . . . 20 25 37
8. Days and months . . . . . . . 9 16 30
9. First words of quotations . . . . . . . 11 21 33 40
10. Names of languages . . . . . . . 31
11. Over-capitalization . . . . . . . 1 8 12 17 26 29 (34)

Student's Name Mc Intire, Judy    Grade 9 10 (11) 12

---

## DIAGNOSTIC OUTLINE--LANGUAGE TEST

### Test 5--Mechanics of English    Advanced Form    Grades 9 to 14

| Battery Summary | Raw Scores | Grade Placement Scores | Sub-test A -- Capitalization |
|---|---|---|---|
| Total Language | 111 | 10.6 | 32 correct out of 40 |
| Mechanics of English | 102 | 11.2 | |
| Spelling | 9 | 8.5 | |

#### Item Analysis for Capitalization

1. Names of institutions and organizations . . . . . . . 2 (19) 23 27 38 39
2. Titles of persons . . . . . . . 3 18 24
3. Titles of literature and drama . . . . . . . 4 14 32 (35)
4. First words of sentences . . . . . . . (5) 15 (28)
5. Names of persons . . . . . . . 6 22 36
6. Names of cities . . . . . . . 7 (10) 13
7. Names of rivers, streets, islands, etc. . . . . . . . 20 25 37
8. Days and months . . . . . . . (9) 16 30
9. First words of quotations . . . . . . . (11) 21 33 40
10. Names of languages . . . . . . . 31
11. Over-capitalization . . . . . . . 1 8 12 17 26 29 (34)

Student's Name Lawrence, Lila    Grade 9 10 (11) 12

# DIAGNOSTIC OUTLINE--LANGUAGE TEST
## Test 5--Mechanics of English   Advanced Form   Grades 9 to 14

| Battery Summary | Raw Scores | Grade Placement Scores | Sub-test A-- Capitalization |
|---|---|---|---|
| Total Language . . . . | 43 | 6.1 | 23 correct out of 40 |
| Mechanics of English . . | 36 | 6.0 | |
| Spelling . . . . . . . | 1 | 7.5 | |

### Item Analysis for Capitalization

1. Names of institutions and organizations . . . . . (2)(19) 23 27 38 39
2. Titles of persons . . . . . . . . . . . . . . . . (3)18 24
3. Titles of literature and drama . . . . . . . . . (4)(14) 32 35
4. First words of sentences . . . . . . . . . . . . (5)15 28
5. Names of persons . . . . . . . . . . . . . . . . (6)22 36
6. Names of cities . . . . . . . . . . . . . . . . . 7 (10)(13)
7. Names of rivers, streets, islands, etc. . . . . . (20)(25) 37
8. Days and months . . . . . . . . . . . . . . . . (9)(16) 30
9. First words of quotations . . . . . . . . . . . . (11) 21 33 40
10. Names of languages . . . . . . . . . . . . . . . 31
11. Over-capitalization . . . . . . . . . . . . . . . (1)(8)(12) 17 26 29 34

Student's Name *Bula, David*   Grade 9 10 (11) 12

---

# DIAGNOSTIC OUTLINE--LANGUAGE TEST
## Test 5--Mechanics of English   Advanced Form   Grades 9 to 14

| Battery Summary | Raw Scores | Grade Placement Scores | Sub-test A-- Capitalization |
|---|---|---|---|
| Total Language . . . . | 35 | 6.0 | 2 correct out of 40 |
| Mechanics of English . . | 29 | 6.0 | |
| Spelling . . . . . . . | 6 | 7.0 | |

### Item Analysis for Capitalization

1. Names of institutions and organizations . . . . . (2)(19) 23 27 38 39
2. Titles of persons . . . . . . . . . . . . . . . . (3)18 24
3. Titles of literature and drama . . . . . . . . . (4)14 32 35
4. First words of sentences . . . . . . . . . . . . (5)(5)28   *Did not*
5. Names of persons . . . . . . . . . . . . . . . . (6)22 36   *complete*
6. Names of cities . . . . . . . . . . . . . . . . . (7)(10)(13)   *items be-*
7. Names of rivers, streets, islands, etc. . . . . . 20 25 37   *yond #15*
8. Days and months . . . . . . . . . . . . . . . . (9)16 30
9. First words of quotations . . . . . . . . . . . . (11) 21 33 40
10. Names of languages . . . . . . . . . . . . . . . 31
11. Over-capitalization . . . . . . . . . . . . . . . (1)(8)12 17 26 29 34

Student's Name *Crow, Harold*   Grade 9 10 11 (12)

323

# DIAGNOSTIC OUTLINE--LANGUAGE TEST

**Test 5--Mechanics of English    Advanced Form    Grades 9 to 14**

| Battery Summary | Raw Scores | Grade Placement Scores | Sub-test A-- Capitalization |
|---|---|---|---|
| Total Language . . . | 99 | 9.6 | 33 correct out of 40 |
| Mechanics of English . . | 85 | 9.2 | |
| Spelling . . . . . . | 14 | 11.0 | |

## Item Analysis for Capitalization

1. Names of institutions and organizations . . . . . . . . 2   19   23   27   38   39
2. Titles of persons . . . . . . . . . . . . . . . . 3   18   24
3. Titles of literature and drama . . . . . . . . . . 4   14   32   35
4. First words of sentences . . . . . . . . . . . . . 5   15   28
5. Names of persons . . . . . . . . . . . . . . . . 6   22   36
6. Names of cities . . . . . . . . . . . . . . . . . 7   10   (13)
7. Names of rivers, streets, islands, etc. . . . . . (20)   (25)   37
8. Days and months . . . . . . . . . . . . . . . . . 9   16   30
9. First words of quotations . . . . . . . . . . . . (11)   21   33   (40)
10. Names of languages . . . . . . . . . . . . . . . 31
11. Over-capitalization . . . . . . . . . . . . . . . 1   8   12   17   (26)   29   (34)

Student's Name _Oliver, Grace_     Grade   9   (10)   11   12

---

# DIAGNOSTIC OUTLINE--LANGUAGE TEST

**Test 5--Mechanics of English    Advanced Form    Grades 9 to 14**

| Battery Summary | Raw Scores | Grade Placement Scores | Sub-test A-- Capitalization |
|---|---|---|---|
| Total Language . . . | 76 | 7.4 | 26 correct out of 40 |
| Mechanics of English . . | 66 | 7.3 | |
| Spelling . . . . . . | 10 | 9.0 | |

## Item Analysis for Capitalization

1. Names of institutions and organizations . . . . . . . . 2   19   23   27   38   39
2. Titles of persons . . . . . . . . . . . . . . . . (3)   18   24
3. Titles of literature and drama . . . . . . . . . . 4   14   (32)   35
4. First words of sentences . . . . . . . . . . . . . 5   15   28
5. Names of persons . . . . . . . . . . . . . . . . 6   22   36
6. Names of cities . . . . . . . . . . . . . . . . . 7   (10)   13
7. Names of rivers, streets, islands, etc. . . . . . (20)   (25)   37
8. Days and months . . . . . . . . . . . . . . . . . 9   16   30
9. First words of quotations . . . . . . . . . . . . (11)   21   33   (40)
10. Names of languages . . . . . . . . . . . . . . . 31
11. Over-capitalization . . . . . . . . . . . . . . . (1)   (8)   (12)   (17)   (26)   29   (34)

Student's Name _Eubanks, Earl_     Grade   9   10   (11)   12

DIAGNOSTIC OUTLINE--LANGUAGE TEST

Test 5--Mechanics of English    Advanced Form    Grades 9 to 14

| Battery Summary | Raw Scores | Grade Placement Scores | Sub-test A--Capitalization |
|---|---|---|---|
| Total Language . . . . . . | 111 | 10.6 | 33 correct |
| Mechanics of English . . | 102 | 11.2 | out of 40 |
| Spelling . . . . . . . | 9 | 8.5 | |

Item Analysis for Capitalization

1. Names of institutions and organizations . . .    2   19   23   27   38   39
2. Titles of persons . . . . . . . . .    3   18   24
3. Titles of literature and drama . . . .    4   14   32   35
4. First words of sentences . . . . .    5   15   28
5. Names of persons . . . . . . .    6   22   36
6. Names of cities . . . . . . . .    7   10   (13)
7. Names of rivers, streets, islands, etc. . . .    (20) (25) 37
8. Days and months . . . . . . .    9   16   30
9. First words of quotations . . . .    11   (21) 33   40
10. Names of languages . . . . . .    (31)
11. Over-capitalization . . . . . . .    1   8   12   17   26    (29) (34)

Student's Name _Durham, William_    Grade   9   10   (11)   12

---

DIAGNOSTIC OUTLINE--LANGUAGE TEST

Test 5--Mechanics of English    Advanced Form    Grades 9 to 14

| Battery Summary | Raw Scores | Grade Placement Scores | Sub-test A--Capitalization |
|---|---|---|---|
| Total Language . . . . . . | 87 | 8.5 | 29 correct |
| Mechanics of English . . | 82 | 8.9 | out of 40 |
| Spelling . . . . . . . | 5 | 6.6 | |

Item Analysis for Capitalization

1. Names of institutions and organizations . . .    2   (19) 23   27   38   39
2. Titles of persons . . . . . . . . .    (3) 18   24
3. Titles of literature and drama . . . .    4   14   32   35
4. First words of sentences . . . . .    5   15   28
5. Names of persons . . . . . . .    (6) 22   (36)
6. Names of cities . . . . . . . .    7   10   13
7. Names of rivers, streets, islands, etc. . . .    20   (25) (37),
8. Days and months . . . . . . .    (9) 16   30
9. First words of quotations . . . .    (11) 21   33   40
10. Names of languages . . . . . .    (31)
11. Over-capitalization . . . . . . .    1   8   12   (17) (26)    (29) (34)

Student's Name _Arron, John_    Grade   9   10   (11)   12

## DIAGNOSTIC OUTLINE--LANGUAGE TEST

Test 5--Mechanics of English    Advanced Form    Grades 9 to 14

| Battery Summary | Raw Scores | Grade Placement Scores | Sub-test A--Capitalization |
|---|---|---|---|
| Total Language . . . . . | 107 | 10.2 | 31 correct out of 40 |
| Mechanics of English . . . | 86 | 9.3 | |
| Spelling . . . . . . . | 21 | 13.8 | |

### Item Analysis for Capitalization

1. Names of institutions and organizations . . . . . . 2 19 23 27 38 39
2. Titles of persons . . . . . . . . . . 3 (18) (24)
3. Titles of literature and drama . . . . . . 4 14 32 35
4. First words of sentences . . . . . . (5) 15 28
5. Names of persons . . . . . . . . 6 22 36
6. Names of cities . . . . . . . . 7 10 13
7. Names of rivers, streets, islands, etc. . . . (20)(25) 37
8. Days and months . . . . . . . 9 16 30
9. First words of quotations . . . . . . (11)(21)(33)(40)
10. Names of languages . . . . . . . 31
11. Over-capitalization . . . . . . . . 1 8 12 17 26 29 34

Student's Name _Adams, Helen_    Grade 9 10 11 (12)

---

## DIAGNOSTIC OUTLINE--LANGUAGE TEST

Test 5--Mechanics of English    Advanced Form    Grades 9 to 14

| Battery Summary | Raw Scores | Grade Placement Scores | Sub-test A--Capitalization |
|---|---|---|---|
| Total Language . . . . . | 116 | 11.0 | 32 correct out of 40 |
| Mechanics of English . . . | 98 | 10.6 | |
| Spelling . . . . . . . | 18 | 12.9 | |

### Item Analysis for Capitalization

1. Names of institutions and organizations . . . . . . 2 19 (23) 27 38 39
2. Titles of persons . . . . . . . . . . 3 18 24
3. Titles of literature and drama . . . . . . 4 14 32 35
4. First words of sentences . . . . . . (5) 15 28
5. Names of persons . . . . . . . . 6 22 36
6. Names of cities . . . . . . . . 7 10 13
7. Names of rivers, streets, islands, etc. . . . (20)(25) 37
8. Days and months . . . . . . . 9 16 30
9. First words of quotations . . . . . . (11)(21)(33)(40)
10. Names of languages . . . . . . . 31
11. Over-capitalization . . . . . . . . 1 8 12 17 26 29 34

Student's Name _Escobar, Paul_    Grade 9 10 11 (12)

# DIAGNOSTIC OUTLINE -- LANGUAGE TEST

Test 5 -- Mechanics of English     Advanced Form     Grades 9 to 14

| Battery Summary | Raw Scores | Grade Placement Scores | Sub-test A -- Capitalization |
|---|---|---|---|
| Total Language . . . . . | *84* | *8.2* | *30* correct |
| Mechanics of English . . . . | *78* | *8.3* | out of 40 |
| Spelling . . . . . . . . . | *6* | | |

## Item Analysis for Capitalization

1. Names of institutions and organizations  . . . . . . . . .   2  (19) 23  27  38  39

2. Titles of persons . . . . . . . . . . . . . . . . . .   3  18  24

3. Titles of literature and drama . . . . . . . . . . .   4  14  32  35

4. First words of sentences . . . . . . . . . . . .   (5) 15  28

5. Names of persons . . . . . . . . . . . . . . . .   (6) 22  36

6. Names of cities . . . . . . . . . . . . . . . . .   (7) 10  13

7. Names of rivers, streets, islands, etc. . . . . . .   (20)(25) 37

8. Days and months  . . . . . . . . . . . . . . . . .   (9) 16  30

9. First words of quotations . . . . . . . . . . . .   (11) 21 (33) 40

10. Names of languages . . . . . . . . . . . . . . . .   31

11. Over-capitalization . . . . . . . . . . . . . . .   1  (8)(12) 17  26
                                                          29  34

Student's Name _Osborne, Rex_     Grade   9 (10) 11  12

Appendix VII-A

COMPREHENSIVE
OBSERVATION GUIDE

Study Form for Use in
Observation Training

Instructions

This is the study form of the Comprehensive Observation Guide. Each guide question is followed by a series of examples of the kind of observed evidence which might be noted by an observer* These examples are only illustrative. Many different kinds of evidence might be observed in various classrooms. This should not be used as a checklist.

## I. THE CLASSROOM

A. How is the physical environment conducive to learning insofar as it is under the teacher's control?

Examples:
a. Teacher attempts to maintain a comfortable temperature by control of heaters, open windows, or fans.
b. Varying sizes of desks are available and properly used to accommodate the needs of different students.
c. Placement of desks takes best advantage of lighting, heating, or cooling, as well as class participation.
d. Sufficient bulletin and chalkboard space provides for displays of work.
e. Room is kept clean; waste materials are disposed of properly.

B. How is the classroom made attractive?

Examples:
a. Color scheme of the room is cheerful.
b. "Permanent" pictures and decorations such as murals, mosaics, and mobiles add color and interest to the room.
c. References, supplies, or apparatus used in the course are attractively displayed on wall shelves and in cabinets.
d. Bulletin board and other displays are attractive and eye-catching.

C. How functional is the seating arrangement in terms of the types of activity going on?

Examples:

a. Movable desks and chairs are arranged in varying patterns around the room.
b. Pupils are not assigned to a desk "permanently"; may change desks during the day, depending on the purpose the teacher has.
c. Arrangement of desks is other than the standard rank and file pattern when activities are such as to use other more functional arrangements.

D. What evidences show that materials, equipment, and facilities are properly cared for?

Examples:

a. Furniture is relatively free of scratches or other marks of defacement.
b. Teacher gives instructions in the proper handling of books.
c. Equipment is neatly stored, covered, and kept ready for use.

E. What evidences indicate a sufficient supply of supplementary materials and instructional aids?

Examples:

a. Classroom bookshelves contain a reasonable number of encyclopedias, dictionaries, and other reference materials (including supplementary texts).
b. Maps, charts, models, or specimens related to the pupils' work are readily available.
c. Various audio-visual aids (such as movie or filmstrip projectors and record players) are in use or are readily available.

F. What evidences in the room illustrate orderliness, good taste, and systematic procedures?

Examples:

a. Supplies are neatly arranged on shelves in cupboards.
b. Equipment and supply storage is labeled, showing where each item belongs.
c. Housekeeping duties are assigned to students, and a schedule or list is posted as a reminder.

G. What evidences are there of a connection between materials seen about the room and what has been or is being taught?

Examples:

a. Bulletin board display is based on the topic under discussion.
b. Teacher-made outlines or work sheets are being used by pupils.
c. "Good examples" of past work are posted around the room.
d. A display of library books pertaining to a specific topic is placed on the study table, book cabinet, or some other vantage point.

H. What are the evidences of instructional and display materials that are pupil-made? Teacher-made? Commercially made?

Examples:

a. Part or all of bulletin board material is obviously pupil-made.
b. Study charts and exercise charts have been prepared by the teacher.
c. Science charts and apparatus are commercially made.
d. Several pupils are working on a display.

I. What evidences of long-range and short-range planning are noted in the room on chalkboards, bulletin boards, tables, or other display areas?

Examples:

a. Outline of present work is on the chalkboard.
b. Committee assignment charts are posted on the walls.
c. Teacher's plan book is opened on her desk and referred to occasionally.
d. Charts on social studies and science indicate a developmental sequence.
e. Assignments (daily or weekly) are posted on the board.

J. What evidences show that the teacher evaluates and returns all work that the pupils are required to hand in?

Examples:

a. Pupils' work on display has been corrected and/or graded.
b. Teacher gives tentative date for return of homework, tests, etc., when taken up.
c. All work returned has been corrected or shows marks of checking.
d. Teacher comments that assignment must be turned in by specific time if pupil expects to have it checked.

K. How are materials arranged to stimulate pupils' curiosity to seek new understandings?

Examples:

a. Bulletin board is captioned with stimulating questions.
b. Astronomy display uses the ceiling of the classroom to represent space.
c. A display of new paperback books is arranged on a table.
d. Bulletin board display of new materials is partially veiled to stimulate interest but remains covered until the appropriate time for its use.

## II. THE TEACHER

A. How does the teacher's appearance set a good example for the pupils?

Examples:

   a. Teacher is clean in appearance and neatly dressed.
   b. Teacher's grooming and clothing are appropriate for the situation.
   c. Teacher takes advantage of opportunities to "freshen up," thereby retaining a neat appearance.

B. What shows that the teacher has a warm, friendly relationship with pupils?

Examples:

   a. Teacher appears cheerful.
   b. Teacher laughs with students and is able to make students laugh while maintaining orderly discipline.
   c. Teacher indicates a high degree of composure when required.
   d. Teacher discusses discipline infraction with pupil on a friendly basis.
   e. Teacher has patience in continuing attempts to make some point known.

C. How does the teacher show enthusiasm for the on-going activities?

Examples:

   a. Teacher willingly engages in activities with the pupils.
   b. At the end of the day, the teacher still exhibits an active interest in the work.
   c. Teacher seems to "lose" self in explanations, discussion, etc.
   d. Teacher exhibits an eagerness to find the solution to problems and the answers to questions.

D. What indicates that the teacher is sensitive to the physical well-being of the pupils?

Examples:

   a. Pupils with physical defects (such as sight or hearing defects) are seated to their best advantage.
   b. During inclement weather, teacher sees that children are properly clothed before leaving the room.
   c. Teacher sees that proper ventilation is provided in the room.
   d. On rainy days, proper steps are taken to see that pupils are kept dry.
   e. Pupils suspected of having a contagious disease are sent to the office or nurse for proper care.
   f. Attention is given to pupils recently ill to prevent overexertion.

E. What indicates that the teacher tries to gain as much knowledge about the pupil as possible in order to understand him better and guide him more effectively?

Examples:

a. A knowledge of the pupil's testing record is indicated when the teacher discusses present status of achievement.
b. Teacher appears genuinely interested when asking pupil about recent happenings in the family.
c. Comments and questions by teacher indicate that she knows number and relative ages of family members.
d. A knowledge of fathers' (and/or mothers') occupations is shown by asking specific pupils about their fathers' work when discussions of various occupations arise.

F. How does the teacher free students from embarrassment, tension, or feelings of insecurity?

Examples:

a. Teacher reassures pupil of satisfactory progress when difficulty is encountered.
b. When pupil makes a mistake in board-work problem or oral report, teacher explains logical reasons for error.
c. Teacher uses a calm, reassuring manner in encouraging completion of work and tests.
d. Teacher gives special attention to a new pupil who is experiencing adjustment difficulties.
e. Discipline problems are handled away from the class or as inconspicuously as possible.

G. How does the teacher attempt to enhance the development of the group as a social unit?

Examples:

a. Any groupings within the class do not remain static for all work.
b. Efforts are made to get pupils to help each other in overcoming work difficulties (except on tests!).
c. Success in group ventures is encouraged through the development of esprit de corps.
d. Teacher has developed a group cohesiveness as indicated by pupils' attempts to see that all class members are involved in class activities.

H. How does the teacher recognize the contributions of pupils?

Examples:

a. Teacher makes a point of showing appreciation for any job well done.
b. Routine duties (such as assignment paper monitor and lab equipment monitor) are rotated among all members of the class.
c. Class "programs" involve all members; behind-the-scenes workers are recognized publicly.
d. Certain types of oral reports are required of all class members.

I. How does the teacher illustrate an understanding and acceptance of the socio-economic levels represented in the class?

Examples:

a. Issuance of free lunch tickets is handled as a matter of course, without sympathy or patronizing attitude.

b. Pupils of obviously better means are shown no special privileges or favoritism nor are needs and interests of the underprivileged pupils regarded as being insignificant.

c. Illustrations and examples used by the teacher in classwork cover all walks of life, not just the more privileged.

d. In lessons on health and sanitation, cleanliness discussions take into account homes which may not have adequate facilities; dietary discussions bring out recommended foods available to persons of varying means.

J. How does the teacher recognize and provide for individual differences in levels of achievement, ability, and interest?

Examples:

a. Many phases of classwork are done by small groups working at different levels of progress.

b. Students are allowed to select from several goals for expected achievement, each succeeding goal representing a higher level of difficulty in work expected.

c. Students exhibiting a particular interest for some topics are allowed to take a major part in preparation and planning of work for the topic.

d. Information sources to which students are referred vary in difficulty according to pupils' abilities to comprehend the contents.

e. Students' special projects reflect individual interests and abilities.

K. How does the teacher maintain harmonious and constructive work in several small groups at the same time?

Examples:

a. Teacher continuously moves among groups to check progress.

b. Initial explanation of assignments indicates what unsupervised groups are to be doing when teacher is involved with one particular group.

c. Teacher maintains a visual check of all groups when working with one particular group.

d. Seating arrangements are changed when pupils in a particular group tend to do too much "socializing."

L. How does the teacher employ democratic principles in conducting the class?

Examples:

a. Each student is given an opportunity to make his desires or opinions known.

b. Certain procedures for the class are determined by majority vote, yet respect is shown for the rights of the minority.

c. Teacher is tolerant of a difference of opinions, but corrects errors in thinking or misinterpretation of facts.

d. Teacher is not autocratic in control; pupils are often given opportunities to lead the class for instructional purposes.

e. Student instigated or elected class council takes part in disciplinary and administrative organization of class.

M. What methods are used by the teacher to provide efficient classroom management?

Examples:

a. On entering room, pupils have developed a routine of hanging up coats, sharpening pencils, and gathering materials needed for the lesson before class begins.

b. Student assistant makes roll check at the beginning of class; teacher prepares or signs absentee report.

c. Money collections are handled in an orderly manner, often by a student.

d. Designated boxes or trays are provided for turning in assigned work.

e. Student monitors handle many of the routine duties such as collecting papers, handling playground equipment, and straightening up the room.

N. What shows the teacher's ability to use various types of instructional materials and aids effectively?

Examples:

a. Movies and filmstrips are used frequently but are always preceded by discussion of what to look for and are followed by discussion of main points illustrated.

b. Bulletin board display indicates a planned development.

c. Classwork extends beyond the textbook to supplementary material, encyclopedias, and other reference sources.

d. Local newspaper is used as an integral part of certain class activities.

O. What is the teacher doing that suggests a well-prepared lesson based on short-range and long-range planning?

Examples:

a. Teacher can suggest sources of information on questions that arise.

b. Duplicated exercise or study sheets have been prepared by teacher and are handed to students at appropriate times.

c. All materials used during lesson are readily available when needed.

d. Demonstrations work properly; teacher knows just what to do and when.

P. What indicates that the teacher has a satisfactory background of knowledge in the subject being taught and keeps informed on new developments?

Examples:

a. Teacher is able to explain reasons for certain procedures (math shortcuts, science practices, or English usages) or underlying causes for certain happenings (historical events, scientific discoveries, or physiological defects).

b. Teacher is not only able to answer questions asked, but also can provide many related facts.

c. New developments or new publications in the field of study are brought out by the teacher.

d. When pupils mention new developments they have read about, teacher seeks more definite information and makes a note of the source.

Q. What indicates that the teacher uses new ideas and develops imaginative approaches to teaching?

Examples:

a. New concepts in math (or in any subject), though not in the text or curriculum guide, are presented in the classroom.

b. Teacher disregards text in developing a new approach to a normally difficult topic (such as worded math problems and improperly used sentence or word forms).

c. Teacher mentions that another class is trying something new and suggests that her class try it also.

d. When a student presents a new idea, teacher states that it has not been tried before, but she is willing to try it if the class desires.

## III. THE PUPIL

A. What indicates pupil enthusiasm for and interest in the lesson?

Examples:

a. Pupils appear anxious to enter the classroom and begin work.

b. Teacher always has several volunteers for any task or to answer any question.

c. Occasionally teacher must exercise additional control to reduce overexuberance.

d. Pupils appear disappointed when class in interrupted by lunch or end of school, thus bringing a temporary halt to the activities.

B. What indicates that pupils' participation in the lesson is active and self-initiating?

Examples:

a. Pupils seek additional aid from references and other supplementary sources without being told to do so by the teacher.

b. Questions on what is being done bring quick, direct, specific answers of immediate goals and major objectives.

c. Nearly all pupils enter into the class activity in helping one another, explaining and correcting mistakes, and suggesting procedures to be used.

C. What indicates that pupils know what they are doing and why they are doing it?

Examples:

a. Pupils go to work following brief instructions with a minimum of confusion or waste of time.
b. Only a few pupils need to request individual assistance from the teacher before they can get started on an assignment.

D. What shows that pupils engage in creative activities?

Examples:

a. Pupils who have used a different procedure for solving a problem (different from the teacher-explained method) give an explanation of their method to the class.
b. Teacher employs creative writing as a means of getting pupils to express themselves freely on the subject being studied.
c. Class programs are developed by the pupils with a minimum of supervision by the teacher.
d. A "brainstorming" technique is attempted to suggest new applications of a specific principle.

E. How is sufficient physical activity on the part of the pupils provided to avoid excessive fatigue?

Examples:

a. When pupils become overly restless, teacher interrupts the class for brief period of physical activity (stand and stretch, calisthenics, or a walk around room).
b. Classwork exercises require more than copying material verbatim from textbook.
c. Certain drill-type activities (such as spelling or the multiplication tables) are made into contests for group or individual competitions.
d. Teacher presents material of a more advanced level to pupils who complete and are no longer challenged by the regular work.

F. What evidences show that the pupils take part in planning the work and in developing the assignments?

Examples:

a. On beginning a new unit of work, pupils and teacher develop an outline of what is to be studied; pupils suggest procedures to use in explaining the specific topics.
b. Pupils suggest exercises which may be used for class or homework (such as science experiments, topics for English papers, and field trips).
c. Teacher actually turns class over to pupils but maintains sufficient supervision to insure progress in learning.

G. How do pupils show signs of self-discipline?

Examples:

a. Teacher very seldom needs to correct conduct.
b. Pupils are free to move around the room to get references, excuse them-selves, etc., but do not abuse the privilege.
c. Misconduct on the part of one student brings reprimand from another.
d. Students instigate the selection (or election) of a disciplinary council and thereby attempt to establish their own control.
e. In discussions, pupils respect the rights of others to freedom of speech and wait for proper recognition before speaking.


IV. THE LESSON

A. What evidences show progress in the fundamental knowledge, skills, abil-ities, attitudes, and appreciations for the subject being studied?

Examples:

a. Work being done shows an advancement over that of the previous grade.
b. Skills being developed show an increased complexity over those previ-ously used.
c. Pupils seem to be more articulate than previously in explaining work being done.
d. More mature pupils show an appreciation for more challenging, difficult work.

B. What indicates that the work being attempted is appropriate with respect to the capacities and abilities of the students?

Examples:

a. Majority of students are able to complete the work and do so within the allotted time.
b. Questions asked about a new topic being studied indicate an understanding of necessary prior knowledge.
c. After explanation, most pupils are able to do individual assignments with little or no additional help.
d. Few "this is too hard" comments are made by pupils; most begin assign-ment without hesitation.

C. What experiences are provided for pupils to put to use the degree of skill gained in a particular area and thereby refine and further extend the skill?

Examples:

a. Laboratory exercises follow classroom lecture and discussion.

b. Pupils write original essays in English, social science, and other similar courses to illustrate or explain their own understanding of some particular topic.

c. Practical problems are provided for applying knowledge gained (such as play store, student council campaign and election, and class panel discussion).

b. Pupils ask questions about points covered previously in different types of activities (such as films, panel discussions, or lab experiments).

c. Plans are made in class for some special activity such as a field trip, class play or program, or study of a special TV program.

F. How does the discussion method lead toward a definite objective?

Examples:

a. Teacher refers to original topic when discussion begins to stray.

D. What indicates the lesson's correlation with other lessons and with the general development of the subject in this and other grade levels?

Examples:

a. Work done in one subject area is related to something done in another area such as preparing graphs in both social studies and math.

b. Teacher points out subject matter which will be needed for later studies or comments on points which had been covered previously.

c. Pupils sometimes "discover" that work done in one subject is related to work done in some other subject.

d. Transition from one lesson or topic to another is a smooth and natural change; no abrupt halt in proceedings.

E. What are the various classroom activities that are employed to stimulate pupil interest and challenge different abilities?

Examples:

a. Reference is made by teacher to previous activities of a different type which have illustrated the same point being studied.

b. During the course of discussion, occasional reference is made to the points which have been covered and others which should be considered.

G. How do the discussion-leading techniques encourage participation by all pupils?

Examples:

a. Teacher asks questions of those who seem hesitant to speak.

b. Teacher restrains those who tend to monopolize the discussion to give others an opportunity to speak.

c. Teacher avoids monopolizing the discussion.

H. How is class discussion developed by appropriate and effective questioning rather than being limited to the recitation of isolated facts?

Examples:

a. Teacher asks questions in such a way that a statement of fact does not give a satisfactory answer.

b. Once the "fact" has been established, teacher calls for discussion of its implications.

c. Teacher adds interest through competitions in which explanations or examples are required.

d. Chalkboard work involves an explanation of errors; pupil may stay at board until he makes a mistake.

e. Pupils make up questions relating to the work, then must be able to verify answer given by classmate.

I. What practices show that the teacher probes beneath verbalisms to see if understanding is present?

Examples:

a. When oral reading is being used, teacher interrupts at intervals to have pupil explain a difficult passage in his own words.

b. In giving reports, pupils are required to explain terms which are new to the class and to be able to answer questions concerning the report.

c. Correction of essay-type tests includes comments of "explain" or "be specific" on points which tend to be "bookish."

d. Teacher asks for illustrative examples of procedures studied and principles learned.

J. What indicates that classroom and homework activities provide worthwhile, substantial units of work?

Examples:

a. Assigned work seems to grow directly out of class discussion or lecture.

b. Duplicated homework (or classwork) sheets lend continuity to the assignments; they are completed in parts over a period of time.

c. Explanation of homework includes values or necessary understandings to be gained; assignment is not given as merely "take the next ten pages."

d. Assignments have been prepared in advance, perhaps written in plan book; they are not developed in the last minutes of class by the teacher thumbing through the text.

K. What indicates that sufficient consideration has been given to the proper development of assignments?

Examples:

a. Sufficient time is given to explaining what is expected.

b. The teacher suggests procedures which may be necessary or sources useful for obtaining information.

c. Quantity of assigned work is reasonable for the group and grade level involved.

d. Better pupils are given more challenging work (and perhaps less drill) rather than just "more of the same."

L. How do classroom and homework assignments indicate that consideration is given to, and use made of, resources of the community and real-life situations of pupils?

Examples:

a. Some assignments are directly related to community affairs or resources.

b. Field trips tie in classwork with the community.

c. Plans are made for the class to have speakers from within the community.

d. A unit of study is developed around the local community and its resources.

e. In geography lessons comparisons are made between the local community and the area being studied.

M. How is the work of the class constantly directed toward certain objectives while maintaining sufficient flexibility to allow the teacher to capitalize on situations as they arise?

Examples:

a. Pupil-suggested activities related to the classwork are discussed and incorporated into the lesson when sufficiently applicable.

b. When discussion begins to get too far afield, yet maintains high interest and and pupil participation, teacher suggests that special reports of the topics be prepared and given to the class at a later date.

N. How is a convincing connection made between subject matter and pupil needs and interests?

Examples:

a. Teacher gives examples of instances where subject matter meets practical needs.

b. Pupils are asked to suggest values of subject being studied.

c. Teacher explains how the subject is useful in developing pupils' individual interests.

d. An outside speaker indicates how a knowledge of the subject is necessary in his type of work.

O. How are pupils encouraged to go beyond the textbook in seeking information?

Examples

a. Teacher makes many references to sources for information other than the text.

b. Encyclopedias and other reference sources are almost in constant use as pupils prepare assignments.

c. When giving individual assistance, teacher suggests pupil "look up" the answer to a question and suggests a reference source.

d. Attention and interest are given to a pupil's explanation of lesson-related information gleaned from outside reading (from such sources as newspapers, novels, or magazines).

P. How does the teacher give direct, specific help for the improvement of study habits?

Examples:

a. Teacher observes work of each pupil during supervised study period; points out incorrect procedures being used.

b. Teacher discusses proper study techniques with class as a whole.

c. Teacher asks different pupils to explain how they arrived at certain conclusions when the same mistake seems to be made by most of the class members; then effort is made to correct general misconceptions.

Q. What methods are used to diagnose individual or group difficulties?

Examples:

a. Teacher circulates about the room, observing how pupils are carrying out assigned tasks.

b. Teacher works with a small group on special problems while other pupils work independently.

c. Teacher leads discussion by asking probing questions designed to uncover weaknesses in understandings.

R. What efforts are made to help the pupils learn to become self-evaluative?

Examples:

a. Pupils are asked to give an evaluation of their work before it is checked by the teacher.

b. Teacher uses symbols (previously explained) to mark major types of errors on papers; pupils make own corrections and resubmit papers.

c. When a mistake is made in classwork, teacher tries to have pupil discover his own mistake and the reason for making it.

S. What procedures and techniques are employed in an effort to make evaluation thorough?

Examples:

a. Teacher checks daily work, makes a note of individual progress.

b. Workbook exercises are discussed, and reasons for correct answers are explained; a check is made on number missed by each pupil.

c. When more active pursuits such as lab experiments are employed, teacher gives an oral evaluation of the work of each pupil.

d. Explanation of method for determining six-weeks, nine-weeks, or term grades includes use of more than test scores.

T. What evidences show that tests and other assignments are used as teaching devices and not merely as measuring devices?

Examples:

a. Daily tests are graded by class members; errors are discussed.

b. Errors made on essay tests are discussed when tests are returned; examples of better work are cited by the teacher.

c. Possible reasons for mistakes and explanation of correct answers are given for objective tests; often pupils correct errors, and corrections are checked by teacher.

d. Tests are returned as soon as possible so that discussion of the material covered is still pertinent to classwork.

e. Mistakes are marked on test papers in such a manner that the pupil can determine the reasons for his error and make necessary correction himself.

U. How do examinations tend to motivate the learning of reasons and relationships rather than the memorization of fragmentary, isolated facts?

Examples:

a. Essay questions ask for the "why" of given events, procedures, or principles rather than merely descriptions.

b. Objective questions are stated in such a way that answers can be obtained only by reasoning based on the fundamental facts.

c. In more involved mathematical processes, teacher gives partial credit for work indicating an understanding of basic principles.

V. What practices indicate an effort to keep parents well informed on pupils' progress?

Examples:

a. A notebook of the week's work is taken home for parents to examine.

b. Certain pupils are told that the teacher would like to have a conference with their parents to discuss difficulties the pupils are having.

W. What types of learning activities are in evidence?

(List one or more of the following or others that are not given here: reciting, practicing, doing research, discussing, creating, copying, studying, planning, dramatizing, making, learning skills.)

X. What types of learning outcomes are in evidence?

(List one or more of the following or others that are not given here: factual information, knowledge, understandings and generalizations, skills, habits, aesthetic appreciations, attitudes, creative abilities, ways of thinking, interests, personality adjustments.)

Appendix VII–B

SAMPLE TEST–OBSERVING FOR DETAILS


Film Clip on a 6th Grade Science Lesson

Please circle correct answers on ANSWER SHEET, not on this test.

1. The number of questions asked by the teacher was

    a. 15-24
    b. 25-34
    c. 35-44
    d. 45 or more

2. The displays on the bulletin board appeared to be

    a. entirely teacher-made
    b. entirely pupil-made
    c. teacher-made and commercially-made
    d. pupil-made and commercially-made

3. The number of times the teacher repeated a student's answer was

    a. less than 15
    b. 15-24
    c. 25-34
    d. 35-44

4. What pattern of questioning did the teacher use most frequently?

    a. Asked a question and then called only on students with raised hands
    b. Called on a student and then asked the question
    c. Asked a question and then called on students without regard to raised hands
    d. Asked a question and allowed any student to answer without calling on one

5. Approximately how many pupils were in this class?

    a. 24-26
    b. 27-29
    c. 30-32
    d. 33 or more

6. Approximately what percent of the students appeared to be Latin-American?

    a. 0-10%
    b. 11-20%
    c. 21-30%
    d. 31-40%

345

7. How many different pupils were called upon to answer questions?

    a. 9-13
    b. 14-18
    c. 19-23
    d. 24-28

8. What type of question did the teacher use most frequently?

    a. Comprehension (Can you give me an example?, etc.)
    b. Recall (Who? What? When?, etc.)
    c. Recognition (Which of these? Was it this way or that way?, etc.)
    d. About equal numbers of each of the above

9. How many times did three or more students raise their hands in response to a question?

    a. 4-8
    b. 9-13
    c. 14-18
    d. 19-23

10. According to the teacher, what type of test was to be given to the class?

    a. Completion
    b. Discussion
    c. Multiple-choice
    d. Short-answer

11. Which one of the following statements is true?

    a. The teacher called upon girls approximately twice as often as boys.
    b. The smallest pupil in the class did not have the smallest desk.
    c. Several examples of pupils' work were posted around the room.
    d. The teacher seated shorter pupils in the front of the room and taller ones in the back.

12. The material on the easel

    a. gave examples of the uses of chemistry
    b. explained the difference between a mixture and a compound
    c. illustrated common elements in nature
    d. illustrated physical and chemical changes

13. The outcomes of the lessons leading to this review appear to have excluded which of the following?

    a. To learn some uses of chemistry
    b. To study physical and chemical changes
    c. To learn the chemical composition of simple materials
    d. To relate chemistry to everyday life

14. Which one of the following statements is false?

  a. The experiment on the demonstration table showed physical changes.
  b. A student explained how sugar was burned to produce carbon.
  c. The first part of the lesson dealt with elements, mixtures, and compounds.
  d. The same student read all three sections of the bulletin board display at the rear of the room.

15. What was written on the chalkboard at the front of the room?

  a. An outline of the class lesson?
  b. Examples of elements, compounds, and mixtures
  c. Some questions to be covered in class
  d. A list of the uses of chemistry in everyday life

16. Which one of the following statements is true?

  a. The teacher failed to give her pupils a chance to ask questions before the test began.
  b. The material on the easel was readily visible to most of the pupils.
  c. The teacher had lesson plans which were opened and referred to occasionally.
  d. There were at least six different evidences of advanced preparation for the day's lesson.

True—False

17. The material on the easel answered the first test question.

18. None of the students took notes or used textbooks during the class period.

19. The displays on the bulletin board were related to the lesson.

20. There were at least five times when the teacher volunteered information that could have been supplied by the students.

Appendix VIII—A

## DESCRIPTION OF TEACHER QUESTION
## AND PUPIL RESPONSE CATEGORIES

Two sets of categories for analyzing teacher behavior are outlined below. Study these categories carefully before using them to analyze a lesson protocol.

TEACHER QUESTIONS

Each substantive teacher question can be categorized in terms of the effect it is likely to have in stimulating cognitive or affective behavior on the part of the students involved. The system to be used in categorizing teacher questions is presented below:

Cognitive Domain

I. Recognition—Which one? Is it true or false?
II. Recall—What? How many? Can you name it?
III. Demonstration of Skill—Can you show us? How do you do it?
IV. Comprehension—Can you give an example? How would you say it in your own words?
V. Analysis—What causes it? How do you explain it? What makes it work?
VI. Synthesis—Can you state a generalization that you see in what we have been discussing?

Affective Domain

VII. Opinion—What do you think? Do you agree? How would you have felt?
VIII. Attitude or Value—Can you explain why you approve?

PUPIL RESPONSES

Teachers secure responses from students in different ways. The pattern of the teacher's response-producing behavior can be determined by categorizing each student response according to the teacher acts (and related conditions) which elicit the response. A system for categorizing pupil responses in this way is presented below:

A. Individual Designated - Teacher offers stimulus to only one designated student.

B. Group Designated - Teacher offers stimulus to all students, but later selects one to respond.

C. No One Designated - Teacher offers stimulus to all students, but some student selects himself to respond.

D. Spontaneous (Undesignated) - Teacher offers no direct stimulus for response. A student is stimulated to originate his own response, independent of any teacher stimulus.

E. Mass Designation - Teacher offers stimulus to all students, but in such a way that a number of students respond simultaneously.

## Appendix VIII-B

## TABULATION WORKSHEET FOR TEACHER BEHAVIOR ANALYSIS

Teacher _____ Grade _____ Subject _____

Time _____ to _____ Date _____ Observer _____

Topic _____

| Behavior Categories | Phase: Time: Activity: | I | II | III | IV | V | No.   Percent |
|---|---|---|---|---|---|---|---|
| 1. Encouraging | | | | | | | |
| 2. Presenting | | | | | | | |
| 3. Assisting | | | | | | | |
| 4. Analyzing | | | | | | | |
| 5. Directing | | | | | | | |
| 6. Discouraging | | | | | | | |
| Total - All Categories | | | | | | | |

*Adapted from instruments developed by various researchers including
R. Anderson, M. Hughes, and D. Ryans.

Appendix VIII–C

TABULATION WORKSHEET FOR BALES' INTERACTION ANALYSIS

Group _____ Observer _____ Date _____ Time _____ to _____

Notes:

| | I. Positive Reactions | | | II. Attempted Answers | | | III. Questions | | | IV. Negative Reactions | | | Totals and Percents |
|---|---|---|---|---|---|---|---|---|---|---|---|---|---|
| | A. Shows Solidarity | B. Shows Tension Release | C. Shows Agreement | D. Gives Suggestions | E. Gives Opinions | F. Gives Orientation | G. Asks Orientation | H. Asks Opinions | I. Asks for Suggestions | J. Disagrees | K. Shows Tension | L. Shows Antagonism | |
| Respondent | | | | | | | | | | | | | |
| Teacher | | | | | | | | | | | | | |
| Girls | | | | | | | | | | | | | |
| Boys | | | | | | | | | | | | | |
| Totals and Percents | | | | | | | | | | | | | |

* R. F. Bales, *Interaction Process Analysis—A Method for the Study of Small Groups* (Cambridge, Mass.: Addison–Wesley, 1950).

Appendix VIII–D

PROTOCOL – THE ELEMENTARY SCIENCE LESSON*

Instructor's Guide

Lesson Topic:  How Plants Grow          Time:  10:20 to 11:35
Teacher:  Mrs. Janie Brown              Subject:  Science
Grade:  Fifth
Number of Pupils:  28
Seating Arrangement:  Conventional, by rows

The following lesson was planned as part of a science program carried on in the regular classroom by the teacher. Mrs. Brown was using a newly developed teachers' guide in an effort to make her teaching more stimulating. The program emphasized the "discovery approach."

The children, grouped heterogeneously, used the basic processes of the new science program to guide the conduct of individual experiments with various seeds. A control group planted seeds with all factors necessary for growth: soil, minerals, air, water, light, and heat. Other groups planted seeds lacking at least one factor essential to plant growth. The children used no text, but were guided in reaching their conclusions by the teacher as she tried to emphasize the use of observing, measuring, inferring, predicting, and classifying as basic processes of the scientific method.

*Analytical work supported by contract O.E. 6–10–108, Division of Laboratories and Research Development, U.S. Office of Education. Diagnostic Analysis of Lesson Protocol by Ben M. Harris and Betty Porter.

352

# THE LESSON

| Teacher and Pupil Acts | Teacher Questions | Pupil Response | Diagnostic Comments |
|---|---|---|---|
| Teacher: Yesterday you did some planting, (1) didn't you? | I | | Teacher recalls fact and adds a recognition question addressed to the entire class. |
| All: Yes, ma'am. (2) | | E | |
| Teacher: I'd like one of you to tell me what (3) you did. Frances, what did you do? | II | | With no pause between first and second question, the teacher converts what might have been group designated cue into an individual designation. |
| Frances: Well, let's see. I took a jar of dirt (4) and put some lima bean and corn seeds in the dirt and put more dirt over the top of them. Then I put some water in the jar so the seeds would grow and put the jar on the shelf. | | A | |
| Teacher: All right. You set it outside then. (5) Peter, what did you do with your seed. | II | | Teacher restates last idea and moves to Peter with the next question. |
| Peter: I put some dirt in a jar and put (6) lima bean and corn seeds in it. I covered it with some more dirt. Then, I set it on the shelf. | | A | |
| Teacher: You set it on the shelf. What else (7) did you do before you put it on the shelf? | II | | A tutorial relationship is maintained by directing still another question to this same student. |
| Peter: I put the lid on it. (8) | | A | |
| Teacher: You screwed the lid down on it, (9) didn't you? Brenda, what did you do with yours? | II | | The teacher moves to Brenda—still a tutorial approach. |
| Brenda: I got a jar and filled it with dirt; I (10) got two lima bean and two corn seeds in the jar, and then, I put some more dirt on top and watered it. | | A | |

353

| Teacher and Pupil Acts | Teacher Questions | Pupil Response | Diagnostic Comments |
|---|---|---|---|
| Teacher: Did someone do something (11) different with his seed? Alice. | II | | Teacher continues to have students recall procedures of experiment. Now the tutorial approach is replaced with a question directed to the entire class. |
| Alice: I got a can of dirt in the jar— (12) about half a jar—and planted seeds on the side, so I could watch them grow up through the glass. I put more dirt on top, watered it, and put it on the shelf. | | B | |
| Teacher: Now, on your study sheet that (13) you received yesterday, you read quite a few things about plants, didn't you? | I | | Mrs. Brown seems satisfied now that experimental procedures have been reviewed. |
| All: Yes, ma'am. (14) | | E | |
| Teacher: One of the first things you found (15) on this sheet was a list of things needed by all green plants in order to live and grow well. Shane, I believe your group worked on the first ones. What things are needed by all green plants if they are to live and grow well? How many things did you find? | II | | The tutorial approach is renewed with Shane. |
| Shane: All green plants need soil, (16) minerals, water, light, air, and heat. | | A | |
| Teacher: Soil, minerals, air, water, light, (17) and heat. Well, what do you think we are trying to prove by the experiment we are doing? What are we trying to prove? Edward. | IV,IV | | After getting students to recall procedures of experiments begun the previous day, the teacher asks a question stimulating a comprehension response. She asks in effect, "What are we doing all of this for?" She repeats the question to emphasize its importance. |

354

| Teacher and Pupil Acts | Teacher Questions | Pupil Response | Diagnostic Comments |
|---|---|---|---|
| Edward: That all green plants need these (18) things to live. | | B | |
| Teacher: Are we trying to prove just that (19) now? Jane, what do you think we are trying to prove? | I<br>IV | | Teacher rejects Edward's answer and shows this by asking a recognition question. In effect, she asks him to recognize that his answer is inadequate. However, she restates her question before allowing Edward to answer; thus she persists in her effort to stimulate comprehension. |
| Jane: That green plants need these (20) things. | | A | |
| Teacher: That green plants need what?— (21) these six things in order to live and grow well? Did all of the seeds that you planted get all six things? | II<br>I | | When Jane answers with nothing to suggest better comprehension than Edward had expressed, the teacher gives in and asks a simple recall question, answers it herself, and follows with even simpler recognition questions. |
| All: No. (22) | | E | The pupils respond en masse. |
| Teacher: Peter, is your plant getting every (23) one of these six things? | I | | The teacher now resumes her questioning in a tutorial fashion. Having been unsuccessful at stimulating responses to the comprehension questions, she tried a probe or two (19). This failed to work, and the simple recognition and recall questions become the pattern again. |
| Peter: No, ma'am. (24) | | A | |
| Teacher: What is lacking? (25) | II | | |

| Teacher and Pupil Acts | Teacher Questions | Pupil Response | Diagnostic Comments |
|---|---|---|---|
| Peter: Water.<br>(26) | | A | |
| Teacher: It's not getting any water? It<br>(27) seems to me there's something else<br>that it's not getting. Look back<br>there on the shelf. What about it? | II | | |
| Peter: Air.<br>(28) | | A | |
| Teacher: Why?<br>(29) | IV | | Teacher asks comprehension question, apparently feeling secure that Peter can respond at this level. |
| Peter: Because the lid is on.<br>(30) | | A | |
| Teacher: The lid is on. Well, what do you<br>(31) think will happen to your plant?<br>Do you think you'll get a plant<br>out of this? | IV<br><br>I | | A comprehension question is asked again, but it is followed so very quickly by a recognition question that the student has no opportunity to respond at the more complex level. The first question has no real effect. |
| Peter: No, ma'am.<br>(32) | | A | |
| Teacher: Well, we won't say for sure that<br>(33) you won't, despite the fact that<br>our instructions state that plants<br>need all six things in order to live<br>and grow well. Do we find that<br>all plants need the same amount? | I | | Teacher does not fully accept this answer. She encourages students to qualify answers. However, the very next question calls for recognition only. In this way the teacher discourages the use of a qualified answer. |
| All: No, ma'am.<br>(34) | | E | The teacher now has the students convinced. They |
| Teacher: —of these things?<br>(35) | I | | are responding enmasse with a "yes" or a "no." |
| All: No, ma'am.<br>(36) | | E | |
| Teacher: What proof do you have of that?<br>(37) What proof do you have that all<br>plants don't need the same | IV | | Mrs. Brown tries again to stimulate a more critical level of thought, but |

356

| Teacher and Pupil Acts | Teacher Questions | Pupil Response | Diagnostic Comments |
|---|---|---|---|
| amount of these things? Alice? | IV | | Alice seems confused now. |
| Alice: (38) Well, some plants—that is, some plants have—. They need more water than others, and some don't need as much water as others. | | B | She's not sure what kind of answers the teacher desires. |
| Teacher: (39) Well, let's think about this. Do we have the same temperature or the same kind of climate all over our earth? | I | | Instead of asking for examples and probing for Alice's meaning, the teacher asks students to |
| All: (40) No, ma'am. | | E | respond to questions for which there is obviously |
| Teacher: (41) But do we find plants almost everywhere on our earth? | I | | only one answer. |
| All: (42) Yes, ma'am. | | E | |
| Teacher: (43) Can you think of some things that plants can stand less or more of? | II | | |
| Alice: (44) Well, some plants can stand cold weather and some can't. And some can stand hot desert weather. | | C | Alice apparently selects herself to respond. |
| Teacher: (45) Well, what about desert plants? What do you know about desert plants? Shane? | II II | | |
| Shane: (46) They don't get very much water. | | A | Without a pause Shane is designated to respond. |
| Teacher: (47) They can get along with less water, can they? | I | | Teacher asks echo question showing acceptance of and reinforcing previous answer. |
| Shane: (48) Yes. | | A | |
| (a) (Bob waves his hand to be recognized so he can respond.) | | D | |
| Teacher: (49) All right, Bob? | | | Teacher recognizes Bob who spontaneously waves hand to be called upon. |
| Bob: (50) Tropical plants can live out of dirt, and desert plants have to be in soil. | | A | |

| Teacher and Pupil Acts | Teacher Questions | Pupil Response | Diagnostic Comments |
|---|---|---|---|
| Teacher: Exactly! So we say that plants (51) have places where they can live best. Now, I'd like you to write some words from your science unit in your science notebook for vocabulary study. Would you expect to find a cactus growing in a tropical jungle? | I | | Mrs. Brown sees in Bob's statement a chance to make a transition to word study. In her eagerness for this transition, she seems unconcerned about the accuracy of Bob's information. |
| All: No. (52) | | E | |
| Teacher: Why? (53) | IV | | Teacher tries to build on Bob's idea, expressed earlier. |
| Bob: Because of the weather. (54) | | C | Bob selects himself. |
| Teacher: Oh? Would you expect to find (55) orchids growing in the desert? | I | | Teacher fails to give Bob a chance to elaborate on his point; instead she forces him to respond at |
| Bob: No. (56) | | A | the simplest recognition level. |
| Teacher: Well, do you know what we call (57) the surroundings in which any plant or animal lives naturally? (Goes to chalkboard. Points to list of words.) Their natural home is called? What's the place called where they do best? We call it their ... ? | II  I  I  I | | Teacher supplies information and asks only for recognition of terminology from word list on board. |
| (b) (Mrs. Brown pauses, looks at Bob, and waits for an answer.) | | | |
| Bob: Environment. (58) | | A | |
| Teacher: Environment. Let's say that. (59) | | | Teacher asks for mass repetition. |
| All: Environment. (60) | | E | |
| Teacher: Now, the word environment (61) means what? Johnny. | II | | This could be asking for comprehension— |
| Johnny: The things that surround. (62) | | B | —but it is right out of the book. |
| Teacher: The things that surround us. Now, (63) plants and animals have an | | | Teacher again does the generalizing and asks |

| | Teacher and Pupil Acts | Teacher Questions | Pupil Response | Diagnostic Comments |
|---|---|---|---|---|
| | environment in which they do best. We say they do best there because they have become what? Tell me what this word is. Shane? | II I | | students merely to recognize term from the word list. |
| (c) | (Mrs. Brown points to a word in a list on the board.) | | | |
| Shane: (64) | Adopted. | | B | |
| Teacher: (65) | Almost. What is it? | II | | |
| Alice: (66) | Adapted. | | C | |
| Teacher: (67) | Adapted. They have become adapted to this kind of environment. Throughout all the many years that our world has existed, many plants, and animals as well, have been able to adapt themselves to different kinds of environment when they have been moved to another place. We might have carried them there, or animals may have carried plants to another place—and after a while they became adapted to the new place, if they were very, very strong. I'd like to call your attention to something that is rather interesting about adaptation. Plants are able to adapt in two ways—they can be transferred to a new place to live, and they may adapt to a small a degree. For example, you might take a dog from a warm climate and move him to a cold climate. What do you think will happen to the dog? In what way would the dog adapt himself to the new cold climate? Diana? | VII II | | Mrs. Brown proceeds to provide information in lecture form. The pressure of time may be worrying her at this point. |
| Diana: (68) | He would grow more hair. | | B | |
| Teacher: | He would grow more hair. And | | | |

| Teacher and Pupil Acts | Teacher Questions | Pupil Response | Diagnostic Comments |
|---|---|---|---|
| (69) after a while he would be adapted and be able to live in that climate. On the other hand, take the same dog out and drop him in the middle of the ocean. Do you think he would be able to adapt there very quickly? | I | | This might have been phrased to encourage comprehension rather than this. |
| Diana: No. (70) | | A | |
| Teacher: He might find it difficult to (71) develop fins and gills in order to swim about and live in the ocean, wouldn't he? | I | | But the teacher supplies the information and merely asks for the class to express agreement. |
| All: Yes. (72) | | E | In this way, even the opinion expressed is given no recognition. Teacher continues to supply information. |
| Teacher: However, this is true also. Many (73) plants and animals have adapted themselves and have made such great changes that if you could have seen the original plant or animal and see that animal today, you could not recognize it as having been the same kind of plant or animal. | | | |
| (d) (Alice waves her hand to volunteer an idea.) | | C | |
| Teacher: Alice? (74) | | | Teacher recognizes Alice who waved hand for recognition. |
| Alice: The first land animal was a fish (75) that was really a kind of frog or something and could climb trees and walk over the ground. | | A | Alice sees in the teacher's previous presentation the direction she wants the lesson to go. Alice tries to help by adding appropriate information. |
| Teacher: He had to adapt himself after he (76) got out of the water, and he had to grow legs and lungs. Yes, you find many theories along that line. Let's get back to green plants again. You said that light was one thing that plants needed. These | | | Teacher accepts Alice's ideas and relates them to concept of adaptation, but does not allow students to show that they understand this relationship. |

360

| Teacher and Pupil Acts | Teacher Questions | Pupil Response | Diagnostic Comments |
|---|---|---|---|
| seeds that you buried in soil, are they getting any light? | I | | |
| All: (77) Yes. No. | | E | Instead of pursuing the concept of adaptation, |
| Teacher: (78) Is there any light going down to them? | I | | Mrs. Brown switches the topic. |
| All: (79) No. Yes. It all depends. | | E | |
| Teacher: (80) Very good. How do you think the seeds that you planted are going to get their start? You said that plants need six things in order to live and grow well, and they need all of these things in order to make food. | II | | Teacher calls for deeper thinking. Potentially, this could call for analytical thinking. |
| (e) (Teacher nods to Alice.) | | | Alice responds to non-verbal cue from teacher. |
| Alice: (81) You see, seeds have food in them that is being stored. | | B | Alice begins to analyze— |
| Teacher: (82) I see. What are seeds? They are simply, what? | II II | | Teacher interrupts thought to get a |
| Alice: (83) Food. Stored food. | | | memorized fragment. Alice obliges! |
| Teacher: (84) Stored food. Back in the fall when the plant became ripe and dropped its seed, it had made provisions for the next season with that stored food, hadn't it. And so, you give the plant the other necessary things, and the seed begins to grow. We planted some bean seeds, and here on the flannel board you can see—what is beginning to happen. | | | Teacher frustrates Alice's efforts to answer analysis question so she can hurry on to the next portion of her lesson. |
| (f) (Teacher calls attention to a flannel seed bed.) | | | |
| Teacher: (85) Here is the seed that has been planted. I'll put this one up here where you can see it. | | | |
| (g) (Mrs. Brown manipulates the | | | |

| Teacher and Pupil Acts | Teacher Questions | Pupil Response | Diagnostic Comments |
|---|---|---|---|
| flannel board so the seeds can be seen.) | | | |
| Teacher: It's very enlarged, of course. This (86) is a little seed. I hope you can see it. It isn't very large. How many of you have watched your mothers shell beans to cook them and have seen this little outer shell come off? Do you see that? Do you see that little beginning of growth right there in the dirt on that seed? Do you know what started it to grow? | I, I<br><br>I<br>II | | Teacher asks for more recall. |
| Shane: It broke in half. (87) | | C | |
| Teacher: That's right. Now, that is the (88) beginning of that seed's growth. To start that beginning, it needed water. That's the young sprout. | | | Teacher accepts incomplete answer, then continues, and answers the question herself. |
| (h) (She points.) | | | |
| Shane: How long ago did it come out? (89) | | D | Spontaneous response from student. He asks the question this time. |
| Teacher: That is drawn in the picture for (90) you here. See this little dome right in here? | I | | Teacher either did not hear Shane's question or is ignoring it. |
| (i) (Mrs. Brown turns to a chart on the wall and points.) | | | |
| All: Yes. (91) | | E | |
| Teacher: From that comes the first little (92) leaves. | | | Teacher's statement is repetitious. It adds no new information. |
| Shane: That's what it was doing when it (93) broke open. | | D | |
| Teacher: Yes. From that came the first (94) little leaves. I believe I have some other outlines that will show better what begins to happen, and what should take place. Let's go over and look at some of the seeds | | | |

362

| | Teacher and Pupil Acts | Teacher Questions | Pupil Response | Diagnostic Comments |
|---|---|---|---|---|
| | we planted near the outside edge of the glass. Now what's happening to this seed? | IV | | Teacher seeks comprehension. |
| (j) | (Mrs. Brown held up a jar with sprouting seeds showing under the soil.) | | | |
| Alice: (95) | It's getting roots. Beginning to take roots. Losing its outer covering. | | C | |
| Teacher: (96) | Yes, it's losing its outer covering. Now, what's beginning–? What's happening here? | IV IV | | Teacher seeks evidence of comprehension. She seems to be urging careful description of observed evidence. |
| Shane: (97) | Beginning to get roots. | | C | |
| Teacher: (98) | But now, you said those plants always need more what? | II | | Instead of restating question, perhaps clearer, the teacher probes without asking comprehension but recall question. |
| Shane: (99) | Water, Air. | | A | Students just guess. |
| Teacher: (100) | They want some light, don't they? So, now, just what has happened here? From the tiny little sprout that you saw has come what? | I IV IV | | Teacher supplies fact with tag question. Teacher probes again for comprehension.— |
| Alice: (101) | A root. Hairs on the root. | | C | —but gets recall. |
| Teacher: (102) | All right. It has made the root part of the plant, but what's happening here? | IV | | Teacher continues to probe for comprehension. |
| Shane: (103) | It's starting to grow. It's growing a stem. | | C | |
| Teacher: (104) | They're growing up toward the ...? | II | | Teacher finally gives up, gives hint of answer, and then asks for completion. |
| Shane: (105) | Air. Light. | | C | Shane guesses. |
| Teacher: (106) | ... to the what? | II | | Others are not involved, except Alice who saves the |

363

| Teacher and Pupil Acts | | Teacher Questions | Pupil Response | Diagnostic Comments |
|---|---|---|---|---|
| Alice: (107) | Light. | | C | day again. |
| Teacher: (108) | They're growing upward toward the light, aren't they? You can see that again with the corn seed. You can see that the stem part of the plant pushes up through the soil toward the light. They want the light. In what way are all green plants alike? Diana? | II | | (rhetorical) Teacher asks for simple fact. |
| Diana: (109) | They need sunlight. | | B | |
| Teacher: (110) | Yes, but there is one thing—there's one particular thing—in science that we know about green plants. And what's the other class of plants? | II | | More recall is urged, but Diana is interrupted with still a different question. |
| Diana: (111) | The non-green plants. | | A | |
| Teacher: (112) | The non-green plants. Now, what about the green plants? All right, Bob? | II | | |
| Bob: (113) | All green plants manufacture their own food. | | B | |
| Teacher: (114) | All green plants manufacture their own food. In order to manufacture their own food they need what? All these things, don't they? Now, in order to understand something about how plants manufacture their own food, we need to know something about another word from your list. About their what? | II I I | | Mrs. Brown seems worried about the time again. She answers her own questions and pushes on to the next word on her list. |
| (k) | (Mrs. Brown points again to a word on the board.) | | | Teacher asks recognition of word from list. |
| Bob: (115) | Structure. | | C | |
| Teacher: (116) | The structure. What do we mean when we talk about the structure of anything? What do we mean when we talk about the structure of anything? | II II | | |

| Teacher and Pupil Acts | Teacher Questions | Pupil Response | Diagnostic Comments |
|---|---|---|---|
| Bob: (117) The skeleton. The material that it is made of and how it is built. | | C | |
| Teacher: (118) The material that it is made of and how it is built. Well, last week we studied about the structure of something else. What was it? | II | | |
| Diana: (119) The mouth. | | C | |
| Teacher: (120) The structure of what in the mouth? | II | | |
| Diana: (121) Teeth. | | A | |
| Teacher: (122) The teeth. And we found out about the materials from which a tooth is built. And so we mean the same thing when we talk about the structure of a seed. We say that plants need these things to build their food. Where do they build their food, these green plant factories? Is it built below the ground or above the ground? | II<br>I | | |
| Diana: (123) Above. | | C | |
| Teacher: (124) Above the ground. Where do they get some of the things that they need to build their food? | II | | |
| Diana: (125) From the roots. | | A | |
| Teacher: (126) From below the ground, don't they? Well, how do these building materials get from the soil to the food building place? And, by the way, what is the food building place? | II<br>II | | |
| Diana: (127) The main root. | | A | Mrs. Brown now appears to be carrying on a dialogue |
| Teacher: (128) Is it? Look at your plants? | I | | with Diana and leaving the rest of the class out. |

| Teacher and Pupil Acts | Teacher Questions | Pupil Response | Diagnostic Comments |
|---|---|---|---|
| Diana: The root hairs. (129) | | A | |
| Teacher: Look at the first drawing at the (130) back of your study sheet. Now, where is the root built, Diana? | I | | |
| Diana: Under the ground. (131) | | A | |
| Teacher: Where is the food built? (132) | II | | |
| All: (Several different answers.) (133) | | E | |
| Teacher: In the leaves, isn't it. Now, they (134) have devised a simple explanation. We're not going to try to get the whole detailed explanation—of how plants manufacture their own food, but very simply, what are the four things that they use? Dennis? | II | | Teacher answers question and then asks for more factual recall. |
| Dennis: Chlorophyll. (135) | | B | |
| Teacher: Chlorophyll. What is chlorophyll, (136) Jane? | II | | |
| Jane: The green covering—I mean the (137) green coloring of a plant. | | B | |
| Teacher: The green coloring of a green (138) plant. That's what we see in plants that make their own food, isn't it? It is this green coloring material, this chlorophyll, which is essential to plants making their own food. I think if you look—on the second page of your study sheet, you'll find the method by which green plants manufacture their own food. What's the first thing that happens? Alice? | I | | (rhetorical) |
| Alice: The plant starts making root hairs (139) or tap roots. | | B | |
| Teacher: Root hairs, what are the root (140) hairs? | II | | |

366

| Teacher and Pupil Acts | Teacher Questions | Pupil Response | Diagnostic Comments |
|---|---|---|---|
| Alice: (141) The little hairs that come out from the main root. | | A | |
| Teacher: (142) The little hairs that come out from the main root. Does the main root itself take in water? | I | | |
| Alice: (143) Yes, ma'am. | | A | |
| Teacher: (144) Does it? | I | | |
| Shane: (145) No. | | C | |
| Teacher: (146) The root hairs are the ones that take in the—what do we call it? | II | | |
| Shane: (147) Soil water. | | A | |
| Teacher: (148) The soil water. What does the soil water contain that is necessary to the life of the plant? | II | | |
| Alice: (149) Water. | | C | |
| Teacher: (150) What is it that water has? | II | | |
| Alice: (151) Minerals. | | A | |
| Teacher: (152) Now, tell me how the soil water gets up to the last leaf where it has to make its food? Harry? | IV | | |
| Harry: (153) The rain. | | B | |
| Teacher: (154) Now, as practice, I want you to begin down here at the bottom, and tell me what happens. | IV | | Mrs. Brown overlooks Harry's answer and tries to encourage him to think. |
| Harry: (155) (Inaudible) | | A | |
| Teacher: (156) How does the soil water get up to the leaves where the food is made? | IV | | |
| Harry: (157) Through the root hairs. The soil water comes through tiny tube-like things that go up to the leaves. | | A | |

367

| Teacher and Pupil Acts | Teacher Questions | Pupil Response | Diagnostic Comments |
|---|---|---|---|
| Teacher: What carries the water through (158) the leaves? Something on the back of the leaves, I think, isn't it? What do we say carries the water? What carries the water on into the leaf part of the plant? | II<br>I<br><br>II<br>II | | |
| Alice: The veins. (159) | | | |
| Teacher: The veins. Haven't you seen the (160) very well defined veins on the back of the leaves? | | | Now that Mrs. Brown has restricted her questioning to simple recognition and |
| Alice: Yes. (161) | | A | recall, she is getting the answers called for. As she |
| Teacher: They show more plainly on the (162) back. The veins carry the soil water on into the leaf, and what happens next? Johnny? | <br><br><br>I | | avoids probing for under-standing, she also makes rapid progress through the lesson. |
| Johnny: That's where the carbon dioxide (163) enters the leaf. | | B | |
| Teacher: What is carbon dioxide? (164) | II | | |
| Johnny: It is a gas. (165) | | A | |
| Teacher: A gas that they take from the ...? (166) | II | | |
| Johnny: Air. (167) | | A | |
| Teacher: Now, they also use some ... ? (168) | II | | |
| Diana: Oxygen. (169) | | C | |
| Teacher: Some oxygen, don't they? (170) | I | | |
| Diana: Yes. (171) | | A | |
| Teacher: Now, we have the soil water; we (172) have the gases they are going to use and, we have the chlorophyll which makes the food, but what must all three of these things have | | A | Teacher continues asking |

| Teacher and Pupil Acts | Teacher Questions | Pupil Response | Diagnostic Comments |
|---|---|---|---|
| before they can start operating? What does anything need before it can function well or do anything–some form of what? | II<br><br><br>II | | for more recall rather than probing for greater comprehension. |
| Dennis: (173) Energy. | | C | |
| Teacher: (174) Energy. Yes. It must have some form of energy. The plant leaf gets the energy from what source? | II | | |
| Dennis: (175) Light. Sunlight. Air and sunlight. | | A | |
| Teacher: (176) Sunlight. Sunlight. We all know that sunlight is the source of energy, don't we? The main source of energy for–actually for our whole world! Now, according to that, do you think that the plant makes food at night? | I | | (rhetorical) |
| Dennis: (177) No, ma'am. It uses the food it made in the daytime. At night it uses the food it made in the daytime. | | C | |
| Teacher: (178) At night it uses the food that it stored during the daytime. What do we call this food? How does the leaf get the air it needs? | II<br>II | | |
| All: (179) (Inaudible) | | E | |
| Teacher: (180) Through what? | II | | |
| Alice: (181) Sunrays. | | C | |
| Teacher: (182) Sunrays? | IV | | Teacher probes for evidence of deeper understanding. |
| Alice: (183) Openings in the leaves let air in and out. | | C | |
| Teacher: (184) Yes. Is there a little breathing apparatus just like we have, a nose that breathes in air for the leaf? | | | |

369

| Teacher and Pupil Acts | Teacher Questions | Pupil Response | Diagnostic Comments |
|---|---|---|---|
| There, the air, gases, the sunlight energy, and the chlorophyll all mix together to make what for the plants? | II | | |
| Shane: Food. (185) | | C | |
| Teacher: Food. What is this food called? (186) (pause) Alice. | II | | |
| Alice: Simple sugar. (187) | | B | |
| Teacher: Simple sugar. Simple sugar. All (188) right. It's not like the sugar that we have on our tables that does come from plants. We do get sugar, don't we, that we can use on the table? What did you find out about that, Alice? You told me yesterday you found out something very interesting about plants and the simple sugar that they make. | II | | Teacher does not pause before designating Alice. |
| Alice: Well, the scientists have estimated (189) that all plants on earth make about four billion tons of sugar in a year. | | A | |
| Teacher: Was it five billion or four? (190) (Looking directly at Alice) | I | | |
| Alice: I think it was four billion. (191) | | A | |
| Teacher: I believe it was four hundred (192) billion, wasn't it? | I | | |
| Alice: Yes. (193) | | A | |
| Teacher: Four...hundred billion tons. Is (194) that a lot of pounds, or not? | I | | Teacher phrases question for simple recognition answer. |
| Alice: Yes. (195) | | A | |
| Teacher: That's a lot of simple sugar, isn't (196) it? | I | | Teacher agrees and asks tag question. |

| Teacher and Pupil Acts | Teacher Questions | Pupil Response | Diagnostic Comments |
|---|:---:|:---:|---|
| Dennis: Yes. Is this all from one plant? (197) | | C | |
| Teacher: Oh, no. All the plants all over the world. That's four hundred billion tons of simple sugar from every living plant. (198) | | | Teacher answers Dennis's question. |
| Dennis: Gosh! (199) | | C | |
| Teacher: That's manufacturing a lot of sugar, isn't it? (200) | I | | Teacher adds tag question to statement. |
| Dennis: What if one plant could do that? What if one plant did that? (201) | | C | |
| Teacher: Oh, no. Not just one plant. You have plenty of (inaudible)— Alice? (202) | | | |
| (1) (Teacher recognizes Alice who sought recognition.) | | | |
| Alice: About 80 percent of this comes from their own sugar contents. (203) | | B | |
| Teacher: From their own sugar content. Now, this content that we just mentioned of sugar-making in a plant, did you find the word that we use, the term that we apply to the food-making process in the leaves? Bob? (204) | | | |
| Bob: Photosynthesis. (205) | | B | |
| Teacher: That is a mouthful, isn't it? (206) | I | | |
| Alice: Photosynthesis. (207) | | C | |
| Teacher: Photosynthesis. Photosynthesis. How did they ever arrive at a word like that to describe the food-making process of a plant? Diana? (208) | II | | |
| Diana: Because it means heat and light. (209) | | B | |
| Teacher: There's a little more than that, | | | |

| | Teacher and Pupil Acts | Teacher Questions | Pupil Response | Diagnostic Comments |
|---|---|---|---|---|
| (210) | isn't there? We might break the word apart to define it—break it into two parts. Who remembers what <u>photo</u> means? Bob? | II | | |
| Bob: (211) | Light. | | B | |
| Teacher: (212) | Light? | II | | |
| Bob: (213) | Heat. | | A | |
| Teacher: (214) | What does the second part of the word mean, Billy? | II | | |
| Billy: (215) | Broken up. | | B | |
| Teacher: (216) | Broken up. So we have the word <u>photosynthesis</u>. What happens to the food in the plant? | II | | |
| Billy: (217) | It is broken up by light. | | A | |
| Teacher: (218) | Broken up by light, isn't it. The energy from the sun—I would like for you to turn to your drawing showing how green plants get materials to make food. Will you, with your pencil, show just how the soil water travels up to the leaves? I would like for you to start by drawing a little arrow point toward the place where soil water enters the plant. Then draw other arrows up the plant to where food is built. Can you see? Where does the soil water enter the plant? Through the root hairs, doesn't it? Now, make the whole trail. Yes, trace it into the root hairs. | | | Students are instructed to illustrate the procedure they've been going over orally. |
| (m) | (Mrs. Brown circulates about the room watching students as they carry out her instructions. She leans over to assist Billy.) | | | |

| Teacher and Pupil Acts | Teacher Questions | Pupil Response | Diagnostic Comments |
|---|---|---|---|
| Teacher: I don't think that you—(To the (219) class) Now where did we say the soil water first enters the plant? | II | | |
| Alice: Through the root hairs. (220) | | C | |
| Teacher: Through the root hairs. So where (221) would your first arrow point? | II | | |
| Alice: To the root hairs. (222) | | A | |
| Teacher: To the root hairs. All right. Now, (223) where is the first arrow? Where does the soil water first enter the plant? Through what? | II II II | | |
| Alice: The root hairs. (224) | | A | |
| Teacher: The root hairs. And where do we (225) find them? I think if we sit down, we can do this better. | II | | |
| (n) (A few students are half standing in their seats.) | | | |
| Teacher: But first, where are the root hairs? (226) Don't we need some arrows pointing to the root hairs from the soil in which your plants are growing? | II  I | | |
| Dennis: And the soil has (inaudible) (227) | | C | |
| Teacher: Yes. (228) | | | |
| Shane: I need to— (229) | | B | Teacher recognizes Shane, apparently hoping he will elaborate on Dennis's point. |
| (o) (The teacher interrupts.) | | | |
| Teacher: I thought we said the soil water (230) enters through the root hairs, and from the root hairs it goes— where? | II | | |
| Brenda: Into the root. (231) | | C | |
| Teacher: To the root, doesn't it? The main | | | Teacher tells students |

373

| Teacher and Pupil Acts | | Teacher Questions | Pupil Response | Diagnostic Comments |
|---|---|---|---|---|
| (232) | root, and from the main root to the plant. Yes, just draw an arrow from the starting point where the soil water first enters the plant on to the place where the food is made. | | | exactly where to draw arrows. |
| Alice: (233) | How is this? | | C | |
| (p) | (Alice holds up her drawing so the teacher can see her arrows.) | | | |
| Teacher: (234) | That's very nice. | | | Teacher compliments Alice's work. |
| (q) | (The teacher glances at the clock.) | | | |
| Teacher: (235) | Our break comes at ten and it's ten now. I'm sure you'd like to be out playing. | | | |
| (r) | (She turns to Dennis who is holding his drawing for her to see.) | | | |
| Teacher: (236) | Yes, it comes in all the roots and goes on up the plant, into all of the leaves, doesn't it? So draw the trail that we traced a while ago. Just remember what we said. The soil water enters what? | II | | Teacher repeats questions on procedures. |
| Alice: (237) | The root hairs. | | C | |
| Teacher: (238) | The root hairs. From the root hairs, it is admitted to what? | II | | |
| Shane: (239) | Top of the leaf. | | C | |
| Teacher: (240) | The main root. I'll tell you some-thing you might try at home if you want to see how water travels. How many of you have some celery at home? | I | | |
| All: (241) | I do. | | E | |
| Teacher: (242) | All right. And do you have some red cake coloring? | I | | |
| All: (243) | Yes. | | E | |

| Teacher and Pupil Acts | Teacher Questions | Pupil Response | Diagnostic Comments |
|---|---|---|---|
| Teacher: (244) Try this tonight. Put some red or green cake coloring in a glass of water; place a celery stem down in the glass; leave it overnight, and see what happens. Take two if you wish, and see what you can prove. Scientists never take just one person's or one authority's word for anything, do they? | I | | Teacher suggests home experiment.<br><br>Teacher gives fact and adds tag question. |
| All: (245) No. | | E | |
| Teacher: (246) They look at several different sources just like you have been doing. What other sources did you use other than your plants? Where did you get your materials? | II<br>II | | |
| Dennis: (247) From the text, from libraries. | | C | |
| Teacher: (248) From the encyclopedia, from library books, from magazines, and the best place to find out something for yourself is to ... ? | II | | |
| Jane: (249) Experiment. | | C | |
| Teacher: (250) To experiment, of course, but? | II | | |
| Alice: (251) Experiment? | | C | |
| Teacher: (252) Now what? | II | | |
| (s) (Johnny is waving his hand eagerly for recognition. Teacher nods recognition.) | | | |
| Johnny: (253) Experimenting with plants. | | A | Johnny responds to non-verbal recognition. |
| Teacher: (254) From your experiments with plants, yes. Do you know what a scientist calls this when he refuses to take one person's word for anything? He looks and listens to several people, and then he | | | She does not pause for |

| Teacher and Pupil Acts | Teacher Questions | Pupil Response | Diagnostic Comments |
|---|---|---|---|
| tries it himself. We have a word for that. Here it is, I'll put it down. | | | answer, so not counted as question. |
| (t) (Mrs. Brown writes on the board.) | | | |
| All: (255) Verification. | | E | |
| Teacher: (256) Verification. He verifies. He never accepts anything as being true just because one authority has said it's true. Never! Especially with something new. We're just doing this experiment to prove what we already know to be true, of course. Do you think scientists who do research and make experiments try something once and when it works say "Oh, boy. I've found it"? Do they do that? | I, I | | Teacher reinforces by asking student what she has just explained. |
| Dennis: (257) No, they try experiments. | | C | |
| Teacher: (258) No, they don't. | | | |
| Jane: (259) They check it. | | C | |
| Teacher: (260) They check it, they check it, they recheck, and then they verify. | | | Teacher repeats. |
| Johnny: (261) Because (inaudible) | | C | |
| Teacher: (262) They did? Well, we are going to try some of those experiments later on after we talk a little more about plants and watch ours grow to see what they do. You may put away your books and things, please. | | | Teacher structures end of lesson. |

## ANALYTICAL SUMMARY FOR
## TEACHER QUESTIONS AND PUPIL RESPONSES

### The Elementary Science Lesson

| Question Categories | Number | % | Response Categories | Number | % |
|---|---|---|---|---|---|
| I. Recognition | 51 | 34 | A. Individual | 45 | 34 |
| II. Recall | 79 | 52 | B. Group | 21 | 16 |
| III. Demonstration | | | C. No One | 41 | 32 |
| of Skill | 0 | 0 | D. Spontaneous | 2 | 2 |
| IV. Comprehension | 18 | 12 | E. Mass | 20 | 16 |
| V. Analysis | 0 | 0 | | | |
| VI. Synthesis | 0 | 0 | | | |
| VII. Opinion | 1 | 1 | | | |
| VIII. Attitude or Value | 0 | 0 | | | |
| Total | 149 | 99 | Total | 129 | 100 |

| | |
|---|---|
| Number of pupils in class | 28 |
| Number of pupil respondents | 13 |
| Percentage of pupils responding | 46* |
| Percent of responses by five most verbal pupils | 76* |

*Mass responses excluded.

Appendix VIII-E

PROTOCOL – THE LEAKING BOTTLE LESSON*

Instructor's Guide

Ellwood Elementary School is located in a working-class neighborhood. The students in the sixth grade, as in the school as a whole, are of varied ethnic origins and socio-economic levels. Twenty-eight students are enrolled in the sixth grade; there are nineteen boys and nine girls. Of these, seven are Negroes, and one girl has emigrated recently from Cuba. (Jay is a new student just transferred from another school system.) The students' I.Q.'s range from a low of 77 to a high of 133. The mean I.Q. is 103. The students range in age from barely eleven years to almost thirteen. Most of the students are eleven. Reading abilities range from a low of 2.0 to a high of 10.0 grade. On the average, the students' reading test scores indicate slightly below normal achievement of 6.1 in the middle of the 6th year. Two students were absent when The Leaking Bottle Lesson was presented.

| Boys | | | Girls | |
|------|------|------|------|------|
| Atlas | Kenneth | Richard | Connie | Pamela |
| Darryl | Kenneth G. | Roy | Deborah | Roxane |
| Glenn | Larry | Russell | Imilse | Sharon |
| Jay | Leonard | Thomas | Kerry | |
| Keith | Michael | Timothy | Marilyn | |
| Kenny | Mike | | Marlene | |

*Diagnostic Analysis of Lesson Protocol by Ben M. Harris and Betty Porter. Prepared in cooperation with the South Park School District in Beaumont, Texas. Analytical work supported by contract O.E. 6-10-108, Division of Laboratories and Research Development, U.S. Office of Education.

380

# Back

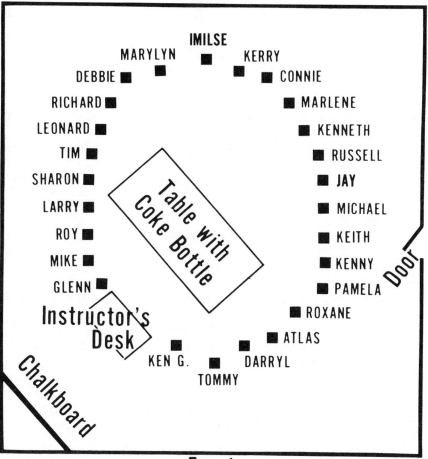

# Front

# SEATING ARRANGEMENT FOR
# THE LEAKING BOTTLE LESSON

LESSON PLAN

Topic:   The Leaking Bottle
                                              Subject:   Science, Grade 6
Instructor:                              Date:   Feb. 1, 1966   School:   Ellwood

Goals

1. To develop more skeptical attitude to avoid assuming things true without proof
2. To develop analytical thinking ability
3. To develop the habit of consciously differentiating between knowledge and assumption in drawing conclusions
4. To develop skill in applying theory and research methods in arriving at conclusions

Objectives

1. To identify assumptions, direct evidence, and supporting evidence (related knowledge) as they all contribute to a conclusion
2. To recognize that very different explanations may apply even when identical evidence is involved
3. To understand that varying our assumptions dramatically changes the explanations that logically apply
4. To understand the use of experimentation for testing an explanation

Overview of the Lesson

1. A Coke is placed on a table in clear view, and teacher briefly introduces lesson about analytical thinking.
2. Focused discussion is initiated and guided by teacher to get pupils to describe and explain condensation phenomenon seen on Coke bottle.
3. Teacher presents logical alternative explanation for observed events.
4. Teacher stimulates free discussion of alternatives with permissive, non-directive procedures.
5. Teacher focuses discussion with questions about testing alternative explanation.
6. Teacher summarizes.

Materials, Equipment and Arrangements

Bottle of Coke or other soft drink in bottle
Thermos jug large enough to chill bottle of Coke
Ice and salt to chill bottle of Coke
Paper towels or cloth to wipe bottle dry and to set bottle upon
Chalkboard, table, desk or stand in the middle of the room
Pupils seated in circle to facilitate pupil-pupil interaction

Procedures

| Time | Activities |
|------|-----------|
| 0 | Introduce lesson. Place Coke bottle on table in clear view. |

"The facts we learn in school are important, but more important is learning how to think. Today, I'd like us to see how well we can think. I mean really think! You know, one of the most difficult things to learn is to think analytically about something we already know."

5       Describing the moisture on the bottle (focused discussion).

Turn to bottle.
"What's happening to our Coke?"
"How do you explain what you see?" (What is on the surface of the bottle? Where is the moisture coming from? How do you know that is moisture we see?)
"How do you know the moisture is coming from the air?"
"What assumptions are you making in explaining what we see?" (Analyze meaning of word "assumption.")

15      Present Summary in Schematic Form on Chalkboard.

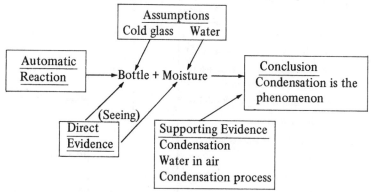

20      Present alternative theory.

1. The bottle and its contents are cold.
2. The bottle is sealed tight.
3. The air in the room is warming the bottle and its contents.
4. The warming contents are expanding and exerting increasing pressure on the inside of the bottle.
5. Under pressure the bottle is slightly porous and the contents are seeping out through the sides of the bottle.

22      Discussion of alternative (free discussion).

"What do you think of my explanation?" "What assumptions am I making?"

40      "How would you test my idea to show me your explanation is more defensible?"

50 - 55   Summary and Adjourn

# THE LESSON

| Teacher and Pupil Acts | | Teacher Questions | Pupil Response | Diagnostic Comments |
|---|---|---|---|---|
| Instructor: (1) | We are going to do something quite different today. We will do mostly talking. | | | |
| (a) | (Instructor gets up from desk and goes to center of room. Students are seated in circle around the room. Instructor wipes off coke bottle and puts coke and cloth on table in the center of room and walks back to desk.) | | | |
| Instructor: (2) | Before we begin, let me make one last bit of preparation for today's session. Let me get that wiped off nice and clean and dry. Guess I don't have to ask anybody what that is! | | | |
| (b) | (Students laugh.) | | E | |
| Instructor: (3) | Isn't that nice and clean, Kenny? We will come back to that after awhile. Isn't this the most peculiar teaching you ever did see? | I | | Rhetorical question |
| (c) | (Students laugh.) | | E | |
| Instructor: (4) | It really kind of tempts you, doesn't it? | | | Rhetorical question |
| Instructor: (5) | Only one bottle. There are 30 of us, aren't there? No.... | | | Procedural question |
| Instructor: (6) | ...twenty-six. | | | |
| Instructor: (7) | You know, today I want to focus with you on how to think. I mean really think. Do you know thinking's hard work? It is, isn't it Pam? When you really get down to doing real thinking.... | I I | | Instructor elicits interest in discussion by his approach to presenting the purpose of the lesson. |
| (d) | (Instructor is seated.) | | | |
| Instructor: (8) | ...so that you really are using that gray matter up there in the head; that's hard work. But it's also kind of exciting and interesting work. | | | |

| Teacher and Pupil Acts | Teacher Questions | Pupil Response | Diagnostic Comments |
|---|---|---|---|
| I think you will agree and I want to give some attention today to a special kind of thinking. It's what we sometimes call analytical thinking or critical thinking which is a special kind. It's a little harder than just ordinary thinking, too! So I hope that you will work at it with me today. Really, don't be afraid to strain the brain. What are we going to think about? Well, we are going to think about that coke bottle. | | | |
| (e)   (Students laugh.) | | E | |
| Instructor: (9)   If you were thirsty, it would be worth thinking about, but not in a very analytical way. That's a casual kind of thinking. The coke bottle is there, and you are thirsty and you think, "Well, I would like to have a drink of that." But, that's not the kind of thinking I'm talking about, is it, when I say analytical thinking? | I | | |
| Now, on the other hand, if that coke bottle was there and you were very, very thirsty and you wanted a drink of some of that coke and you didn't have any way of opening it and you had to think, "How am I going to get that bottle open?" Now, that might be analytical thinking. Now you've got a real problem. Now you have to really get those gray brain cells working, to figure out, how do I get the coke bottle open? Well, we're going to think about that coke bottle. But not in terms of being thirsty. Remember, I wiped that coke bottle very carefully with this rag! | | | Rhetorical question

Rhetorical question |
| (f)   (Instructor wipes coke bottle with | | | |

| Teacher and Pupil Acts | Teacher Questions | Pupil Response | Diagnostic Comments |
|---|---|---|---|
| rag and walks around circle giving students the opportunity for a close view of the coke bottle as he continues to remind students that he had previously dried it carefully.) <br> * * * * * * * * * | | | |
| Instructor: (10) Now let's put it right back there. All right, what's happening to our coke? Pam? | V | | Instructor asks open-ended question to stimulate more student response. |
| Pam: (11) It's thawing out and the bottle is sweating out. | | B | |
| Instructor: (12) It's "thawing out" and the bottle is "sweating." Could you talk a little louder, Pam? I can hardly hear you. Say it again. | | | Teacher repeats unique phrases used by student. Procedural question to make certain response is audible. Teacher shows acceptance of student's idea by asking to have it repeated. |
| Pam: (13) It's thawing out and the bottle is sweating. | | A | |
| Instructor: (14) Kenneth? | V | | Kenneth is both answering open-ended question (10) and reacting to Pam's response. |
| Kenneth G.: (15) It's condensing. | | B | |
| Instructor: (16) "It's condensing." All right. Do you all agree? | II | | Teacher accepts but asks for other views. |
| (g) (Keith nods "yes.") | | C | Keith selects himself for non-verbal response. |
| Instructor: (17) Is that what Pam means? What does Pam mean by "sweating out"? | I <br> IV | | Teacher encourages contrasting of ideas expressed by Pam and Kenneth G. |
| (h) (Keith raises his hand.) | | C | |
| (i) (Instructor nods to him.) | | | |
| Keith: Well, warm air holds more | | A | Keith responds to non- |

| Teacher and Pupil Acts | Teacher Questions | Pupil Response | Diagnostic Comments |
|---|---|---|---|
| (18)      moisture than cold air, so the warm air outside is going where it is cold. Cold water and air on the inside is making it sweat. Making it have water on the out- side. | | | verbal recognition. He senses that teacher wants fuller explanation of what has been described as "sweating" and "condensing." Keith tries to provide analysis. |

\* \* \* \* \* \* \* \* \*

The instructor encourages students to talk through their explanation of the moisture on the bottle. Then in a much more highly structured fashion, he questions them about how they know what they are saying is true:

"How do you know that the bottle is cold?"

"How do you know those beads of liquid are water?"

"How do you know that bottle is made of non-porous glass?"

Each such question causes a flurry of efforts to answer. Some students even suggest testing procedures:

"Well we could taste it."

"We could feel that it is cold or not."

"We could tap it with a pencil to see if it sounds like glass...."

At this point the instructor moves to the chalkboard and begins to sketch a diagram.

"You saw the bottle. You saw moisture. So, through the process of seeing, you drew your conclusion? No, you needed more evidence. Was there some supporting evidence? Some facts, information, knowledge?"

ANALYTICAL THINKING
ABOUT "MOISTURE" ON THE BOTTLE

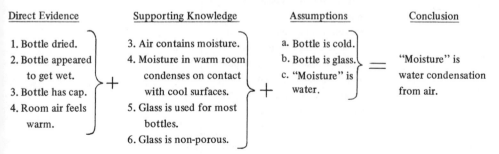

The students respond readily, telling how they were using what had previously been learned.

Kenneth G.:   We knew something about rain. We knew that warm air holds more moisture than cold air.

Michael:   Warm air loses water as it's cooled off.

Mike:   Well, I went to the _____ Bottling Company downtown, and they showed us _____. They said it was glass.

The instructor includes these ideas in his diagram as the students talk. He labels each column to show the difference between "direct evidence" and "supporting knowledge."

Finally, the instructor asks: "Now, you were making some assumptions, weren't you? What were the assumptions to go along with your evidence and supporting knowledge?"

| | |
|---|---|
| Mike: | We were believing that was moisture on the bottle. |
| Pamela: | Well, when you set it down on the table, it had a sound like glass. |
| Richard: | There was ice in the bottle. |
| Instructor: | We are assuming that the bottle is colder than the air. I didn't let you touch the bottle, did I? If you had, we would then have coldness as direct evidence rather than an assumption. |

The instructor completes the diagram on the chalkboard. "Boys and girls, notice what we're saying. These assumptions about the bottle, about the moisture, about the temperatures of the bottle are important to our conclusion. Without these assumptions we cannot really draw a conclusion."

A stretch break is called by the instructor now. He senses some restlessness. The students stand and talk informally among themselves. Some are still talking about the bottle.

\* \* \* \* \* \*

| Teacher and Pupil Acts | Teacher Questions | Pupil Response | Diagnostic Comments |
|---|---|---|---|
| (j)          (The instructor sits down and students follow.) | | | |
| Instructor: (19)          I might say to you boys and girls that in a way now, we're acting like scientists. We're being very critical, very analytical. As scientists we try to avoid making assumptions. We try to avoid reaching conclusions unless we have all the evidence and if we don't have all the evidence, if we have made some assumptions, then we're cautious about our conclusion. | | | |
| (k)          (Instructor points to diagram on board.) | | | |
| Instructor: (20)          We say, "Well, we believe that this is condensation which occurs this way. But, until I know for sure that it's cold, until I know for sure that it's water, I cannot be certain of my conclusion." And, this is | | | |

| Teacher and Pupil Acts | Teacher Questions | Pupil Response | Diagnostic Comments |
|---|---|---|---|
| the thing that makes the difference between a scientist and just ordinary people who just look at it and say, "Sure it's cold and it's moisture." And never give it another thought. Now, I want to do something with you and move your thinking along just a little bit. You've explained this moisture on the bottle quite well for me. Quite well for most people. But, I'm going to explain it in a different way. I want you to listen to my explanation now, a different one. That bottle is cold. I had it on ice. Quite cold. This room is warm. I can feel it. Therefore, that liquid is getting warmer inside that bottle. Now, I know that bottle is sealed tight because I felt the cap, and as a liquid gets warm it tends to expand. So, that liquid is getting warmer. It is expanding. As it expands, the pressure inside that bottle increases! The substance that the bottle is made from is porous under pressure and that liquid is seeping out through that bottle and forming on the surface. | | | |
| (l) (Instructor pauses; students laugh.) | | E | |
| Instructor: (21) It's a good logical explanation, isn't it? What's illogical about my explanation, Sharon? | V | | |
| Sharon: (22) I don't understand it. | | B | |
| Instructor: (23) All right, if you didn't understand, then maybe it isn't logical. Keith, do you understand the logic of my explanation? | I | | Instructor asks recognition question, but student gives analytical answer. |

| Teacher and Pupil Acts | Teacher Questions | Pupil Response | Diagnostic Comments |
|---|---|---|---|
| Keith: (24) Well, you said that it was seeping through the glass, and I don't think that a coke or anything, water or liquid, could seep through the glass. | | B | |
| Instructor: (25) All right. You're assuming that it's glass. | | | |
| Keith: (26) Well, even a rock! | | A | |
| Instructor: (27) I assume that it is a porous material. | | | |
| Keith: (28) Well, even if it was a rock, it would take about a thousand years, I guess, for the water to seep through it and cut through it. Plastic of some... might.... | | A | |
| Instructor: (29) You think my assumption that it's a porous material is not a good assumption? | I | | |
| Michael: (30) I thought that when water gets warmer, that it contracts, not expands. | | | |
| Instructor: (31) All right. Michael thinks that my explanation is wrong, that when liquids get warm, they contract instead of expanding. Kenny, do you know about that? | I | | |
| Kenny: (32) Well, they expand. | | A | |
| Instructor: (33) So you say that they expand. So then my explanation is logical to that degree, isn't it? | I | | Instructor asks recognition question, but student responds on higher level of thinking. |
| Kenny: (34) Cause if you had a balloon and you put it over a warm spot, well, the balloon would expand. | | A | |
| Instructor: (35) Gases expand when they're warm at least, and I said liquids do. Richard? | IV | | |
| Richard: (36) Before you put it in, maybe you didn't have ice in it and put it in | | B | |

390

| Teacher and Pupil Acts | | Teacher Questions | Pupil Response | Diagnostic Comments |
|---|---|---|---|---|
| | a cold place like in the thermos, and it contracted and made ice. | | | |
| Instructor: (37) | Tim? | IV | | |
| Tim: (38) | You said just a while ago about how the moisture got on the out-side, sort of bringing it out, as the air from the coke goes up, it comes out through the top of the cap, around the cap, on the sides. | | B | |
| Instructor: (39) | You're saying that my explanation would be improved if we assumed that the pressure forced the moisture up to the point where the cap would leak? | IV | | Instructor reinforces Tim's idea that it's more than heat expansion and contraction and relates to analysis of the alternative explanation. |
| Tim: (40) | Sort of around the sides. | | A | |
| Instructor: (41) | You wouldn't have to assume a porous bottle. You would only assume a leaky cap. All right. Pam? | | | |
| Pamela: (42) | Well, Roxane had an idea that— well, let her explain it. | | B | |
| Instructor: (43) | All right, go ahead, Roxane. | | | |
| Roxane: (44) | Well, if the coke got hot and more pressure builds up, well—if it got more and more pressure in there, that the whole thing would just explode. And, then you would have water everywhere. | | B | |
| (m) | (Students laugh.) | | E | |
| Instructor: (45) | You're saying that either I'm right that there's enough seeping taking place to keep it from exploding or we're going to have an explosion any minute now! | | | |
| (n) | (Students laugh.) | | E | |
| Roxane: | No, sir, when it gets hot, ... | | C | |

| Teacher and Pupil Acts | Teacher Questions | Pupil Response | Diagnostic Comments |
|---|---|---|---|
| (46)          (inaudible) | | | |
| Instructor: Well, this kind of supports my (47) explanation, doesn't it? That maybe there's seepage occurring there because it isn't exploding. Darryl, what do you think? (Darryl looks blank. Frowns.) Can't tell right at this moment, can you? That's all right. Glen, what are you thinking about? Do I have you confused now? Mike, go ahead. | V | | Instructor asks recognition question, shifts, elaborates, and then rapidly rephrases question to require analytical thinking. |
| Mike: If you put a pot of water on the (48) stove and you let it boil over night and you come back, you might have no more water. And Michael said that water was the same as gas, and when it gets so cold, it evaporates. | | B | |
| Instructor: Keith? (49) | V | | |
| Keith: Well, I agree with you that it (50) expanded and then the air—the air is brought up on the top of the bottle where there is no coke and it forced the coke down and the coke can't seep out of the top that way, cause the air is trying to get out. And if you were to open the bottle—I mean the lid to it—you would open it a tiny bit, it might fuse up and then that way—I think you are wrong because water can't go out of the bottle. I don't believe it can. | | B | |
| Instructor: All right.———Kenny? (51) | V | | |
| Kenny: Well, there's air in the top of the (52) bottle and the coke in the bottle is cold, and so, naturally, the air in the bottle would be cold, and as it gets warmer, the coke ex- | | | |

| Teacher and Pupil Acts | | Teacher Questions | Pupil Response | Diagnostic Comments |
|---|---|---|---|---|
| | pands and it pushes the air—it's still cold—and it pushes the air through the sides of the cap and the bottle. And as that cold air reaches the warm air, as it gets through the cap, well, it changes into water as the cold vapor hits the warm air. Then it changes into water. | | | |
| Instructor: (53) | What do you think, Sharon? | V | | |
| Sharon: (54) | I agree. | | B | |
| Instructor: (55) | Kenneth? | V | | |
| Kenneth G.: (56) | Well, I agree with Kenny cause it had so much pressure in the bottle, well, that it would steam up when you open the top a little bit. It wouldn't have air holes in it because if it was to expand, it would be so much pressure in it— it couldn't have air holes in it. | | B | |
| Instructor: (57) | Uh huh.———Michael? | V | | |
| Michael: (58) | Well, as Kenneth says, the pressure makes it fuse up, and I want him to explain it to me why it fuses up. | | B | |
| Instructor: (59) | All right, Kenneth. He wants more information. | | | |
| Kenneth G.: (60) | Why it fuses up? Because it has so much pressure in it. It has no air holes. | | A | |
| Michael: (61) | Do you mean when the air gets into the bottle, it pops open? | | C | |
| Kenneth G.: (62) | It has no place for the air to seep out and it expands.... | | A | |
| (o) | (Many hands go up.) | | | |
| Instructor: | Go ahead. I don't have to call on | | | Instructor encourages |

| | Teacher and Pupil Acts | Teacher Questions | Pupil Response | Diagnostic Comments |
|---|---|---|---|---|
| (63) | you. You can talk. Go ahead. | | | more student to student interaction by instructions not to wait to be called on. |
| Mike: (64) | Well, the bottle when it is made, has to be put into a mold and when the mold is put together, so much heat is on it where it's put together, it seeps in there and when it expands it—or something—it lets air out. And there is air in the coke when you shake it up, it spews out. | | C | |
| Imilse: (65) | Why is ice coming up to the top now? (Ice crystals seem to be forming at the top as a cluster.) | | D | |
| Richard: (66) | Because the air in the top is pushing the liquid down and ice is lighter than water and therefore it floats up. | | D | |
| Imilse: (67) | What is it doing now? It wasn't doing that a while ago. | | D | |
| Richard: (68) | Well, the ice is breaking up, and it's not getting warmer in the room. It's not getting warmer in the room, I mean, the bottle has been in the room a certain time, and the ice is beginning to melt and break up and that's why it's there now. | | D | |
| Marilyn: (69) | You said the water—the air was pushing the coke down? Well, where does the coke go when it pushes it down? | | D | |
| Richard: (70) | It goes to the bottom, I mean top, I think Kenny said that a while ago. | | D | |
| Mike: (71) | A gas floats up and a liquid goes down and it's not like a gas. It doesn't—it doesn't go up by itself. You have to have either pressure through it or air pushing it up. | | D | |

| | Teacher and Pupil Acts | Teacher Questions | Pupil Response | Diagnostic Comments |
|---|---|---|---|---|
| Roxane: (72) | I say that when they made that bottle, they used so much pressure on it they made it so it just wouldn't leak, and so that water just could not come out through there either. I say that it comes from the air that melts it. | | D | |
| Instructor: (73) | Uh huh! | | | Instructor's reaction encourages further response. |
| Roxane: (74) | Yea, but it couldn't expand through the bottle. | | C | |
| Instructor: (75) | Go ahead, you speak up. | | | |
| Tim: (76) | Well, I say Roxane is wrong because if there's pressure up in there, it would explode, and if it's got to come out somewhere, it would come out around the cap. | | B | |
| Student: (77) | (Asking questions) Maybe there's not enough pressure in there to make it explode? | | D | |
| Kenny: (78) | The ice has some oxygen in it or it wouldn't come up to the top, and when the ice melts, it releases the oxygen and that causes more pressure in the bottle. | | D | |
| Instructor: (79) | Pressure? | IV | | Instructor narrows the focus by question about pressure. |
| Tommy: (80) | More pressure inside the bottle. | | C | |
| Instructor: (81) | Can you explain that a little further for me? How do you feel.. | IV, V | | Instructor encourages Tommy to relate idea about pressure to analysis of theory. |
| Tommy: (82) | Well, Roxane said that the water in the bottle couldn't get out because they filled it so tight—insulated cap cork.... | | A | |
| Keith: | Well, the coke has water in it—I | | C | |

395

| | Teacher and Pupil Acts | Teacher Questions | Pupil Response | Diagnostic Comments |
|---|---|---|---|---|
| (83) | mean it's mixed with water. Well, the carbonated water and it's frozen and—but the ingredients are not—and when the warm air on the outside is pushing it, it warms it up and it just melts, I mean, it just melts.... | | | |
| Instructor: (84) | Kenny? | V | | |
| Kenny: (85) | Uh, if you left the coke in the refrigerator a long time, it would just—the whole bottle would freeze and the coke inside would freeze and you wouldn't have as much room at the top as you would if the coke were still a liquid because the oxygen in the ice.... | | B | |
| Instructor: (86) | Uh huh! | | | |
| Kenny: (87) | And then when it melts, the oxygen goes to the top and the liquid goes to the bottom. | | C | |
| Instructor: (88) | I'm not sure I understand. Do you folks understand what Kenny's saying here? Do you Marilyn? Can you try to put it into some other words for us? | IV IV IV | | |
| Marilyn: (89) | Well, I understand what he is thinking about, but I don't think I could tell it. | | B | |
| Instructor: (90) | These are difficult things to talk about because they are complicated, aren't they? Well, where are we? | | | |
| (p) | (Students laugh.) | | E | |

\* \* \* \* \* \* \* \* \* \*

The Leaking Bottle Lesson

| Question Categories | Number | % | Response Categories | Number | % |
|---|---|---|---|---|---|
| I. Recognition | 10 | 33.3 | A. Individual | 11 | 22 |
| II. Recall | 0 | 0 | B. Group | 15 | 30 |
| III. Demonstration of Skill | 0 | 0 | C. No One | 8 | 16 |
| IV. Comprehension | 10 | 33.3 | D. Spontaneous | 11 | 22 |
| V. Analysis | 10 | 33.3 | E. Mass | 5 | 10 |
| VI. Synthesis | 0 | 0 | | | |
| VII. Opinion | 0 | 0 | | | |
| VIII. Attitude or Value | 0 | 0 | | | |
| Totals | 30 | 100 | | 50 | 100 |

Number of pupils in the class     26
Number of pupil respondents     13
Percentage of pupils responding     50**
Percent of responses by five most verbal pupils 24/50     49**

---

* Prepared in cooperation with the South Park School District in Beaumont, Texas.
Analytical work supported by contract O.E. 6 - 10 - 108, Division of Laboratories and
Research Development, U.S. Office of Education.
** Mass response excluded.

Appendix VIII-F

PROTOCOL – A CREATIVE WRITING LESSON*

Lesson Topic:        Writing original stories, story endings, and imaginative descriptions

Teacher:             Mrs. Betty Black

Grade:               Second Grade

Number of Pupils:    23

12 Girls      11 Boys

## The Lesson in Brief

Mrs. Black organizes four subgroups for the following writing activities:

Group I.    (Listening to part of a story on tape and then writing the ending to it.) The six children in this group listen to "The Pied Piper of Hamelin" by Robert Browning to the point where the Pied Piper led the children into the mountain, and the door closed behind them. The story takes about five minutes, and then the children spend the remainder of the time writing their own endings.

Group II.    (Using a mirror to make a written description of themselves.) Each of the five children in this group is given a stand-up mirror and asked to make a written description of himself. Several children write much more than visual descriptions and reveal many things about their own self images.

Group III. (Using "story starters" for individual stories.) Each of the seven children in this group receives a slip of paper containing an opening phrase and is asked to write an individual story from his "story starter." The starters are inside a large cardboard pencil made by the teacher. One of the slips of paper reads as follows: "This morning, I opened the closet door, and there was . . ."

Group IV. (Writing imaginative stories about objects.) Each of the five girls in this group chooses a story starter from pictures of eyes, lips, fingers, toes, thumb, etc., and writes an autobiographical story about her picture.

## Lesson Plan

I.    Background Information

Pupils in this class began writing original sentences and paragraphs in September. They wrote second lines to rhymes and also short poems. They have written songs, letters, stories, and book reports. They may attempt a play before school is out.

II.    Teacher Objectives

A.    To motivate a desire toward creative writing

---

* Prepared in cooperation with the South Park School District in Beaumont, Texas.

    B.   To emphasize independence in writing
    C.   To create a relaxed environment for writing
    D.   To assist with spelling
    E.   To improve written and oral language

III.   Pupil Activities

    A.   Listening to part of a story on tape and writing the ending to it.

        The story will be "The Pied Piper of Hamelin" by Robert Browning. The children will be hearing the story for the first time. They will hear only up to the point where the mountain opens and the children go inside. What happened to them?

    B.   Using "story starters" for individual stories. The "story starters" are contained in a large cardboard pencil made by the teacher. A chart next to the pencil will give the following directions:

1. Handle carefully. It is magic.
2. Take off the magic eraser.
3. Tip the pencil slightly until the magic papers show at the end.
4. Pull one of the magic papers out gently.
5. Push the other papers back into the pencil.
6. Read your paper and write your story.

The slips of papers will contain the following story starters:

1. This morning, I opened the closet door, and there was . . . .
2. If I were a giant I would . . . .
3. On the way to school I saw . . . .
4. If I were a space man I would . . . .
5. The prettiest thing I ever saw was . . . .
6. One day I was a moon man and I . . . .

    C.   Using a mirror to make a written description of themselves.

        Pupils of this group will each have a stand –up mirror and will write what they see.

    D.   Writing imaginative stories about objects.

        This group will choose a story starter from pictures of eyes, lips, fingers, toes, etc., and then they will write about the picture.

Note: If any child wishes to write a story without a story starter of any kind, he is completely free to do so.

IV.   Materials to be used

    A.   Tape recorder and earphones
    B.   Pictures
    C.   Bulletin boards

D.    Pencil, paper
E.    Mirrors
F.    Charts

V.    Sequence of Events - Teacher Working with Groups

A.    Tape, earphones - listen to story (5 minutes)
B.    Teacher working with story starters (5 minutes)
C.    Writing about objects (7 minutes)
D.    Teacher working with mirror describing group (5 minutes)
E.    Reading stories written using pictures of objects (15 minutes)

<u>Physical Arrangements</u>

At the front of the room, a U-shaped pattern of individual desks and chairs is arranged facing the left side of the room. The seven children in Group III, seated here, are facing a chart rack and a chart with directions for using a magic pencil. A large, teacher-made cardboard pencil containing "story starters" is on the floor beside the chart rack.

The six children in Group I use a table and an earphone panel on the right side of the room. A tape recorder, on a small table nearby, is also provided for this group.

The five children in Group II are seated in a semi-circle of individual desks and chairs near the chalkboard at the back of the room. Each child is provided with an individual stand-up mirror.

The five children in Group IV are seated in a semi-circle of individual desks and chairs facing an easel near the left side of the room.

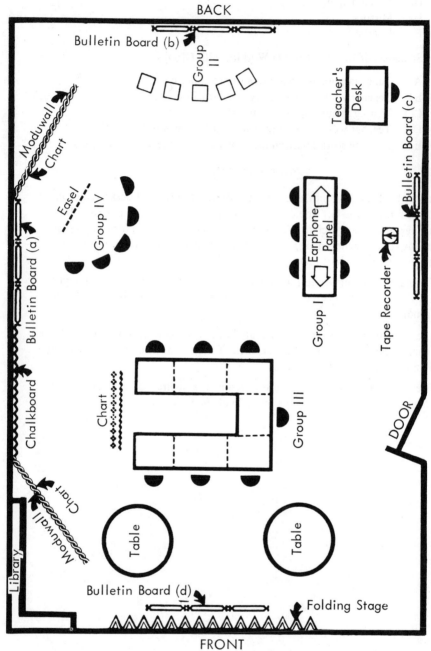

BACK

Bulletin Board (b)

Group II

Teacher's Desk

Bulletin Board (c)

Moduwall

Chart

Easel

Group IV

Bulletin Board (a)

Earphone Panel

Group I

Tape Recorder

Chalkboard

Chart

Chart

Group III

DOOR

Moduwall

Library

Table

Table

Bulletin Board (d)

Folding Stage

FRONT

CREATIVE WRITING—IMAGINATIVE STORIES

## The Lesson

In Group I, five boys and one girl are seated around a table at the right side of the room. An earphone panel is on the table. A tape recorder is on a smaller table behind the group against the right wall. The teacher has planned for the earphones to be used by the children to hear, for the first time, a pretaped beginning of Robert Browning's story, "The Pied Piper of Hamelin." Their assignment is to write their own ending to the story.

(a)       (As the lesson begins, Mrs. Black stands at end of table before Group I and faces the front of the room. She holds a book in her hands. She turns several pages to show illustrations to children.)

Teacher:   This is a story of "The Pied Piper of Hamelin." After you listen to this story, (1)       you are going to write something for me, and I can help you. So you must listen very, very carefully to this story because you are going to write the ending of this story.

Gary:      Ending! (Giggles.)
(2)

Teacher:   You've never done that before, have you? Well, I'm going to let you write (3)       the ending of the story—how do you think this story ends?

(b)       (As Mrs. Black explains, she closes the book, places the edge of the book on the table, and rests her hands upon it. Brad rests his head on his hand. The teacher then places the book flat on the table. Freddy, in Group II, swings his feet under his desk, places his hand in his mouth, and gives a small hand wave.)

Mark:      Sad?
(4)

Teacher:   However you want it. Sad—if you want it to be sad. If you want it to be glad— (5)       you can make it any way you want it to be. Do you understand?

Mark:      Yes, ma'am.
(6)

Teacher:   Well, it might take you a long time to write it. It might not. Just however you (7)       think it will end. Now get your earphones on. Get them adjusted and if they're uncomfortable on your ears, tell me.

(c)       (The teacher places hands on earphone controls. Sharon brushes her hair back and puts on her earphones. Wayne puts his earphones on and adjusts his own control.)

Teacher:   They're not comfortable? How does that feel? Does that feel O.K.? Mark, (8)       are they comfortable? Are they comfortable, Sharon? O.K. Let's hold our noise down now, and I'm not going to show you the pictures since we have just a few pictures. When you get through if you know how to unplug this take it over and put it there. When you finish your story if you have some time left you may draw a picture of how your story ends. Can you do that for me? Are you ready?

(d)       (All children nod. The children seem eager to hear the story on the tape. Mrs. Black checks the earphones of four children and then adjusts the volume of controls. She shows the children how to unplug the headsets when they have finished. The teacher leans over Mark, shows him about the headsets, and says something to him.)

| Mark: (9) | Yes, ma'am. |
|---|---|
| Joe: (10) | Just put it sad or–? (He looks a bit uncertain.) |
| (e) | (Mrs. Black moves to a table behind the children, turns on the tape recorder, adjusts it, and then reverses the tape. She turns around and looks at Joe.) |
| Teacher: (11) | If you want it to be sad–fine. If you want it to be happy–fine. You fix it the way you want it to be. O.K.? |
| Joe: (12) | O.K. |
| (f) | (Mark turns around and talks to the teacher. She answers, stops the recorder, and connects the recorder to the earphone panels. Evidently this had been forgotten. Again she starts the recorder.) |
| Mark: (13) | I heard you talking. (Whispers.) |
| (g) | (Mrs. Black moves back to the table with a microphone in her hand.) |
| Teacher: (14) | Do you hear? |
| Sharon: (15) | Yes. |
| (h) | (The teacher places her hands on Wayne's shoulders.) |
| Teacher: (16) | (She then places her hands on table.) Are you ready? |
| (i) | (The children nod. When the tape recorder squeals, the children laugh.) |
| (j) | (Three other groups have been waiting while Mrs. Black worked with Group I. She now moves quickly to the side of the room, picks up four mirrors on stands, and moves to Group II.) |

Group II has five children, two boys and three girls. They are seated in a semi-circle of individual desks at the back of the room and to the left of Group I. The teacher plans for pupils to write what they see in the individual mirrors.

| Freddy: (17) | Mirrors! Make a picture of yourself! |
|---|---|
| (k) | (The pupils giggle. Mrs. Black places a mirror on each desk and flips one to show the magnifying side. John smiles at himself, puts his hands back of his chair, and stretches. He looks again, smiles at himself. The other children laugh. They all seem to be very excited.) |
| John: (18) | He's making faces at himself. |
| Teacher: (19) | Who do you see? |
| Becky: (20) | I don't know? |
| Teacher: (21) | You don't know who that is? |

Becky:     Uh-huh.
(22)

(1)        (The teacher moves to Louisa, adjusts her mirror, leans down, looks in the
           girl's mirror.)

Teacher:   Who is it?
(23)

Louisa:    Me.
(24)

Teacher:   You?  Who do you see?
(25)

Louisa:    Me.
(26)

(m)        (Mrs. Black moves to the next desk and looks in another mirror.)

Teacher:   What a handsome gentleman!
(27)

(n)        (John smiles at himself.)

Teacher:   Do you see yourself?
(28)

John:      Yes, ma'am.
(29)

Teacher:   (To the whole group.)  Now, this is what I want you to do.  On your paper,
(30)       I want you to write me all about the person you see in the mirror.  Tell me
           how you look to yourself.  Describe yourself.  Tell me about you.  Then you'll
           need to look in the mirror to find out about you, won't you?

(o)        (John looks detached as Mrs. Black gives the explanation of the assignment.
           He props his elbow on the table, briefly rests his head on his hand, tilts his
           mirror, and gazes steadily at himself.)

Louisa:    (Giggles.)  If I were writing a story like that, I'd say I was beautiful and every-
(31)       thing.  (Giggles.)

Teacher:   It's nice to think you're beautiful.  All right, can you do that?  Can all of you do that?
(32)

(p)        (Freddy smooths his hair as he looks at himself in his mirror.)

Judy:      Yes, ma'am.
(33)

Teacher:   O.K., get your paper and let's get started.  Tell me all about the person you
(34)       see.  If you want to turn your mirror over, you'll see yourself magnified.

(q)        (The teacher flips a mirror to show both sides.)

Teacher:   Look how much bigger you are.  You can turn it over and see yourself.  O.K.,
(35)       can you get busy working on that?

John:      Yes, ma'am.
(36)

(r)        (The teacher turns John's mirror to magnifying side.  He asks her a question,
           and she turns his mirror back to original position.)

| John: | I'm going to make my picture big. |
| (37) | |

| Teacher: | If you'd rather do it magnified—all right, you may do it that way. |
| (38) | O.K. Can you get busy working on that? |

| (s) | (John grins as teacher moves away. He talks to Freddy. John moves his paper closer and takes a pencil from a box on his desk. All the children move paper and begin to work.) |

Group III has seven children, four boys and three girls. Their desks are placed together forming a large U at front of the room, opposite Group II and to the left of Group I. The opening of the U is at the left, and the chart rack is directly before the opening. On the floor, beside the chart is a large cardboard pencil labeled "Magic Pencil." The pencil contains "story starters" or sentences for beginning a story. Mrs. Black's plan calls for each child to receive a different opening sentence to use in stimulating him to write an individual story.

| (t) | (Mrs. Black moves quickly to this group and places a chart on the chart rack at the end of the table. The chart gives directions for using the "Magic Pencil." She picks up a large teacher-made cardboard pencil labeled "Magic Pencil" and holds it horizontally before her. The children are very excited; they laugh and giggle.) |

| Teacher: | Here comes your surprise. |
| (39) | |

| Alan: | Oh, boy! |
| (40) | |

| David: | I just love a surprise. |
| (41) | |

| Sandra: | Are we going to write a story? |
| (42) | |

| Jim: | It's a big surprise. |
| (43) | |

| Alan: | Magic Pencil! |
| (44) | |

| Teacher: | Didn't I tell you you were going to get something magic? |
| (45) | |

| Richard: | Oh, boy! Yes. It looks like a crayola. Does it really write? |
| (46) | |

| Teacher: | (She pretends to write with the pencil.) It writes magic. Maybe you're not |
| (47) | magic. Maybe you can't do it. |

| Rhonda: | Magic pencil. Funny magic pencil. (Giggles.) |
| (48) | |

| Teacher: | (She holds pencil in her hands.) Magic is in here. O.K., let's look here. I |
| (49) | want you all to— |

| (u) | (The children in Group I laugh aloud, and children in Group II turn around.) |

| Teacher: | They're listening to a story. Let's just turn around. They have a good story |
| (50) | going there. First of all, the magic pencil—and look at number one, David. |

|  | This tells us how to operate this magic pencil. |
|---|---|
| (v) | (The teacher holds the pencil, looks toward the chart, and asks the children to read.) |
| Teacher: (51) | "Handle carefully. It is magic." Oh, I'd better handle it carefully. (She handles pencil very gently.) |
| Teacher: (52) | What does number two say? |
| David: (53) | "Take off the magic—uh—eraser." |
| Teacher: (54) | (She removes eraser.) All right. The magic eraser is down here, and I've taken it off. Then what does it say to do, Rhonda? |
| Rhonda: (55) | "Tip the pencil slightly till the magic papers . . . ." |
| Teacher: (56) | All right, it says, "Tip the pencil . . . ." What does tip mean? Slightly tip it this way and something is going to appear at the end. |
| (w) | (The teacher tips the pencil. Slips of paper show when the end of the pencil is turned toward the children. The children exclaim, with "oh's" and "ah's." |
| Rhonda: (57) | Candy? |
| Pupils: (58) | (Giggles.) |
| Teacher: (59) | Let's go on and read. Number three says, "Tip the pencil slightly till magic paper shows at the end." And what does number four say, then, Teresa? |
| Teresa: (60) | "Pull one of the magic papers out." |
| Richard: (61) | (He looks toward Group I.) Mrs. Black, I can hear the story over here. |
| Teacher: (62) | Ssh! "Pull one of the magic papers out." Then, what does it tell us to do? Sandra—number five. |
| (x) | (The teacher places her hand inside the tube of the pencil to demonstrate pushing papers back and gets just one paper.) |
| Sandra: (63) | "Push the—push the other papers back." |
| Teacher: (64) | (She pushes all the papers back inside the pencil.) You'll push the others back and just get one paper. And then what does it tell us? David—number six. |
| David: (65) | "Put—put the magic eraser back on." |
| Teacher: (66) | (She replaces the eraser.) All right. We'll put the magic eraser back on, and what does number seven say, Richard? |
| Richard: (67) | "Read your paper and write a magic story." |
| Teacher: (68) | Now all of you are good story writers. That's right, Theresa. All of you are very good. You write wonderful stories. |

| | |
|---|---|
| Theresa: (69) | That's why you put us over here. |
| Teacher: (70) | That's why I put over here. You write delicious—we'll call them delicious stories. Now, I'm going to let you operate the magic pencil. I think I should help you though, don't you? |
| Richard: (71) | Yes, ma'am. |
| Teacher: (72) | Cause it's sort of big. We'll start over here, and don't tell anyone what your paper says. It's all secret, and it's all magic. Beware—it's magic. (She smiles about the magic.) |
| David: (73) | I'll bet the answer is really good. |
| Teacher: (74) | O.K., let's start over here. |
| Pupils: (75) | (Giggles.) |
| Teacher: (76) | First, you tip it. |
| (y) | (Mrs. Black tips the pencil and goes to David. He pulls out a paper and reads it silently, and she bends down to read it also. She whispers to David. He says, "Oh!" and smiles. The teacher then moves to Alan. He takes a slip and reads it, and the teacher bends down again. Alan places both hands on his face and moves his shoulders up. The teacher wants to be certain each child understands exactly what his sentence or "story starter" says before he begins to write.) |
| (77) | Shhh! |
| (z) | (The teacher moves around the table and repeats the above procedures. Rhonda and Theresa take slips, and Theresa laughs.) |
| Teacher: (78) | Shh! Get a paper and get busy. Are you ready? |
| (aa) | (Jim reads his slip and smiles happily. He whispers to teacher, and she laughs with him.) |
| Teacher: (79) | Don't tell. You might need to change that word to <u>wonderful.</u> |
| Jim: (80) | Oh, boy! |
| Teacher: (81) | O.K. |
| Jim: (82) | What's the—uh—title? |
| Teacher: (83) | You title it. |
| David: (84) | Richard is ahead. |

| | |
|---|---|
| (bb) | (Richard reaches in, takes a slip, reads it, and then exchanges the slip for another one. He puts the first slip back inside the pencil.) |
| Teacher: (85) | Richard is a good writer. That's all that counts. (She laughs.) Do you know what you are going to write about? (To Richard.) |
| Richard: (86) | Yes, ma'am. |
| Teacher: (87) | O.K. |
| Teacher: (88) | Why don't I put the magic pencil right here. |
| (cc) | (Mrs. Black lays pencil on the floor in front of the chart rack. She folds her hands, stands at the head of the group, and smiles.) |
| Sandra: (89) | How much do you write? |
| Teacher: (90) | How many stories? |
| Sandra: (91) | Yes, ma'am. |
| Teacher: (92) | Why don't we just write one right now, and at the end, we'll get the magic pencil and take it back with us. This is our pencil. |
| David: (93) | Oh, boy! |
| Teacher: (94) | We can write more stories if you want, but not today. |
| Alan: (95) | It's not theirs. |
| Teacher: (96) | No, it's not theirs. It's our pencil. |
| Alan: (97) | Oh, boy! |
| Teacher: (98) | Shhh! (She points to Group III.) Go on with your work. |
| (dd) | (The teacher moves to Group I and shows the children where to place their earphones. She picks up a headset for a boy and then hands the set to the child to put away.) |
| Teacher: (99) | Here, you take your own earphones and put them over there very carefully. |
| Pupil: (100) | Mrs. Black, come here. |
| Teacher: (101) | All right. |
| (ee) | (As the teacher moves away, she stops to place a chair under a table. The children in Group I return to the table and sit down again. They begin to draw pictures of their stories. One boy stands up and stretches and then bends over.) |

Teacher:      Now, do you know what to do right here?
(102)

Pupil:        Yes, ma'am.
(103)

Teacher:      O.K.
(104)


    Group IV has five girls whose desks are arranged in a semicircle on the left side of the room, opposite Group I. The desks are facing an easel placed near the left wall. On the previous day each girl chose a picture of a part of the body (eyelash, nose, lips, toe, thumb) and wrote an autobiographical story about her picture.

Teacher:      (She moves to Group IV, leaves the group briefly, then brings a chair, and sits
(105)         down.) I'm ready to hear your stories. Are you ready to read them?

Ann:          Yes, ma'am.
(106)

Teacher:      O.K. Let's get a chair. Now, read so that I can hear you. (She looks at Wayne
(107)         in Group I.) Wayne, will you get busy over there?

Teacher:      Let's start over here with our Bluebird. Do you know how to clip your picture
(108)         up here? (She points to the easel.)

(ff)          (Cheryl rises to clip her picture on the easel.)

Teacher:      Are you ready?
(109)

Ellen:        They're comfortable.
(110)

Teacher:      Do you like the desks? Are they comfortable?
(111)

Ellen:        I wish we could have them in our room.
(112)

Teacher:      Need some help?
(113)

(gg)          (Mrs. Black gets up to adjust Cheryl's picture on the easel.)

Cheryl:       Yes. (Giggles.)
(114)

(hh)          (The teacher places her hands on Cheryl's shoulders and shows her where to
              stand. Cheryl smiles and stands, holding her paper.)

Teacher:      Now! Will you stand about right here, Cheryl, so that we can see the picture
(117)         and so that we can hear. About right there. Is that O.K.? (She returns to her
              seat.)

Teacher:      You can all see the picture. Now, let's listen to Cheryl's story. These are auto-
(118)         biographies that you wrote yesterday over at that table, and I didn't check
              them or read them or anything.

Cheryl:       Mrs. Black, I call myself Snuffy.
(119)

Teacher:      Do you? Well, an autobiography is a story about yourself, but instead of
(120)         being yourself, you're going to be something else. What are you, Cheryl?

| | |
|---|---|
| Cheryl:<br>(121) | The nose. (She points to her picture of a nose.) |
| Teacher:<br>(122) | What? I didn't hear you. |
| Cheryl:<br>(123) | The nose. |
| Teacher:<br>(124) | You're the nose. |
| Cheryl:<br>(125) | Yes, ma'am. |
| Teacher:<br>(126) | Now read real loud, Cheryl, so I can hear you. And read clearly. |
| Cheryl:<br>(127) | "I am a nose. My name is Snuffy. The girl who owns me is Sunset. Sunset leans up against me like a soft, furry bunny. I like it when she rubs her soft fur against me. I like her to rub her soft fur on me, but I do not like to smell the stinky bunny. Sometimes, she rubs her baby cat against me, and her mother is my mother's nose." |
| (ii) | (Cheryl reads aloud and smiles at her story.) |
| Teacher:<br>(130) | Uh—your mother is on Sunset's mother's face? In other words, your mother is Sunset's mother's nose? Oh, that's good. O.K., go ahead. Excuse me. |
| Cheryl:<br>(131) | "I don't like to be pulled on or smushed in. Mrs. Lips is always talking. Mrs. Eyes is always blinking at me, and Hair—Mrs. Hair always tickles me. They always say, 'Hello, Snuffy.' I say, 'Hello, Mrs. Eyes. Hello, Hello, Mrs. Hair.' Sometimes when she says, 'Hello, Snuffy,' I say, 'Hello, Mrs. Hair.' Sometimes Mrs. Hand scratches me. I don't like that a bit. One day my owner played clowns and painted me all up with red paint and a big blue dot. Would you like to be me? Sunset's mother made her take the paint off. I was glad too." |
| (jj) | (Cheryl laughs. The others in the group laugh also.) |
| Teacher:<br>(132) | You mean you got painted, Mrs. Nose? |
| Cheryl:<br>(133) | Yes, ma'am. |
| Teacher:<br>(134) | Oh. Like a clown? I'll bet you did like that, didn't you? |
| Cheryl:<br>(135) | Yes, ma'am. (Giggles.) "One day someone hit me and made me bleed, and when they did, they didn't say, 'I am sorry.' " |
| Teacher:<br>(136) | Aw. |
| Cheryl:<br>(137) | "Sunset bandaged me up, and soon I was well again, and now I— and now I— and now all I did was sniff again." |
| Teacher:<br>(138) | Oh. I'm so glad you're well and have been bandaged, and you can sniff, Mrs. Snuffy. |
| Pupils:<br>(139) | (Giggles.) |
| Teacher:<br>(140) | O.K. Thank you, Cheryl. I thought that was wonderful. Did you like that? |

| (kk) | (The teacher helps Cheryl take down her picture. Cheryl returns to her seat.) |
| Pupils: (141) | Uh-huh. (Giggles.) It was funny. |
| Teacher: (142) | What part did you like best, Stella? |
| (11) | (Stella thoughfully places a hand to her face and answers.) |
| Stella: (143) | When there was—uh—somebody painted her up. |
| Teacher: (144) | You like when Snuffy got painted? (Stella nods.) What part did you like, Sue? |
| Sue: (145) | Mmmmmm. |
| Teacher: (146) | I'm sorry somebody hit Mrs. Snuffy and made her bleed. |
| Cheryl: (147) | (Giggles.) |
| Teacher: (148) | O.K. Ellen, would you like to be next? |
| (mm) | (Ellen moves forward and places her picture on the easel. Her picture is a large mouth, gaily painted.) |
| Ellen: (149) | Uh-huh. |
| Teacher: (150) | Who are you today? |
| Ellen: (151) | Miss Lips. |
| Teacher: (152) | You're Miss Lips? You're not Ellen today, are you? |
| Pupils: (153) | (Giggles, laughter, and noise.) |
| Teacher: (154) | Oh, how pretty you look today! |
| Ellen: (155) | (Giggles.) Oh, thank you. |
| Teacher: (156) | You're welcome. Stand over a little to the side and read real loud for me, Ellen. |
| Ellen: (157) | "Hello. My name is Miss Lips. I like to smile, I like to—" |
| (nn) | (The children whisper as Ellen begins to read.) |
| Teacher: (158) | A little fast. |
| Pupils: (159) | (Whisper.) |
| Teacher: (160) | Pardon us, Ellen, while we move. Why don't you start over and slow down a little bit? Will you? |
| (oo) | (Ellen, smiling and laughing occasionally, reads quickly.) |

| | |
|---|---|
| Ellen: (162) | "Who are you? You look like little baby toe. You sure are little, but you sure are fat. I live on a face. My lips are red. What color are you? Who me? I'm tan. You should see my father. He—he is—here he comes. Bye. Oh, he is gone. I hate when that old lady puts lipstick on me, but that's to make me look good. That old lady puts red, orange, and pink, and other colors. That old lady sure is lucky to have me. I made that old lady look good. Some-times I like it when she puts red stuff on me. I do not like sticky lips. She sure looks good with lips. So that's the end of lips. Good-bye." |
| Teacher: (163) | Oh, that was good, Ellen. Very good. |
| (pp) | (Ellen flips her paper, almost a wave, and backs away. Then she takes her picture from the easel as the teacher reaches up, still seated in chair at left, to help her. Ellen sits down.) |
| Teacher: (164) | Now, how about the little toe. I'll put your picture up. |
| (qq) | (Ann comes forward. The teacher rises and puts the picture on easel. She shows Ann where to stand. The teacher sits down as Ann begins reading.) |
| Teacher: (165) | Look at those pictures. Ann is little baby toe today. She is going to tell us the adventures of being a toe for one day. Do you want to stand over here? Read a little bit slow and real loud for me so I can hear you. |
| Ann: (166) | "Little Toe"—"I'm a little toe, so chubby and fat. I do not wiggle so much like the other toes. I hardly move. One day somebody came and touched me. I didn't mind very much because I am used to it. I don't sneeze, I don't walk— all I ever do is lay on a sheet—that's all I ever do. My little toe everybody pushes me all around. This big, mean thing right beside me is so mean to me, but cute, little me—I just don't do anything, I just let him push me around. I belong to a little boy. He is also chubby and fat." |
| Pupils: (167) | (Giggles.) |
| Ann: (168) | "But I don't care. Probably you want to know who this is. It is my brother. All of his toes are my family. I have other brothers, but they are not mean and fat as he is. My daddy doesn't care. He just makes me mad. Mother said, 'Why do you treat your little baby brother like that?' " |
| (rr) | (Other children remain quiet.) |
| Teacher: (169) | A little louder. |
| Ann: (170) | "And he didn't and I was glad. But he did it again, and I was going to tell my little father on him. I hope he gets punished, and he will stop, and he will start again, but I have had enough of this. I am just going to tell my little father. I think it will work. Oh, let's forget about that. On with the story! One day I heard somebody say, little toe. The baby's name was Billy. They did name me. They named me Willie because his name was Billy. All my brothers were mad. But I just minded my own business and ignored them. Oh, that's the end of the story of the little toe." |
| Teacher: (171) | Oh, good. You really have problems there with all those little brothers and sisters. |
| (ss) | (The teacher rises from chair and helps take down the pictures. Ann sits down.) |

Teacher:     O.K., good. Tom Thumb, let's hear about you. You want me to help you put
(172)          it up? Let's see. Which way do you go, Tom Thumb—this way, or this way?
              O.K., move over a little bit. Let's stand over a little bit—just a little bit, Lisa.
              Right there.

(tt)          (The teacher hangs picture of thumb and shows Lisa where to stand.)

Lisa:         "Tom Thumb."
(173)

Teacher:     Wait just a minute. Read slowly and loud.
(174)

Lisa:         "Tom Thumb can do many things. He can feel things. He can button a coat.
(175)          He can pop balloons. He can turn pages of a book. Tom Thumb likes people.
              He can do many things. Although he is the smallest one of us, he is a good
              helper. He can play marbles, too. He loves to help you. I don't know what
              we would do without you, Tom Thumb. You can turn the dial on the tele-
              phone. Your fingernail is sharper than a knife. He can even rip his own pants
              and shirt." (Giggles.)

Teacher:     You are pretty important, Lisa. Because it would be sort of hard to get around
(176)          without a thumb, but I have never dialed a telephone with a thumb. Do you?

(uu)         (The teacher takes down the picture and hands it to Lisa.)

Teacher:     O.K. Let's hear from Eyelash.
(177)

(vv)         (Stella moves to the easel. The teacher moves to the easel and hangs up pic-
              tures of a very large eye.)

Teacher:     O.K. You want to read real nice and loud for me.
(178)

Stella:       (She reads aloud from her paper.) "Little Lost BoBo Eyelash. Who are you?
(179)          I don't like to hear stories, but I like to tell them. So I will tell you what
              happened to me once. Once upon a time there was an eye. He had a lot of
              eyelashes, and the best one was BoBo eyelash. She was the smallest, prettiest,
              and funniest eyelash of them all, but she had done some things she did not
              like. She hated to be combed at all. And then one day in September, '65,
              she cut me off of her eye, but I didn't care because I just ran away. Then
              BoBo, that's me, went free and ran and played and most of all did not have to
              be combed. Then one day I said, 'We must go out and find BoBo. She might
              be lost.' So all the eyelashes and the eye went to look for little lost BoBo.
              They looked in cabinets, streets, and on every eye. They looked in the grass.
              There in the middle of the grass was little BoBo. How glad they were! Oh,
              how happy BoBo was! She was so glad to see eye and eyelashes that she
              jumped up in her place, and BoBo stayed there forever. I lived happily ever
              after." And that's the story of little lost BoBo eyelash. I will tell you another
              story very soon. (Sits down.)

Teacher:     (She takes down the picture.) Oh, that was good. Did you like your story?
(180)          Yes, everyone read their story. O.K., Ellen's story was about the lips, remem-
              ber? Pick up your chairs and move them.

(ww)        (Mrs. Black stands facing the girls with her hands clasped behind her.)

Teacher:     Cheryl, you don't need to bring yours.
(181)

(xx)         (The teacher moves to the table holding earphones. The children from Group
              IV bring chairs to table and sit down.)

| Teacher: (182) | Bring your chair over here. Now, plug in. |
|---|---|
| (yy) | (Mrs. Black shows the children how to plug in the earphones, adjusts the controls, untangles the wires, and plugs in the recorder. It squeals. The children in Group IV laugh.) |
| Teacher: (183) | Shh! |
| Pupils: (184) | (Laughter.) (Giggles.) Yeah! (Giggles.) |
| Teacher: (185) | Now, for a while you'll be hearing some things on the tape recorder. Can you hear? |
| (zz) | (Children in Group II, with mirrors, are smiling and looking at themselves.) |
| Teacher: (186) | Do you hear? I would like for you to get your stories right now, and let's come over here, and sit around, and listen in a circle right here by the easel. Bring your stories over this way. |
| (aaa) | (Group II, using mirrors to write descriptions, moves to the semicircle before the easel.) |
| Teacher: (187) | Come on, John. If you're not through, come anyway, John, and we'll listen. We'll let you just stand there because you're going to be first. O.K.? |
| (bbb) | (Mrs. Black shows the children in Group I where to place their chairs in the area where Group II worked.) |
| Teacher: (188) | Sit here, Freddy. Then Marie, you may sit here. John, get a chair. Right over here. Why don't you sit here? Are you still making faces at yourself? |
| (ccc) | (Wayne, a boy in Group I, sticks out his tongue at the mirror.) |
| Teacher: (189) | All right, let's listen to this story which she wrote while she was looking in the mirror. Becky, why don't you step up and read slow and read nice and loud, will you? |
| (ddd) | (The teacher places her hands on Becky's shoulders. Becky begins to read from her paper.) |
| Becky: (190) | "My name is Becky. Well, I have blonde hair and blue headband, blue eyes and some white in them. Two of my teeth are out. My collar is low. I am wearing a red dress. My eyebrows are light brown. My eyelashes are not dark black. I think I am very pretty. I think I should be prettier. My cheeks are pink. My lips are pink. I think I am very—I am very pretty. I have little bangs, and that's the story of myself." |
| Pupils: (191) | (Clap.) |
| Teacher: (192) | That was good. Becky, I think you're pretty, too. You want to sit here? |
| (eee) | (Mrs. Black pats Becky on her back and moves from Becky's chair to opposite chair as Marie gets up to read.) |
| Becky: (193) | (Giggles.) |
| Marie: (194) | "Myself"—"I see myself. Hi! My name is Marie." |
| Teacher: (195) | Read aloud now so I can hear you. |

Marie:          "I see myself. Hi! My name is Marie. My hair is pretty. See I am pretty too.
(196)           I have pretty teeth too. They are shiny too. I brush them every day. My hair
                is curly. I wash it. That is why it is shiny and curly. I have a nose too. It is a
                big one. I have a mouth too. It is to talk with. Well, I had better go. Good-
                bye."

Teacher:        Oh good, Marie. I think you're nice looking, also. O.K., John, would you like
(197)           to—John, did you get through?

John:           No, ma'am.
(198)

(fff)           (The teacher stands with arms folded as she talks to John.)

Teacher:        Would you like to read just what you have, and I'm going to let you finish be-
(199)           cause I thought you started out very, very good. Now, John, you'll have to
                read real loud and clear. Let's step up to that line here so I can hear you.
                Fine. Right there.

(ggg)           (The teacher points to show John where to stand.)

John:           "Myself"—"He can be sad—he can be glad."
(200)

(hhh)           (John reads from his paper.)

John:           "He can be nice, but he's mostly happy. He can be helpful and not helpful.
(201)           He falls down, and he stands up. He has brown eyes and black . . . ."

Teacher:        Oh, well, John, you can be all those things when you want to. Is that the way
(202)           you feel all the time?

John:           Not all the time.
(203)

Teacher:        I'm glad you're happy most of the time.
(204)

(iii)           (John sits down and puts his paper to his mouth. Freddy rises and begins to
                read. The teacher stops him.)

Teacher:        Wait just a minute—I didn't hear your title.
(205)

Freddy:         "Me."
(206)

Teacher:        Oh, that's your title? Oh, O.K.
(207)

Freddy:         "I live behind a farm. There are big, fat cattle and pigs. I have on a striped
(208)           shirt. There is a wall behind me. You can see I am writing—I have sort of
                green eyes, and I also have brown hair. My shirt is blue, gold, white, and
                black stripes. I have a short neck. My ears are big. John and Becky are sit-
                ting behind me. I have very big lips."

Teacher:        Good. Sit down. Who were you talking to? Were you talking to yourself?
(209)           Where was the world?

Freddy:         (He points upward.) Up there.
(210)

Teacher:        Oh, where is the farm?
(211)

Freddy:         In the mirror. (He points to his mirror at the desk across room.)
(212)

| | |
|---|---|
| Teacher: (213) | Oh, you were looking at it in the mirror? That's good. Are you through with your story? |
| (jjj) | (The teacher leans over to talk to the boy. He returns to his seat.) |
| Freddy: (214) | No, ma'am. |
| Teacher: (215) | Would you like to go back and work on your picture at the bottom of the page? John wants to go back and work on his story. |
| (kkk) | (John and Freddy leave the group and go back to desks across the room to complete stories.) |
| Teacher: (216) | (She looks at Group III—magic pencil group.) Are you through? |
| Richard: (217) | Yes, ma'am. |
| Teacher: (218) | Oh, that's good. How many of you in here are through? |
| (lll) | (Several children raise hands.) |
| Teacher: (219) | David—how about you? |
| David: (220) | Yes. |
| Teacher: (221) | Are you? (To Sandra.) |
| Sandra: (222) | Yes, ma'am. |
| Teacher: (223) | All right, do you want to come over here? Are you through? Come over here and let us hear what you've written. Bring your little magic slip. |
| (mmm) | (The children rise, take chairs, and move to the reading circle.) |
| Jim: (224) | Bring your magic slip? |
| Teacher: (225) | Yes. |
| Richard: (226) | Why bring your magic slip? |
| Teacher: (227) | Bring it right over here. |
| (nnn) | (The teacher points to the circle and then moves around circle and turns paper over.) |
| Teacher: (228) | You want to sit over there? Just turn this paper over. |
| Alan: (229) | May I sit here? |
| Teacher: (230) | No, I want you to sit over here. O.K., David, get up and read what you've pulled out of the magic pencil and then read your story. |
| (ooo) | (David rises, goes to center of circle, and begins to read from his paper.) |

David:          "If I were a giant, I would—"
(231)

Teacher:        Wait just a minute. Excuse me. Let's put it up here. Now turn around and
(232)           read it for them. I don't believe they heard you.

(ppp)           (David reads from his paper.)

David:          My title is "I'm a Giant." "If I were a giant, I would stomp all over the houses
(233)           and squash everyone but Mrs. Black and my family."

Teacher:        Oh, thanks for saving me.
(234)

David:          "A million—a million, hundred, and two thousand cows, a hundred and fifty
(235)           girls with pigtails. I wouldn't eat—I would drink two million gallons of
                monkey beer."

(qqq)           (David grins and moves toward his desk. Teacher takes his magic slip from
                easel and hands it to him.)

Teacher:        Are you through with that story?
(236)

David:          No, ma'am.
(237)

Teacher:        You're not through? You're going to do some more?
(238)

David:          I'm going to do some more.
(239)

Teacher:        Well, thank you for saving me and your family, Giant.
(240)

Alan:           He kills me!
(241)

Teacher:        Do you want to go back to your table?
(242)

David:          Yes, ma'am.
(243)

Teacher:        Do you want to read your story?
(244)

Richard:        It's pretty long.
(245)

Teacher:        That is all right. I don't mind. Now, this is—you wrote an imaginary story,
(246)           didn't you?

(rrr)           (Richard rises and comes forward. He hands his slip of paper to the teacher.
                She reads the "sentence starter" and places it on the easel. The boy reads his
                story before the group. The teacher stands at the back of the group.)

Richard:        Yes, ma'am.
(247)

Teacher:        This is the imaginary story of "On the way to school I saw a little . . . ."
(248)

Richard:        "Donkey man. He said, 'You better get off my land before I make you a
(249)           donkey boy.' Then he made me a donkey boy. The donkey man said, 'I came
                out of the ground. I am a bugger man.'"

| Pupils:<br>(250) | (Giggles, laughter.) |
|---|---|
| Richard:<br>(251) | "He looked—he looked—I forgot that word—strange. He looked strange." |
| (sss) | (Mrs. Black starts toward Richard, stops and goes back.) |
| Richard:<br>(252) | "He was about six foot tall. I was about five foot tall. He ran away from me. I did not know why. The donkey man was laughing because he wanted to, I guess. But I am still a donkey boy. Goodbye." (He sits down.) |
| Teacher:<br>(253) | You mean you got on this man's land, and he was a donkey man, and he turned you into a donkey boy? |
| Richard:<br>(254) | Yes, he was a bugger man. |
| Teacher:<br>(255) | Well, I'm glad I'm not a bugger man. Thank you, Alan. Are you going to read yours next? |
| (ttt) | (Alan rises, takes the magic slip of paper from the easel and sits down.) |
| | (End of recording as lesson continues.) |

## Appendix IX-A

## REACTIONS TO INTERVIEW

Instructions:

For each of the following questions, circle the number that best describes your reaction to the interview that you have just observed. Circle any one of the five options for each question.

A. If you were the parent, how would you feel toward the interviewer?

5 strongly positive
4 somewhat positive
3 neutral
2 somewhat negative
1 strongly negative

B. If you were the parent, how would you feel about accepting the interviewer's suggestions?

5 highly accepting
4 somewhat accepting
3 neutral
2 somewhat rejecting
1 highly rejecting

\* This was interview

number 1 2 3

(circle one)

C. If you were the parent, how would this interview affect your self-confidence?

5 supporting, bolstering
4 somewhat supporting
3 neutral
2 somewhat shattering
1 shattering

D. If you were the parent, to what extent would the interviewer have been effective in helping you to be a better parent?

5 highly effective
4 somewhat effective
3 neutral
2 somewhat ineffective
1 highly ineffective

\*\* Record and add the numbers you circled here

A. _____

B. _____

C. _____

D. _____

Total _____

## GROUP DISCUSSION REACTIONNAIRE

### DIRECTIONS

Circle the number which best represents your reaction to each of the five questions below. Total your circled reactions in the space provided at the bottom of this sheet. This is confidential.  Please be frank!

I.  How much satisfaction did you derive from your participation?

  5 Completely satisfying experience
  4 Quite satisfying
  3 Intermediate between satis-
    fying and dissatisfying
  2 Quite dissatisfying
  1 Completely dissatisfying

II. How much did you agree with the final group ranking?

  5 I agreed completely
  4 I agreed quite a bit
  3 I agreed and disagreed equally
  2 I disagreed quite a bit
  1 I disagreed completely

III. How effective was your leader in helping the group to reach agreement?

  5 Completely effective to work with
  4 Quite effective
  3 Neither effective nor ineffective
  2 Quite ineffective
  1 Completely ineffective to work with

IV. How good was the final ranking by the group?

  5 Best possible
  4 Quite good
  3 Neither best nor poorest
  2 Quite poor
  1 Poorest possible

V. How much responsibility for the final group ranking did you feel?

  5 Felt completely responsible
  4 Felt somewhat responsible
  3 Felt neither responsible nor lack of responsibility
  2 Felt somewhat a lack of responsibility
  1 Felt total lack of responsibility

### TOTAL REACTION SCORE

I.  _____        IV. _____

II. _____        V. _____

III. _____

422

Appendix IX-C

## FIRST SESSION: MARY'S REPUTATION

### PROBLEM:

Mary, a high school senior, comes into the principal's office in tears. Mary, whose parents are very strict and very religious, has acquired a "reputation" as a result of having dated soldiers from a nearby military post. The purpose of her tearful visit to the principal's office is to report that a classmate named Steve called her a "bitch" last week. Then, this morning, Mary returned to class from the library to find Steve and some other boys looking through her notebook (containing personal notes) and laughing about the contents, including a few comments added by the boys. Mary insists that she will notify her parents if action is not taken by the principal. The principal recalls that Steve is not only a star athlete, but is ordinarily a good school citizen.

The task for your group is to decide on the best course of action for the principal to take. Rank order the following actions the principal might take. Place a 1 by the best suggestion, a 2 by the next best, and so on.

_____ a. Have a joint conference with Mary and Steve
_____ b. Call the boys in and reprimand them
_____ c. Have a teacher find out why boys are mistreating Mary
_____ d. Call Mary's parents for a conference
_____ e. Instruct Steve to apologize to Mary
_____ f. Reassure Mary and let the matter drop

## SECOND SESSION: BOBBY'S THEME

### PROBLEM:

Bobby, a seventh grade boy, has been under treatment at the Child Guidance Clinic for four years. His mental and emotional stability remain in a precarious balance, but he has not been a serious behavior problem. Mrs. Satterwhite, the auditorium teacher, assigns Bobby and four other boys a five-page theme on George Washington as punishment for misbehavior. The four other boys hand in their themes on time, but Bobby refuses. Mrs. Satterwhite tells Bobby in the presence of the class that he cannot return to her room without the theme. Bobby goes to the principal and calmly explains that he does not consider theme writing suitable punishment, that he feels he should have some other kind of punishment, but that spankings, expulsion from school, or any other form of coercion will not succeed in getting him to write the theme. The principal knows that Bobby means what he says.

The task of your group is to decide on the best course of action for the principal to take. Rank order the following courses of action by placing a 1 by the best alternative, a 2 by the next best, and so on.

    _____  a. Back up the teacher by insisting that Bobby write the theme

    _____  b. Reassure Bobby and try to get the teacher to change the punishment

    _____  c. Talk to the teacher and Bobby together to seek a compromise

    _____  d. Change the punishment and readmit Bobby to class

    _____  e. Allow Bobby to spend the auditorium period in the office or the library for the remainder of the semester

## THIRD SESSION: THE OLD GROUCH

### PROBLEM:

Miss Carsner, who is known as an "old grouch," and who seems to have a lot of discipline trouble, habitually sends boys to the office because of misbehavior in her typing classes. The offenders are usually, but not always, the mischievous type who get into minor difficulties at times, but who get along well enough in most of their classes. Today, three boys (who have been sent to the office by Miss Carsner before) appear again with the following note: "These boys have been talking and making a nuisance of themselves. They should be expelled." The boys insist that the entire class misbehaves continuously, doing the same things for which they have been sent to the office.

The task for your group is to decide on the best course of action for the principal to take. Rank order the following alternatives by placing a 1 by the most desirable, a 2 by the next most desirable, and so on.

_____ a. Reprimand the boys, but no punishment
_____ b. Tell the teacher to be more understanding of boys
_____ c. Visit the classroom before doing anything else
_____ d. Have a conference with both teacher and boys
_____ e. Punish the boys by having them stay after school
_____ f. Calm the teacher down and let the matter drop

# INDEX

## A

Achievement, analysis of, 118–30
  Answer Sheet-Charts, 121, 122, **127**\*
  Growth Profile Chart, 121, 122, **126**
  growth scores, 120, **125**
  Individual Profile Chart, 120, **124**
  Item Analysis Worksheet, 121, 122,
    **126**, 128
  Mental Maturity Record, 120, 122, **125**
  Mental Maturity Test, 120, 122, **124**
  Pupil Record Card, 120, 122, **124**
  tests, 118, 128
Achievement Test Report, 119, 122, **123**
Activities, basic, 233–69
  brainstorming, 234, 236–40
  buzz sessions, 241–46
  conferences, 233
  demonstrations, 234, 235, 247–54
  group discussion, 233, 234, 235,
    255–62
  in-service programs, selection for, 234
  objectives, 233–35
  role-playing, 234, 235, 263–67
Alabama, in-service programs in, 54
Answer Sheet-Charts, 121, 123, **127**
Aptitude tests, 118

## B

Bales' categories, 195, 202
Bales' Interaction Analysis, **170**, 171, 183,
  195, 202
Bessent, Wailand, 57
Bloom, Benjamin S., 217
Brainstorming, 36, 45, 234, 236–40
  and analyzing lesson protocols, 166
  and audio recordings, 238
Burnham, Reba M., 7
Buzz sessions, 36, 241–46

## C

Classroom observation, 131–44
  Comprehensive Observation Guide,
    135, **135**, 137, 146, 147, 153
  film clip observations, sample of group
    test results, 139, **139**
  films and videotapes, application in,
    137–39, **139**, 142, 143
  instruments, development of, 133,
    134–36

\*Boldface indicates an Exhibit on that page.

levels of observation related to skills
   employed, 141, **141**
objectives, 132–33, 144, 161
reliability of observations as a function
   of number of visits, 140–41, **140**
Teacher-Question Inventory, 91, 136,
   137, **149**, 154–57, 166, 171–72
Classroom observation guides, 144–62
   COG Recording Form, 150
   COG Study Form, 147
   Comprehensive Observation Guide,
      135, **135**, 137, 146, 147, 153, 154
   sample questions from each section,
      **146**
   and lesson protocols, analysis of,
      164–79
   objectives, 144–45, 161
   Pupil Response Inventory, 157–60
   recording evidence, four problems in,
      148–50, **149**
   recording procedures, 147–48
   Teacher-Question Inventory, 154–57
   sample lesson analysis using the, **155**
Closed circuit TV, in demonstrations,
   250
COG Recording Form, 150
COG Study Form, 147
Communication, group, 196–213
   Bales' categories, 202
   and buzz groups, 196
   and group discussion, 196
   Group Discussion Reactionnaires, 197,
      198, **198**
   objectives, 196–97, 202
   reactionnaire results, summary analysis
      of, 199, 200, **200**, 201
   schedule for problem-solving sessions,
      198, **198**
   Tabulation Worksheet for Reaction-
      naire Results, 198, **198**, 199, 201
   vignettes, use of, 197
Communication patterns, 186–213
   feedback, effect of in communications,
      186, 202–12
   group communication, three styles of,
      186, 196–202
   interviewing, three styles of, 186,
      187–96
Communications, directions for, 204,
   **205, 206**
Comprehensive Observation Guide, 135,
   **135**, 137, 146, 147, 153, 154
   sample questions from each section,
      **146**
Conferences, 233
Confidence score (C-score), 208
Content, activities, objectives, and goals,
   216, **216**
Criteria, stating, 223, **224**

D

Demonstrations, 247–54
   definition and objectives, 247, 248,
      251, 254
   personnel selection for, 248, 250
   in reality simulation, 51
   videotapes and closed circuit TV, use
      in, 250
Design for Learning, 46
Diagnostic flexible grouping, 106–18
   and "Capitalization" scores, 111, 116
   Diagnostic Outline-Language Test,
      108, **109**
   master plans and materials kits for, 117
   Worksheet for Diagnosing Learning
      Needs, 111, **113–14**, 115
   Worksheet for Language Sub-test A—
      Capitalization, 111, **112**
   Worksheet for Mechanics for English,
      108, **110**
Diagnostic Outline-Language Test, 108,
   **109**
Directions:
   for communication, 204, **205, 206**
   for receiver, **207**, 208, **209**, 210
   for scoring feedback exercise, 208, 210,
      **210**

E

"Eavesdropping," in buzz sessions, 242,
   245
English, Worksheet for Mechanics of,
   108, **110**
Environmental change, in in-service
   education, 24–25
Experience impact of activities, 34, **35**,
   42

F

Feedback:
   and brainstorming, 237
   effect of:
      on classroom observation, 142, 165
      on data analysis, 45, 47, 48, 54
      on personal interviewing, 186, 195,
         200
   effect of communications in, 202–13
   confidence score (C-score), 208

directions for communication, 204,
    **205, 206**
directions for receiver, **207,** 208,
    **209,** 210
directions for scoring feedback
    exercise, 208, 210, **210**
objectives, 202–3, 211, 212
one-way communication, 186, 203,
    204, 210
two-way communication, 186, 203,
    204
verbal, 208, 211
visual, 208
written, 203
Feedback exercise, directions for scoring,
    208, 210, **210**
Film clip observations, sample of group
    test results, 139, **139**
Film clips, application in classroom
    observation guides, 153
Films, use of:
    in personal interviewing, 195
    in reality simulation, 51
Films and videotapes, use of:
    in analyzing lesson protocols, 164, 180,
        184, 185
    in classroom observation, 137–39, **139,**
        142, 143, 153
    in group discussions, 257
    in training to use classroom observa-
        tion guides, 153
Florida, In-service programs in, 54
Free interaction, in buzz sessions, 242,
    245, 246
Functional change in in-service educa-
    tion, 25

**G**

Group Discussion Reactionnaires, 197,
    198, **198**
Group discussions, 255–62
    and brainstorming, 233, 234, 235,
        236–37, 238, 240
    and case discussion method, 258, 262
    definition and objectives, 233, 234,
        255, 261–62
    films and videotapes, use of, 257
    and free interaction, 261
    leaderless discussion method, 258–59,
        262
    and recording outcomes, 257
Grouping:
    grade:
        using "Capitalization" scores, 111,
            116
        using sub-test scores, 116

homogeneous, 103, 104, **105**
instructions for, 97, **98–99**
interclass or "sectionizing," 106, 128
Group reactions to three styles of inter-
    views, summary for, 192, **193**
Growth Profile Chart, 121, **126**
Growth scores, 120, **125**

**H**

Harris, Ben M., 34, 57, 233
Hermanowicz, Henry J., 4

**I**

Ideals, Selected Goals and Specified
    Objectives, 32
Individual Differences, Worksheet for
    Analyzing, 101, **102**
Individual Profile Chart, 120, **124**
Initial Teaching Alphabet, 37–38
In-service, the Organizational Context
    for, **16**
In-service design grid, 36, **37**
In-service education:
    activities in, 5–6
    as component in larger design, 40–42
    conceptual framework, 15–28, **16**
    definition, 1–3, 15–17
    and functional specialization, 22–23,
        26–27
    and instructional change, 15–55
    and instructional staff development,
        2, 3
    involvement as key, 3–4, 9–10, 47, 54
    and leadership, for planning, 6–9
    and organizational change, 21–28
    organizational context for in-service,
        16, **16**
    and personnel development, 25, 27–28
    and planned change, 18–21, **24**
    process for change, 17–18
    programming and resources, 5–6
    and sources of change, 23–26, 27–28
    staff needs, 2, 3, 5, 6
*In-Service Education: Materials for
    Laboratory Sessions,* 165
In-service program design, 29–43
    experience impact of activities, 34, **35,**
        42
    in-service design grid, 36, **37**
    for learning, **46**
    for specific objectives, 30–33, 36–40,
        38–40, 42, 43

Instruction:
  grouping pupils for, 94–106
    activities sequence, 96, 103–4
    homogeneous grouping, 103, 104,
      **105**
    procedures, 96–97, **97–100**, 105–6
    Sample Data on One Pupil, **97**
    Worksheet for Analyzing Individual
      Differences, 101, **102**
  individualizing and grouping for,
    94–130
    achievement, analysis of, 118–30
    diagnostic flexible grouping, 106–18
  observing and analyzing, 131–62
    classroom observation, 131–44
    classroom observation guides, train-
      ing to use, 144–62
    criteria for, 131–33, 144, 153
Instructional change, 15–55
Instructional objectives:
  preparing, 218, **218**, 219, 220, 222,
    223, 225, 227
  setting, 214–29
    clarifying conditions for, 222, **223**,
      227, 229
    content, activities, objectives and
      goals, 216, **216**
    criteria, stating, 223, **224**
    criteria for, 214–15, 222–23, 227,
      228, 229
    outcomes, evaluating, 225, **226**, 227,
      228
    outcomes, specifying for, 218–20,
      **219**, 221, 227, 228–29
    *Programmed Instruction, Preparing
      Objectives for*, 214
    stating, in performance terms,
      220–21, **221**, 227, 229
    *Taxonomy of Educational Objec-
      tives*, 37, 215
Instructional television, 17, 22, 26, 27
Instruments, observation:
  checklist, 136
  free response, 134–35, **135**
  rating, 136
  tabulation, 136, **136**
Interaction:
  free, in buzz sessions, 242, 245, 246
  free, in group discussion, 261
  and role-playing, 263
Interviewing, personal, 187–96
  and Bales' interaction categories, 195
  definition and objectives, 187, 195–96
  evaluation of, 192–95
  and film, "The Conference," 195
  group reactions to three styles of inter-
    views, summary form for, 192,
    **193**

procedures, 188–96, **189**, **193**
reactionnaires, 190–93
and role-playing, 194, 195
teacher-parent, as pattern for, 187
vignette, "Being a Parent is Too Much
  Work," 188, **189**, 191
Interviewing, three styles of, 187–96
Item Analysis Worksheet, 121, 122, **126**,
  128


# K

King, Martha L., 7
Krathwohl, David R., 217


# L

Laboratory approach, to in-service program design, 9–10, 44–45
  definition, 45–46
  learning principles, 46, 50–51
Laboratory sessions, illustrations of,
  57–229
  communication patterns, study of,
    186–213
  instructional objectives, setting, 214–29
Language Sub-test A—Capitalization,
  Worksheet for, 111, **112**
Language Test—Diagnostic Outline, 108,
  **109**
Learning, principles of, 50–51
Learning Needs, Worksheet for Diagnosing, 111, **113–14**, 115
Lesson protocols, analysis of, 163–85
  Bales' interaction analysis, categories
    and illustrations for, **170**, **171**,
    183, 195, 202
  brainstorming procedures, 166
  and buzz groups, 167
  creative writing lesson, 184
  elementary science lesson, 184
  *Instructor's Guide protocol*, 166,
    171–78
  instruments for, 180–85
  leaking bottle lesson, 184
  objectives and advantages, 163–64,
    184–85
  Pupil Response Inventory, Sample
    Protocol Analysis Using the, **166**,
    **168**, 171, 172
  and role-playing, 180
  "Russian Revolution" protocol, 165,
    171, 172–78

Teacher Behavior Inventory, 180–83
  sample tabulation on, **169**, 171
Teacher Question Inventory, Sample
  Protocol Analysis Using the, 166,
  **167**, 171, 172
using video and audiotape recordings,
  164, 180, 184, 185
Levels of observation related to skills
  employed, 141, **141**

# M

McIntyre, Kenneth E., 34, 53, 57
Mager, Robert F., 214, 217
Marking Pupils' work, problems of,
  61–78 (see also Pupils' work,
  marking)
Mental Maturity Record, 120, 122, **125**
Mental Maturity Test, 120, 122, **124**
Missouri, in-service programs in, 54

# N

National Defense Education Act, 20
National Science Foundation, 20
New Mexico, in-service programs in, 54

# O

Objectives:
  affective, broad-spectrum, and
    cognitive, 37–40, **38–40**
  clarifying conditions for, 222, **223**,
    227, 229
  stating, in performance terms,
    220–21, **221**, 227, 229
Observation, levels of, related to skills
  employed, 141, **141**
Observations, reliability of, as a function
  of number of visits, 140–41, **140**
Organizational change:
  authority, hierarchy of, 22, 26
  functional specialization, 22, 23, 26
  rules and regulations, reliance on, 22,
    23
Organizational drift, 19
Organization context for in-service, 16,
  **16**
Outcomes:
  affective, broad-spectrum, and cogni-
    tive, 37–40

evaluating, 225, **226**, 227, 228
specifying, 218–20, **219**, 221, 227,
  228–29

# P

Personnel change in in-service education,
  25
Planned Change in School Organizations,
  **24**
Problem-solving sessions, schedule for,
  197, 198, **198**
*Programmed Instruction, Preparing
  Objectives for,* 214
Psychodrama, 263
Pupil, Sample Data on One, **97**
Pupil performance, evaluation of, 60–93
Pupil Record Card, 120–22, **124**
Pupil Response Inventory:
  categorizing responses, 158–60
  objectives and procedures, 157–60,
    166, 171
  sample lesson analysis using the, **159**
  sample protocol analysis using the,
    166, **168**, 171, 172
Pupils' work, marking, 61–78
  activities, 64, 78
  arithmetic tests, 66, **74**
  English themes, 65–66, 69–73
  instruments, description of, 64–78
  procedures, 63–64
  spelling tests, 66–67, **75–77**

# R

Ratios:
  sex, 106
  supervisor-pupil, 7
  supervisor-teacher, 7
Reactionnaire results:
  summary analysis of, 199, 200, **200**,
    201
  tabulation worksheet for, 198, **198**,
    199, 201
Reactionnaires, 197, 198, 200, 201
  reactions to interview, 190
  summary form for group reactions to
    three styles of interviewing, 192,
    **193**
Reality simulation, and role-playing,
  51–52, 54
Receiver, directions for, **207**, 208, **209**,
  210

Recorders, use of in buzz sessions, 242, 245
Recording evidence, four problems in, 148, **149**, 150
Reliability of observation as a function of number of visits, 140–41, **140**
Role-playing, 234, 235, 263–67
  definition and objectives, 263, 266–67
  and feedback, effect of, 212
  and interaction, 263
  in personal interviewing, 194, 195–96
  in protocol analysis, 180
  and psychodrama, 263
  and reality simulation, 51–52, 54
  and sociodrama, 263

## S

Schedule for problem-solving sessions, 198, **198**
School organizations, planned change in, 24
School Principalship Project, 57
Sociodrama, 263
Structural change in in-service education, 25
Supervision, in in-service education, 1, 2

## T

Tabulation Worksheet for Reactionnaire Results, 198, **198**, 199, 201
*Taxonomy of Educational Objectives*, 37, 215
Teacher Behavior Inventory:
  and analysis of lesson protocols, 180–83
  sample tabulation on, **169**, 171
Teacher-learning process, dynamics of, 137, 152, 165
Teacher-made tests, 79–93, 118
  essay, 89–90
  matching, 86–89
  multiple choice, 83–85
  true-false, 85–86

Teacher-Question Inventory, 91, 136, **149**, 154–57, 166, 171–72
  effective questions, 156–57
  cognitive questions, 154, 156
  question-response-acceptance sequence, 157
  sample protocol analysis using the, 166, **167**, 171, 172
Television, instructional, 17, 22, 26, 27
Test construction, 79–93
Texas, University of, School Principalship Project, 57

## U

University Council for Educational Administration, 3

## V

Variability:
  intragroup, 107
  trait, 106, 107
Variability reduction, 97
Videotapes:
  and closed circuit TV, use of, in demonstrations, 250
  use of, in brainstorming, 238, 239
Vignettes, use of, 51, 197
  "Being a Parent is Too Much Work," 188, **189**, 191
Virginia, in-service program in, 54

## W

Wolfe, Wendell, 3
Worksheet:
  for analyzing individual differences, 101, **102**
  for diagnosing learning needs, 111, **113–14**, 115
  for language sub-test A—Capitalization, 111, **112**
  for mechanics of English, 108, **110**